BY SIDNEY ASTER:

Ivan Maisky and Parliamentary
Anti-Appeasement, 1938–1939
(in *Lloyd George, Twelve Essays,*
A. J. P. Taylor, ed.), 1971

English Poetry in Quebec,
John Glassco, ed., 1965

1939
THE MAKING
OF THE SECOND
WORLD WAR

Sidney Aster

SIMON AND SCHUSTER · NEW YORK

ACKNOWLEDGEMENTS

I have greatly benefited by the assistance in correspondence and conversation from the following, to whom I am most grateful: the Hon David Astor, Mr Frank Ashton-Gwatkin, Mrs Ruby Beaumont-Nesbitt, Princess Marthe Bibesco, Lord Boothby, Lord Boyd, the late Major-General Nevil Brownjohn, Lord Butler, Lord Chilston, the late Mrs Zelda Coates, Sir Laurence Collier, the late Major-General Francis H. N. Davidson, Mr Sefton Delmer, Professor David Dilks, Sir Alec Douglas-Home, Professor Noel Fieldhouse, Brigadier R. C. Firebrace, Lady Kirkpatrick, Sir Thomas Preston, Mr Jasper Rootham, Captain Stephen Roskill, Mr Andrew Rothstein, Sir Arthur Rucker, Lord Salter, Lord Sherfield, the late Lady Strabolgi, and Major-General Sir Harold Wernher.

Access to unpublished papers and, where necessary, permission to quote has kindly been given by Mrs Barbara Agar, British Library of Political and Economic Science, Mrs Dorothy Burgin, Lord Caldecote, Lord Chatfield, Mr Michael Dawson, the First Beaverbrook Foundation, Mrs B. M. Godfrey, the Earl of Halifax, Mrs Joan Heywood, Lord Kennet, Lady Liddell Hart, Mrs Dorothy Lloyd Mrs Mary McManus, Lieutenant-Commandar H. W. Plunkett-Ernle-Erle-Drax, Colonel J. W. Pownall-Gray, Public Archives of Canada, Mr William Rees-Mogg, Franklin D. Roosevelt Library, Lord Simon, the late Mr Laurence Thompson, Transport House, Lady Vansittart, and the Marquess of Zetland.

Crown copyright documents are used by permission of the Controller of Her Majesty's Stationery Office. The map illustrating European Diplomacy is based with permission on one taken from *Recent History Atlas* (1966) by Martin Gilbert. I wish to

5

thank all the archivists and librarians who have facilitated my research.

I acknowledge with thanks permission to quote copyright material from David Dilks, ed., *The Diaries of Sir Alexander Cadogan, 1938–1945* – Cassell; *Ciano's Diary, 1939–1943* – Chicago Daily News; John Harvey, ed., *The Diplomatic Diaries of Oliver Harvey, 1937–1940* – Collins; *Harold Nicolson Diaries and Letters*, I, *1930–1939*, and the Sir Harold Nicolson Diaries – Collins, and Mr Nigel Nicolson; *The Ironside Diaries, 1937–1940* – Constable; Birger Dahlerus, *The Last Attempt*, Ivan Maisky, *Who Helped Hitler?* – Hutchinson; Keith Feiling, *The Life of Neville Chamberlain*, Sir Ivone Kirkpatrick, *The Inner Circle* – Macmillan; Waclaw Jedrzejevicz, ed., *Diplomat in Berlin 1933–1939*, *Papers and Memoirs of Jozef Lipski, Ambassador of Poland* – Columbia University Press.

TO JOYCE

Contents

Illustrations

Introduction

LEGISLATION passed in May 1967 by the British Parliament reduced the period of secrecy for State papers from fifty to thirty years. The critical documents for the eve of war in 1939, therefore, were declassified and made public on January 1st, 1970. Here, among thousands of bound volumes and files of loose papers of all Government departments, is contained the vital evidence which finally reveals the making of the Second World War.

These massive archives can also be supplemented now by a virtual explosion of other official documents and collections of private papers. The published and unpublished State papers of Europe, including the USSR, and North America have been consulted in the writing of this book. In Britain, especially, the private papers of more than sixty-five participants in events have been used. They encompass the ten currently available collections of British Cabinet Ministers, and some extracts from the letters of the Prime Minister, Neville Chamberlain.

These are the records which contain the revelations in private letters, the closely argued memoranda, the often hastily penned minutes, the suggestions for action, and the crucial decisions which influenced decisive events. This material usually eclipses the published memoirs of many who took part in the events here described. Constrained by rigid standards of discretion and sometimes handicapped by fading memories, former officials were generally their own worst apologists.

The documents now available, particularly the full archives of the Foreign Office used here for the first time, reveal that the Second World War only became inevitable on March 15th, 1939.

The seeds of potential conflict with Nazi Germany were planted in earlier events, in the clash of personalities, and in the conflict of policies. On March 15th, however, Hitler's armed forces occupied Czechoslovakia, whose frontiers had been redrawn and whose continued independence was recognised at the Munich conference. By this single action, Hitler cast irrevocable doubt on his integrity as a responsible spokesman for German aspirations. Instead, he had exhibited potentially insatiable ambitions.

On that day, too, appeasement was destroyed. Confidence and good faith, the bases of appeasement, disappeared. A cloud of disillusionment, mistrust and intimidation settled over Europe. Britain, France and the United States found that Hitler had again broken his pledged word. He became a diplomatic pariah. The democracies decided that the first step in reconstructing peace in Europe must be an overture from Hitler. They waited for his "sign". They waited for him to indicate concretely that he had erred in the destruction of Czech independence, and that the new problems facing Europe – the dispute over the Free City of Danzig and Germany's differences with Poland – could be discussed in an atmosphere free of intimidation. They waited, prepared to grasp any initiative from Berlin, and maintained in the meantime what became known as a policy of "menacing silence". Hitler, for his part, also waited, but for the democracies to make him a new offer. He was convinced that they had become unreasonable and unwilling to offer further concessions to the Third Reich.

The Second World War, fought for more than five years and involving more nations than ever before in the history of conflict, emerged from this unresolved crisis of confidence of less than six months.

Meanwhile, Britain and France frantically prepared for war. They guaranteed the independence of Poland, Greece, Rumania and Turkey. They negotiated an alliance with the Soviet Union which, had it succeeded, would have also guaranteed Finland, Estonia and Latvia. The British government engaged in military conversations with the French, the Poles and the Turks. Massive rearmament programmes speeded ahead, and sales of munitions were made to new allies. An anti-German deterrent front became the diplomatic and military framework of a policy with one aim: to convince Hitler that it was not worthwhile to go to war to redress grievances which could be peacefully resolved.

The lives of officials working against a background and under conditions of intolerable strain are vividly depicted in these new records. In the 172 days between March 15th and September 3rd, 1939, Czechoslovakia and Albania lost their independence and the Lithuanian port of Memel was seized. Throughout the European continent troops were daily on the move, and armoured columns perfected techniques. Air forces practised tactics, navies demonstrated their strength, and armament factories turned out the weapons of war. German and Polish, French and Italian, Hungarian and Rumanian troops eyed each other menacingly across their fortified frontiers. War scares, crisis and invasion were the order of the day. Plans of diplomatic pacification, drafts of warnings and counter-threats, intelligence reports, and diplomatic assessments were hourly prepared and scrutinised. The documents poignantly exhibit the thoughts and actions of statesmen, politicians and civil servants daily faced with the ultimate decision: peace or war.

The secrets, the unexplained events, and the missing details of a contentious period in history can now be disclosed after almost thirty-five years. Here is revealed Britain's speedy disillusionment with the euphoria of the Munich conference, the subsequent plans to hasten rearmament, and the intelligence sources and impact of the previously underestimated war scares of January 1939. Here, too, is revealed for the first time the intriguing story of the "Tilea affair", which set in motion the deterrent front and the policy of guarantees.

With fresh perspectives from new evidence it is possible for example to understand the failure of Allied grand strategy to offer direct military assistance to Poland, or to evaluate how intelligence about the attempts by the German and Soviet governments to negotiate secretly a treaty forced the British and French to continue their own alliance discussions with the Soviet

Union. It is possible to destroy such myths as British culpability for the outbreak of appeasement in July, or the long-held view that the British government would have reached a settlement with Germany at the expense of Poland. And finally, the full story can be told of how a Cabinet revolt at No. 10 Downing Street on the night of September 2nd brought the British and French governments into the Second World War.

Evidence gathered from archival sources has been elaborated during conversations with many individuals possessing personal experience of events in 1939. Most have been named among the *Acknowledgements*. I must express my gratitude more fully, however, for the assistance of the late Dr Viorel Virgil Tilea, Rumanian Minister in London from February 1939 to July 1940. Although writing his memoirs, Dr Tilea generously gave me the most valuable information derived from his own experiences and from Rumanian sources. He fully explained his actions and struggle to preserve the independence of Rumania. During the two years before his death, he read parts of the manuscript, correcting and adding many points of detail. He was unsparing of his time and invariably hospitable.

To Sir William Seeds, who served as British Ambassador in Moscow from January 1939 to January 1940, I am grateful for his having spoken for the first time of his experiences on the eve of war. He illuminated the hazards faced by an ambassador in Moscow, charged suddenly with the onerous and thankless task of negotiating an alliance with the Soviet government. I am also grateful to three former members of the Chamberlain Cabinet. Sir Reginald Dorman-Smith discussed with me numerous aspects of British policy. Above all, he elaborated on his motives and actions and those of his colleagues involved in the Cabinet revolt of September 2nd. Lord De La Warr and the Rt Hon Malcolm MacDonald confirmed points of detail. Arthur Primrose Young generously put at my disposal documents recording his experiences as a secret link between the Foreign Office and the German resistance, and explained his efforts to inspire confidence in Hitler's dissidents.

My debt to Martin Gilbert extends over a long period, during which I have profited from his encouragement and advice. His generosity both with information and the unique sources at his disposal, and his gracious hospitality have been most appreciated. He read the manuscript and made numerous suggestions of great value. Lord Gladwyn, Lord Strang, Mr Anthony Harbour, and Mr Trevor Burridge also read the manuscript. Their observations have been most useful. Mr Philip Herbison assisted me for a time with research, and, although not a historian, quickly adapted to provide help for which I am very grateful. My ultimate expression of gratitude belongs to my wife, Joyce, for her encouragement and advice, and assistance with research, typing and revision.

London 1972   SIDNEY ASTER

CHAPTER ONE

A Bloodless Triumph

On the morning of March 15th, 1939 the citizens of Prague awoke to find their capital occupied by the armed forces of Nazi Germany. At about 4 a.m. their ageing President, Dr Emil Hacha, had signed a document thrust before him in Berlin by Adolf Hitler. It "placed the fate of the Czech people into the hands of the Führer of the German Reich". Hitler took the Czechs of Bohemia and Moravia under his "protection". He had acquired his first imperial possession in which the majority of inhabitants were not German speaking.

Germany's military machine had been put into operation even before Hacha's arrival in Berlin. On March 14th two important Czech industrial centres, Mährisch-Ostrau and Vitkovice – the latter containing extensive armament works – had been occupied. After the signature of the agreement in Berlin, Czech radio from early in the morning broadcast appeals to the population to offer no resistance, to keep calm and go about their work as usual. At 6 a.m. German troops crossed the Czech frontier at three points. Two thousand paratroops landed at Prague airport the same morning. The Gestapo quickly followed the advancing armies.[1]

When Hacha returned to his capital, he was first met at the railway station by a German guard of honour. He was then driven to the ancient Hradcany castle in the old town. There he found Hitler already comfortably installed and admiring the splendours of the former palace of Bohemian kings. By the evening of March 15th the military occupation of Czechoslovakia, affected swiftly and with the minimum number of troops, was complete.

Hitler felt confident he had won another bloodless victory. He had never miscalculated since assuming office in 1933. His sense of timing and his exploitation of opportunities had brought him one dazzling success after another. The Rhineland in 1936, and Austria and the Sudeten-German areas of Czechoslovakia in 1938 had been incorporated in Germany with an ease which won him the admiration of the German masses and the army, worried the British and French governments, and to the American people seemed the inevitable pattern of European events. For each of these bloodless victories, despite the bitter criticisms aroused, an adequate case in the name of German appeasement could be reasonably made. The methods used – intimidation and threat – were contemptible; but they did not seem cause for war. Each move by Hitler was designed to satisfy some grievance arising from the Versailles peace settlement of 1919. The emotional slogan of national self-determination was turned to use against the democracies with magnificent effect and rich results.

In 1939, however, Hitler miscalculated twice. He was to gamble later in August that the British and French would not make the quixotic gesture of coming to the assistance of Poland. This miscalculation led to the Second World War. But he also made an earlier error. He underestimated the shock aroused by his occupation of Czechoslovakia. For the first time Hitler had absorbed, not a German minority, but a whole Slav nation into the Third Reich.

The crisis which gave Hitler the unexpected opportunity to intervene in the affairs of his Slav neighbour began as an internal Czech dispute. For several days it had all the characteristics of an east European minorities squabble. It could have been resolved by the principals involved without great power intervention. The Czech army was adequate to deal with the situation, by force, if necessary. But happening as it did on Germany's eastern frontier, Czech involvement, as Hitler so well calculated, became inevitable.

The Slovak government with its capital at Bratislava had been established on November 22nd, 1938. It had a wide degree of autonomy, but its foreign relations were to be managed by the central government at Prague. Within a few months the Slovak government remodelled its domestic affairs to include many of the usual totalitarian trappings, such as a one-party system and the Hlinka Guard, closely modelled on the German SA. Furthermore, several Slovak Ministers maintained unofficial contacts with Berlin which encouraged their separatist tendencies.

Such activity worried the harassed government in Prague, who used the main lever left to them. Either Slovakia must submit to the established constitutional order, or the newly autonomous state would be denied financial support. On March 9th President Hacha dismissed the separatist Slovak Premier Tiso, banned the Hlinka Guard, and installed the more moderate Dr Sidor as Premier. He then sent in the Czech army to maintain order. Tiso fled to Berlin. There he was ordered by Hitler to encourage the Slovak Diet to declare its independence. This was done on March 14th with Tiso at its head.

That afternoon Hacha asked for his meeting with Hitler in Berlin. He left Prague at 4 p.m. still President of a crumbling republic. He returned the next day a broken man, to take the puppet position of State President of the German protectorate of Bohemia and Moravia. He died in 1945, awaiting trial as a war criminal.

These events were being watched by all concerned with varying degrees of ignorance and concern. By March 10th the Czech general staff secretly obtained the German plans for a military deployment against Czechoslovakia. They also knew that March 15th was the target date. Rumours to the same effect were available to the French and brought to the attention of the British Foreign Office. However, it could not be confirmed: it had come through secret sources.[2]

The news was not surprising, nor was it entirely unexpected. It was simply more convenient in London to cast a half-closed and sceptical eye on events. Few believed the Germans would brazenly occupy Czechoslovakia.[3] No one believed the action could be stopped.

As the famous "Ides of March" approached, the favourite date for surprises on the continent, more exact information poured into the Foreign Office. From the British Legation in Prague came news that the Germans were withdrawing police from all over the country and organising them into semi-military formations. This concentration of police was to be effected by about March 15th. Similar action had preceded the occupations of Austria and the Sudetenland the previous year. These police had then been employed to keep order in the newly acquired territories.[4]

It was Saturday, March 11th which gave Sir Alexander Cadogan, the efficient and meticulous Permanent Under-Secretary of State, another of his nightmarish days. In the morning he walked with the Secretary of State for Foreign Affairs, Lord Halifax, to the Foreign Office and discussed the Slovak crisis. "For God's sake don't let's do anything about it," Cadogan urged the tall bowler-hatted figure at his side. But at his office a stream of bad news awaited him. First came information from a secret source that the German press had been instructed to exploit the Slovak crisis with the usual tales of persecution and harassment by the Czechs. Then the Hungarian Minister, George de Barcza, arrived for a chat. A talkative member of the propaganda service connected with the German Embassy had just secretly related to him that "things" would be happening by March 14th–15th at the latest.

Cadogan's next visitor brought yet more information. He preferred a private talk to a telephone message. Major-General Sir Vernon Kell, founder in 1902 and since director of MI5, the counter-intelligence service, sat alone with Cadogan. He came, as Cadogan noted in his diary, "to raise my hair with tales of Germany going into Czechoslovakia in next 48 hours". After thanking him for this piece of news, Cadogan rushed off to tell Halifax. Both men decided to play it cool. They were now used to war scares. And in any case, what was Britain to do? There never was any question of fighting Germany to save the diminished Czech state. Halifax agreed he would go off to Oxford to fulfil a previous engagement at All Souls College. But Cadogan decided he had better warn the Prime Minister, Neville Chamberlain, about the MI5 report.

The day was not yet at an end for the overworked Cadogan. As he was finishing his dinner at home, Gladwyn Jebb, his Private Secretary, telephoned. Jebb was responsible for liaison with the intelligence services. He rang "to say SIS [Secret Intelligence Service] have some hair-raising tales of Czechoslovakia for the 14th", Cadogan noted in his diary later that evening and added: "It can wait."[5]

The next three days, March 12th–14th, found the Foreign Office in a mood of deep despair and gloom. The situation in Czechoslovakia was confused and the information obscure. The British government had not been represented diplomatically in Bratislava, the capital of Slovakia, until January 1939. The new Consul, Peter Pares, had then been taken ill. It was not till late February that he was able to report anything definite about the Slovak government's policies or its personalities.

To a large extent the press, with its well informed continental correspondents, provided the main source of news for the Foreign Office. While this news made clear that the Czech state was breaking up, and while the intelligence services reported ominously on Hitler's intentions, the Foreign Office fiddled and dissembled. Germany's encouragement of the Slovak separatists was known and considered very disturbing. The form that Hitler's intervention would take, however, was a matter of speculation and debate. But the early end of the federal Czech state was gloomily forecast. "I do not think there is any action which H.M.G. can take to prevent or hinder such an outcome," was the opinion of Roger Makins of the Central Department. From this there were very few dissenting voices either in the Foreign Office or in the government. The replies given in the House of Commons on March 14th by Neville Chamberlain to Clement Attlee, the Labour Party leader, on the events in central Europe were deliberately uninformative. Luckily Chamberlain was not asked to comment on reports of German troop movements towards Czechoslovakia. The Foreign Office had preferred him not to say anything.[6]

The close attention being paid to the internal affairs of Czecho-slovakia was not indulgence or idle curiosity. It was an interest based on fear that war could erupt from the dying agonies of a state which had once before brought Europe to the brink. In September 1938 Neville Chamberlain had twice flown to Germany to help find a solution of the German-Czech crisis. His third flight culminated in the historic Munich conference of September 29th–30th. Peace was bought at a heavy price. The Sudeten-German areas of Czechoslovakia returned to Hitler's Reich. Czechoslovakia remained an independent but mutilated state. Britain and France agreed to participate in an international guarantee of the new Czech frontiers. Germany and Italy were also to join in the guarantee as soon as the questions of the Hungarian and Polish minorities in Czechoslovakia had been settled.

The Anglo-French guarantee of Czechoslovakia was born of a guilty conscience. It was a concession authorised by Chamberlain to satisfy the French and give confidence to the Czechs. It proved to be awkward, embarrassing and potentially dangerous. It was also strategic suicide. A militarily strong Czech state had been forced to accept Hitler's demands. No one would dream of fighting for the truncated remains.

Yet the British government had taken its commitment very seriously. On October 4th, 1938 the Minister for Co-ordination of Defence, Sir Thomas Inskip,* had spoken on the subject to the House of Commons. His words were carefully chosen and made on Chamberlain's authority. While the guarantee was not technically in force, Inskip declared, the British government "feel under a moral obligation to Czechoslovakia to treat the guarantee as being now in force". Should Czechoslovakia be subject to an "act of unprovoked aggression" Britain would come to its assistance.[7]

These fateful words had transformed a statement of intent into a public embarrassment. They were uttered in the con-

* On January 29th, 1939 Inskip became Secretary of State for the Dominions. He was replaced as Minister for Co-ordination of Defence by Admiral of the Fleet Lord Chatfield.

fident hope that a treaty binding all interested powers would replace this unilateral act. There was political sense in the gesture. If Hitler would add his signature, it could be used against him. It might deter him from taking action against his helpless neighbour. However, if he disregarded his own guarantee, his pledged word would be exposed as valueless.

Encouraged by this reasoning, the Foreign Office set about its task of getting a German signature. A lengthy paper was completed on November 12th for discussion at Cabinet level. It set out the possible participants, the form a guarantee should take, and the circumstances in which it should apply. In an almost prophetic vein, the case was mentioned where the guarantee would not apply: "Were Slovakia or Ruthenia to break away from Czechoslovakia . . . [or] were Czechoslovakia to join in a union with Germany which was so close as to amount to a virtual alienation of independence of the republic."

When Chamberlain visited Paris on November 24th, 1938, he stressed what he hoped would be the deterrent nature of any guarantee. He made it quite clear that it was not a practical measure designed to lead to a confrontation with Germany so narrowly avoided two months before. He need not have been so blunt. The French shared his evident distaste for this possibility. Their policy in late 1938 was to weaken their diplomatic links with eastern Europe. It would have been perverse to begin adding new obligations.

Chamberlain and Halifax returned to London and reported to the Cabinet on November 30th. The situation was becoming potentially dangerous. It was necessary to avoid a position, Halifax warned, in which Britain and France might be asked to take action against Germany and Italy "on behalf of a State which we were unable effectively to defend". When the guarantee was discussed a week later at the Foreign Policy Committee of the Cabinet, every Minister seemed to agree that it must only come into effect if three of the four guarantor powers – Britain, France, Germany and Italy – decided to act.[8]

The Czechs themselves were next sounded as to their views. The new government which had replaced the one led by President

Beneš, who had fled into exile, meekly replied on December 10th that anything agreed upon by the four Munich powers would be acceptable. The Czechs were in no mood to air any independent views to the Germans. They had just agreed to allow Germany to construct and administer a new motorway from north to south across their territory. They much preferred silence and concessions. This tightening grip of Germany upon Czech independence was very closely watched by the Foreign Office with resigned pessimism.[9]

Then came the turn of the Italians. Perhaps Benito Mussolini would use his influence in Berlin to get the negotiations started. With the question of the Hungarian and Polish claims against Czechoslovakia settled, it seemed the appropriate moment to turn to the Axis Powers. The Foreign Office prepared a brief on the subject for Halifax and Chamberlain to use during their visit to Rome in early January 1939. This suggested "that Czechoslovakia has alienated her independence to such a degree that any guarantee from other States would be futile". Still, why not try to learn the views of the Italian government as to the best way of giving effect to the guarantee?

On January 12th Neville Chamberlain and Lord Halifax dutifully sat down before Mussolini's desk in his vast room at the Palazzo Venezia. The Duce fiddled with a double sheet of foolscap. After a vague exchange of views on disarmament, and before a discussion on the adjustment of boundaries between Ethiopia and British Somaliland and the Sudan, Chamberlain raised the question of the guarantee. There seemed an instant meeting of minds. Mussolini felt central Europe would remain quiet. Chamberlain agreed it was best to leave the question of the guarantee open.[10]

Only the German government remained to be sounded out. In London there seemed little point in continuing these inquiries. When the German Foreign Minister, Joachim von Ribbentrop, had visited Paris on December 6th, 1938 he had treated the subject with great reserve. The Czechs did not yet deserve any guarantee. There was still the possibility of "another Beneš" governing that intractable little nation.

The Foreign Office in London soldiered on with waning enthusiasm. "We are . . . coming to think that the question of the Czechoslovak guarantee is becoming an academic one," William Strang, head of the Central Department, commented on January 9th. "Czechoslovakia has become in a large degree a vassal State."[11]

Chamberlain whole-heartedly agreed. He was extremely annoyed with this need to continue exchanging views. The Munich conference was important to him for its significance in the appeasement of Germany. He feared the Czechs would once again bring Britain and Germany into a confrontation. Yet the time was approaching to ask the German government for their views on the question.

The appropriate telegram was dutifully drafted by the Foreign Office. But at this point Halifax feared the effect on the volatile Germans. He submitted the draft to the Prime Minister, whose response was petulant and critical. "I was under the impression," he minuted, "that the Foreign Secretary had agreed with me that it was best to let this matter alone for the present & that there was a chance that if not stirred up the guarantee might fade out." He lamely agreed, nevertheless, to make the desired inquiry in a very general way.[12]

Although the German Ministry for Foreign Affairs was asked on February 8th what it intended to do about the guarantee, it was not until March 3rd that the reply reached London. The British and French were told to mind their own business. Czechoslovakia did not yet deserve a guarantee. Her internal developments and her foreign relations were too unsettled. The reply also hinted plainly that any interference by the Western Powers in central Europe would aggravate the situation. That area fell within the German sphere of influence.

A "somewhat curious document in places impertinently worded", Roger Makins minuted on March 11th after examining the reply in the Foreign Office. William Strang drew the obvious conclusion: Germany was keeping her hands free to deal as she pleased with any situation that might arise, or which she might provoke.

The more authoritative opinion of Sir Orme "Moley" Sargent, Assistant Under-Secretary of State, had already been given on this impasse. He viewed the German reply as a blatant excuse, "somewhat ominous" when related to "recent rumours" regarding Germany's intentions towards Czechoslovakia. Arguing with Hitler would be useless. The whole question, therefore, should be allowed to lapse until some future date. "One trouble," Sargent pointed out, was the unconditional moral guarantee declared by Sir Thomas Inskip on October 4th, 1938. Britain was still tied by this "dangerous commitment". The only way of wriggling out, Sargent concluded, was to say nothing, and hope that the Czechs would never call on Britain to invoke this pledge.

Sir Alexander Cadogan pondered this desperate advice and minuted:

> I am afraid one probably has to be cynical about this, and to recognise that, with the passage of time, the question of the guarantee loses more and more of whatever it had of actuality. If in Sept.–Oct. last we couldn't save Czechoslovakia from what was then done to her, it is plain that we shall not be able to save her from further consequences. And therefore I feel we can do no more than act as Sir. O. Sargent suggests.[13]

On March 14th, with reports of Germany about to march into Czechoslovakia multiplying hourly, Sargent, Strang and Sir William Malkin, Legal Adviser to the Foreign Office, sat down to find the best evasive statement. They based themselves on some random notes prepared by Halifax several days earlier. The essence of the apology was that Inskip's statement of October 4th, 1938 "was designed to tide over an uncertain transitory period, pending agreement on the terms of an international guarantee ... it was never contemplated that in default of a more general agreement this country should be placed permanently in a position of special obligation." A draft telegram was prepared along these lines to inform the French and to keep them from making any independent move.[14] This telegram was cancelled. The French were equally unenthusiastic.

All such evasions and legal squirming proved in twenty-four

hours to be quite unnecessary. While still tinkering with a draft reply to Germany, Czechoslovakia ceased to exist as an independent state. The form of German intervention, foreseen with apprehension months previously, offered an obvious escape.

———

At 11 a.m. on March 15th the British Cabinet assembled at 10 Downing Street. It met while the newspapers of the world were publishing details of Germany's swift and sudden occupation of Prague.

For just another hour the strategists and servants of appeasement talked in the familiar style of concession, pacification, and conciliation. The methods by which Neville Chamberlain, ever since becoming Prime Minister in May 1937, had struggled so passionately for an Anglo-German settlement still motivated the conversation. But for the bewildered, uncertain men huddled together that morning, this was the last appeasement Cabinet. When they met three days later they were already preparing for war. In these three days old style appeasement died. The word itself is recorded only once in the Cabinet minutes of the remaining meetings before war was declared on September 3rd.

The first object of the Cabinet meeting of March 15th was self-preservation with the least loss of face. The guarantee was uppermost in everyone's mind. Lord Halifax presented the arguments prepared for him by the Foreign Office. He need not have bothered. The nimble mind of the Prime Minister took advantage of the fragmentary morning's news. The "fundamental fact", he pointedly remarked, "was that the State whose frontiers we had undertaken to guarantee against unprovoked aggression had now completely broken up." It was very likely, he continued, "that the disruption of Czechoslovakia had been largely engineered by Germany, but our guarantee was not a guarantee against the exercise of moral pressure."

"Moral pressure" was a bad euphemism. But this was the voice of expediency, not cynicism. Whatever shock or anxiety he must have felt, Chamberlain was determined to carry through this Cabinet with a business as usual manner. The remaining decisions he also forced through with an abruptness designed to hide his real feelings; at least until he could assess in solitude the meaning of Hitler's latest coup and lay plans for the future. The Cabinet agreed to postpone, but not to cancel, the scheduled visit to Berlin of Oliver Stanley, President of the Board of Trade. This "signal mark of our disapproval" was considered sufficient. The suggestion made by Halifax to recall the British Ambassador in Berlin, Sir Nevile Henderson, was icily dropped.

Yet, beneath the surface, the first rumblings of discontent and suppressed shock made themselves heard, despite Chamberlain's low-pitched approach. He read out to the Cabinet a short parliamentary statement which he had himself drafted for delivery that afternoon. In it he intended merely to express "regret" at the German occupation of Czechoslovakia. Hitler was disappointed last September in not being able to stage his military demonstration against the Czechs. Chamberlain "thought that the military occupation was symbolic, more than perhaps appeared on the surface". Symbolic gestures, therefore, presumably needed no immediate response.

This reasoning was too facile for the normally phlegmatic Foreign Secretary to stomach. He had already indicated that the British government must take some overt action to show its disapproval of Germany's move. Of course, it was necessary, he had argued, "to steer a course between, on the one hand, pious and futile lectures and, on the other hand, the undesirability of leaving public opinion in any doubt as to our attitude to Germany's action in this matter." Above all, he feared the reaction on public opinion in the United States and south-east Europe if Britain remained inert.

After Chamberlain finished reading his intended statement, Halifax returned to the attack. Was it not obvious, he pointed out,

> that this was the first occasion on which Germany had applied her shock tactics to the domination of non-Germans. He thought that it was important to find language which would imply that Germany was now being led on to a dangerous

path. . . . He also stressed that Germany's attitude in this matter was completely inconsistent with the Munich agreement. Germany had deliberately preferred naked force to the methods of consultation and discussion.

This last remark was calculated to hurt the Prime Minister, to awaken him to the seriousness of what had happened just a few hours ago in central Europe. For these words poignantly brought to mind the Anglo-German declaration, signed by Chamberlain and Hitler on September 30th, 1938.* This was the document which Chamberlain had waved to the world on his return to London. It was Halifax's personal loyalty to the Prime Minister which gave him the courage to voice such honest criticism. Everyone else was silent. Chamberlain's reply, if any, remains unrecorded in the Cabinet minutes. But it was agreed that his proposed statement should be further discussed after the meeting.[15]

Meanwhile, Sir Alexander Cadogan had been at work in his office preparing a statement for his chief, Lord Halifax, to be made in the House of Lords. At 12.30 p.m. he went across to 10 Downing Street to discuss it with Chamberlain, Halifax, and Sir Horace Wilson, Chief Industrial Adviser to the government, and intimate confidant of the Prime Minister. Chamberlain promised he would base his own address to the Commons on Cadogan's draft. But would he stand by the advice coming from the Foreign Office?

At 3 p.m. the Prime Minister rose to speak to an expectant assembly of MPs. The looks of recrimination must have pained him deeply. But it also reinforced his stubborn streak. He would tell the Commons of the decisions taken earlier that morning in the Cabinet. He declared in slow and deliberate tones that his decision to sign the Munich agreement four and a half months

---

* The Anglo-German declaration stated in part: "We are resolved that the method of consultation shall be the method adopted to deal with any other questions that may concern our two countries, and we are determined to continue our efforts to remove possible sources of difference and thus to contribute to assure the peace of Europe."

earlier was the right one in the circumstances. On this, he had no regrets.

He would also satisfy the critics in the Foreign Office. Of course, he continued, the occupation of Czechoslovakia was contrary to the spirit of the Munich agreement. Indeed, Germany had expanded for the first time beyond her ethnic and linguistic frontiers.

But then the Prime Minister made two comments which should have been carefully noticed by anyone who desired to assess him accurately. He firstly observed that what Hitler had done was to "administer a shock to confidence" when it was just beginning to revive. And then he added: "It is natural, therefore, that I should bitterly regret what has now occurred." These words pointed towards every action he would approve in the remaining months of peace. Hitler had personally slapped him in the face. Hitler would have to make amends.

Unfortunately, Chamberlain did not end his speech there. He was not a man to humble himself before the Commons where he had faced daily abuse and savage criticism. In a last flourish of bravado, he concluded with a personal postscript. His government would continue to promote the substitution of the "method of discussion for the method of force in the settlement of differences". "Appeasement? Fatal!" Sir Alexander Cadogan dejectedly wrote in his diary that night.[16]

While he was treating the Commons to a holding operation, events behind the scenes were moving quickly. As the seriousness of Hitler's latest coup sank into the minds of officials, Tory Party leaders, members of Parliament, and public and world opinion, the Government slowly shrugged off its shock and lethargy.

Lord Halifax was the first to vent his spleen. Herbert von Dirksen, the German Ambassador, came to see him to fulfil the diplomatic nicety of conveying a copy of the communiqué signed that morning between Hitler and Hacha. Dirksen was one of Hitler's less enthusiastic admirers. None the less, he dutifully stated the German case as to why changes had been inevitable in central Europe. His soothing words were met by a barrage of rage. Hitler had repudiated the Munich spirit, the Foreign Secretary retorted. He had lied when he publicly said that Germany had no more territorial ambitions. Halifax continued:

> The immediate result was that nobody felt the assurances of the German Government to be worth very much, and that everybody asked themselves in what direction the next adventures would be framed. I could well understand Herr Hitler's taste for bloodless victories, but one of these days he would find himself up against something that would not be bloodless.

The only conclusion to be drawn, Halifax added, was that the German government was not interested in a settlement with Britain, cared nothing for world opinion, and "were seeking to establish a position in which they could by force dominate Europe and, if possible, the world".[17]

These last words had been a commonplace utterance of appeasement's opponents for years. This was the first time they had been used by a British Foreign Secretary to any of Hitler's Ambassadors in London. The view soon became a cliché in government circles. But from thought to action was another matter. It took just another forty-eight hours.

One other member of the Foreign Office left his outrage on the record. The former Permanent Under-Secretary of State, Sir Robert Vansittart, now isolated in his honorary and impotent position as Chief Diplomatic Adviser to the Foreign Secretary, watched his every prediction of events realised. Hitler had not surprised him; but the British government had. Something more was required than merely the cancellation of Stanley's visit to Berlin.

The Czech coup "will go down to history as one of the greatest and most gratuitous outrages ever perpetrated", Vansittart wrote on March 15th to Halifax. "There seems to be no longer any strength in our loins or capacity for moral indignation in our natures." Britain's passive attitude would have a deplorable effect on opinion in the United States. "I must conscientiously place on record my conviction that if we cannot show more resolution and reprobation than this, we shall certainly lose any possibility of effective cooperation from the United States when our own hour comes."[18]

American opinion of British policy was always uppermost in the minds of officials in London. No war could be fought without American money; nor won without American involvement. In 1939 London looked at Europe while casting nervous glances across the Atlantic. Vansittart's criticism struck a sensitive nerve. Nor was he alone in demanding a strong riposte to Hitler.

The News Department of the Foreign Office was being besieged by American correspondents eager for news of what Britain intended to do. They pointed out that the apparent complacency in London was making a deplorable impression in the United States. The Czech colony there, which now included the former President Beneš, was numerous, well organised and prosperous. They would get a sympathetic hearing and could cause a good deal of embarrassment. Charles Peake, an official of the News Department, recommended some gesture be made to show Britain's "displeasure" at Hitler's action.[19]

It remained to the credit of the French that any protest was at last sent. France's determination to oppose Nazi Germany changed as often as her governments. In 1939, however, Paris was beginning to nudge a reluctant London along the lines of tougher measures and responses. The Czech occupation was one such occasion. On March 14th Georges Bonnet, the French Foreign Minister and former Ambassador to Washington, had let it be known that the less London and Paris interfered in Czechoslovakia the better. But two days later, Charles Corbin, the French Ambassador, called on Sir Alexander Cadogan in the early morning. The Quai d'Orsay had had a change of heart. It now wanted to lodge a formal protest with Hitler even if this meant doing it alone. Would Britain join in?

No one in the Foreign Office was enthusiastic. Protest notes to Germany were an impotent gesture. Still it was useful for the record, and very desirable for internal political reasons.[20]

Chamberlain's speech in the Commons had proved one of the major disasters of his political career. The country had expected fighting words from its Prime Minister: they had received a curious apologia. Talk in the parliamentary lobby was already of the Prime Minister's resignation. Lord Halifax was tipped as his likely successor.[21]

Cadogan prepared a strongly worded telegram of protest. But under the cautious gaze of Chamberlain, Halifax watered it down. References to the "subjugation of nearly 8,000,000 Czechs" as being a denial of the right of self-determination and contrary to Hitler's own racial principle were crossed out. The note, as delivered, merely informed the Germans that Britain considered their actions illegal. At the same time Henderson was recalled from Berlin to report. He was not withdrawn.[22]

Having given the masses what seemed desirable, Chamberlain then took Halifax aside for more important business. The Prime Minister had a speaking engagement at the annual meeting of the Birmingham Unionist Association on March 17th. It was the eve of his seventieth birthday. Here, for people dear and familiar to him, he had long ago prepared a speech on domestic questions and social service. Even he could see this would not now do. Opinion in every corner of the country demanded an explanation and a new policy. He would have to talk about foreign policy. For several hours he argued back and forth with Halifax, trying at once to appease his critics yet maintain his principles. By the end of the day the impression was that he had "been binged up to be a bit firmer".[23]

The impression was precisely correct. The Prime Minister's speech of March 17th at Birmingham, broadcast to America and the Empire, was the most important he made in 1939. It was in many ways a far more exact statement of his position and future policy than has usually been credited. When Chamberlain spoke in public, he may have been discreet; he may, as he once wrote, "go further in the direction of understatement than is good for my popularity"; but he was always honest. This occasion was no different.

He assured the packed hall that he was "sound in mind and limb". Challenging any rumours of his resignation, he added that he intended to continue in office. As for what had happened in the Commons, two days before, he begged his audience to understand. The information coming from central Europe was both fragmentary and unofficial. He went on:

We had no time to digest it, much less to form a considered opinion upon it. And so it necessarily followed that I . . . was obliged to confine myself to a very restrained and cautious exposition, on what at the time I felt I could make but little commentary. And, perhaps, naturally, that somewhat cool and objective statement gave rise to a misapprehension, and some people thought that because I spoke quietly, because I gave little expression to feeling, therefore my colleagues and I did not feel strongly on the subject. I hope to correct that mistake to-night.

This Chamberlain went on to do with clarity and balance. He again defended the Munich settlement as a contribution towards the European appeasement he so deeply desired. He had relied on Hitler to abide by that agreement. Instead, Hitler had taken the law into his own hands. He had negated those very principles which had been mutually agreed upon. This inevitably raised the question, Chamberlain continued, as to what reliance could be placed on any of Hitler's assurances. It also raised the momentous question of Hitler's motives and ambitions: "Is this the end of an old adventure," Chamberlain asked, "or is it the beginning of a new? Is this the last attack upon a small State, or is it to be followed by others? Is this, in fact, a step in the direction of an attempt to dominate the world by force?" By his actions Hitler had completely "shattered the confidence which was just beginning to show its head", and which could have made 1939 a year of sanity and stability.

The Prime Minister did not end his speech there. Once more he added a different, more personal, note to balance his speech. Despite his outspoken condemnation of the Prague coup, he warned that he was not joining the warmongers' camp. The reference was slight and tacked on. He stated that he was "not prepared to engage this country by new unspecified commitments operating under conditions which cannot now be foreseen". In other words, he would have nothing to do with anti-German alliances. He would keep his hands free, press on with rearmament and wait for Hitler, in some concrete way, to re-establish the confidence he had just shattered.

Replying to a resolution expressing confidence in his leadership, and unanimously adopted, Chamberlain related a little-known anecdote. While visiting Rome in January, a lady had given him a photograph. It was a bust of Augustus, the Roman Emperor, on which was inscribed: "The Peace-maker of the World."

"When I got home and opened the parcel containing the photograph I was shocked to see that the bust had been so mal-treated that there was nothing left of the nose, and hardly any of the features were recognisable. So that photograph now stands in my room at Downing Street, with the inscription: 'This is what happens to peace-makers'."[24]

Chamberlain's speech was a deeply personal statement, expressing his bitterness and regret at Hitler's slap in his face. He had gauged the public's mood and reassured it. He had acknowledged the arguments of his critics, but he had rejected their methods. He did abandon appeasement; but only that which stemmed from military weakness; which was based on mutual confidence, good faith and the sanctity of agreements. Reassured by the fact that rearmament had been gathering speed in the six months since Munich, he grasped a new appeasement: the appeasement which he would follow from strength, which left the next move to Hitler. When that finally came, it proved to be war. Hitler never understood the message of Prague.

CHAPTER TWO

War in the West?

THE numbed nerves, the paralysis of will and the blank stares exhibited by the British government when Hitler seized Czecho-slovakia were a pathetic spectacle. Four months of almost continuous war scares and the delusion of a peace lull had induced this state of shell-shock.

Neville Chamberlain returned from the Munich conference in a state of euphoria and fatigue. From a window of 10 Downing Street he waved a piece of paper to the crowds below and said, in words for ever associated with his name, that he had brought back from Germany "peace with honour. I believe it is peace for our time." Chamberlain was not indulging in an orgy of self-congratulation. He was publicising the fact that Hitler had made a commitment on paper to behave. Meetings with Hitler had left Chamberlain with many reservations, not least that he was dealing with a "fanatic".[1] But he hoped that the Anglo-German declaration they had signed would be honoured. He also anticipated that "active steps" would be taken to follow up the Munich agreement.

"Our Foreign Policy was one of appeasement," Chamberlain told the Cabinet on October 31st. "We must aim at establishing relations with the Dictator Powers which will lead to a settle-ment in Europe and to a sense of stability."[2]

These hopes had been shattered within a few weeks. In public speeches during October and early November, Hitler boasted of his latest bloodless conquest, abused the democracies and stormed against such "warmongers" as Winston Churchill, Anthony Eden and Alfred Duff Cooper. The Secret Intelligence Service provided disturbing information that Nazi leaders were unsatisfied and bent on some irresponsible action.

Confirmation came from the strangest source to influence the Foreign Office in the coming months. Dr Karl Friedrich Goerdeler, a former *bürgermeister* of Leipzig and a prominent member of the German political resistance, with excellent contacts in the German civil service and among the generals, had been introduced to the Foreign Office in July 1937. The man responsible had been Arthur Primrose Young, an ebullient electrical engineer, inventor, and expert in industrial management. With Young's assistance, Goerdeler had relayed precise details of Hitler's plans against Czechoslovakia during August and September 1938, and advised counter-action. Goerdeler's advice had been ignored, but his accurate forecasts had forced respect for him as a reliable secret source.

On October 15th, after receiving a letter asking for another conversation, Young travelled to Schaffhausen in Switzerland. There he had a long meeting with Goerdeler who lamented that "his gospel of firmness" had been ignored. The next six months would decide the future of the British Empire, he warned. Only a determined attitude would stem the tide of totalitarian expansion. The dictators were being impelled towards further conquests. The Mediterranean would soon become a Fascist sea, while Japan would attack Hong Kong. Goerdeler believed "that Hitler has not conceived a great destructive plan, but rather, the onward rush of future events would impel him and his allies to achieve further conquests". This made war inevitable.[3]

Further information followed from Goerdeler on November 6th and 7th. Himself unable to make the secret journey to Switzerland, Young had delegated his original intermediary with Goerdeler, Dr Reinhold Schairer, a German refugee and educationalist at the University of London, who in 1940 departed for America.

Germany was facing financial chaos, Goerdeler explained in authoritative detail, derived directly from the German Finance Minister, Hjalmar Schacht, with whom he was in touch. Hitler was oblivious to sound financial remedies and was becoming "more and more mad". His entourage was dividing into reasonable and extremist Nazis. The extremists, including Joachim von Ribbentrop, were urging him on towards a grandiose programme of expansion. The Balkans and Asia Minor were to be conquered, opening the door to India. The Arabs, armed by Italy and Germany, would be encouraged to begin war. Holland, Belgium and Switzerland would soon be brought under German rule. Field-Marshal Göring was trying to act as a restraining influence. But Hitler was "entirely in the hands of the extremists who have warped and changed his nature beyond redemption". Goerdeler warned: "If anyone, anywhere, still believes in anything that Hitler promises, he is an utter fool."[4]

A meeting of the Foreign Policy Committee had been scheduled to discuss ways of improving Anglo-German relations. It finally met on November 14th under the shadow of a horrifying and destructive outbreak of anti-Semitism throughout Germany. It had been sparked off by the assassination in Paris of a German Embassy official by a distraught Polish Jew. Ministers agreed they had no effective method of protest or retaliation. Britain was "not in a position to frighten Germany".

These events seemed to confirm the picture of Hitler's mind and intentions drawn by Goerdeler. His information was described to the Committee. Lord Halifax pointed out how it coincided with reports received from other informants. Government and party circles in Berlin were "riding a very high horse". They felt the "Germans now had Europe in their pocket". Party wits were openly discussing the partition of the British Empire. Hitler himself was quoted as saying that if the British had not introduced conscription by the spring of 1939, "they may consider their world Empire as lost". Ribbentrop had received instructions on future German policy which included disrupting the Anglo-French alliance, supporting Italian and Japanese expansionist aims, and aggravating British difficulties in the Near East. "Meanwhile Hitler will concentrate on extending and consolidating his position in South Eastern Europe."

The conclusion Halifax put before this Committee was that "no useful purpose would be served by a resumption at the present time of the contemplated Anglo-German conversations".

Instead, rearmament must be stepped up in order to correct the impression that the British "were decadent, spineless and could with impunity be kicked about". Although Chamberlain had his doubts about the secret sources, they contained no definite dates for immediate action, he shared the Foreign Secretary's concern at the deterioration in the situation. He agreed on the need to encourage the moderate elements in Germany, and to hasten rearmament wherever practicable.[5]

Until December, "SIS information was to the general effect that Hitler intended to move East in the Spring and not West".[6] The main focus of this was not Czechoslovakia, as might have been expected. Rather, Germany was supposedly intent on encouraging Ukrainian nationalism in the hope of eventually disrupting the USSR. Europe was soon ridden with rumours of Hitler's next move eastwards.

This programme of action was distressing as to what it foretold of Nazi aims. It did not, initially, cause undue alarm in London. The more cynically minded viewed the prospect of a direct Nazi-Bolshevik battle with perfect equanimity. It would at least ensure the safety of the British Empire. The more practically minded felt that if Germany was to undertake an intensive *Drang nach Osten* – a drive to the east – the British and French should best keep their noses out.

In the major policy review undertaken after the Munich conference, Sir Alexander Cadogan advised a defensive attitude to the affairs of central and south-east Europe.[7] And the Ukraine, straddling parts of Poland and the USSR, was much further eastwards. Support for this policy came from British diplomats on the continent. The Berlin Embassy, in particular, pointed out that the *Pax Britannica* was ineffective in central and eastern Europe, Britain could no longer hope to be the "policeman of Europe". Nothing could stop Hitler from creating a system of vassal states. To maintain Germany's goodwill necessitated Britain recognising this basic fact. A conflict between Germany and Russia, such as over the Ukraine, was of no concern to Britain. This was one issue on which Chamberlain adamantly laid down the law when the subject was briefly discussed at the Cabinet.

Such views aroused criticism in the Foreign Office. Sir Orme Sargent pointed out that the "free hand" in eastern Europe might in fact strengthen Germany until she constituted a threat to France and, ultimately, to Britain. Roger Makins bluntly called such a policy "short-sighted". The experts in dealing with the USSR and able to offer first-hand information, the Northern Department of the Foreign Office and the British Embassy in Moscow, were both sceptical. They did not believe the "frontiers of the Soviet Union were likely to crumble at the horn blowings of a handful of Ukrainian emigrés".[8]

The picture of Hitler and his policies derived from secret sources, "tested over a long period", and which emerged until mid-December, was sombre and chilling. It was described later, on January 19th, 1939, by Gladwyn Jebb:

> Germany is controlled by one man, Herr Hitler, whose will is supreme, and who is a blend of fanatic madman and clear-visioned realist. His ambition and self-confidence are unbounded, and he regards Germany's supremacy in Europe as a step to world supremacy. He has been particularly susceptible, since Munich, to extremist influence. At present he is devoting special attention to the Eastward drive, to securing control of the exploitable riches of South, and possibly more of, Russia. He also intends to subject Eastern and South-Eastern Europe to Germany's political and economic hegemony, to vassaldom, if not worse. Polish and Roumanian integrity are threatened. He means to secure the return, sooner or later, of Germany's former Colonial possessions, or a satisfactory overseas equivalent; but that does not seem at present to be the primary objective. . . . The Eastward drive – the Ukraine in particular – is the order of the day. But Herr Hitler is *incalculable*, even to his intimates. He is capable of throwing the machine he has created, regardless of settled policy, and on his own initiative, in any direction at short notice. He can personally precipitate a conflagration, whatever the consequences to his regime may be.[9]

The obsession with Hitler's eastward expansionist plans died down in a short time. The Foreign Office then had to admit that the intelligence had not come from very reliable sources.[10]

The rosy prospects of a battle of European giants, from which Britain and France could stand aloof, came to an abrupt end. In December intelligence as to Hitler's aims suddenly changed, throwing the Foreign Office and 10 Downing Street into a panic.

Ivone Kirkpatrick had served as First Secretary to the British Embassy in Berlin since 1933. There the Irish-born diplomat, a veteran of the First World War, with a reputation as a raconteur, cultivated a network of acquaintances who habitually leaked secret information to him. On December 10th, 1938, before leaving Berlin to work in the Foreign Office as the expert on Germany, he attended a farewell dinner party. The guests included a retired German Secretary of State, associated with dissident military commanders. The next day Kirkpatrick received a note from the man, begging him to come immediately to his home. There Kirkpatrick was told the telephone had been disconnected and was made to promise not to telegraph anything to London. The Germans had broken the British cyphers. "What I have to tell you", the informant said, "is not a bazaar rumour or a story obtained from any dubious source. It is first-hand information from the War Office and the Air Ministry. Hitler has ordered preparations to be made for an air attack on London in peace time." Aircraft, airfields and material were to be prepared and the selection of targets completed within three weeks. Britain, therefore, must take all necessary precautions.

The signal that Hitler had finally approved the *Blitzschlag* – the bombing of London without warning – was to have been a small bookseller's catalogue, sent to Kirkpatrick's London club.

A "sensational and rather lunatic little episode" was how Kirkpatrick later described this meeting. On December 15th, when he rushed into the Foreign Office with his intelligence, he caused a minor panic. Sir Fabian Ware, deputy head of MI5, had also heard the story from agents in Germany. Neville Chamberlain was at once informed and, although sceptical, felt that it could not be disregarded. A meeting of Ministers was summoned for the next morning. Absolute secrecy was maintained to the point of excluding lesser Foreign Office officials from knowledge and prohibiting any written records to be kept. An anti-aircraft regiment parked their guns in Wellington barracks, clearly visible to the German Embassy across the park.

The Committee of Imperial Defence, which directed and supervised the whole defence structure, discussed this report, and decided to accelerate all branches of air raid defences. A state of readiness was ordered within three months.[11] The Secret Intelligence Service also prepared an intelligence summary to be given to the American government. The information was never sent. The bookseller's catalogue never arrived in London.

The Kirkpatrick story had produced a minor panic. Rather than reciprocating the goodwill extended to him by Chamberlain, the Führer instead was believed to be planning the aerial bombardment of London: the one form of attack which sent shivers down the spines of all Whitehall officials. The fear of the bomber, dramatised by the destruction it was bringing during the Spanish Civil War, had been one of the many reasons compelling accommodation with Germany during the Czech crisis of 1938. Measures had been authorised after the Munich conference to increase the air raid defences of the capital, but these were by no means complete. They were sufficient to convince both the Foreign Office and the War Office that London could meet and survive the threat from the air.[12]

While this panic further increased Foreign Office disillusionment with Hitler, Chamberlain resigned himself to await some gesture of goodwill from Germany. He had decided not to take any initiative and "more or less leave Germany alone" for the meantime. By November 30th he had recognised that the "prospects of appeasement were not very bright in Berlin". Speaking to the House of Commons on December 19th, he stated he was "still waiting for a sign from those who speak for the German people" that they shared his desire to make their contribution to peace.

Optimistic as ever, the Prime Minister thought he detected

this sign in Hitler's New Year proclamation. "We have as always only one desire," Hitler declared, "namely that in the coming year it may be possible to succeed in contributing to the general pacification of the world." It took the experience of the Foreign Office to convince 10 Downing Street that Hitler's words represented nothing more "than the usual commonplace uttered on such occasions".

Although disappointed, Chamberlain was not deterred. He was also by this time inclined to discount the possibility of a German attack in the west.[13] During the next three weeks, even further shocks awaited him. His optimism was challenged, but his faith that war was not inevitable remained as deeply rooted as ever.

The Kirkpatrick story was actually not the first post-Munich war scare which threatened the western powers. The earlier report from Dr Karl Freidrich Goerdeler, "X" Document No. 4 of November 6th–7th, had had a less immediate response. He had made a passing reference to German aggressive aims against Holland, Belgium and Switzerland. In early December Arthur Young was asked to see Goerdeler and question him about this, among other things.

The contact on December 4th was again made in Switzerland, but this time in Zurich. Goerdeler told Young that his information about Hitler's designs in the west "was based on what he had been told by '*a man who is in daily contact with Hitler*'."* The first objective was Switzerland. "And on the principle that a Dictator only thrives by 'having a *new kill* for breakfast every morning,' X. [Goerdeler] feels that the danger ahead of Belgium and Holland is very real."[14]

This began to fit in with other information reaching London. From the Secret Intelligence Service came news that the extremists surrounding Hitler, notably Heinrich Himmler, head of the Gestapo, and the Foreign Minister, Joachim von Ribbentrop, were becoming more and more convinced that England could be successfully blackmailed. A certain "Herr Q", "an important member of the Nazi Party", had passed information to Sir Robert

* The Foreign Office thought this may have been Captain Fritz Wiedemann, a confidant of Hitler. (FO371/22961, C864/15/18.)

Vansittart in London that Himmler was advocating a surprise lightning blow against the west. Herr Q's conclusion was that the "extremist leaders are advocating a course which is likely to lead to a general war in the spring".[15]

Secret sources were not alone in coming to this conclusion. The British Military Attaché in Berlin, Colonel F. N. Mason-MacFarlane, despite many swashbuckling aspects to his character – such as plans to assassinate Hitler personally – was a very well-informed and astute observer. The despatch he wrote on December 26th, 1938, analysing military possibilities for the coming year was circulated to the Cabinet. There was little comfort to be drawn from his pessimistic conclusions. "We can be very nearly certain that military action for next year is contemplated and in preparation." It could be expected at a comparatively early date.

Foreign Office officials, already saturated with similar information, noted their entire agreement. Sir Alexander Cadogan, on January 6th, 1939, summarised the gloomy prospects:

> There is no doubt that 1939 will be big with fate. We cannot guess what Hitler will decide, or much less can we guess at the probable outcome of his decision. We can only prepare for the worst shocks.[16]

Still the information kept coming. In the second week of January, Goerdeler, back again in Germany, communicated more confidential information which was conveyed via Paris. Hitler was continuing to ignore warnings that the financial situation was incurable without a balanced budget. He was "convinced that England is degenerate; weak; timid; and never will have the guts to resist any of his plans". He had given orders to the general staff to prepare detailed plans of action and to complete mobilisation by February 15th against the Swiss and Dutch frontiers. "Both countries will not be conquered but only 'occupied' as security that the Western countries will satisfy German demands" as regards colonies, loans, raw materials and access to world markets. France will also be menaced and pressed to concede the northern part of her territory and Belgium as part of a German "zone of security".[17]

Sir Robert Vansittart's sources confirmed this picture of Hitler's intentions. At the same time, the Foreign Office was flooded with stories describing feverish preparations in Germany for military action. This included the calling up of reservists, the cancellation of Christmas leave, the widespread movement of ammunition, and the purchase of Czech agricultural produce.[18]

A German attack on the west appeared imminent. The weight of evidence seemed irrefutable and action was necessary to meet the danger. The Foreign Office prepared a lengthy paper, analysing its intelligence of German intentions. An introductory note warned: "All the reports seemed to show that Hitler is contemplating a coup early this year, the danger period beginning towards the end of February . . . he may decide that the moment is propitious for dealing an overwhelming blow at the Western Powers." The attached analysis of secret intelligence bleakly confirmed the likelihood of Germany "coming west" in 1939. Its chilling conclusion read:

> . . . there is incontrovertible evidence that at any rate many of the Führer's entourage are seriously considering the possibility of a direct attack on Great Britain and France during the next few months – perhaps during the next few weeks. It does not even seem to be at all unlikely that the Führer himself is thinking on such lines as these. At any rate all our sources are at one in declaring that he is barely sane, consumed by an insensate hatred of this country, and capable both of ordering an immediate aerial attack on any European country and of having his command instantly obeyed.[19]

A special meeting of the Foreign Policy Committee was called on January 23rd to discuss this intelligence. Lord Halifax was aware that some Ministers were not convinced as to its reliability. At the outset, therefore, he explained "that while it was derived from many different well tested sources it showed on the whole considerable unanimity". Pressures within Germany were "compelling the Mad Dictator of that country to insane adventures". It would be as wrong to "get into a state of panic" as it would be "to minimise the dangers".

47

The Committee quickly agreed as to their future action. On the insistent recommendation of Sir Robert Vansittart, making a rare appearance on this Committee, President Roosevelt was to be asked to speak out before Hitler's scheduled address to the Reichstag on January 30th. *Following a very strong appeal from the Foreign Office, and with the full approval of the Prime Minister, the Chiefs of Staff were invited to report on whether Dutch territorial integrity was so vital a strategic interest as to necessitate intervention in case of a German attack. If the answer was affirmative, what military response did the Chiefs of Staff advise?

On January 25th the Cabinet considered the situation. Fearing possible leakages of secret information, Lord Halifax only summarised the Foreign Office paper. In general, he stated, "The atmosphere was much like that which surrounds a child, in which everything was possible and nothing was impossible".

The Prime Minister supported his Foreign Secretary. The intelligence could not be ignored, Chamberlain said, "since we might be dealing with a man whose actions were not rational". On the other hand, allowance must be made for the "rather disturbing atmosphere in which those who received these reports necessarily worked". And they had not always forecast events accurately.

The Chiefs of Staff had meantime decided to be prepared. Their report to the Cabinet recommended immediate action to tighten the defences of western Europe. A German invasion of Holland was a "direct challenge" to British security. This was generally accepted by the Cabinet. Acceding to Chamberlain's reluctance to be bound too closely in all cases to the defence of Holland, no public statement about this decision was to be made. Steps designed to put the defence services into a state of readiness to meet any emergency were instead authorised.

Further discussion was left to the Foreign Policy Committee which met the next day, January 26th. The second report of the

* On February 1st Halifax referred the Cabinet, with obvious satisfaction, to Roosevelt's evidence before the Military Affairs Committee of the Senate, in which the President had said he would support the democracies short of a declaration of war and sending American troops.

Chiefs of Staff, who were present with the Service Ministers, added a note of realism to their previous advice. Britain, in fact, "could do little or nothing to prevent Holland from being over-run". The restoration of her territory would depend on the later course of the war. Chamberlain took a strong lead in pointing out that the object of any intervention would really be to resist German aggression ultimately directed against Britain and France. The fight would then be "in defence of the freedom of all neutral countries". The advice of the Chiefs of Staff was accepted.

The decision to defend Holland raised new problems of military planning. The Foreign Policy Committee agreed to open staff conversations with France on the basis of war against Germany and Italy combined.[20]

The momentum for action was sustained by further intelligence. On January 25th Sir Robert Vansittart noted that three "trustworthy sources" now confirmed that Hitler intended to thrust westwards. One of these sources gave March 3rd as the date by which German preparations must be completed. Yet another Goerdeler report arrived at the Foreign Office through Dr Reinhold Schairer. On January 26th information came that Hitler would present Britain with a three-day ultimatum towards the end of February or in March. The Führer would then proceed to occupy Holland and Switzerland if his demands were not met. Sir Alexander Cadogan at once advised that Britain must declare her intention to defend the Dutch.[21]

When the Cabinet assembled on February 1st, Neville Chamberlain was eager for military talks to proceed. It was recognised that this "was a big step forward and almost tantamount to an alliance", but justified by the threatened crisis. French insistence that Switzerland should be accorded the same treatment as Holland was readily granted.

Immediate steps were taken to plan for a series of Anglo-French military conversations. The question of similar talks with the Belgians was to await further negotiation. They were known to be reluctant to embark upon them and rather preferred to continue the intimate relations secretly established between the British and Belgian general staffs.

Only the tip of the iceberg was publicly revealed when Neville Chamberlain, addressing the House of Commons on February 6th, stated: "Any threat to the vital interests of France, from whatever quarter it came, would evoke the immediate co-operation of Great Britain." One MP, Harold Nicolson, described Chamberlain as "an astonishing and perplexing old boy". The announcement "startled the House", and appeared to be a "complete negation of his 'appeasement' policy".

"In our foreign policy we were doing our best to drive two horses abreast, conciliation and rearmament. It was a very nice art to keep these two steeds in step", Chamberlain had told the Cabinet on November 7th, 1938.[22] Three months later his balancing act was in shambles.

The British government had fought and won the first, fictitious, battle of 1939. The possibility of war had been contemplated with despair, but with none of the equivocation so prevalent in 1938. The challenge, even though unfounded, had been accepted. The response to this New Year panic had been firm and decisive. The western front had been strengthened. The war scare had convinced many that Munich had been a concession which had failed. The sacrifice of Czechoslovakia had apparently satisfied neither Hitler nor his extremist advisers.

Living through days marked by reports of Germany's aggressive intentions had its lessons. There emerged in the Foreign Office a consensus of opinion as to the kind of man who held supreme power in Germany. It began to be assumed that Hitler kept his own counsel. He had laid plans that winter both for an attack in the west and for a drive to the east. German military preparations were assumed to be proceeding to cover both possibilities. It was convenient for Hitler, meanwhile, "to hide behind a smoke-screen of uncertainty" until his plans matured.

This held great dangers for the western allies. Assuming that Hitler alone made the final decision to act, and that he acted on the spur of the moment in response to particular events, what trust could then be placed on secret intelligence, even if gleaned from Hitler's immediate entourage?

In 1939 a glut of intelligence poured into London. From the middle of December 1938 to the middle of April 1939, the Foreign Office had to ponder and evaluate no less than twenty definite intelligence reports indicating aggressive action by the Axis. There was intelligence about German military plans and preparations. The dates allegedly set by Hitler for action against one or other state on the continent were leaked. What intelligence sources could not do, however, was to say categorically whether Hitler would in fact act as reported.

The Foreign Office fell back on the only possible response. William Strang opted for moderation: "The Prime Minister's motto – not defiance or deference, but defence – seems to strike this middle line." Ivone Kirkpatrick added the following advice on February 20th: "Our policy should continue to be to emphasise our confidence in Germany's intention to keep the peace, whilst putting our defences in order as soon as possible and emphasising the non-aggressive nature of our rearmament." A day later, Cadogan issued his own warning: "Any slackening of effort on our part, or any relaxation of vigilance, would be extremely dangerous. I shall continue to hope for a real change of heart in the German Gov't., but I shall never believe in it until I see it proved."[23]

So well had the British government adjusted to dealing with the incalculable Führer that his next move, the march into Prague, caught many in London quite unaware. By mid-February reports of Hitler's intentions underwent one of their periodic and unexplained changes. The Foreign Office believed this was due to the progress in British rearmament, the firm response to the war scares of January, the reaffirmation of the Anglo-French alliance, France's refusal even to discuss Mussolini's Mediterranean claims and, not least, to the stiffer attitude adopted by President Roosevelt towards the dictatorships.

The first straw in the wind was Hitler's eagerly awaited speech on January 30th to the Reichstag. Again he directed personal attacks against "such agitators" as Churchill, Duff Cooper and

Eden. The American Secretary of State for the Interior, Harold Ickes, was for the first time admitted to that select circle. Hitler also made an angry attack on the United States, blaming the Jewish influence there for anti-German feeling. However, he derided the recent war scares as "lies born out of morbid hysteria" and stated he had no intention of entering into a conflict with Britain.

Prophecies of doom could be drawn as easily as crumbs of comfort from this speech. The Foreign Office took a cautious view. "Whilst we can congratulate ourselves that Hitler's speech has not aggravated the situation", Kirkpatrick wrote on January 31st to Halifax, "it is clear that we are not justified by anything he [Hitler] has said in relaxing our vigilance, our preparations or the measures we are taking to concert with the French and other Governments." Likewise, Gladwyn Jebb, noting the "recent absence of alarmist reports from all our secret sources", warned on February 16th that "we have still to reckon with the well-known 'incalculability' of Herr Hitler, and it would certainly be fatal . . . to assume that we are yet out of the wood".[24]

Even Lord Halifax, when speaking to a meeting of Dominion High Commissioners the next day, mentioned that the situation had generally improved. But "he would not like to go further than this for the very next day might belie it". As late as March 11th, Sir Alexander Cadogan, who despite his usual austere comments was quite capable of breaking out into poetic prose, noted: "I hope we may be able to continue between the Scylla of ostrich-like complacency on the one hand and the Charybdis of 'potential hysteria' on the other."

"Ostrich-like complacency" was of course more palatable than hysteria. From many quarters came assessments which buttressed this attitude. On February 3rd MI5 reported the view of Dr Fritz Hesse, press adviser to the German Embassy in London. He had stated on his return from Berlin that Hitler's current policy was "appeasement in the West and peaceful penetration in the South-East". The Secret Intelligence Service supported this conclusion.[25]

No less an authority than the Deputy Director of Military

Intelligence at the War Office, Brigadier Frederick Beaumont-Nesbitt, affirmed on February 8th that general military measures, short of actual mobilisation, were aimed at placing Germany in a high degree of readiness. Otherwise, there were "no other measures pointing to early military action either in the West, East or South". The War Office was not blind, however, to the inherent danger of the European situation. While there was a lack of evidence pointing to any immediate move, the peace establishment of German formations was very nearly up to war strength. Hitler had "under his hand a fighting machine which can be moved in support of his policy in a matter of hours and in any direction".[26]

The desire to play it cool and be done with the more extravagant war scares strongly prevailed during February. On the 16th, the United States Under-Secretary of State, Sumner Welles, received the British Ambassador, Sir Ronald Lindsay. Welles had been very much impressed by the "gloomy news" he had of Italian and German military preparations which pointed towards a crisis or even war by the end of March. President Roosevelt, who was at the time on board a train for a fortnight's cruise with the US fleet, had told the press, after hearing of these reports, that he might be obliged to cut short his vacation.

Lindsay's telegram reporting this conversation was sent for expert examination to the head of the Secret Intelligence Service, Admiral Sir Hugh "Quex" Sinclair. The Admiral "was inclined to take the view that it represented alarmist rumours put forward by Jews and Bolshevists for their own ends". A soothing reply was returned to Washington.[27]

A strong reaction against threatening rumours and panic intelligence also set in. It became necessary for Sir Alexander Cadogan to come to the defence of the Secret Intelligence Service and specifically absolve it of any blame. On February 28th he wrote:

Our agents are, of course, bound to report rumours or items of information which come into their possession: they exercise a certain amount of discrimination themselves, but naturally do not take the responsibility of too much selection and it is our job here to weigh up the information which we receive and try to draw more or less reasonable conclusions from it. In that we may fail and if so it is our fault, but I do not think that it is fair to blame the SIS. Moreover, it is true to say that the recent scares have not originated principally with the SIS agents in Germany, but have come to us from other sources.[28]

Perhaps the greatest single inspiration for this "February lull" was Sir Nevile Henderson, the British Ambassador in Berlin. He had an almost apocalyptic belief in his mission of Anglo-German reconciliation. "I had been chosen, under the guidance of Providence, for the special task of helping to preserve the world from the horror of another and more ghastly war than the last", he wrote before his death in 1942. While he often persisted in views opposed even by Chamberlain, the two men shared one common deep-rooted belief. Representing a country where anti-totalitarian opinion proved more eloquent than the voices urging Anglo-German rapprochement, both had by necessity to redress the balance. Nazism and Fascism were equally despicable to both. But the claims and grievances of Germany and Italy had to be heard, objectively assessed, and then redressed.

Henderson's dedication aroused violent emotions, yet he was undeterred. Almost every day while in Berlin he wrote out in longhand personal letters to those whom he suspected of being sympathetic: the Prime Minister, Sir Horace Wilson, Lord Halifax and, sometimes, Sir Alexander Cadogan. Henderson was despised and undiplomatically abused by Vansittart. Foreign Office officials confined themselves to penning savage, often sarcastic, criticisms of his telegrams and letters when circulated for comment.

In October 1938 Henderson had returned to London on leave. It was then that he learned he was suffering from a malignant growth in the mouth. A successful operation left him able to carry on, though still physically unfit, after a long and arduous spell in hospital. The question of replacing him was raised in the Foreign Office, but no decision was taken. He returned to Berlin in February, eager to carry on his mission, and repair the damage to Anglo-German relations caused by the recent war scares. The Ambassador quickly arranged interviews with leading Germans to gauge the temperature in Berlin. On February 15th he had a long talk with Ribbentrop, whom he found calm and very self-confident. Ribbentrop's greatest annoyance was reserved for the anti-German attitude of America.

Three days later Henderson called on Field-Marshal Hermann Göring, Minister for Air and Commander-in-Chief of the *Luft-waffe*, who proudly announced that he had lost forty pounds in weight. The fatigue resulting from such a strenuous diet had forced him to plan a complete rest cure at San Remo for early March. "People can make what mistakes they like while I am away; I shall not care," he said. The exchange of views on the intentions of British and German rearmament which followed left Henderson with the "definite impression . . . that Herr Hitler does not contemplate any adventures at the moment and that all stories and rumours to the contrary are completely without real foundation". Memel, Danzig, and Czechoslovakia, Henderson added, would no doubt be the next objects of German attention. Hitler would not force the pace unless his own hand was forced. "I believe in fact that he would now like in his heart to return to the fold of comparative respectability," Henderson prophesied.

This conversation evoked pages of minutes from the pens of Foreign Office officials. They simply could not stomach Henderson's facile optimism as to Hitler's intentions. It was their common view that any soft-pedalling on Hitler's part was due solely to the firmness displayed by Britain and France during the last crisis. Sir Robert Vansittart was incensed by what he called the Ambassador's "dangerous rubbish". "Sir Nevile Henderson does not seem to be in touch with reality." As for the future, Cadogan wrote in a personal minute to Halifax, "I have the profoundest suspicion of Hitler's intentions: I believe they are strictly dishonourable, and I know what he would like best, if he could do it, would be to smash the British Empire. . . . The only one thing certain in a very uncertain world is that we must be prepared as best we can for anything."[29]

Neville Chamberlain, still searching for some soothing words or hopeful signs from Berlin, found that Henderson's prognostications made exciting reading. In letters to his sister he bubbled with confidence. He was now quite optimistic. All his information pointed to the way of peace. Germany was in no mood for war. She was occupied with her own internal economic problems. And he repeated the view he had so often, mistakenly, expressed about European affairs that he had finally got the better of the dictators. On February 17th he called in the American Ambassador, Joseph Kennedy, for a long talk, and freely spoke of his disagreement with the Foreign Office pessimists. Hitler remained "impractical and fanatical", Chamberlain said. But the "only hope of doing business with Hitler is to take him at his word". Up to date, Kennedy reported to the State Department in Washington, Chamberlain had no reason to disbelieve it.[30]

So excited did Chamberlain become at this point as to the prospects opening up, that he wrote Henderson a personal letter. This sketched a picture of a pacified Europe that, had it succeeded, would have left him with the glory rather than the obloquy of being the "man with the umbrella".

> Things look as though Spain might clear up fairly soon. After that the next thing will be to get the bridge between Paris & Rome into working order. After that we might begin to talk about disarmament, preferably beginning with Mussolini, but bringing in the Germans pretty soon. If all went well we should have so improved the atmosphere that we might begin to think of colonial discussions. But people have got so frightened and "het up" about them that we should have to approach the subject with the greatest care.

Halifax was shown this extraordinary letter. He could not let it pass without comment, and at once wrote to Henderson that the Prime Minister was being too optimistic. What was needed from the leading Nazis was "more than smooth words as evidence of friendly hearts". Sir Alexander Cadogan confided his opinion to his diary. "Nevile H. is completely bewitched by his German friends."[31]

Chamberlain's euphoria, in retrospect, seems distinctly irresponsible. To have staked so definite an assessment on such meagre signs was wishful thinking. Lulls had occurred many times before when Hitler was hesitating before action. Hopes had so often been rudely shattered. But approaching the end of his second year as Prime Minister, Chamberlain was impatient for large-scale results.

For the more sceptically minded, the European scene was still full of danger, of unresolved possibilities. Those searching beneath the surface of Nazi Germany found enough to disturb them. At the same time as the Secret Intelligence Service was reporting an absence of alarmist rumours, Sir Robert Vansittart was telling a different story. The tragedy, however, was that his sources, among others, had been discredited because of the New Year panic. This was particularly true of information coming from Dr Karl Goerdeler. Lord Halifax began to wonder how the German moderates appeared to know the plans of the dictators in such detail. Sir Orme Sargent regretfully commented on what a pity it was that Goerdeler "tries to curdle our blood by overstating his case". More important was that Cadogan was getting very bored with almost daily alarms. "Our sources of infn. have lately become so prolific (and blood-curdling)", he minuted, "that I am beginning to regard them all with a degree of suspicion."[32] The Foreign Office was soon to be awakened from their almost drunken passivity to panic reports.

Vansittart did his best to keep alive the immediate danger of further German action. Until the middle of February, he was still convinced Germany's next move would be westwards. When the mobilisation date of February 15th, which he had predicted, passed without being put into action, he suddenly had more alarming intelligence. It came from Professor T. Philip Conwell Evans, an important and very secretive figure in Vansittart's remarkable intelligence network, known to some as his "Private Detective Agency". Conwell Evans was a prominent British Germanophile, a Joint Honorary Secretary of the Anglo-German Fellowship, and had lectured at the University of Königsberg. He was on friendly terms with Ribbentrop and had actually been his confidant when the Foreign Minister had been Germany's Ambassador in London. In this capacity Conwell Evans had regularly visited the German Embassy. But the fact that Germany's actions during the 1938 Czech crisis had turned the Welsh professor against the Nazis was still unknown to Ribbentrop.

In late February Conwell Evans hastily returned from Berlin where he had attended the annual *Deutsch-Englische Gesellschaft** meeting and spoken privately to leading Nazis. The story he brought back was startlingly different from Henderson's assessments. Where the British Ambassador had exchanged pleasantries and platitudes with Ribbentrop, Conwell Evans had been treated to bluster, ranting and raving. Ribbentrop felt he was in safe company and gave vent to his megalomania. He warned that Britain should no longer interest itself in the Czech situation. As for President Roosevelt, he was a thorn in the flesh. Ribbentrop abused him "as the mouthpiece of Judah and the instrument of the Comintern".

After further conversations and secret contacts with the German moderates, Conwell Evans submitted to Vansittart a memorandum which was uncanny in its forecasts. Hitler had decided to incorporate within the Reich the rest of Czechoslovakia, Conwell Evans wrote.

> He will apply the familiar method of creating unrest by stirring up factitious claims for self-determination, this time on the part of the Slovaks. The Czechs will naturally resent this attempt at a second partition of their country. Hitler will then be furnished with a pretext to intervene by military force, and will end by wiping out Czechoslovakia as an independent state. . . . Hitler seems to have decided to undertake the adventure which runs the least risk of provoking the armed intervention of Britain and France, but which nevertheless inflicts the greatest possible humiliation on the western Democracies.

Where Conwell Evans erred was in placing the date for this operation as "probably" in May. He reserved his final word of

---

* The German counterpart of the Anglo-German Fellowship.

warning for Henderson: "I regret to say that Sir Nevile Henderson is completely out of touch with the situation in Germany."

Vansittart arranged an appointment with Lord Halifax to discuss this news. He feared the "orgy of optimism" being indulged in by the Government would rebound to their discredit. The meeting never took place. Halifax was taken ill. Sir Alexander Cadogan was very sceptical about Conwell Evans, even hinting that he was being used by the Nazis to spread alarmist reports. By the end of February, there were also "rumours" from intelligence sources of Hitler's plans to destroy Czechoslovakia. On March 6th Vansittart received further information from Conwell Evans, confirmed by the Secret Intelligence Service, that leave had been stopped for the German army and air force.[33]

Despite these disturbing indications, the order from 10 Downing Street was to maintain the semblance that the golden age of European appeasement was on the doorstep. Cabinet Ministers spoke publicly in this sense. So, too, did Chamberlain himself when speaking off the record to a meeting of lobby correspondents in the House of Commons on March 9th.[34] The shock of the March 15th occupation of Czechoslovakia was rudest to those who had postured with ostrich-like blindness.

———

Hitler must have watched western statesmen with some amusement in 1939. The frantic activity in London and Paris, the continuous speeches and parliamentary declarations, the ebb and flow of press rumour and speculation were all very useful. They helped to mask a period in his military planning which was limited, yet full of possibilities. Poland, isolated between her two powerful neighbours, Germany and Russia, could be easy game. The return of Memel to the Reich could be a simple matter of "addressing a registered letter to Kaunas", the Lithuanian capital. The Carpatho-Ukraine, the eastern part of Czechoslovakia given autonomy after the Munich settlement, could be manipulated as a centre for the disruption of both the Polish and Soviet Ukraine. Rumania could not withstand a German drive, especially if undertaken with the connivance of the Hungarians. There was finally the possibility of an attack in the west. But a war on two fronts, the nightmare of German military planners, was to be avoided. It is not surprising, therefore, that at least until the end of December 1938, some Germans with access to Hitler had the impression that he was still undecided in what direction to turn next.[35] His basic freedom of action could be exercised against the west or into any corner of eastern Europe.

Caught on the horns of this dilemma, Hitler took the path of the safer and cheaper glory. The British and French governments prepared for an attack in the west. President Roosevelt, from across the Atlantic, muttered approval and issued vague warnings to Germany. Meanwhile, Hitler kept his own counsel and laid his plans. These had in fact only one limited aim: to complete the subjugation of Czechoslovakia interrupted by the Munich conference; or in the bitter words of Sir Robert Vansittart: to "indulge in the desecration of the corpse (*Die Leichenschändung*)."[36]

No sooner had Hitler said goodbye to Neville Chamberlain, Edouard Daladier and Benito Mussolini at Munich and returned to the Berghof, than he sent for General Keitel, Chief of the High Command of the *Wehrmacht*. Hitler inquired as to the strengths and dispositions needed to break Czech resistance in Bohemia and Moravia. There the matter rested until October 21st, 1938. On that day a new directive was issued to the German armed forces: to prepare the defence of Germany against surprise air attack and the "liquidation of the remainder of the Czech State". The latter would only be put into action should Czechoslovakia pursue an anti-German policy.

This directive was superseded on December 17th. The army was to continue making its preparations against Czechoslovakia, but on a less grand scale. Troops would only leave their stations on the night prior to attack. There was no need for any large-scale mobilisation. The Czechs could hardly resist. The whole operation was to have the appearance of a peaceful undertaking.[37]

Having made all the necessary military arrangements, Hitler sat back to await the inevitable bungling of the politicians and diplomats. Events for him held no surprises.

CHAPTER THREE

Viorel Virgil Tilea

At 6 a.m. on March 17th Viorel Virgil Tilea, the Rumanian Minister in London, was awakened at his home in Belgrave Square by a mysterious telephone call from Paris. The voice said in Rumanian: "Do you know who is talking?" Tilea recognised it immediately. The informant gave him details of the harsh economic and political demands the Germans had made on his country.

Tilea then went downstairs to his study where he found on his desk a telegram which had arrived from his Foreign Minister, Grigore Gafencu. It instructed him to warn the British government of the consequences to the entire European continent of Hitler's seizure of Prague. The belief was growing that Hitler alone was the arbiter who decided the fate of nations. So far no statement or action had come from the Western Powers to dispel this belief.[1]

Tilea pondered these instructions and his anonymous telephone call. What was he to do? As he reflected, echoes of a conversation he had had the previous day came to mind. Worried by the destruction of Czechoslovakia, he had rushed to the Foreign Office to speak to Sir Orme Sargent. He had told him that "from secret and other sources" – the Rumanians had very efficient intelligence services – his government believed Germany had plans to reduce Hungary to vassalage and to destroy Rumania. Then, emphasising that he was speaking "entirely personally", he had asked Sargent how far Rumania could count on British assistance in case of need. Armaments to equip four divisions, of the kind previously ordered from Czechoslovakia, were desperately required. Would Britain now be prepared to

61

grant Rumania a credit of £10 million to purchase war material? Tilea had made this particular request, unsuccessfully, several times before.

Sir Orme Sargent had listened sympathetically. He was by now one of the most outspoken of Foreign Office officials and quite disillusioned with appeasement. But he offered no definite reply. The proposals put forward, he explained, raised "questions of high policy", and Lord Halifax would be informed.

Tilea had left the Foreign Office empty-handed. He might have been encouraged, however, had he known that day of the indirect support he was receiving from his government which was soon to abandon him in humiliating circumstances. At ten minutes past noon on March 16th a telegram was received at the Foreign Office from the British Minister in Bucharest, Sir Reginald Hoare. The Rumanian monarch, King Carol II, a great-grandson of Queen Victoria, had asked that both Britain and France would "on some occasion which appears to them suitable let it be known that they have not lost interest in South Eastern Europe". This telegram reached Sargent's desk the next day. He took immediate action. He "strongly" urged that Ministers in their forthcoming speeches should emphasise that the British government was "still as interested as we ever have been in South-Eastern Europe".

Sargent took another important step. "I have called the attention of the Private Secretaries to this", he minuted, "in case it is still possible for the *Prime Minister* to insert a suitable passage in his speech this evening." Neville Chamberlain was caught on the telephone before making his speech at Birmingham and included the desired reference.[2]

But of all this Tilea knew nothing when he decided to act yet again. He had his official instructions to approach the British government. This was also backed by private information. For weeks he had followed, with mounting anxiety and incomplete information, the delicate commercial negotiations proceeding in Bucharest between his government and a high-powered German delegation. Tilea's next moves set in motion a chain of events which, in the opinion of the American Ambassador,

Joseph Kennedy, "changed Chamberlain's policy." It ended five and a half months later in the outbreak of the Second World War.

On his way to the Foreign Office, where he had been given an interview later that afternoon, Tilea called in at the American Embassy. He had only a few weeks before made the acquaintance of Joseph Kennedy. He liked and trusted the Ambassador and decided he must be informed. Tilea revealed that the German demands, made about a week or ten days before, "were economic and really meant the end of Rumania". They had been rejected. Kennedy immediately telegraphed this news to the State Department in Washington.[3]

Tilea then went on to the Foreign Office where Oliver Harvey, Private Secretary to Lord Halifax, escorted him into the Foreign Secretary's first floor office. Moments before the Minister's arrival, Harvey had told Halifax of a message which he had just received. Walter Elliot, the Minister of Health, had rung up to say that he had been speaking to Robert Bernays, an MP and junior Minister. Princess Marthe Bibesco, a Rumanian writer and intimate friend of Lady Violet Bonham-Carter, had revealed to Bernays that the President of the Council in Bucharest, Armand Calinesco, had told her on the telephone of Germany's economic ultimatum.[*]

* Exhaustive inquiries made, both by the author and others, directly to Princess Bibesco, confirm that the luxuriant description in the diaries of Sir Henry Channon (pp. 186–7) of a meeting between her and Bernays on March 17th is "incorrect ... pure fantasy" and "sheer invention". On the one hand she explains that in early March Bernays had visited her residence in Posada, in the Carpathians, eleven miles from the royal residence at Sinaia. Bernays had been recommended by Baroness Asquith. He was introduced to King Carol, told about the German ultimatum, and returned to London to inform the Foreign Office. On the other hand Princess Bibesco maintains that President Calinesco in fact did telephone to her on March 17th with the story of the ultimatum. She then contacted Bernays who at once got in touch with Walter Elliot, another of her friends. He, in turn, informed Oliver Harvey. The details of how the news of the German ultimatum reached the Foreign Office may be contradictory. In the rumour-ridden world of Rumanian politics everything was possible; except perhaps the likelihood of President Calinesco speaking to

With his usual polite demeanour, Halifax expectantly listened as the Rumanian Minister repeated what he had related to Sargent the previous day. But Tilea now reinforced the general appreciation with his urgent private information. During the last few days, he recounted, the German mission in Rumania, negotiating a new commercial treaty, had asked his government to grant Berlin a monopoly of exports and to restrict Rumanian industrial production in German interests. In return, Germany would guarantee the frontiers of Rumania.

"This seems to the Roumanian Government something very much like an ultimatum", Tilea stated, having picked his words deliberately in order to avoid giving the impression an actual ultimatum had been presented. Could the British government, therefore, give a precise indication of the action they would take in case Rumania was attacked by Germany? A solid bloc of Poland, Rumania, Greece, Turkey and Yugoslavia, supported by Britain and France, might save the situation. Halifax replied that he would lay the question "with all urgency" before the Prime Minister and the Cabinet.[4]

Tilea felt he could not ask for more. Before leaving, he handed the Foreign Secretary a copy of the telegram containing Grigore Gafencu's instructions. He then went to see Sir Alexander Cadogan to repeat his story. While waiting to be received, Tilea had had a few words with Cadogan's Private Secretary, Gladwyn Jebb. They discussed the general situation. Would Rumania ever accept aid from the USSR, the one country able to offer effective military support? Jebb asked, expecting a negative reply. To his surprise, Tilea answered: "Of course they would. There was no question about it." Jebb seemed convinced of the degree of danger to Rumania.

There was one last momentous call Tilea made at the Foreign Office. He visited Sir Robert Vansittart, whose office was situated directly below that of the Foreign Secretary. Here Tilea repeated

---

Princess Bibesco over tapped telephone wires from Bucharest to London. (Letter, Princess Bibesco to the author, June 7th, 1971. I am grateful to Lord Boyd and V. V. Tilea for permission to read their correspondence with Princess Bibesco.)

his information, and received the most sympathetic hearing and encouragement. Vansittart's own intelligence network broadly confirmed Tilea's story. He agreed that it would be useful if the Minister would leak the story to the press. This was done both in London and New York.

On his way back to the Rumanian Legation, Tilea stopped in for a late tea with the Turkish Ambassador, Dr Tevfik Rüstü Aras. They were joined by the Greek Minister, Charalambos Simopoulos, and the Soviet Ambassador, Ivan Maisky. The threat to Rumania posed dangers to each of their countries. Tilea confided to this gathering that he had seen Halifax, Cadogan and Vansittart and then related what he had learned on the telephone that morning. According to the report which Maisky sent that evening to Moscow, Tilea revealed that the ultimatum, "made about a week ago" and rejected, had been repeated the previous day "in a yet more threatening form". On returning at last to his Legation, Tilea compared notes with his Military and Assistant Military Attachés. They had simultaneously been to see the Secretary of State for War, Leslie Hore-Belisha, to underline on strategic grounds the implications of the information and the appeal the Minister had conveyed to the Foreign Office. Hore-Belisha, one of the youngest Ministers and the only Jew in the Cabinet, was deeply impressed and promised to help. That was an encouraging sign.[5]

At the Foreign Office Halifax, Cadogan and Sargent met to discuss Tilea's information. They agreed on the obvious: Britain herself was in no position to offer direct aid. But what about Rumania's neighbours and potential allies? By ten o'clock that evening telegrams had already been sent off to Moscow, Warsaw, Ankara, Athens and Belgrade. To all capitals, except Moscow, went a simple request for information: what would be their attitude if Germany attacked Rumania? The Russians were a separate problem. They were asked whether they would, if requested, help Rumania. So ended a day described by a weary Cadogan in his diary as "Politically, awful. Really worse than last September" – the height of the Czech crisis.[6]

A revolution in British foreign policy had just been triggered off by the unsubstantiated information brought to the Foreign Office by a relatively unknown diplomat from a distant country. Who was this man who succeeded in stirring into action a government which had since the Munich conference virtually written off eastern Europe and seemed blindly dedicated to reaching an accommodation with Hitler's Germany?

The diplomat responsible, Viorel Virgil Tilea, was young, intelligent, ambitious and had been for a long time well-disposed towards Britain. Partly educated at the London School of Economics, he was President of the Anglo-Rumanian Society, was awarded a CBE for this work in 1938, and had been in the entourage of King Carol during the state visit to Britain in November 1938. He was reputed, according to the British Embassy in Bucharest, to be an intimate of the King and to have been aiming for a long time at representing his country in London. In actual fact, he had refused the post three times. Being, as well, one of the five leading industrialists in his country, he had a direct interest in Rumania's political and economic orientation. But it was his whole background, passionately Anglophile, humanistic in education and outlook, which made him a devout patriot and a fervent opponent of Nazism and German expansionism. Despite Tilea's obvious dedication, the British Minister in Bucharest, Sir Reginald Hoare, unfortunately regarded him as giving an "impression of untrustworthiness". This description, supported by no evidence and concealed from him, was to haunt all of Tilea's activities and make his mission more hazardous.

Before leaving Bucharest in January 1939, to take up his position as the newly appointed Minister to London, Tilea had a long conference with King Carol. The King agreed to Tilea's comprehensive plan of action. This was designed to tie the Rumanian economy closer to British interests and strengthen the political links between the two countries. If successful, such a campaign would prevent Germany from having a virtual monopoly on the fabulously wealthy natural resources of Rumania. Her oil, gold, timber and wheat were a vital prize for the war machine of any country. Tilea was instructed to secure that prize for the British, using whatever means and discretion he thought necessary. Armed with this broad mandate, Tilea arrived in London aboard the Golden Arrow from Paris on February 1st.

Time was desperately short, but Tilea's energy was unlimited. He was determined his country would not go the way of Austria and Czechoslovakia. For more than a month, the new Rumanian Minister hurriedly made the rounds in London. Private meetings with potential investors, planning the formation of a new Anglo-Rumanian trading organisation, and urging the despatch of a commercial mission to Bucharest all took time and effort. From the Foreign Office, to the Board of Trade, to the Treasury and back again, Tilea planned, persuaded, argued and cajoled. But with little success. Looking back thirty years later on this period of his life, Tilea reflected: "Negotiating with British officials in February 1939 was like playing one man tennis. I hit many balls into their court, but they were never returned."[7]

The winter of 1938–39 was not the right moment to be asking the British government to extend its political and economic influence in south-east Europe. The "spirit of Munich" – the hoped-for period of conciliation and accommodation with Hitler – still preoccupied, if intermittently and without response from Berlin, the mind of the British government. King Carol, when visiting London in November 1938, failed miserably in his efforts to interest the British government in the fate of his country. His economic proposals were turned down as being commercially unsound. It was agreed privately that Rumania was a bad credit risk. Besides, the policy of political subsidies for economic schemes, while typical of German trading methods, was not recognised by the more conservative, genteel, British economists.

The crux of the matter, hinted at but rarely discussed, was the political issue. Did the Rumanians have the will to preserve their independence before the massive German offensive in central and south-east Europe? The Foreign Office thought not. The Treasury and Board of Trade agreed. Neville Chamberlain himself, always more practical than his colleagues, "was very much influenced by the fact that the political situation in Rumania was so uncertain and unstable". It was best, in his opinion, "to keep the pot boiling". Sir Frederick Leith-Ross, Chief Economic Adviser to the Foreign Office, disagreed. "I like M. Tilea," he once wrote, "and I think that one can talk frankly with him." He also thought it was worthwhile trying to save Rumania. In the end his point of view prevailed.

Tilea's arrival in London, therefore, could not have come at a worse time. Yet he was undeterred and passionately determined. He approached his mission as a businessman, not as a diplomat. At his introductory meeting with Sir Alexander Cadogan on February 1st, he took the opportunity "to make a general appeal to His Majesty's Government to assist Roumania to save herself from the clutches of Germany". Cadogan replied with generalities and platitudes.

Two days later it was the turn of E. M. B. Ingram, head of the Foreign Office Southern Department, to receive the persistent Minister. Ingram was told that Rumania was faced with the prospect of vigorous political and economic pressure from Germany. Bucharest was stalling in its commercial negotiations. But London must show a greater eagerness to invest in, and assist, Rumania if she was to avoid being monopolised by the Germans. Ingram listened patiently, but neither he could offer any encouragement.[8]

On March 1st Tilea discussed the political situation with the Soviet Ambassador, Ivan Maisky. In case of German aggression, Maisky assured him, Rumania could count on Russian support. While doubtless pleased to have this assurance, Tilea knew that such a commitment only from the Bolsheviks would earn him few friends in London, and would be violently opposed by many around the King and in the Foreign Ministry at home. However, he continued his efforts. On March 10th, when speaking to Philip Nichols, another member of the Southern Department, Tilea advanced a scheme for a "Black Sea 'Gentleman's Agreement' ", designed to weld together the nations of south-east Europe in opposition to Hitler's Germany.[9]

Events did not wait on such well-planned schemes of mutual assistance. By March 14th all of Europe was watching Czechoslovakia's agony. Fearing the worst, Tilea went to the Foreign Office to seek an interview. He was received by Sir Orme Sargent, to whom he poured out his anxiety about the situation in central Europe. Yugoslavia and Rumania, he pointed out, could be as easily disintegrated as Czechoslovakia. Could not the British government at least make a gesture? Why not announce at once the immediate despatch of a commercial mission to Bucharest; cancel the forthcoming visit to Berlin of the President of the Board of Trade; and raise the Legations in Bucharest, Belgrade and Athens to Embassies. To all this Sargent wearily replied that the suggestions would be considered.[10] There were more urgent problems to deal with; more ominous telegrams waited on his desk for attention. The events which followed in the next forty-eight hours produced the crisis background which allowed Tilea to succeed where others had failed.

The "Tilea affair" has mystified inquirers and provoked more than its share of controversy since 1939. What explains the impact his story had in the Foreign Office, leading to such a formidable change in British foreign policy? What were his motives: personal gain or patriotic loyalty? Was he acting on official instructions and did he exceed them? Where did he get his information?

The question of why Tilea should have set the Foreign Office machinery working so quickly is partly answered, of course, by the impact of the Czech coup. Hitler had outraged the Foreign Office and humiliated Chamberlain. The only response could be a diplomatic protest which, as was well known in London, would fall on deaf ears. But then Tilea appeared at the exact moment with relevant news. Here was the opportunity to react; and react firmly. The occasion was immediately seized. If Hitler was on the march, as was believed in London, he must be stopped. The telegrams had therefore gone out to the east and south-east European governments.

But was the Foreign Office taken in by Tilea? Were such astute observers as Cadogan and Sargent the willing tools of an elaborate hoax? A report in the *Völkischer Beobachter* from its London correspondent claimed that the "panic reports" of a trade ultimatum were the combined invention of Tilea and Sir Robert Vansittart: the former worried about his career after failing to secure closer Anglo-Rumanian trade relations; the latter anxious to force a military confrontation with Germany in south-east Europe.[11]

At mid-day on March 18th a brief, but urgent, message arrived from Sir Reginald Hoare, advising the cancellation of the Foreign Office inquiries in east and south-east Europe. Three hours later came a telegram of explanation. Grigore Gafencu, the Rumanian Foreign Minister, had asserted that the economic negotiations with Germany were proceeding normally. There was no immediate threat to Rumania's independence. While he regretted that Tilea "should in an excess of zeal have misrepresented the situation", he asked the British government to retain its confidence in the Minister.

At once a telephone call was made to Tilea at the Rumanian Legation. He repeated his belief in the truth of the information at his disposal. Still unsatisfied, Cadogan asked Tilea to come down to the Foreign Office to explain his actions. The whole affair, in view of Gafencu's denial, was proving in London to be "rather disconcerting".

Tilea knew he was on the carpet, yet he was undeterred. He first translated for Cadogan a telegram, just received from Gafencu, ordering him to deny the story of the ultimatum. Cadogan's minute of the conversation continues:

He [Tilea] then went on to explain to me that he was quite convinced that the story of the ultimatum was true, but he added that it had been presented by the Germans about ten days before the recent Czech crisis and had been turned down at once by the Roumanian Government. He said that he had received it from a private source, which, on further questioning, he declared to be the general manager of a big Roumanian industrialist, who had come specially to Paris to pass the news on to him. . . . I said that it was not clear to me that M. Tilea had at any time obtained knowledge of the ultimatum directly from his Government. . . . Nothing would shake M. Tilea as to the truth of his story about the ultimatum. He said that there were many cross-currents in Roumania, but that he was convinced that it was true that the ultimatum had been presented and had been refused: his fear was that the refusal might not be maintained. He saw that it was somewhat disconcerting for us to have this conflict of information: he himself realised that he was in a delicate position: he did not mind so much about his position vis à vis the authorities in Bucharest, but he was afraid that his position here might be compromised. . . . Finally M. Tilea said that on the whole the appearance of this story in the press in London had not done any harm. . . . I do not think that my interview with M. Tilea increased my confidence in him.[12]

Tilea himself was not blind to his embarrassing predicament. The next evening, March 19th, he went to see Lord Lloyd, President of the British Council. The work of this organisation in promoting closer Anglo-Rumanian cultural relations had brought the two into intimate contact. Lloyd himself was a firm believer in the need to rescue south-east Europe from German domination. As a result of his conversation with Tilea, Lloyd wrote to Halifax the following day:

I had a long talk with Tilea last night, who is anxious that you should be assured that whatever news you get from Rex Hoare or anyone else, the German economic ultimatum was in fact given. He was told so on the telephone by Tatarescu [the Rumanian Ambassador in Paris] and Bonnet had confirmed the information. . . . Tilea is very anxious that you should realise the delicacy of the internal situation in Roumania, but cannot tell you so officially. I think that Gafencu is not a strong man and has all along been in favour of concessions to Germans, whilst the King is surrounded by people having German economic interests pressing him in the same direction. Personally, I think the King will stand very steady, especially if he gets encouragement from here, but I know that Tilea is right about the pro-German influences that play upon the King from industrialists and other business people in Roumania.

Tilea now rested his case. He had acted not on impulse, but out of consideration for the safety of his country. In his belief, this lay in closer relations with Britain. He had exceeded his instructions only in a strictly legal sense. His appointment to London carried a very broad mandate from King Carol, which he did not fear to use. The denial from Gafencu was expected. Tilea had little regard for his Foreign Minister and considered him a defeatist.[13] Finally, he had gone as far as he dared when justifying his actions in revealing something of the identity, but not the name, of his informant. *

In his conversations with Cadogan and Lloyd, Tilea tried discreetly to picture the turbulent, confused and often vicious, circle of influences which played upon King Carol. He was convinced he enjoyed the full confidence of his monarch; himself playing off competing interests against each other. Rumanian politics were not for the weak or the indecisive, and Tilea was neither. He had hoped the British government would understand and act. They did, in fact, act immediately and understood later.

Written evidence of the German ultimatum never turned up in 1939, nor since, indeed, in any archive. Perhaps it may never come to light. The Germans could have made their demands orally. As the months passed and further information about the Tilea "ultimatum" trickled out of Bucharest, the Foreign Office began to think twice about the Rumanian Minister in London. In June came a curious story from Sir Reginald Hoare. A Secretary of the German Legation in Bucharest had committed

---

* The precise identity of the informant was never revealed by Tilea. To Cadogan he spoke of the "general manager of a big Roumanian industrialist", while with Lord Lloyd he mentioned Tatarescu. If in fact the former was the informant, Tilea was referring to a representative from the anti-German economic camp in Rumania. The four major Rumanian industrialists were Gigurtu, Malaxa, Ausnit and Bujoiu. Max Ausnit was negotiating through Tilea in London for the formation of an Anglo-Rumanian Trading Company. Ausnit had returned to Bucharest in February and was expected in Paris during the criticial days of early March. He might have been responsible for relaying information to Tilea.

suicide in April because "he had chattered about the famous 'Tilea ultimatum' to Roumania while in his cups in a night club". Sir Reginald Hoare commented, when forwarding this evidence to the Foreign Office: "The long and short of it seems to be that Tilea was perhaps not so wide of the mark!"

In November 1939 it was learned that between March 18th–20th King Carol had ordered intensive military preparations to resist any pressure from Germany. Hoare, who submitted this new evidence, concluded "that the language held in London by Monsieur Tilea corresponded more closely with the facts than that held to me by either the Minister for Foreign Affairs or the King himself, though why the King should be willing to give information in London which he withheld here is not readily comprehensible." An official of the Southern Department minuted: "In fact M. Tilea may have been nearer the truth than we supposed." Sargent, Cadogan and Halifax added their initials. Vansittart felt once more vindicated: "I never supposed that, on this occasion, he was anywhere else, and I did my best to make that plain."[14]

The other clue which explains Tilea's success concerns less the story he brought to the Foreign Office, but rather the spectre haunting London of a Germany on the march to continental domination. During the early weeks of 1939 the French had consistently predicted Germany would shortly undertake the subjugation of Rumania. In January the Secret Intelligence Service had information directly from the German Foreign Office that, after the Italian-French quarrel was settled, the Führer "would then turn to Roumania as the next country to be brought under German domination".

When Germany occupied Czechoslovakia, the news from Rumania reaching London was ominous. General Popescu, First Deputy Chief of the Rumanian general staff and responsible for intelligence, was in a state of shock. He told Geoffrey Macnab, the British Military Attaché, that according to his information German military preparations went far beyond the immediate task of occupying Czechoslovakia and "were intended eventually for some wider and far reaching adventure". As a result Rumania had called up certain reservists and strengthened her frontier guards on the Hungarian border during March 15th–16th.[15]

This news was no surprise in London. As soon as Prague had been occupied, Gladwyn Jebb got in touch with the Secret Intelligence Service. He wanted all the information they had regarding Germany's military intentions. It seemed unlikely to the Foreign Office that Hitler's infantry and armour would spend their time in Prague, viewing the baroque and rococo splendours of the old city.

On March 18th Jebb produced his vital report. According to the Secret Intelligence Service, there was no indication of large military concentrations in the west. However, most of the German tank and motorised divisions, the offensive forces, were advancing east and southwards beyond Prague. Bulgaria was reported to have mobilised some classes and strengthened her north-east frontier with Rumania. "It seems therefore clear", Jebb concluded, "that, from the purely military point of view, Germany may be preparing for a drive through Hungary to Roumania, in concert with Bulgaria, accompanied by defensive action only in the West."[16]

It was this information, as much as Tilea's story, which galvanised the machinery of the British government into action. It also further explains why, when Tilea was virtually disowned by his government, London continued to formulate plans and gather allies. The problem was to lay the plans and find the allies.

———

Old style appeasement was dead. What was to be the new policy? No one in London was very sure. One obvious alternative was an alliance system – the "grand alliance" – Winston Churchill had advocated in March 1938. This was repugnant to Chamberlain for personal reasons: it was Churchill's policy. It was politically distasteful as well, because the "grand alliance" was to have included the USSR. Chamberlain also believed the First World War had been caused by the creation of two opposing blocs of nations. This would surely lead once again to another war, which he was determined to prevent.

Lord Halifax was more open-minded. The United States Ambassador, just back from a trip to Rome, came to see him on March 17th. Halifax knew he had to speak frankly, if he was to reassure American opinion. He told Kennedy that the British government had for years followed a policy of avoiding any commitments and keeping out of any conflict unless Britain herself was attacked. The events of the past few days, Halifax continued, were leading many people to examine afresh another method of security: "to rally all the forces of order and peace and announce in advance a joint decision to resist any violation of either." Kennedy responded sympathetically. He was in favour of President Roosevelt taking some action quickly in regard to the United States neutrality act.[17]

Sir Alexander Cadogan, who might have been expected to provide fresh ideas, seemed the most depressed and bewildered. "Don't know *where* we are. We ought perhaps to take a stand (whatever that may mean)", he wrote on March 16th. Several days later he was only a little clearer on what to advise:

> . . . I'm afraid we have reached the cross-roads. I always said that, as long as Hitler could pretend he was incorporating Germans in the Reich, we could pretend that he had a case. If he proceeded to gobble up other nationalities, that would be the time to call "Halt!". That time has come, and I must stick to my principle, because on the whole, I think it right. I don't believe that he can gobble all Europe, or at least I don't believe that, if he does, it will do him much good. But we must have a moral position, and we shall lose it if we don't *do* something now.[18]

With such a general poverty of ideas and confusion of aims, there seemed only one answer: to call in the military to advise. This move was as preposterous as it was barren. The British Chiefs of Staff, like those of any country, could only plan the military consequences of political decisions, once taken. Alternatively, they could furnish advice as to the feasibility of plans of action. They could hardly advise when there were neither political plans nor decisions.

It had taken the Chiefs of Staff two sessions at their Georgian offices in Richmond Terrace, at 11.15 a.m. and 3 p.m. on March 18th, to thrash out something for the politicians to go on. The discussions were helped by the presence of Sir Horace Wilson, Sir Orme Sargent and the three Service Ministers. The advice of the Chiefs of Staff was sombre and cautious. Britain could only defeat Germany through the combined efforts of economic warfare – a continental blockade – and by forcing Hitler to fight both in the east and west simultaneously. German political domination of Rumania, which was bound to follow the economic ultimatum, would be a major disaster. Rumania's oil and agricultural products, once organised with German efficiency, could hinder indefinitely the effects of a blockade. Furthermore, once in possession of Rumania, Germany could easily threaten Turkey and Greece. Britain depended on these two powers to maintain a south-east front in Europe and protect the eastern end of the Mediterranean. The outcome of a conflict with Germany in such circumstances "would be problematical".

How was Britain therefore to act? The Chiefs of Staff advanced two suggestions: "We should use diplomatic endeavour to induce the United States of America to range herself more definitely on our side", was the unattainable advice. The revolutionary suggestion was as sensible as it was repulsive to the politicians: "Get an alliance between Great Britain, Russia, Poland and France now and issue an ultimatum ... [which] might deter Germany from her intention to absorb Roumania."

To this bold advice several cautious notes were then added. Even if Poland and the USSR were allies, the situation could still prove desperate. The Poles would be surrounded on three sides by Germany. While the Russians, helpful as they might prove, were "militarily an uncertain quantity". The Chiefs of Staff, therefore, advised that from the military point of view they did not feel justified in recommending to the Cabinet that Britain alone should challenge Germany over the Rumanian question.

To further underline their caution, the military advisers repeated their favourite dogma, which alone made sense of every political decision taken by Chamberlain since he became Prime

Minister. Even if Britain were allied with France and the USSR, a war against Germany, Italy and Japan simultaneously would "place a dangerous strain on the resources of the Empire". No foreseeable strengthening of British defence forces, they concluded, was designed to meet such a war on three fronts.[19]

The military advisers had met and they had agreed: Rumania was the key to a war with any chance of success against Germany. Britain could not assist her unilaterally. The only policy was to gather allies. The next five and a half months were spent trying to make sense out of this advice in rapidly changing circumstances.

At 5 p.m. on March 18th a very belligerent Cabinet assembled at 10 Downing Street. Neville Chamberlain apologised to his colleagues for having disturbed their weekend. But Britain was "entering upon another rather troubled period".

The Cabinet was treated to a breathless survey by Halifax of events, discussions and decisions taken since their last meeting three days ago. Gafencu's denial of Tilea's story was mentioned, yet Halifax thought it opportune to consider the British position should a similar situation arise in the future. At this point, Lord Chatfield, the Minister for Co-ordination of Defence, summarised for the Cabinet the advice given by the Chiefs of Staff. He agreed that the right course of action was to organise political support in south-east Europe.

Chamberlain, however, had his own views on European events. He refused to allow the discussion to centre on whether or not Britain should fight for Rumania. He reminded the Cabinet of his Birmingham speech. That speech he regarded "as a challenge to Germany on the issue whether or not Germany intended to dominate Europe by force". An attack against Rumania, which he considered unlikely, would only illustrate Hitler's Napoleonic intentions. Therefore, "if Germany was to proceed with this course after warning had been given, we had no alternative but to take up the challenge." Did the Cabinet agree to this change of policy? he asked. "The question of the moment at which we should make our stand was a separate issue."

The British Cabinet was to hear the individual voices of weakness right up to the outbreak of war. There were those who wanted yet more time to prepare, who feared the encirclement of Germany and dreaded the outcome of battle. But on March 18th the important Ministers, Lord Halifax, Sir John Simon, the Chancellor of the Exchequer, Leslie Hore-Belisha, the Secretary of State for War, and Lord Chatfield supported Chamberlain's new policy. They agreed that the next act of German aggression, proof that Hitler had accepted Chamberlain's challenge, would mean war.[20] During the following agonising months, these men prepared British defences and found allies. They wrestled with their conscience, had moments of doubt, spells of weakness and disappointed hopes. However, when the challenge was made by Hitler on September 1st, they decided on war.

CHAPTER FOUR

Making a Stand

ON March 31st, 1939 Neville Chamberlain astonished the world. He had done this many times before in pursuit of his own conception of appeasement. But on the afternoon of March 31st, speaking before a hushed and expectant House of Commons, Chamberlain declared that Britain would come to the help of Poland should there be any threat to her independence. He had himself chosen the country on which his government would make its stand. He had not intended two weeks earlier, however, to lay down the gauntlet to Hitler so soon, nor quite in such lonely circumstances.

During the Cabinet meeting of March 18th, Chamberlain had asserted that Britain could not and should not resist alone any future German aggression. Instead, she must "ascertain what friends we had who would join with us". If sufficient assurances were forthcoming from other countries then a public pronouncement could be made. Such a step might temporarily deter Hitler. The time this gained would be used to implement further defensive steps. Lord Halifax entirely agreed. "The attitude of the German Government was either bluff," he suggested, "in which case it would be stopped by a public declaration on our part; or it was not bluff, in which case it was necessary that we should all unite to meet it, and the sooner we united the better."

Not everyone in the Cabinet chose their words so carefully. Leslie Hore-Belisha, Secretary of State for War, and fearless in speaking his mind, asked why should Britain not contract "frank and open alliances" with Poland and Russia? This was exactly the advice of the Chiefs of Staff. His only support, unfortunately, came from Walter Elliot, the Minister of Health.

Mention of Russia grated on Chamberlain's ears. At once he

stopped any loose talk about the Bolsheviks. "Poland was very likely the key to the situation", he dogmatically stated. Why he should have said this, if he was interested in organising resistance among the states of south-east Europe, may appear enigmatic. It was probably intended to avoid introducing the controversial and thorny problem of the Russians. He felt they were best left in their byzantine isolation, outside the scope of European affairs. This fundamental view he never changed. But his emphasis on Poland did have some strategic relevance. As the strongest state bordering on Germany's eastern frontier, Poland was necessary to bolster the military power of any south-east European bloc. It would complete a deterrent front which would then stretch from the Baltic Sea in the north to the Mediterranean in the south.

The Cabinet conclusions saw Chamberlain overruled on the Russian issue. It was agreed to "make approaches to Russia, Poland, Yugoslavia, Turkey, Greece and Roumania with a view to obtaining assurances from them that they would join with us in resisting any act of German aggression aimed at obtaining domination in South-East Europe". Providing "satisfactory assurances" could be obtained, a "public pronouncement of our intention to resist any such act of German aggression" would be made.[1] The desperate search for assistance in deterring Germany had begun in earnest.

Perhaps it was the sobering effect of having to meet on a bleak Sunday morning in March. More likely Chamberlain, Halifax, Sir John Simon and Oliver Stanley who met at 10 Downing Street the following morning to carry out the Cabinet decision were having second thoughts.[2] The replies already received from the east and south-east European governments as regards their intentions in view of Viorel Virgil Tilea's information were extremely discouraging. To the Foreign Office question as to what they intended to do, these governments astutely threw the ball back into the opposite court: "What did Britain intend to do?"

Chamberlain claimed he had foreseen this. He always felt the Foreign Office was unproductive in bringing out new ideas. No wonder so much of British policy emanated from his fertile mind.

80

In these circumstances, he told his colleagues, he had overnight conceived a more limited plan of action. He wished in the first instance for Britain to invite only Russia, France and Poland to join in making a declaration of a general character. The importance of such a move was that it "would constitute a warning to the world. . . . There was no harm done in his view if this warning was in somewhat general terms and kept people guessing". Meanwhile, efforts would be made behind the scenes to encourage common action. Chamberlain then wrote out a draft declaration.

Nor was the Prime Minister finished with presenting his new ideas to this meeting. He revealed his plan to write to Benito Mussolini, whose friendship he had so carefully cultivated for many months. Chamberlain wanted to ask Mussolini to use his influence in Berlin to express Britain's anxiety about Hitler's intentions. As he explained in a letter to his sister later that day, he wanted to restrain Mussolini.[3]

The Foreign Office had also been thinking of the Italian dictator, even before the Prime Minister. But it was anxious lest Mussolini might try to imitate Hitler. An Italian journalist source in London had suggested that Mussolini might issue an ultimatum pressing his colonial claims against France. Sir Alexander Cadogan preferred, therefore, to caution Mussolini: Britain intended to stand by France. Cadogan's main concern was to prevent the Italian dictator "from touching off the Mediterranean powder-magazine". He feared the impression given by Chamberlain's letter was that this country "was seeking another Munich".[4]

When Chamberlain raised the question at this meeting of Ministers, Halifax pressed the Foreign Office plan of action. Chamberlain was unmoved. He feared a "rebuff from Signor Mussolini, who might think we were interfering in his business". But he did accept for consideration a copy of the draft produced by the Foreign Office. The meeting then adjourned for a long Sunday lunch and further informal discussions.

In the interval, Lord Halifax had the difficult task of receiving the Soviet Ambassador, Ivan Maisky. Alone among the east Europeans governments canvassed, the USSR had replied with a concrete proposal for a six-power conference at Bucharest to plan deterrent action against Hitler. Attending international conferences symbolised for the Russians the Great Power status they craved. To the Foreign Office, it was a headache and a complication. Halifax had to tell Maisky that no "responsible Minister" could be spared during the crisis and that any conference which failed would be highly dangerous.

The Soviet proposal had never been put to the Cabinet. It had been instantly rejected that morning in the Foreign Office. This reaction has always been puzzling, except for the further reason which Halifax revealed three days later to the Dominion High Commissioners. A conference in a European capital, compelling delegates to refer important questions back to their governments, Halifax explained, involved the "added danger of telephoning over Europe for instructions over wires which would certainly be tapped".[5]

The four Ministers, with Sir Horace Wilson now also present, met again at 4.30 p.m. The mood of the meeting was to still further weaken the proposed plan of action. The draft telegram they agreed to submit to the Cabinet the next day emphasised the formal four power declaration itself. It dealt only in general terms with the projected subsequent consultations.

In the meantime, the Americans were very much in the minds of these assembled Ministers. If Britain was to be involved in war against Germany, and possibly Italy, something had to be done to steady the Far East situation. Chamberlain recalled that in the September 1938 crisis the United States "had adopted a very friendly attitude in Naval Affairs". He therefore considered asking the American government to despatch a fleet to Honolulu. This gesture might discourage Japan from siding with the Axis. On March 22nd Roosevelt agreed to resume the secret Anglo-American naval talks, to be carried on through the respective Naval Attachés in Washington.

When Chamberlain and Halifax confronted their Cabinet colleagues the next morning, March 20th, they had to explain why they had had to back-track on a far reaching decision taken by a determined and bellicose Cabinet. First Halifax and then

Chamberlain discussed the reasons for the more limited public declaration now contemplated. "Not a very heroic decision", Halifax conceded, but the Government wished to act quickly, impress world opinion and not be tied down to definite commitments in indefinite or unforeseeable circumstances.

It was Chamberlain who again tried to keep fundamentals, as he saw them, before the Cabinet:

> The real issue was that if Germany showed signs that she intended to proceed with her march for world domination, we must take steps to stop her by attacking her on two fronts. We should attack Germany, not in order to save a particular victim, but in order to pull down the bully.

He wished therefore to "make it clear that the declaration did not constitute a guarantee of the existing frontiers and of the indefinite maintenance of the *status quo*. The declaration was concerned with a far wider issue, namely, security and political independence of European States against German domination."

Such a declaration, which bound Britain to do nothing more than to consult, left many in the Cabinet dissatisfied. How could such a loose statement inspire confidence in the threatened European states that Britain would really resist Germany?

Chamberlain was obstinate. He considered his new policy both startling and bold. It was a considerable advance on any action he had previously advised. He was even reluctant, he candidly admitted, to go as far as the proposals for mere consultation. Yet he expected people to have confidence in his intentions and faith in his resolve. A simple pledge to consult together in case of a threat to European peace was in his opinion sufficient to warn Hitler. The Cabinet was doubtful. They left the final wording of the declaration to Halifax.[6]

Before adjourning, Chamberlain received Cabinet approval to write to Mussolini. He would not accept Halifax's advice, supported by the Foreign Office, that his letter gave an impression of weakness and alarm.

When it came to personal diplomacy with the dictators, Chamberlain still felt he knew best. "I don't want to convey the impression that I am seeking another Munich", he wrote privately, "but I want to make M[ussolini] see that if Hitler goes on as he has begun it will mean war and induce him to warn his partner." For the Foreign Office suggestions, Chamberlain had only contempt: A "monument of clumsiness" he derisively commented to Sir Horace Wilson. That night, after some final corrections in his room at the House of Commons, Chamberlain despatched his letter to Mussolini.

The Foreign Office instinct in dealing with Mussolini may not have been entirely correct. Mussolini was badly shaken by Hitler's sudden occupation of Prague. On March 15th Hitler had sent Prince Hesse, the German son-in-law of the Italian King Victor Emmanuel III, to pacify the Duce and explain his latest coup. Mussolini "did not wish to give Hesse's news to the press ('the Italians would laugh at me; every time Hitler occupies a country he sends me a message')." By March 17th the British Ambassador in Rome, Lord Perth, had found out about Hesse's mission.[7] Perth also strongly suggested the time was ripe to improve Anglo-Italian relations. At the same time the Foreign Office had received indirect "feelers from other quarters suggesting that Italy would be prepared to do a deal with the Western Powers". The "most serious of these approaches", in the opinion of Sir Andrew Noble of the Southern Department, came from the Marchese Medici, the Under-Secretary of State to Mussolini. He described Mussolini as very anxious and therefore willing to moderate his demands if Franco-Italian negotiations were reopened.

Foreign Office officials had no objection to giving reasonable consideration to Italian demands, if reasonably put forward. But unlike the Prime Minister they were sceptical "that by buying off the Italians now we shall in fact weaken the Berlin-Rome Axis". As Philip Nichols minuted: "no assurances that we can obtain from Italy today are worth the paper they are written on." Italy must herself make the first move away from the Axis. In the meantime everything must be done to avoid any action likely to strengthen the relations between Hitler and Mussolini. Cadogan had also given a lot of thought to this dilemma and on March

24th wrote: "Doubtless Italy's historic policy has always been to sell herself to the highest bidder." But, he added, "is anyone ready to put up the price necessary to buy Italy? Would there not be grave danger in making an approach to her (by giving the impression of fear and weakness)? Could we be ever sure that Italy *was* bought?"

After flirting briefly with buying off the Italians, the British government dropped the idea. Meanwhile, the Italians had to be kept happy, and even this more limited policy could be endangered. For Lord Perth, a passionate devotee of amicable Anglo-Italian relations, warned the Foreign Office of the dangers of losing Italy forever if Britain followed up her budding policy of associating the Bolsheviks with the deterrent front. Chamberlain particularly was susceptible to this advice. Nor was the Foreign Office immune. It must be borne in mind, Cadogan observed, "that too open association with the Soviet may tend to strengthen the Axis. If the problem could be so simplified as to be put in the form of a question – Italy or Russia? – I wd. unhesitatingly plump for the former."[8]

Events later forced the British government to reverse this appraisal. In the meantime, the mirage of Italian friendship helped further to isolate the Russians.

Mussolini's dejection at Hitler's policies over Czechoslovakia was short-lived. The temperamental Duce soon fell back into line. "We cannot change our policy now. We are not prostitutes," he told his Foreign Minister and son-in-law, Count Galeazzo Ciano. And as for Chamberlain's personal letter, he regarded it as yet further "proof of the inertia of the democracies". He took his time before replying. When his letter reached the Foreign Office on April 1st it was found to be curt and self-righteous. Chamberlain was advised to reread the Duce's public pronouncements. Italy would take no pacific initiative until her own rights had been recognised. So snubbed did Chamberlain feel by the reply that he even refused to preserve among his personal files the original copy of Mussolini's reply. It was returned to the Foreign Office.[9]

If Chamberlain felt content with his restricted formula for a four-power declaration, he quickly discovered others had serious reservations. In the late afternoon of March 20th, Charles Corbin, the French Ambassador in London, called on Cadogan to hear details of the British plans for action. Corbin at once "expressed horror". The text of the declaration, he argued, "would confirm the impression that the Powers were not disposed to take any action and would only talk when a threat arose". Neither Poland nor Rumania would cooperate in such circumstances. The "publication of this bare declaration would have a much worse effect than publishing nothing at all. If consultation were decided on," Corbin angrily concluded, "let us consult at once, but do not let us announce that we should meet together to consult when the danger arose."

Cadogan was won over by these arguments. He at once collected Sir Horace Wilson and both rushed off to the House of Commons for further consultations with Chamberlain and Halifax. This time Chamberlain deferred to Foreign Office advice. He thereby upset all his cautious arguments advanced so persistently during the previous two days. Such concessions increased in the following months. It was not so much that Chamberlain became less obstinate or more open to Foreign Office persuasion; rather the acute European crisis, demanding almost daily debate on foreign policy, made him less sure, less confident of his own expertise. The four-power declaration was finally telegraphed to the British Ambassadors in Paris, Warsaw and Moscow at 11.5 p.m. on March 20th. It suggested that, as the threat to the security or political independence of any European state was a matter of common interest, the four governments "undertake immediately to consult together as to what steps should be taken to offer joint resistance to any such action".

That evening Cadogan pondered the significance of this step. Britain had now decided to call a halt to German expansion. There were enormous risks involved of goading Hitler into aggressive action. But there seemed to be no alternative. "Life is Hell," he wrote and then closed his diary.[10]

On March 21st the French President, Albert Lebrun, accompanied by Georges Bonnet, the Foreign Minister, arrived in London on a four-day state visit. A banquet at Buckingham Palace, theatrical entertainments arranged with the assistance of Sir Robert Vansittart in the courtyard of the India Office, and a gala performance at Covent Garden provided the façade which attracted press attention. But behind the scenes the politicians and diplomats debated, argued, and planned foreign policy.

Late in the afternoon of March 21st, Lord Halifax and Georges Bonnet discussed developments since Hitler's occupation of Prague. Both Foreign Ministers agreed that the next act of German aggression must be resisted. Conscious of the many treaty commitments France had in eastern Europe and her inability to offer effective military assistance, Bonnet felt that it "was desirable . . . to go to the utmost limit, even to the extent of threats, to bring Poland in." Only then could Russian help be useful. To this Halifax replied carefully: "the primary question would not be: can we give direct assistance to Poland or Roumania? but: can we conduct a successful war against Germany?" Polish support would be forthcoming, Halifax concluded, if Britain and France "were prepared to take a very firm line". That was the reason for proposing the four-power declaration. It was also the reasoning which guided British policy until the outbreak of war.

When the Cabinet met at 10 o'clock the next morning, the first topic of conversation was naturally the declaration proposal. Although no official replies had yet been received, Halifax was able to offer some indication as to the attitude of the powers canvassed. The French were generally favourable. The Poles still hesitated and appeared reluctant to come to the assistance of Rumania. The Russians were "somewhat perturbed". The only comment Chamberlain himself made on this subject was that he found the probable attitude of both Poland and Russia "somewhat disagreeable".

The main news story that morning was an item which, not surprisingly, aroused little Cabinet comment. The return of the German-speaking port of Memel and its surrounding territory, detached from Germany by the Treaty of Versailles and then seized by Lithuania in 1923, was expected at any moment. "There was, of course, more justification for this course than for certain recent events", Halifax stated. This latest German mini-coup, accomplished that night, was to occasion little reaction. It merely confirmed the need to press on with defensive plans.

A further two-hour conversation with French officials took place later that afternoon in Chamberlain's room at the House of Commons. Bonnet was then able to report full French agreement to the four-power declaration. But it was still the Polish attitude which dominated the conversation and proved most intractable. The main difficulty, as had been foreshadowed by the British Ambassador to Warsaw, Sir Howard Kennard, after a conversation with the Polish Foreign Minister, Colonel Jozef Beck, was Poland's concern to preserve a balance between her two giant neighbours, Germany and the Soviet Union.

Chamberlain felt Poland would assist Rumania if the Soviet Union were excluded. Bonnet was not so optimistic. He pointed out that Rumania had so far not asked for Polish assistance against Germany; and according to his information some of the Rumanian "upper class preferred Hitler to Stalin". Despite Bonnet's arguments, Chamberlain expressed considerable sympathy with Polish objections against identifying the Soviet Union too closely with efforts to build a Polish-Rumanian front. Halifax at once pointed out the dangers of giving the "Soviet Government the idea that we were pushing her to one side".

The current of the discussion, however, was already pushing the four-power declaration proposal out of the picture. And Chamberlain was the first to perceive this. As Poland's reply was expected to be either "negative or evasive", he saw no point in pressing them any further. Instead, a new procedure was to be explored. As Rumania was the country most immediately threatened, Poland had to be persuaded to assist her. If this was successful, then Britain and France would give the Poles a "private undertaking" to join in rendering assistance.[11]

This decision to switch from an ambitious four-power

declaration to a more limited plan of Polish-Rumanian mutual assistance, backed by Anglo-French support, proved more significant than was apparent at the time. The Soviet Union, after a brief diplomatic appearance, was being nudged back into its isolation. Despite the scepticism now surrounding Tilea's information regarding the German "ultimatum", Rumania remained a prime concern. It was Poland, however, which was emerging as the dominant political force in eastern Europe. She had a common frontier with Germany; was in a position to assist Rumania; and seemed, to Chamberlain particularly, to be the one eastern European country able to threaten Germany with the prospect of a war on two fronts.

This gradual switch to Poland was largely due to Chamberlain. He readily sympathised with the Poles' reluctance to associate with Bolshevik Russia. The Poles feared to provoke Hitler into violent action; so did Chamberlain. The Poles did not want to burn all their bridges to Berlin; neither did Chamberlain. Both the Polish government and Chamberlain hoped to gain time, refused to accept the inevitability of war, and considered caution the safest form of defence. Writing to his sister on March 26th, Chamberlain explained why he had agreed to keep the Russians at bay. "I must confess to the most profound distrust of Russia", he wrote, adding that the Soviets had no offensive military power, and were "concerned only with getting everyone else by the ears". Countries such as Poland, Rumania and Finland, which "hated and suspected" the Soviets, could offer more effective help than the Russians. He had reached the conclusion, therefore, that it was impossible to advance further with the declaration proposal.[12]

Broad defensive plans continued to be laid in the days following the Anglo-French talks. On March 24th Count Edward Raczynski, the Polish Ambassador, called on Lord Halifax to deliver the official reply to the declaration proposal. He immediately apologised for bearing a message which "would rather complicate an already complicated situation". Would Britain agree to a "confidential bilateral understanding" to consult together in case of a new threat from Germany?

Halifax's suspicions were aroused, but so was his curiosity. Secret diplomacy of this kind was dangerous. It also raised difficulties with the French. Last, but not least, such a proposal would place too vast an obligation upon the British government.[13] Hitler's March 15th coup had initiated in London a search for large scale assistance in eastern Europe. Was Britain after all her efforts to be isolated in solitary support for Poland?

This new Polish plan, communicated by Raczynski, was motivated by no tender regard for the difficulties being experienced in London or Paris. Unknown to the British and French governments, the Poles were deep in secret negotiations with the Germans. On March 21st Ribbentrop had warned the Polish Ambassador in Berlin, Jozef Lipski, of Germany's concern at a "gradual stiffening in German-Polish relations". Both he and Hitler therefore wished to make a "fresh attempt" to reach a settlement on outstanding issues with Polish representatives. Hitler personally would welcome a visit from Colonel Beck. The basis for any discussion, Ribbentrop concluded, would be the return of Danzig to Germany, and the establishment of an extra-territorial railway and road between the Reich and East Prussia. In return, the Corridor would remain Polish and Germany would guarantee Poland.

Lipski, who had just had his offer of resignation rejected by Beck, returned hastily and in deep gloom to Warsaw. There he found the Foreign Minister not unduly perturbed, and in a belligerent mood. Danzig, Beck declared to a meeting of senior officials, was a "symbol" for which Poland would fight. The Polish state would never "join that category of eastern states that allows rules to be dictated to them". He considered it "wiser to go forward to meet the enemy than to wait for him at home." Beck then revealed the basis of his exuberant confidence: "We have arrived at this difficult moment in our politics with all the trump cards in our hand."

The main trump card was of course Britain's new interest in

eastern Europe. This knowledge enabled Beck to send his depressed Ambassador back to Berlin with Poland's reply. It received there, in Lipski's words, a "distinctly cold reception". While willing to continue negotiations, Ribbentrop was told on March 26th, Poland rejected Hitler's proposals. Instead, Poland wished to have a bilateral German-Polish guarantee of Danzig and to offer traffic concessions across the Corridor.

Ribbentrop's reply was to warn Lipski that these suggestions "could not be regarded by the Führer as satisfactory". But Hitler, who had tactfully removed himself from Berlin during these negotiations, had no immediate plans for military action against Poland. He did not wish to facilitate any Anglo-Polish agreement.[14]

Direct negotiations between Germany and Poland, neither broken off nor suspended on March 26th, did not resume until August 31st at 6.30 p.m., ten hours before the attack on Poland commenced. But in late March Beck had no fears that his policy of balance between Germany and the USSR, supported by an amenable British government, was succeeding.

Throughout the long hours of the weekend of March 25th–26th, officials of the British Foreign Office had intensively discussed how to deal with the Polish proposal for a "gentlemen's agreement" and the need to strengthen Rumania. On the 26th Chamberlain approved in principle the idea of a guarantee to Poland. Cadogan, who took part in these talks, felt quite discouraged, even sceptical: "Whole situation looks as murky as it can be, and all the little States are weakening and showing funk." Still, he hoped that speedy and firm action "*might* act as a deterrent to avert war".[15]

The increasing complications of the international situation finally forced Chamberlain to summon a meeting of the Foreign Policy Committee on March 27th. It was their first meeting since February 8th. But rather than cause "undue publicity" by summoning an emergency meeting of the Cabinet, as Chamberlain shortly explained, he preferred firstly to consult with the Foreign

Policy Committee. The discussion which followed was lengthy, bitter, and at times confusing.

In a detailed opening statement, Chamberlain described the reasons which had forced him to abandon the plan for a four-power declaration of consultation and adopt an alternative approach. If Poland and Rumania were prepared to resist a German attack, then Britain and France would support them. It would also be useful for Poland and Rumania to assist each other in case either were attacked. Sensing how revolutionary this plan would be to some of his colleagues, Chamberlain explained the difficulties. At once he warned that attempts to build up a deterrent front were likely to be frustrated if Russia was closely associated with the scheme. Countries such as Poland and Rumania, and Catholic opinion in Spain and Portugal, resented any flirtation with the Bolsheviks. Most important, it would destroy the opportunity "to exercise influence on and establish good relations" with Italy and Japan. "It looked, therefore, as if a failure to associate with Soviet Russia would give rise to suspicion and difficulty with the Left wing both in this country and in France, while on the other hand insistence to associate with Soviet Russia would destroy any chance of building up a solid and united front against German aggression." This was the dilemma. The decision – Russia must as a result be temporarily excluded.

Chamberlain then reminded the Committee of the immediate danger. Rumania, with her rich resources of oil and agricultural products needed by Germany to break any allied blockade, was threatened. If she were overrun, Poland would be almost encircled and the states of south-east Europe demoralised. "The inclusion of Poland in the scheme was vital because Germany's weak point was her inability at present to conduct war on two fronts, and unless Poland was with us Germany would be able to avoid this contingency."

The Prime Minister then went on to observe that although "this plan left Soviet Russia out of the picture", Moscow "might be indirectly and secretly brought into the scheme". Chamberlain envisaged a "secret agreement between Russia and Great

Britain under which Russia would come to the help of Poland or Roumania in case either of these countries became involved in war with Germany." Although events were shortly to overtake this scheme, this was not the result of any lack of effort on the part of Chamberlain.

The surprising aspect of the discussion which followed was the vehement opposition voiced to the exclusion of the Soviet Union from the first line of defence in eastern Europe. Most astonishing was the emergence of the chief advocate of this view – Sir Samuel Hoare, the Home Secretary. In 1954 Hoare published his memoirs, *Nine Troubled Years*, and made an impressive defence both of appeasement and Chamberlain's cold-shouldering of the USSR. This was largely due to his sympathy for Chamberlain, who since his death in 1940 had been most savagely abused.

Yet in 1939 Hoare was one of Chamberlain's most persistent opponents. "I was constantly trying to push Neville into more resolute action", Hoare wrote several years later. This was particularly true with regards to Chamberlain's Soviet policy. On no less than five occasions during the discussion, Hoare intervened to hammer home his main concern: "that the dropping out of Russia would be regarded in many quarters as a considerable defeat for our policy." His concern was based on no sympathy for the Bolsheviks. Possibly worried by the reactions from his colleagues to such outspoken views, he felt compelled almost to apologise: "No one could accuse him of any predilections in favour of Soviet Russia." But he firmly believed "Russia constituted the greatest deterrent in the East against German aggression. All experience showed that Russia was undefeatable and he was apprehensive of the possible consequences that might result if at this juncture the enmity of Soviet Russia towards this country was increased." Only Oliver Stanley, President of the Board of Trade, and Lord Chatfield, Minister for Co-ordination of Defence, gave their support.

But Hoare's insistence on including Russia led, at this very late stage, to some discussion on military strategy as opposed to political gestures. Chatfield, who should have been able to offer definitive military advice, hid instead behind a classic statement of equivocation. "On the whole Poland was, from the military point of view, probably the best of potential eastern allies," he declared, "but he thought Soviet Russia would act as a greater deterrent so far as Germany was concerned." As the Foreign Office spokesman, Halifax also added his own view, quite astonishing in retrospect. If Britain "had to make a choice between Poland and Soviet Russia, it seemed clear that Poland would give the greater value." Nevertheless, Colonel Beck would be encouraged to consider Russia as a source of munitions and supplies in an emergency. The Russians showed later what they thought of this particular idea.

The military appreciations available in the Foreign Office, Halifax continued, reaffirmed that the purges had destroyed Soviet offensive power, but left intact her defensive qualities. As for a Polish military appreciation, Halifax dolefully admitted "there was nothing very recent. The Polish Army consisted of some 50 Divisions and might be expected to make a useful contribution." However, there was no need to worry. Germany appeared unprepared to fight a war on two fronts.

The amateurish and ill-informed opinions reflected how absorbed the British government had become with politics, with making a gesture to deter Hitler. It also brought the assembled Ministers to a moment of truth, never publicly admitted and rarely privately pronounced:

THE SECRETARY OF STATE FOR FOREIGN AFFAIRS said that . . . there was probably no way in which France and ourselves could prevent Poland and Roumania from being overrun. We were faced with the dilemma of doing nothing, or entering into a devastating war. If we did nothing this in itself would mean a great accession to Germany's strength and a great loss to ourselves of sympathy and support in the United States, in the Balkan countries, and in other parts of the world. In these circumstances if we had to choose between two great evils he favoured our going to war.

THE MINISTER FOR CO-ORDINATION OF DEFENCE said that he agreed with this appreciation of the situation. In a sentence we were in a weak military position to meet a political situation we could not avoid. . . .

THE PRIME MINISTER pointed out that by manning the Maginot Line we should be holding up large German forces which would otherwise be available for overrunning Poland and Roumania. This argument applied both to the East and to the West and that was why we attached so much importance to the inclusion of Poland in the Pact.

Whatever criticism could be laid against the guarantee of Poland, blindness was definitely not one. The Prime Minister and his senior advisers had no illusions as to what Britain could, or could not, achieve militarily in eastern Europe. They had no illusions that, despite great strides in rearmament, the help Britain could give to the threatened states east of Germany was puny.

What Chamberlain hoped was that the proposals being considered "would greatly strengthen the morale of other States and tend to bring them on to our side." If Hitler was impressed by this message, peace could result. If not, then the Ministers meeting on March 27th knew war would break out. They sensed with little enthusiasm that the telegrams they had met to discuss committed Britain to fight Germany for an eastern European state for the first time since 1914. They agreed "to approve, generally" the policy proposed by Chamberlain and Halifax.[16]

Late that night telegrams containing the Anglo-French guarantee proposals were sent to the British Ambassadors in Warsaw and Bucharest. They were not to act on these instructions until further notice. The French, who were firstly to be asked to consider similar and simultaneous action, notified their agreement the next day.

Lord Chatfield's obvious embarrassment at being unable to offer any solid military information finally led to some action being taken. He had in fact asked the Chiefs of Staff on March 21st to analyse, "when time permitted", the strategic aspects of the four-power declaration proposal. He had particularly sought information as to the armed strength, efficiency and mobilisation plans of the Poles and Russians. Conscious also of Anglo-French inferiority in aircraft and infantry, he asked for a report on the number of divisions and aircraft Germany would be compelled to dispose in east and south-east Europe if Poland and Russia were allies. As the four-power declaration proposal failed, no action was taken by the military advisers.

On March 28th Chatfield again turned to the Chiefs of Staff. He apologised for the short notice, but asked for a report "as a matter of great urgency" on the military implications of an Anglo-French guarantee to Poland and Rumania. The report was to assume that the USSR would remain a "friendly neutral to the extent of being willing to supply war material to Poland and Roumania".

The Chiefs of Staff and their Joint Planning Sub-committee, responsible for preparing draft reports, met in almost continuous session throughout the 28th. The preliminary report they produced and signed that day was calculated to put a brake on the grandiose, even militarily irresponsible, scheme of the political guarantees contemplated by the Cabinet. It sternly warned that with these guarantees "we will have surrendered the issues of peace and war with Germany to the action of Governments over whom we have no control, and at a time when our defence programme is far from complete." The benefit of threatening Germany with a war on two fronts, however, was not overlooked. Poland and Rumania would no doubt be easily conquered. But "having regard to the internal situation in Germany, the dispersion of her effort and the strain on her rearmament programme, we should be able to reduce the period of Germany's resistance and we could regard the ultimate issue with confidence." The general conclusion reached can only be read as a military protest against the scope of the contemplated guarantees:

. . . neither Great Britain nor France could afford Poland and Roumania direct support by sea, on land or in the air to help them to resist a German invasion. Furthermore, in the present state of British and French armament production, neither Great Britain nor France could supply any armaments to

Poland and Roumania. This emphasises the importance in this respect of assistance from the U.S.S.R.[17]*

The Chiefs of Staff had been expressly asked by Chatfield to have their report ready for the Cabinet meeting the next day, March 29th. At 11.0 a.m. the Cabinet assembled at 10 Downing Street for the first time since March 22nd. As British plans had changed so drastically in the intervening week, Halifax explained the reasons for the failure of the four-power declaration. He reminded his colleagues, however, of the Government's continued concern "to take effective steps to organise action against further German aggression". He then explained the projected Anglo-French guarantee of Poland and Rumania.

Once again Halifax and Chamberlain found themselves strongly criticised for having excluded the Soviet Union. Sir Samuel Hoare, this time supported vocally by Walter Elliot, the Minister of Health, desperately put forward ideas on how to give the Russians a positive role in this new plan. Their criticisms proved effective and forced some concession. Halifax agreed that "it was desirable that we should try to get as much assistance from Russia as was practicable . . . he would take what steps were possible to keep in with Russia." He had already done so. The telegrams containing the guarantee proposals to Poland and Rumania pointed out the role envisaged for the USSR. Halifax wrote that the "benevolent neutrality" of the USSR was vital in order to ensure the supply of war material to the Poles and Rumanians. "It is important not to reinforce their [Soviet] tendency towards isolation", Halifax ominously warned, "and I propose to consider in due course how best to retain their close interest."[18]

Besides foreign policy, the Cabinet of March 29th had before

---

* The importance attached by the Chiefs of Staff to military assistance from the USSR was curiously not shared by the Secret Intelligence Service. A senior member of the Foreign Office, Sir Lancelot Oliphant, minuted on March 29th that "as regards any material help wh. the Soviet might supply to either Poland or Roumania, C [Admiral Sir Hugh Sinclair] told me today that in his belief they could do nothing of real value." (FO371/23061, C3968/3356/18.)

them a crucial item of domestic legislation. It was not on the agenda for the meeting; and its urgency and importance was emphasised by its being introduced by the Prime Minister himself. The issue was the question of conscription. Ever since he had become Prime Minister in May 1937, Chamberlain had been haunted by his election pledge that he would not introduce conscription in peace time. The deterioration in the European situation forced him to reconsider this pledge and allowed a possible rationalisation. He now told the Cabinet: "although we were not actually at war, the state of affairs in which we now lived could not be described as peace-time in the ordinary meaning of the word." Therefore, while he feared that the Labour Party and the trade union movement would categorically oppose conscription, it was still possible to increase the Territorial Army.

Chamberlain had arrived at this decision under heavy pressure. For many months the French government had harangued the British Foreign Office to introduce conscription. To which the usual British reply had been to point at France's own festering sore: its meagre aircraft production. Equally important were the determined efforts of the Secretary of State for War, Leslie Hore-Belisha. Throughout March 28th, Hore-Belisha, Chamberlain and Sir Horace Wilson had exchanged letters and minutes, and consulted together over lunch. They were concerned, in the words of the Secretary of State for War, with the "over-riding political necessity of doing something on an impressive scale." He received strong support from Halifax, equally determined to "make an announcement wh. will impress foreign opinion," and "Europe as to our military determination".[19]

Such combined pressure and reasoned argument Chamberlain could not resist. When Sir John Simon, Chancellor of the Exchequer, who so consistently chose economic stability over the financial burdens of rearmament, stated he was impressed by Halifax's arguments, the day was won. The Cabinet agreed to raise the Territorial Army from 130,000 men to its war strength of 170,000 and then double it in size. Leslie Hore-Belisha had also cogently argued the case for adding another 50,000 men to the regular army. At this Simon closed the purse strings. The

Cabinet concurred. But Halifax added prophetically that sooner or later it would be found necessary to go even further. To gain the maximum publicity for this move, Chamberlain himself agreed to make the announcement in the Commons that afternoon.

When the Cabinet finished its business before lunch Ministers had still not been informed of the objections of the Chiefs of Staff to the projected guarantees to Poland and Rumania.

During the afternoon, Lord Halifax was shown an important message from the American Ambassador, Joseph Kennedy. On the previous day, March 28th, Herschel Johnson, the Counsellor at the American Embassy, had called upon Sir Orme Sargent. He brought an urgent communication which Kennedy "was most anxious" to have conveyed immediately to the Foreign Secretary. The United States Ambassador in Poland, Anthony J. Drexel Biddle, had been told by a friendly, and previously reliable, German journalist that Hitler was under the thumb of Ribbentrop. Furthermore, Ribbentrop was "now pressing for immediate action against Poland, pointing out that Great Britain and France will fail to support Poland and that this failure would serve to alienate American opinion from France and Great Britain." Halifax was deeply impressed. The impact of this warning was to influence in a decisive manner the British decision to guarantee Poland without waiting for Beck's reply to the larger four-power scheme.[20]

At 6 p.m. that evening, March 29th, Ian Colvin, 26 years old and one of the two Berlin correspondents of the *News Chronicle*, was escorted by Cadogan and Halifax into the Prime Minister's room at the House of Commons. Sir Walter Layton, Editor of the *News Chronicle*, had asked the Foreign Secretary to receive the young journalist who was already well known in the Foreign Office. Both Colvin and his colleague, H. D. Harrison, were under sentence of expulsion from Germany where their reports had come under strong criticism. The Foreign Office hoped that Colvin at least would be allowed to remain in Berlin as, in the opinion of Ivone Kirkpatrick, he "is a much better informed and sensible journalist, though he trips up sometimes from lack of caution".

The story Colvin began to tell to this gathering, which now included an official of the Secret Intelligence Service, was on the surface quite unremarkable. Information had been communicated to him in January "from a reliable source". A victualling contractor to the German army had been instructed to deliver supplies for army use to forward dumps in east Pomerania. This area formed a rough wedge pointing towards the railway junction of Bromberg at the head of the Polish Corridor. These deliveries were to be completed by March 28th. Already the German press had begun a typical propaganda campaign reporting the excesses by Poles against the German minority in Bromberg. Colvin added that all his information pointed to an "attack on the Polish Republic in twelve hours, three days, a week or a fortnight".

As Colvin spoke, Chamberlain "plucked away at the loose skin of his throat in deepest indecision". After Colvin had finished, Cadogan suddenly asked: "How would it affect people in Germany if we gave a guarantee to Poland?" "It would help", was Colvin's reply. He and the others then left the Prime Minister's room.

Halifax stayed behind with Chamberlain. According to Cadogan, who had himself not been quite convinced by the journalist's story, Halifax had "seemed impressed". The result of this tête-à-tête was that the Prime Minister "agreed to [the] idea of an *immediate* declaration of support of Poland, to counter a quick putsch by Hitler".[21]

Colvin then returned to Berlin, where five days later the German government relented and allowed him, but not Harrison, to stay, provided his reports were "more objective". Sir Walter Layton, however, disliked the seeming favouritism being shown by the Foreign Office to Colvin whom he considered "rather highly strung". He asked both journalists to return to London.* In a revealing letter to William Strang on April 13th, Sir George Ogilvie-Forbes, Counsellor of the British Embassy in Berlin, denied that any discrimination had been shown between Colvin

---

* After his return to London in April, Colvin worked for a time in the Foreign Office. On July 7th he returned to Berlin for a short visit.

and Harrison. The German government itself had decided to let Colvin remain. Ogilvie-Forbes continued:

There is also friction between Harrison and Colvin, the former complaining that the latter has not recently been very attentive to his duties as a journalist. I have no doubt too that the "News Chronicle" did not like their junior correspondent being received by the Prime Minister and the Secretary of State and entrusted with certain work outside normal journalism.

Personally I am sorry that Colvin is leaving because of his good contacts but perhaps this is as well since he has been indulging in activities most dangerous to himself and possibly to the Embassy also.

"I agree", Strang minuted in the margin of this letter.[22]

The most fascinating aspect of Colvin's story was that his information had already been filed away in the Foreign Office for several weeks. On March 2nd the British Consul in the German port of Bremen, Thomas Wildman, had telegraphed Sir Nevile Henderson "With all reserve . . . that a German demonstration or attack against Poland is intended during this month". The only confirmation available to the Military Attaché at the British Embassy, Colonel F. N. Mason-MacFarlane, was the report of a contractor instructed to collect foodstuffs in east Pomerania by March 28th. Both the Consul's telegram and the Military Attaché's minute on it were sent to London on March 3rd. "There's no smoke without a fire", Frank Roberts, of the Foreign Office Central Department, minuted on March 15th.

By the middle of March such information had multiplied ominously. The Secret Intelligence Service had received at that time "various reports" indicating that German military preparations for an attack against Poland were to be concluded by March 28th. The Secret Intelligence Service confidently asserted that among their flood of information "this is the only case in which they have been able to substantiate rumours of definite dates fixed for action".[23]

In the following days, particularly after the German seizure of

Memel, the pace quickened alarmingly. Europe was seething with rumours of dates for a German seizure of Danzig or for an attack against Poland. By March 24th Poland had called up a considerable number of reservists and specialists of various classes. Warsaw had three days of practice air raid protection blackouts. Within days, upwards of half a million men were mobilised. The situation in Danzig, which had previously remained calm, suddenly grew tenser on March 28th.[24] Yet the Polish government itself had no information of troop movements or other measures in Germany indicating a possible Danzig coup. But they let it be generally known that, while ready to negotiate, they would forcibly resist any German ultimatum against Danzig.

Likewise the Hungarian-Rumanian border was a hive of military activity, ever since Hitler permitted the Hungarians on March 15th to occupy Ruthenia, the most easterly part of Czechoslovakia. The Rumanians, who now saw a further section of their north-east frontier becoming Hungarian territory, and who had themselves previously entertained hopes of a slice of Ruthenia, grew alarmed. Reports reached London that Germany had invited Hungary to join in military action against Rumania. This was firmly denied by the Hungarian Director of Military Intelligence himself.[25] Both Hungary and Rumania began to mobilise. The British and French governments sent frantic telegrams urging moderation and demobilisation to both Budapest and Bucharest. Demobilisation finally took place in mid-April.

Nor was western Europe spared rumours of yet more German military plans. In early March the French press had begun publishing scare stories that Hitler intended to attack Holland and Switzerland. Similar reports in January had led the British and French governments to secretly agree that a German invasion of Holland or Switzerland would be a *casus belli*. This agreement was leaked in Paris to the intense embarrassment of all concerned. By March 21st the Dutch seemed to be thoroughly alarmed. The Swiss, despite repeated efforts to appear blasé, on March 27th ordered further troops to strengthen their frontier defences.

The British government at first did not accept the stories of German troop concentrations in the west, assuming them to be a ploy. War Office intelligence also discounted them.[26] But after the occupation of Prague the danger could no longer be ignored. A series of special meetings, beginning on March 18th, involved various government departments and committees concerned with preparations for the outbreak of a war. Sir Horace Wilson explained to one such committee on March 21st that "owing to a series of rebuffs over the last few days, Herr Hitler was now in a towering rage, and we could not disregard the possibility, however remote, that in his present mood he might embark upon some 'mad dog' act." The danger, Wilson explained, "was a bolt from the blue in the air." Immediate defensive steps were taken. A special committee was set up to advise on an extensive programme of accelerated rearmament. By March 23rd eighty-three anti-aircraft guns and fifty-two searchlights were deployed around London.[27]

It was this prospect of a continent on the brink of the final conflagration which haunted the minds of western statesmen. There seemed to be only one response possible: an unmistakable warning to Hitler.

———

Late in the evening of March 29th and into the early hours of the morning Halifax, assisted by Cadogan and R. A. Butler, Parliamentary Under-Secretary of State for Foreign Affairs, prepared a draft declaration of a Polish guarantee and appropriate telegrams to Paris and Warsaw.

The Cabinet was called together at short notice at 11 a.m. on March 30th to consider these documents, which they now examined for the first time.[28] Would they approve yet another new departure in British policy? Halifax firstly described the information given him from American sources and from Colvin. He admitted this "was necessarily uncertain evidence." He admitted there were powerful objections to any statement at this point: not least, that it gave Beck what he had secretly requested on March 24th; it might upset the prospects of Poland and Germany reaching an accommodation; it might provoke Germany; and it left Rumania out of the picture. "Finally, the draft statement was rather heroic action to take, on the meagre information available to us."

Halifax wished to take "some prior action so as to forestall Herr Hitler's next step." If successful this could discredit Hitler in army circles and warn German public opinion of the dangers of a two-front war into which Hitler's policies were leading. He asked the Cabinet, therefore, to approve the draft declaration. It could then be issued at a moment's notice should the situation deteriorate. He continued:

> . . . plans had been prepared by Germany for a number of adventures, including an attack on Poland. The real question was which adventure Germany proposed to undertake next and at what date. . . . Our policy was to resist Germany's attempts at domination. If Poland was the next object of aggression, we must face the situation at once, and the best means of stopping German aggression was almost certainly to make it clear that we should resist it by force.

Asked whether he intended to distinguish between a seizure of Danzig by Germany, and a German attack on Poland, Halifax was quick to reply, perhaps too quick. He "thought it was difficult to find any better test than the decision by Poland whether to regard such an attack as a threat to her independence which she must resist by force." Later in the discussion, Chamberlain added his fullest agreement. If the Poles regarded the Danzig issue as a threat to their independence, and were prepared to resist, "then we should have to come to their help."

The implication that Britain could find itself at war because of a decision by the Polish government aroused the immediate criticism and anxieties of the waverers in the Cabinet: the Lord Chancellor, Lord Maugham, the Secretary of State for India and Burma, the Marquess of Zetland, the Secretary of State for Air, Sir Kingsley Wood, and the Chancellor of the Exchequer, Sir John Simon. Chamberlain understood the critics in his Cabinet. His own mind had doubtless pondered similar views. He sympathised that the action proposed "was a serious step and was the actual crossing of the stream. It was right that all his colleagues should consider the matter carefully before they took any irrevocable step."

What was troubling Chamberlain and others in the Cabinet was the implication of the draft declaration prepared by the Foreign Office. This committed Britain in stiff terms to go to war should Germany attack Poland. It gave neither Britain nor Germany any freedom of manoeuvre. What Chamberlain had in mind, however, was the difference between deterrence and an outright challenge. He hoped desperately that his policy would deter Germany from action; he hesitated at uttering threats of war. That such a subtle policy differentiation might be lost on an unsubtle Hitler never seems to have occurred to him. He had lost faith in Hitler's ability to respect agreements; he still hoped Hitler was open to rational persuasion; he still refused to believe war was inevitable.

As the discussion progressed through sometimes hesitant, sometimes belligerent phases, Lord Chatfield intervened. As the Cabinet spokesmen for the Chiefs of Staff views, his comments carried considerable weight.

The Chiefs of Staff report on the strategical implications of a guarantee to both Poland and Rumania had not been presented at the Cabinet meeting on March 29th, for which it had been called. Yet Chatfield, when beginning his statement on the 30th, said that the "position had been examined from the military point of view by the Chiefs of Staff." But was this true? There is no record of a subsequent meeting of military heads to report on a guarantee to Poland alone, excluding Rumania. Chatfield then went on to assert that the Chiefs of Staff

> had come to the fairly definite conclusion that, if we have to fight Germany, it would be better to do so with Poland as an ally, rather than to allow Poland to be absorbed and dominated by Germany without making any effort to help her. No doubt it would be impossible to prevent Poland from being overrun . . . within two or three months. . . . Nevertheless, the Chiefs of Staff thought that if Germany were to attack Poland, the right course would be that we should declare war on Germany.

This summary of the views of the Chiefs of Staff was tendentious. They had never advised the Government to declare war should Germany attack Poland. They were even critical of the whole idea of guaranteeing Poland and Rumania. Their main fear in both their reports of March 18th and 28th had been the Allies' inability to prevent the destruction of Poland. That was the reason they had twice advised Chamberlain to bring in the USSR, which alone could militarily help the Poles. Chatfield ignored this aspect.

Had the March 28th report of the Chiefs of Staff, therefore, been deliberately suppressed? It was in fact circulated "only to those who normally receive copies of Chiefs of Staff papers." Presumably this did not include most members of the Cabinet. Hore-Belisha was allegedly refused permission to circulate the report. Chamberlain's objection was that the Chiefs of Staff views would be "tantamount to a criticism of his policy." It was only on April 3rd, three days after the guarantee was publicly announced, that the Foreign Office and the Cabinet were permitted to see the Chiefs of Staff report, and then in a revised version.[29]

The views of the Chiefs of Staff, as Chatfield interpreted them for the Cabinet, had their desired effect. A guarantee to Poland was considered necessary. But Chamberlain objected to the Foreign Office draft. He wanted a "somewhat less defiant note", indicating the desirability of settling differences by discussion and not force.

The wisdom of this suggestion was confirmed moments later. Chatfield read out a memorandum, which had just been handed to him from the Chiefs of Staff. War Office intelligence had no evidence of any preparations for an attack against Poland. German military dispositions were "designed to cover a *coup d'état* against Danzig only". Should the Government nevertheless announce a guarantee, the Chiefs of Staff wanted the Poles to make a simultaneous declaration of reciprocal aid. "Otherwise there would be no two-front war for Germany." In a final word of admonition, the Chiefs of Staff asked the Cabinet to make sure Rumania's resources were denied to Germany in the event of war.[30]

It was Chatfield who suggested a compromise between the tough Foreign Office declaration and the limited military intelligence available. The Cabinet agreed it would be better to issue a "more general statement at an earlier date, which would give more timely warning" and would be less provocative to the German government. Chamberlain then read out an alternative draft he had prepared. But after some discussion, and no doubt with the approach of lunch time, the Cabinet decided that the final wording should be left to the more expert Foreign Policy Committee. In the meantime, telegrams would be sent to Paris, asking the French government to make a similar declaration, and to Warsaw, informing the Polish government of the intended action.

"We separated with a feeling almost of relief with the knowledge that a definitive decision had been taken", the Marquess of Zetland, Secretary of State for India and Burma, wrote five days later, "even though we realised that we were burning our boats and that we might be committed to war over a principle which we have all come to think transcends even the vital material interests of this country . . . you . . . see how far we have travelled in the past few months."[31]

Little progress was in fact made that afternoon when the Foreign Policy Committee met. Instead, even further doubt was cast upon the supposed German intention to attack Poland. According to Sir Horace Wilson, War Office inquiries "indicated little, if any, sign of the concentration of German troops against the Polish frontier." Besides the normal number of German divisions poised on both sides of the Corridor, there were only the fourteen divisions used in the invasion of Czechoslovakia. "The Prime Minister agreed that this information did not support the theory that Germany was contemplating an immediate military *coup de main*."[32]

Action seemed now to depend on the reliability of military intelligence. As the hours passed it appeared even less certain that Germany was prepared to invade Poland or seize Danzig. When the Foreign Office received that afternoon the daily War Office "Summary of Information" – the same one presumably which Sir Horace Wilson referred to during the Foreign Policy Committee – it was not impressed. "This doesn't look to me very formidable as yet", Cadogan minuted, even though a telegram had just arrived from the Military Attaché in Berlin repeating Colvin's story of the previous day.[33]

Meanwhile, Foreign Office officials were busily set to work summarising and assessing the flood of European telegrams describing Hitler's intentions. Richard Speaight of the Central Department drew up on March 29th a five-page memorandum dealing with a possible German coup in Danzig. He concluded: "there is no concrete evidence that the Germans are planning one." Ivone Kirkpatrick assessed the information available as to German military plans. He found himself faced with "somewhat conflicting" reports. On the one hand various sources reported March 28th as being the date either for the delivery of supplies or for the completion of military concentrations on the Polish frontier. Other "secret sources", indirectly in touch with Hitler's personal staff, claimed that the Führer was anxious to avoid a conflict with Poland.

"The conclusion to be drawn", Kirkpatrick equivocally noted, "is the usual one in so far as Hitler's plans are concerned." His ultimate aim remained to eliminate or neutralise Poland and Rumania. But the "final decision may, as in the past, be precipitated by events which Hitler can neither foresee nor control." For the meantime there was little reason to think Hitler was committed to an early attack against Poland.[34]

It was against this background of uncertainty that the Foreign Policy Committee once more assembled on March 31st at 10 Downing Street at 9.45 a.m. Mounting pressures and difficulties from all sides seemed to force the pace of events towards an immediate decision on the Polish guarantee.

Chamberlain described how he had resisted efforts made that morning by three Opposition Labour leaders, Hugh Dalton, Arthur Greenwood and A. V. Alexander, to include even a slight reference to Russia in his parliamentary statement on the Polish guarantee. They had warned that the Government might otherwise expect "trouble". Chamberlain, without any apparent prompting from his colleagues, further recalled what he had told this Labour delegation. The absence of Russia in the declaration "was based on expediency and not on any ideological consideration. He had impressed upon them the danger of alienating Poland at the present juncture."

The Prime Minister was angry, as well, because the Opposition leaders had leaked details both of the crisis and of contemplated action to the press. Any further delay in making a declaration, it was also pointed out, would have a depressing effect on financial circles in the City of London.

Finally, Chamberlain once again returned, in a rather troubled mood, to the military justification for the proposed action. The latest available information, he stated, "seemed to point to it being unlikely that the Germans were contemplating any immediate *coup de main.*" Would it not be better, he suggested, to omit any reference to rumours in the proposed declaration? To which an unnamed colleague sharply replied that to do so would negate the justification for the declaration.

Caught on the horns of this dilemma, the Foreign Policy Committee agreed to take the plunge. Ministers acted against the best military advice tendered by the Chiefs of Staff. They doubted Hitler's immediate intentions to attack Poland or seize the Corridor. But reluctant to withdraw their offer at the last moment, the Foreign Policy Committee gave Chamberlain authority to address Parliament. In a last rearguard action, Ministers agreed that Ambassador Kennard should warn the Poles of two strings attached to the guarantee. Firstly, Poland must herself resist any threat to her independence. Secondly, "she would not indulge in provocative behaviour or stupid obstinacy either generally or in particular as regards Danzig."[35]

At once Chamberlain rushed off to the House of Commons to report briefly that his Government did not necessarily accept as true rumours of a projected attack on Poland. This was intended to calm public opinion and financial circles, thereby avoiding any risk of a heavy fall in prices in the City. He then hurried to a meeting of the full Cabinet in his Commons' room at noon. There was no agenda and only one topic: the international situation.

Only one decision had to be taken: to let the Cabinet see the proposed statement and authorise its issue.

Hoping perhaps for quiet assent, Chamberlain again found himself deeply involved in the thorny Russian issue. He reviewed the attempts he had made behind the scenes to convince the Opposition leaders of his intention to include the Russians at some point. But he feared the Labour party especially were convinced "that the Government were prejudiced against Russia and were neglecting a possible source of help". The Cabinet was worried that the questions following the statement in Parliament could be highly embarrassing to the Government. Someone suggested making the statement as late as possible to shorten the time for such inquiries. It was thought best, however, for Halifax firstly to see the Soviet Ambassador, Ivan Maisky, and then say something to Parliament in light of this conversation.

The latest assessment of military intelligence again brought confusing results. Early in the discussion Chamberlain observed that "further enquiries had failed to confirm the alleged German troop movements." Nor did the French government fear any imminent coup by Germany. Leslie Hore-Belisha, who had remained conspicuously silent during several Cabinet meetings, later intervened to read out a statement of the up-to-the-minute military information. "This showed that Poland had already mobilised a considerable number of reservists, and that the indications were that Germany intended either to occupy Danzig on the 1st April or to intimidate Poland, at a time when that country appeared to be drawing closer to the Western Powers."

No one bothered to question what had suddenly made the Intelligence Department of the War Office, from whom Hore-Belisha's report was derived, be so categorical as to Hitler's intentions regarding Danzig.* Instead, this information ended any further discussion. The declaration to Parliament was

---

* The full War Office report did not reach Chamberlain until the early evening. The most dramatic item of intelligence listed was a "Most Secret Report", received on March 29th, that Germany intended to occupy Danzig without the Corridor: "Action imminent". (PREM/331.)

approved. Joseph Kennedy and Benito Mussolini were to be given advance notice of the guarantee.

The Foreign Office at once telephoned Chamberlain's personal message to Mussolini. "I feel sure that you will approve my motive", the Prime Minister stated.

Cadogan was delegated to inform Kennedy. The Ambassador surprisingly felt the guarantee "would be regarded in America as a 'subterfuge'." Cadogan disputed this "rather hotly". Kennedy promised he would do his best with the "beastly" American newsmen in London.

Later in the afternoon Kennedy telephoned the Foreign Office. He had just had a call from President Roosevelt "who thought the statement excellent and said that in his judgement it would have a very great effect. The United States he thought would consider that war was imminent, but the President did not think that this would do any harm." As regards the American newsmen in London, Kennedy had done his job well. Their despatches were, in his opinion, "very good."[36]

The most awkward mission was placed on Halifax's shoulders. He was given the task of conciliating the Soviet Ambassador and eliciting, if possible, some gesture of approval. Since the failure of the four-power declaration, Ivan Maisky had been kept largely in the dark as to British policy. Undeterred, but stung and snubbed, he had continued his activities behind the scenes. At this the peppery little Ambassador was an expert. His unofficial contacts were many and well placed, including the Labour MP, Hugh Dalton, a frequent visitor to the Soviet Embassy, and Sir Robert Vansittart. Little that was discussed in the Cabinet and Foreign Office did not soon reach his ears. The substance of every briefing that Chamberlain gave to the Opposition leaders was certain to be conveyed to Maisky. He "is a very nice little man", Vansittart remarked about the Ambassador months later, "But the trouble about Maisky is that he knows nothing about Russia. He knows a lot about England, a very great deal, but then I know a lot about England myself and I do not want to hear about England from a foreigner."

When Halifax finally confronted Maisky at the Foreign Office in the early afternoon, the Soviet Ambassador was not entirely ignorant of what was wanted of him. Halifax first read out the proposed parliamentary statement which he suggested was a "grave and momentous decision." In order to avoid "any unnecessary appearance of divisions" between Britain and the USSR, could Chamberlain tell Parliament the Soviet government approved of the statement? The request was as outrageous as it was clever. Not unnaturally, Maisky refused. He did consent to Chamberlain making some reference to the fact that British action accorded with the principles of Soviet policy. But he twice warned Halifax that the USSR "had no wish to force themselves on anybody, and would therefore take no initiative."

Maisky then returned to the Soviet Embassy to sulk and commiserate with his sympathisers. A. J. Sylvester, Private Secretary to David Lloyd George, was waiting there and related to Maisky what Chamberlain had that day confidentially told Lloyd George about British policy.

"I think Mr Lloyd George is right in saying of Poland", Maisky said, "that this is a reckless gamble on the part of the Prime Minister to believe that he can really stop Hitler by combining Britain, France and Poland."[37]

At 3 p.m. Chamberlain stood at the despatch box in the House of Commons. Slowly and impressively, he read the following statement:

His Majesty's Government have no official confirmation of the rumours of any projected attack on Poland and they must not, therefore, be taken as accepting them as true. . . . In their opinion there should be no question incapable of solution by peaceful means, and they would see no justification for the substitution of force, or threats of force for the method of negotiation.

As the House is aware, certain consultations are now proceeding with other Governments. In order to make perfectly clear the position of His Majesty's Government in the meantime before those consultations are concluded, I now have to inform the House that during that period, in the event of any action which clearly threatened Polish independence, and which the Polish Government accordingly considered it vital to resist with their national forces, His Majesty's Government would feel themselves bound at once to lend the Polish Government all support in their power. They have given the Polish Government an assurance to this effect.

I may add that the French Government have authorised me to make it plain that they stand in the same position in this matter as do His Majesty's Government.

Replying to questions from Arthur Greenwood, the deputy Labour leader, Chamberlain emphasised that his statement covered only an "interim period". Furthermore, the "principles" of British policy were "fully understood and appreciated" by the Soviet government. The visit shortly expected from Colonel Beck would be an opportunity "to accumulate the maximum amount of co-operation in any efforts that may be made to put an end to aggression".

Three days later, in the Commons, Chamberlain returned to his declaration. The guarantee which had been given to Poland, he explained, "constitutes a portent in British policy so moment-ous that I think it is safe to say it will have a chapter to itself when the history books come to be written." As Chamberlain pointed out, Britain had agreed to protect a country in eastern Europe. This had only been undertaken because he now felt Germany's appetite to dominate other nations was insatiable. All Hitler's previous assurances that his foreign policy had only limited aims "have now been thrown to the winds. That is the new fact which has completely destroyed confidence and which has forced the British Government to make this great departure."

Throughout this speech Chamberlain made an impassioned plea for Hitler to come to his senses; to pull back from the brink while there was still time; and not to force the Prime Minister into a war he did not want.

I am no more a man of war to-day than I was in September [1938]. . . . These recent happenings have, rightly or wrongly, made every State which lies adjacent to Germany unhappy, anxious, uncertain about Germany's future intentions. If that is all a misunderstanding, if the German Government has never had any such thoughts, well, so much the better. In that case any agreements which may be made to safeguard the independence of these countries will never have to be called upon, and Europe may then gradually simmer down into a state of quietude in which their existence even might be forgotten. . . . [But] we cannot live for ever in that atmosphere of surprise and alarm from which Europe has suffered in recent months. The common business of life cannot be carried on in a state of uncertainty. As far as it is possible for His Majesty's Government to help to restore confidence by plain words, we have done our part. In doing so I am certain that we have expressed the will of this people. I trust that our action, begun but not concluded, will prove to be the turning point not towards war, which wins nothing, cures nothing, ends nothing, but towards a more wholesome era when reason will take the place of force and threats will make way for cool and well-marshalled arguments.[38]

With such words Europe was set for a trial of strength. A stand had finally been taken. But it was a lonely position. On March 18th Chamberlain had hoped to rally the countries of south-east Europe into a deterrent front. He had refused even to contemplate the possibility of Britain and France alone having to fight Germany.

Yet the hesitations of the threatened but divided states of south-east Europe forced him to look further north for support. He stubbornly insisted Poland was the "key" to the situation: she was the pivot of the political and military problems of eastern Europe; she was the pivot of a two-front war. On March 31st Poland was given an Anglo-French guarantee. The British had arrived in eastern Europe for the first time since 1914. They now had to find further company.

German troops in front of the Hradcany Palace in Prague on March 15, 1939.

Prime Minister Neville Chamberlain leaves 10 Downing Street on March 15th, 1939 to make a parliamentary statement on the German occupation of Czecho-slovakia. He is followed by Sir Horace Wilson, Chief Industrial Adviser to the Government, Secretary to the Treasury, and Head of the Civil Service.

Lord Halifax, Secretary of State for Foreign Affairs, and his Chief Diplomatic Adviser, Sir Robert Vansittart, in Downing Street.

German Ambassador Herbert von Dirksen, recalled to Berlin, prepares to leave on March 19th, 1939 from Victoria Station.

Dr Karl Friedrich Goerdeler,
a leading member of the
German resistance, kept the
Foreign Office informed of
Adolf Hitler's plans.

Keystone Press Agency Ltd.

Viorel Virgil Tilea, Rumanian
Minister in London, leaving
the Foreign Office after a
visit on March 20th, 1939.

United Press International (UK) Ltd.

Sir William Seeds (centre) with Soviet Foreign Minister, Maxim Litvinov (left), and Mikhail Kalinin, Chairman of the Presidium of the Supreme Soviet, on January 28th, 1939 when the new British Ambassador presented his credentials.

Ivan Maisky, Soviet Ambassador in London, with Robert Hudson, Secretary of the Department of Overseas Trade, at Victoria Station on March 16th, 1939 before the start of the Minister's tour of northern European capitals, including Moscow.

Polish Ambassador Count Edward Raczynski, and his Foreign Minister, Colonel Jozef Beck, leave the Foreign Office during the Anglo-Polish conversations in London, April 3rd–6th, 1939.

Radio Times Hulton Picture Library

King Zog of Albania and Queen Geraldine visit a church in Sweden in July 1939 during a stop on their travels in exile.

Keystone Press Agency Ltd.

Alexis Léger, Secretary-General of the French Foreign Ministry, Foreign
Minister Georges Bonnet, and Prime Minister Edouard Daladier at the War
Office in Paris on May 20th, 1939, after talks with Lord Halifax on the Anglo-
French-Soviet negotiations. *United Press International* (UK) *Ltd.*

Sir John Anderson, Lord Privy Seal, and Lord Zetland, Secretary of State for India and Burma, after a Cabinet meeting on January 18th, 1939.

William Morrison, Chancellor of the Duchy of Lancaster, and Malcolm MacDonald, Secretary of State for the Colonies..

Keystone Press Agency Lt.

Lord Maugham, the Lord Chancellor, and Sir Thoma Inskip, Secretary of State for the Dominions, in Downing Street on March 15th, 1939.

Keystone Press Agency L.

Oliver Stanley, President of the Board of Trade, and Lord Chatfield, Minister for Co-ordination of Defence, in Downing Street on March 31st, 1939.

Keystone Press Agency Ltd.

Robert Hudson, Lord Runciman, Lord President of the Council, and Leslie Burgin, Minister of Supply, leave Buckingham Palace on August 24th, 1939 after a meeting of the Privy Council.

Keystone Press Agency Ltd.

Sir John Simon, Chancellor of the
Exchequer, September 3rd, 1939.
United Press International (UK) Ltd.

The Anglo-French military mission to
Moscow ready to depart aboard the *City of
Exeter* at Tilbury. Admiral Sir Reginald
Plunkett-Ernle-Erle-Drax, General Joseph
Doumenc, Air Marshal Sir Charles Burnett,
Major-General Thomas Heywood, General
Valin, and (extreme right) Captain Willaume.
Radio Times Hulton Picture Library

German State Secretary
Ernst von Weizsäcker
(right) accompanies
Foreign Minister Joachim
von Ribbentrop on
August 22nd, 1939, to
Berlin airport where a
Condor airplane waits to
take the Foreign
Minister to Moscow.

Associated Press

Joachim von Ribbentrop,
Friedrich Gaus, Legal
Director of the German
Foreign Ministry, Joseph
Stalin, Soviet Foreign
Minister Vyacheslav
Molotov, and Gustav
Hilger, Counsellor of the
German Embassy in
Moscow, after the
signing of the German-
Soviet Non-aggression
Pact of August 23rd,
1939.

*United Press International (UK)
Ltd.*

Italian Prime Minister, Benito Mussolini.

President Franklin D. Roosevelt and Sir Ronald Lindsay, retiring British Ambassador in Washington.   *Associated Press*

American Ambassador Joseph P. Kennedy and Mrs Rose Kennedy, followed by their sons, arrive at the House of Commons during the crisis in late August 1939.   *Radio Times Hulton Picture Library*

Crowds watch the arrival on August 24th, 1939, of Neville Chamberlain at the House of Commons to rush through the Emergency Powers (Defence) Bill.

Associated Press

Sir Nevile Henderson, British Ambassador in Berlin, and Sir Alexander Cadogan, Permanent Under-Secretary of State for Foreign Affairs, cross to 10 Downing Street on the morning of August 28th, 1939.

Associated Press

General Lord Gort,
Chief of the Imperial
General Staff, and Leslie
Hore-Belisha, Secretary
of State for War (centre)
in Downing Street.
United Press International (UK)
Ltd.

Air Chief Marshal Sir
Cyril Newall, Chief
of Air Staff, and
Sir Kingsley Wood,
Secretary of State for Air,
leave 10 Downing Street
on September 5th, 1939.
United Press International (UK)
Ltd.

Chancellor Adolf Hitler at the Kroll Opera on the morning of September 1st, 1939, announcing the beginning of the German-Polish conflict. On Hitler's left is Dr Otto Dietrich, Reich Press Chief. Behind sits Field-Marshal Hermann Göring, Minister for Air.

Associated Press

Neville Chamberlain's draft of the telegram proposing the guarantee to Poland.
Crown Copyright

On Thursday, 31st August, 1939, the House will meet at 2 45 p m.

Debate on the International situation, and consideration of any necessary emergency business.

Your attendance at 2 45 p.m. is particularly requested

DAVID MARGESSON.

NOTE.   IMPORTANT.

In view of the uncertainty of the course of events,

the House may be called together before Thursday, 31st August

Should this be necessary, it may only be possible to

give Members 24 hour's notice.

A notice from the office of the Conservative Chief Whip, Captain David Margesson. Parliament was actually forced to meet two days early, on August 29th, 1939.

Martin Gilbert Archive

CHAPTER FIVE

"A Long, Solid and Durable Front"

WHEN Neville Chamberlain had finished announcing the guarantee to Poland, he sat down to listen to parliamentary reaction. The Conservative Chief Whip, Captain David Margesson, suddenly approached him and they exchanged a few words. The Prime Minister scribbled a note which Margesson then passed to a former Prime Minister, the ageing and outspoken David Lloyd George. He looked at Chamberlain with surprise and with a nod of his head signalled his assent. One of the most virulent critics of appeasement had just been invited to discuss events privately and be given the "latest information".

When they were seated in the Prime Minister's room in the House of Commons, Lloyd George asked why he had risked involving Britain in a war with Germany? According to the account which Lloyd George later passed to Ivan Maisky:

> The Prime Minister replied, that, according to information at his disposal, neither the German General Staff nor Hitler would ever risk war if they knew that they would have to fight at the same time on two fronts – the West and the East. Lloyd George then asked just where this "second front" was. The Prime Minister answered: "Poland." Lloyd George burst into laughter. . . . "Your statement of today [is] an irresponsible game of chance which can end up very badly."[1]

The game of chance was not so lunatic as Lloyd George charged, for reasons which Chamberlain could not fully explain. In British government circles it was accepted that Germany could smash

Poland. The only argument concerned the length of Polish resistance. However, intelligence reports and political assessments gave some ground for hope that the guarantee would prove an effective deterrent. "The German propaganda machine presents the world with an imposing façade of German strength, but we know that there are many chinks in the German armour", Ivone Kirkpatrick had noted on March 30th. Weariness among the German people produced by shortages of food and intensive war preparations, lack of raw materials, insufficiency of officers, shortage of equipment and the necessity of a pause to reorganise Czechoslovakia were specific indications that Germany was not in a position to wage a protracted general war.

Secret Intelligence Service information on conditions inside Germany had drawn attention to internal weaknesses in the event of a major war and had given confidence to the Foreign Office in organising resistance. "We are in a stronger position than we were last September to resist pressure and perhaps even to call a bluff", was how Frank Roberts had summed up the situation on the eve of the guarantee to Poland.[2]

Colonel F. N. Mason-MacFarlane, the British Military Attaché in Berlin, got carried away by the implications of these assessments. He was convinced that the military situation was changing in Britain's favour and that Germany was entirely unprepared for a war on two fronts. In a memorandum on March 28th, which had arrived in London two days later, he sounded a call for a preventive war against Germany within the next three weeks. "War, and war now" to hit Germany hard and quickly had been the essence of his advice. Sir Alexander Cadogan derisorily dismissed Mason-MacFarlane's "hysterical outpouring". On April 10th he flew to London in order, in his own words, to "ginger-up the War Office". A month later he left Berlin to take up an appointment in the War Office.[3]

The confidence gained from the belief that Germany was unable to fight a war on two fronts had added impetus and courage to the decision to guarantee Poland. It was this conviction which Chamberlain had tried, unsuccessfully, to convey to Lloyd George. This did not mean, however, that the British or

French were themselves fit to fight or possibly even to deter Germany.

On March 31st the first defensive outpost against Germany had been established in eastern Europe. The next urgent problem was a defensive front determined and able ultimately to resist Germany. But what states were available and where was the second front? A dangerous confusion had been forced on to Anglo-French strategy by pinning the key to the eastern front on the shoulders of Poland.

British strategy in early 1939 was not based on a two-front European war. It was planned to defeat Germany by a defensive strategy at the outset on the western front, giving way later to the offensive and backed by the strangulating, though long term, effects of the allied blockade. This strategy eventually won the Second World War.

A massive report, entitled "European Appreciation, 1939–1940", had been signed by the three Chiefs of Staff on February 20th, 1939. It laid down the strategy to be pursued in case of war after April 1939. The Chiefs of Staff drew up plans for Europe only for a war on the western front. In their opinion, Britain could give no effective direct help to any of the countries in east and south-east Europe. The Foreign Office, advising the Chiefs of Staff, had reassuringly observed that France would never fulfil her treaty commitments to Poland and the USSR without a guarantee of British assistance. Britain need never be involved, therefore, in a war started by Germany in eastern Europe. But the Chiefs of Staff had made a vital recommendation. They attached the "highest importance to the military advantages to be derived from having Turkey and Greece as our allies, in a war against Germany and Italy."

This advice was central to Anglo-French strategy. The defence of the Mediterranean had been divided equally between the British and French navies: the former being responsible for the eastern half, the latter for the western end. A German penetration of the Balkan countries would have been a deadly threat to the British naval presence in the Adriatic, Aegean and eastern Mediterranean. The Chiefs of Staff hoped Greece would help in a war against Italy by assisting in the control of the Aegean, isolating the Dodecanese islands, strengthening British naval control of the central Mediterranean, and providing bases for the use of the British navy.

For the Turks, the Chiefs of Staff had made more ambitious plans. An alliance with Ankara would bring the allies vital benefits. The Dardanelles, scenes of bloody fighting in 1915, would be closed. This would strangle Italy's Black Sea trade, especially oil on which she was dependent. The Italian possessions in the Dodecanese islands would become commitments for defence as opposed to vantage points for attack. The harbour at Smyrna, and Turkish air bases would be invaluable for the war effort in south-east Europe. "For these reasons it is difficult to overemphasise the influence which Turkish intervention on our side would have on the position in the Eastern Mediterranean and the Aegean", the Chiefs of Staff had written on February 20th.[4]

Here was a priceless ally whose association with Britain was urgently requested as the cornerstone of Mediterranean policy. The Foreign Office recognised this and described Turkey as a "Small Great Power". Her policies would benevolently influence those of the other Balkan countries and, as a Moslem state, bolster Britain's influence in her numerous Moslem colonies.

Yet tragically the politicians had equivocated despite many assurances from Turkey of the basic coincidence of her own and British interests. In February 1938, Dr Tevfik Rüstü Aras, then Foreign Minister, had told the British Ambassador, Sir Percy Loraine, that once Italy had entered into a war, no matter on what side, "Turkey would fight on the side of England." On July 28th Loraine had urged the Foreign Office to regard these assurances as sincere and take up the offer of political friendship. Political co-operation in the Middle East, appointment of full-time service attachés in Ankara, and enough money to buy the Turkish press was the mixed bag of suggestions the Ambassador proposed. His letter remained unanswered. So long as closer Anglo-Italian relations was Chamberlain's goal, and hopes remained to detach Italy from Germany, he could not risk upsetting Mussolini by warming up to the Turks.

Sir Percy Loraine's successor, Sir Hughe Knatchbull-Hugessen, was an equally determined advocate of Anglo-Turkish solidarity. "I admire the Turks. They are gentlemen, straight and frank and one knows where one is with them", was one of the first impressions he recorded in his diary after arriving in Ankara. On March 10th, 1939, he reminded the Foreign Office that Loraine's letter of the previous year had had no reply. He warned that Turkish goodwill would have to be met with positive inducements offered in advance of any hostilities.[5]

The highly expert Strategic Appreciation Sub-committee* had been set up on February 24th to discuss the Chiefs of Staff "European Appreciation". At their third meeting on the morning of March 17th, they agreed that events had outrun that appreciation and called for a partial reassessment. The reply was evident from remarks made the following day by Air Chief Marshal Sir Cyril L. N. Newall. They laid the basis of the kind of two-front war now envisaged.

> Once Germany has access to the Mediterranean we can no longer regard Greece and Turkey as potential allies. We should, therefore, have to fight Germany in the west and could only rectify the Balkan situation by defeating her there. The outcome of the conflict would be problematical. Our aim should be to ensure that Germany becomes engaged on two fronts.

The first step was to secure alliances with Poland and the USSR. In their definitive reply, the Chiefs of Staff were adamant on the vital importance of securing alliances with Turkey and Greece, even at the risk of alienating Italy.[6]

Here for the first time was Britain's new strategy. Germany had to be prevented from reaching the Mediterranean. This

---

* The members included: Lord Chatfield, the chairman, Sir John Anderson, Lord Privy Seal, W. S. Morrison, Chancellor of the Duchy of Lancaster, the three Service Ministers, and the Chiefs of Staff – Admiral Sir Roger Backhouse, Chief of the Naval Staff, General Lord Gort, Chief of the Imperial General Staff, and Air Chief Marshal Sir Cyril L. N. Newall, Chief of the Air Staff.

could help to make an economic blockade effective. A strong Polish-Russian northern front, calculated to assist Rumania and deter Germany, was vital. Alliances with Greece and Turkey would give encouragement and strength to the south-east Balkan front, deter Italy and protect British naval defences in the eastern Mediterranean. Cabinet reaction to this advice was initially enthusiastic. It evoked from Sir Thomas Inskip an emotional warning that "if Roumania was overrun and Germany advanced to the Mediterranean and the Aegean, we should be in danger of becoming a second-class Power."

While the Chiefs of Staff tendered advice on how to tackle Germany in a two-front war, Chamberlain and Halifax were as anxious to deter Germany with the same tactics. "If the threat of action was to be an effective deterrent", Halifax told the Cabinet on March 29th, "Germany must be faced with a war on two fronts simultaneously. Poland was therefore the key to the situation."[7] It is hardly surprising that the Balkan end of the eastern front, in dangerous disarray, was temporarily ignored.

At the same time Chamberlain was aware that Germany's strength and easy victories were undermining the morale of the Balkan states. Hitler's occupation of Czechoslovakia had terrified them. The new Turkish Foreign Minister, Sükrü Saracoglu, at once urged Britain and France to take the lead to counteract the "increased magnetic attraction acquired by Germany".

The signature of the German-Rumanian commercial agreement on March 23rd caused further despondency in Ankara. The chill wind of German influence was beginning to be felt on the Dardanelles. Saracoglu warned of the growing impression that the Western Powers were washing their hands of south-east Europe down to the Bosporus. Sir Hughe Knatchbull-Hugessen was himself greatly disturbed. The "critical moment with Turkey" has arrived, he telegraphed to London on March 25th.

Despite the dangers their governments were now exposed to, the Greek and Turkish representatives in London continued to assure the Foreign Office of their goodwill, but they preferred to wait for Britain and France to take the lead in organising Balkan resistance. * Only the Turks were lavish in their assurances. Their Ambassador, Dr Tevfik Rüstü Aras, told Lord Halifax on March 21st: "If assured of Anglo-Turkish co-operation, if England went to war Turkey would do the same."[8]

Instead of encouragement, the response was a mixture of soothing words, pacifying gestures and vague generalisations. Foreign Office officials even had to remind Halifax to keep the Balkan Ministers informed of British plans.

With politics obscuring strategy and immediate considerations overriding long-term aims, Sir Orme Sargent completed on March 27th a pungent memorandum. The policy of the British government in resisting German aggression, he wrote, was to stand on the line of Poland, Rumania and Yugoslavia. But Hitler's successes had "inspired such terror in Central Europe that we cannot hope that these countries will be ready to resist German pressure on the strength of vague British promises . . . [and] will no longer be willing to occupy the front trenches". Since the Munich conference, Sargent continued, he had always feared that the only tenable front was formed by Turkey and Greece. "Now I am beginning to doubt whether we shall hold even this one unless we take immediate and decisive action to secure our position." The question of alliances with Greece and Turkey should be immediately considered "before Germany's insidious penetration has undermined these two countries' present loyalty to the British connexion".

Such outspoken opinions provoked discussion. The head of the Eastern Department, Sir Lancelot Oliphant, agreed Turkey had to be brought in "on the ground floor" in any negotiations designed to resist Germany's advance in south-east Europe. An Anglo-Turkish alliance was "essential . . . and urgent whether or not a rot sets in in Roumania". These suggestions unfortunately reached Cadogan when he was in a depressed and indecisive mood. He doubted "whether if Germany *really* does

---

* All previous attempts to organise the states of south-east Europe had miserably failed. The only agreement ever reached, the Balkan Entente, weakly united Rumania, Yugoslavia, Greece and Turkey specifically against Bulgarian irredentist claims.

gobble S[outh] E[ast] Europe she will really be stronger to attack us". In principle he had no objection to an alliance with Greece and Turkey, though he preferred concentrating on the Polish-Rumanian defensive barrier first, and then hitching on Greece and Turkey as a second line of defence. He felt such a plan would be less provocative to Italy. The time had come, in his opinion, to take the Greeks and Turks fully into the confidence of the British government and be invited into the eastern front. A decision on alliances rested with the Cabinet.[9]

Lord Halifax did not see the minutes of this discussion until April 10th. Meanwhile, under Foreign Office prompting, the Greek Minister, Charalambos Simopoulos, and the Turkish Ambassador, Dr Aras, had been fobbed off with further assurances of British goodwill and friendship. The unexpected guarantee to Poland seemed to further isolate the Balkan countries. It was only at Sir Orme Sargent's insistence that the Rumanian government was assured on March 31st that it was not being permanently abandoned. The scheme for a joint Polish-Rumanian front would be implemented.

The next day, Radu Florescu, who was in charge of the Rumanian Embassy while Viorel Virgil Tilea was in Bucharest, visited the Foreign Office. He was confused and anxious. He asked whether the guarantee to Poland meant Britain was abandoning Rumania and making her help to Rumania dependent on Poland. "I did my best to dissuade him of this idea", Sargent minuted afterwards, "and to explain to him that we were treating Poland and Roumania on a footing of complete equality". Britain had certainly not lost interest in Rumania's fate.

These soothing words earned Sargent a double reprimand. Cadogan was the first to attack: "in point of fact is it not the case that 'we would only intervene on behalf of Roumania if and when Poland did so?' I thought it was a condition of our larger scheme that Poland *should* be ready to go to the assistance of Roumania? We have said repeatedly that Poland is the 'key'."

"That is certainly my view," was Halifax's brief comment. Sargent tried to defend himself. "I was concerned to reassure the Roumanian Chargé d'Affaires," he minuted, and continued:

... I would deprecate giving the impression to Roumania that Poland is in a position to veto any plan for guaranteeing Roumania. We do not want to discourage the Roumanians at this stage unduly, and even though Poland is the key to the collective security system we are trying to set up in Eastern Europe, it would, I think, be dangerous to tell the Roumanians now in so many words that we shall abandon them to their fate if Poland refused or having agreed fails to come to Roumania's assistance.

Cadogan had the last word. If Colonel Beck agreed to guarantee Rumania all would be well. "If he refuses", Cadogan laconically added, "we may have to explain to the Roumanians that the bottom has dropped out of the whole scheme put to them by Sir Reginald Hoare."[10] That scheme was for an Anglo-French joint guarantee of Poland and Rumania. The implication that there would consequently be no eastern front, only a single isolated ally in eastern Europe, was ignored by Cadogan.

––––––––

London expectantly awaited the arrival of the Polish Foreign Minister, Colonel Beck, whose visit had actually been arranged in January. Despite the March crises in Europe, he had decided to fulfil his London engagement. On a previous trip to England in November 1936, he had made an unfortunate impression at the Foreign Office. Owing to his "fatigue and his weak head", his Ambassador, Count Edward Raczynski, noted in his diary, "the few glasses he had to drink made him arrogant and aggressive". This time, confident of the success so far of his diplomacy, Beck was tough and efficient. On April 3rd he arrived at Victoria Station and was welcomed by Lord Halifax. Beck was also greeted by the "usual red carpet", a "specially erected stand for several dozen photographers," and an "interested and friendly crowd". He was finally driven off to the "usual suite at Claridge's".

Having paid his preliminary respects, Halifax then joined his colleagues at the Foreign Office. They had gathered to discuss "how to take Beck". Massive briefs, ranging from the Danzig question to the problem of Polish Jews and Palestine, had been laboriously prepared. Yet on the vital issues relevant to building an eastern front – a Polish commitment to assist Rumania against German aggression, and the pressing need for Soviet military assistance to Poland – no considered briefs were drawn up.

There is no doubt that at the Foreign Office gathering on April 3rd these problems were discussed. The records of the conversations with Beck dramatically illustrate how hard he was pressed on these problems. But the main concern was with another question which has never previously been revealed. Should Britain threaten to withdraw her guarantee if Beck did not reciprocate? The meeting decided against such a threat and to maintain the guarantee in any circumstances.

The implication that Germany could thereby hold in the east and safely attack westward seems to have been ignored by everyone except Gladwyn Jebb. To guarantee "Poland unreciprocally, indefinitely and unreservedly would be, if not positively dangerous, at least a shade quixotic", he wrote to Cadogan the next day. Jebb felt there were powerful arguments in favour of abandoning the unilateral guarantee and thus reserving complete freedom of action. A defenceless Poland would tempt Hitler, force the Poles, as seemed likely, to resist, and in this way ensure Germany fought on two fronts. "All possible pressure including threats", should be applied therefore to get a reciprocal guarantee. This might "lead to war, but to a war for which the nation is ready and which we should probably win."[11]

Jebb's fears proved quite unfounded. Both he and the Foreign Office underestimated Colonel Beck's astuteness as a diplomat. Travelling in the Nord Express from Warsaw to London, Beck stopped in Berlin for a brief conversation with his Ambassador, Jozef Lipski. He warned Beck that a reguarantee from the Polish side would be considered by the Germans as the final break with Poland. Beck was undaunted. Any controversy in London would be avoided, he confidently assured Lipski. An Anglo-Polish agreement would be reciprocal but defensive. Poland had no intention to join any anti-German coalition.[12]

In the first of their conversations, Beck faced Halifax in the Secretary of State's room at the Foreign Office. Almost in his opening words, when referring to Britain's unilateral guarantee, Beck casually stated: "it was clear that the engagement must be reciprocal. . . . This was the only basis that any self-respecting country could accept." Answering confidence with flattery, Halifax replied that "he had expected this to be M. Beck's attitude . . . because of the position Poland occupied in the world".

Having thus lulled the British Foreign Secretary with an important concession, Beck then quickly laid down the line on other issues. Poland preferred to preserve a totally independent and "correct" policy towards the Russians. Any pact with them would provoke the Germans and "would possibly accelerate the outbreak of a conflict". Polish survival depended on preserving her independence from both Russia and Germany. Should Britain and Russia sign any agreement, Poland would have to publicly dissociate herself. On the question of a Polish guarantee to Rumania against a German attack, Beck again proved obstinate. Such action would force Hungary into the German camp and he wished to see Hungary and Rumania at peace. He could only agree to consult with Rumania on future policy.

There was little pressure, no threat and less conviction in the arguments Lord Halifax then put forward to persuade Beck to view the problems of European security on a continental scale. Could Britain count on the support of Poland if Germany attacked such vital Anglo-French interests as Holland, Belgium, Switzerland, Denmark and Yugoslavia? This "might be discussed", Beck replied. Was not Rumania's security vital to Poland? Yes, he stated, but Hungary must not be antagonised. Was it not important for Poland at least "to be able to use the Russian route for the supply of war material?" The Polish government "had not a very high opinion of Soviet Russia" was Beck's retort.

Halifax had exhausted himself. When the discussions resumed late that afternoon, Neville Chamberlain was present to try his hand. He also firstly tried flattery to weaken Beck's position. The "destruction of Polish independence would constitute the most serious attack on the British Empire that we had ever experienced", Chamberlain said. Germany's piecemeal absorption of her neighbours could only be prevented by the deterrent of an eastern front. Of course, "Poland's forces would no doubt put up a gallant fight". But only Soviet Russia could replenish their supply of munitions should war break out. Only a guaranteed Rumania could secure Poland's southern frontier. And only an agreement which included, for example, Belgium, Holland, Switzerland and Denmark would provide security in western Europe.

To all of Chamberlain's insistent and diverse arguments, Beck politely reiterated his previous replies. After less than two hours the meeting adjourned. Everyone at the Foreign Office agreed afterwards that, besides his concession on reciprocity, Beck had proved "very sticky". A certain suspicion of the Polish Foreign Minister was also coming to the surface. As Halifax told the Cabinet on April 5th, it was obvious that Beck "would prefer that Roumania rather than Poland should be over-run by Germany".

Halifax also retained a sense of overall strategy. He advised the Cabinet that consultations on how best to preserve Rumanian independence should continue. And he wished to press forward, "irrespective of Poland's reactions, with a view to strengthening the Balkan Entente". Despite strong Cabinet support for these views, Chamberlain had other ideas. He sympathised with Beck's outlook. While the talks had not been "unsatisfactory, they had not turned out quite as we had expected." The Prime Minister explained to the Cabinet:

> The general attitude adopted by both the Liberal and Labour Oppositions was that we had returned to the policy of collective security. They were thinking in terms of arrangements under which we should have an agreement with Turkey, Greece, Roumania and perhaps other Balkan States, the Baltic States and Russia – in effect, a Grand Alliance against Germany.

The Prime Minister said that at the outset of these negotiations he had thought that we might perhaps have an understanding with Poland, Russia, Roumania, and later on with Turkey and Greece. It was clear, however, that we should not secure an arrangement with Poland on these lines.

The alternative, which he "was by no means indisposed to negotiate", was an Anglo-Polish alliance. "After all, Poland was the key to the situation," he expansively repeated to his colleagues, "and an alliance with Poland would ensure that Germany would be engaged in a war on two fronts." He was very conscious of the fact that it would be necessary to take the "utmost care as to the presentation" of an exclusive Anglo-Polish alliance in order to avoid a "considerable outcry and criticism".[13]

Chamberlain expressed no regrets and no disappointments. He admired Beck's confidence and trusted his assurances that Germany had no immediate intention to attack Poland. An alliance with Warsaw held every prospect of deterring Hitler. It could even help Beck to negotiate, from a position of strength, a peaceful settlement with Germany. But the strategic muddle continued. The advice of the Chiefs of Staff was ignored. Beck's objections to co-operating with the Russians, even indirectly, were shared by the Prime Minister. While the Balkans seemed destined to be abandoned. The eastern front against Germany was to rest on the shoulders of the "gallant" Poles.

During the afternoon of April 5th Neville Chamberlain confronted Colonel Beck for the last time and appealed to him, unsuccessfully, to be more accommodating on the wider issues involved. The Prime Minister pointed out that the conversations were bound to arouse suspicion and to disappoint public opinion which had been led to expect an arrangement where various states "would band themselves round Great Britain, France and Poland as a nucleus". Instead what had emerged from the talks could be regarded "as a selfish arrangement" between London and Warsaw.

Beck softened enough to help Chamberlain out of his difficulties. The public communiqué announced that Poland had reciprocated the guarantee. A permanent agreement would be temporarily deferred. In the meantime, both governments were free to pursue suitable arrangements with any other state. A secret document summarising the talks and initialled the next day left the British government free to continue its negotiations with Rumania, the Balkan Entente and the Soviet Union.

Had Chamberlain and his Cabinet any serious intention to extend the eastern front southwards into the Balkans? Exhausted by the conversations with Beck and faced with his stubborn arguments, it seemed the Balkan pot was to be left to simmer.

Three interviews within two hours was how Sir Alexander Cadogan disposed of the thankless task entrusted to him by Lord Halifax. Following the Anglo-Polish conversations, the Balkan representatives in London were called to the Foreign Office. Cadogan told them that they would be kept informed of developments. Forms of co-operation would be discussed as soon as Poland and Rumania had agreed on future policy. Viorel Virgil Tilea, who had just returned to London from Bucharest, had no time for platitudes. He had been discussing the results of the conversations with Beck and was now searching for the British assessment. Tilea immediately embarked on a "regular catechism" and "cross-examination". He finally drew from Cadogan the brutal truth that Britain would only guarantee Rumania if Poland did likewise.[14] It seemed that the Balkan countries would just have to wait for Colonel Beck. Or would they?

"This proves Mussolini a gangster as Czechoslovakia proved Hitler, and we must set up a barrier with Greece and Turkey", Sir Alexander Cadogan advised Lord Halifax at the Foreign Office on Good Friday, April 7th. All day news was coming into London of what seemed like an Italian invasion of the tiny kingdom of Albania. Within twenty-four hours King Zog's outnumbered army had surrendered. With his wife and three-day-old child, he fled to Greece.

After weeks of typical indecision and wavering, Benito Mussolini had decided on March 23rd to settle the "Albanian question". The speed of German expansion by turns depressed and agitated him. Italy had not kept up with its Axis partner. After Hitler's Prague coup, Mussolini felt impelled to shower the Italians with the fruits of an Albanian occupation. "Satisfaction and compensation: Albania", was Count Ciano's war cry. Diplomatic pressure and military preparations speeded ahead. Ciano expected a bloodless victory. He gauged King Zog as a devoted family man who would prefer capitulation to seeing his wife, Queen Geraldine, "running around fighting through the mountains of Unthi or of Mirdizu in her ninth month of pregnancy".[15]

Rumours of Italian preparations travelled the European diplomatic grapevine. But there is no evidence that before April 4th anyone in London believed the Italians would be so rash as to invade Albania. By mid-March the Southern Department of the Foreign Office, dealing with Albanian affairs, was quite convinced that "Italian designs on Albania have been put into cold storage". On March 29th Sir Orme Sargent himself observed: "I don't suppose Mussolini will attempt a coup in Albania in present circumstances – unless Yugoslavia agreed to collaborate (which she won't)." The next day a top level discussion at the Foreign Office came to the seemingly rational conclusion that too many factors made an Italian adventure unlikely. That the Italians might act irrationally was confidently ignored. As late as April 3rd, Sir Andrew Noble of the Southern Department wrote: "I . . . still incline to the view that Italy is not going to pounce on Albania just now".[16]

There is no evidence that the Secret Intelligence Service gave any substantial advance warning of the occupation. On March 22nd they had a report from a "secret source in Italy", the accuracy of which could not be vouched for, that a move against Yugoslavia, probably accompanied by a landing in Albania, would take place about April 1st. This intelligence, forwarded to the Yugoslav Regent, Prince Paul, brought a reassuring reply. He considered the report "out of date".

The considerable military activity in Italy was very carefully watched. War Office intelligence officials assumed, for example, that the activity at the Adriatic port of Bari was merely preparation in case of a general war. An actual occupation of Albania, they wrote on April 4th, "does not appear likely". Neither did the Intelligence Department of the Admiralty guess the destination of the assembled Italian troops. While to the Southern Department of the Foreign Office, all the activity, if aimed at Albania, was as silly as "training an elephant to smash a flea."[17]

Without accurate advance intelligence, the British government had refused to believe that Mussolini would strike at Albania. Britain was quite prepared to see him gain total control of internal Albanian affairs. Italian men, money and materials already flooded the country. Albania had been recognised by treaty as an Italian sphere of interest since 1921. This gave her the right even to intervene with troops, but only in case of danger to Albania's borders from a third party. But would Mussolini be so short-sighted as to tear up the Anglo-Italian Agreement, brought into effect on November 16th, 1938, which recognised that the territorial *status quo* in the Mediterranean area should be maintained? Neville Chamberlain had fought against loud opposition to push through this agreement. He was shocked to have Mussolini now disregard it with impunity. By instinct, as on March 15th, he tried to minimise the latest coup by the dictators.

When the Albanian situation first came up for a brief discussion at the Cabinet on April 5th, Halifax appeared unworried. Any action Mussolini took in Albania, he reassuringly suggested, "would be taken in a manner which, on formal grounds, would not perhaps be open to strong criticism." He was not yet thinking of an invasion.

A day later Halifax was becoming anxious. Information was conflicting, he told the American Ambassador, but the evidence suggested that the Italians were going to make "some definite move". Without being prodded, Kennedy was quick to offer advice on how to defend a policy of British inaction. Take the line, he confided to Halifax, that an attack against Albania did not threaten world domination.

After a meeting at the Foreign Office, Lord Halifax instructed his Ambassador in Rome, Lord Perth, to urge the Italian Foreign Minister not to take any violent action in Albania. The British government appreciated Italy's special interest there. Surely

Mussolini shared the common desire to preserve the Anglo-Italian agreement? Halifax cancelled his plans for a quiet Easter weekend at his Yorkshire estate. Chamberlain stayed in Scotland, fishing.

Lord Perth finally saw Ciano on April 7th. The Italian Foreign Minister had just returned from a flight over Durazzo to watch the occupation. Italy "had sent troops to restore peace, order and justice in Albania," was how he described the operation. Perth did not object. He was about to retire from the diplomatic service. He preferred to end his days in Rome with a whimper and not a bang; a frame of mind which incensed the Foreign Office.

On an unofficial level, the British and Italians saw eye to eye over the Albanian invasion. The soothing message passed in telegrams from Rome to London was that Britain need have no fears: Italian aims were limited. The telegrams in the other direction pleaded with Mussolini to avoid excess bloodshed, respect the Mediterranean *status quo*, and preserve the Anglo-Italian Agreement. Such words were designed to prevent a clash over Albania which both Britain and Italy wanted to avoid. No one in either Cabinet or Foreign Office circles dreamed of fighting Italy now, when a confrontation had been so painfully avoided throughout the Spanish Civil War.

"If possible we don't want this comparatively minor question", Sir Orme Sargent cautioned on April 6th, "to wreck such prospects as there are of weaning Italy from the Axis, bringing about a Franco-Italian detente & getting Italian troops out of Spain – all matters of far greater moment than the bullying of the Albanian Govt. however deplorable and disturbing this may be. In a word we cannot stand on the 'Albanian front'."[18] But another front was readily available.

"We must not forget that the British are readers of the Bible", Mussolini had told Ciano on March 19th, "and that they combine mercantilism with mysticism. Now the latter prevails, and they are capable of going into action."[19] But like Hitler, Mussolini underestimated the British, because the seizure of Albania proved to be for Anglo-French strategy in south-east Europe what the Prague coup had been for their strategy in eastern Europe. In March a defensive outpost had been established in Poland. In April two more outposts were to be set up in Greece and Rumania, and in May another was established on the Dardanelles. There would probably have been no deterrent front in south-east Europe had Mussolini not frightened the British and French governments into an active response.

In late February when Mussolini was first reported as having designs against Albania, the Foreign Office had drawn up a single plan of action. An alliance with Greece assisted by Turkey and France should be the democracies' response.[20] And the democracies were learning to react swiftly.

Only ten Ministers out of a Cabinet of twenty-two had decided to spend their Easter weekend in London. This "scratch crew" was hastily gathered at 10 Downing Street on Saturday morning, April 8th. Cadogan and Sir Horace Wilson were also invited to attend.

The constantly recurring word in the record of this meeting is "obscure". Communications with the British Minister in the Albanian capital, Sir Andrew Ryan, had been cut since April 6th. Even the Albanian Minister in London, Lec Kurti, embarrassingly had to ask the Foreign Office for news. The extent of resistance and Italy's ultimate intentions were unknown. The only sure fact was that troops had landed at Albania's ports. Consequently, as Halifax pointed out, there were only two questions to be considered: what should be done about Albania itself, and what should be the wider political response?

Sending a British fleet to the Adriatic to bombard Italian forces in the Albanian ports was "impossible". Seven British warships were in the Italian ports of San Remo, Naples and Sorrento. The *Warspite* at San Remo had on board Admiral Sir Dudley Pound, the Mediterranean Commander-in-Chief.

The Balkan countries most directly affected, Yugoslavia and Greece, were watching impassively. Nor did Mussolini's actions merit sending him an ultimatum which would start a European war. The episode showed, however, the insecurity of south-east Europe. The one viable response, in Halifax's opinion, was to reach agreements with Greece and Turkey which would indicate Britain would tolerate no interference in their affairs. This step should be taken at once, even before Poland and Rumania ironed out their differences, and even if Mussolini was offended. This was the only possible reaction, even if, as Halifax also feared, American public opinion would feel that while the British government "used brave words", its "action was less heroic". Later that afternoon Halifax was to receive indirectly an assurance from President Roosevelt "that American opinion was not . . . disposed to jump off in the sense of expecting Great Britain to take any drastic action."

In a rare demonstration of Cabinet unity, not one of the ten Ministers disagreed. Sir John Simon, normally so cautious in his views on European diplomacy, applauded Halifax's analysis.[21] Yet, strangely, no definite proposals of guarantee or alliance with Greece or Turkey were advanced. Was there to be more delay?

Just as Germany's seizing of Czechoslovakia on March 15th had set rumours of further coups circulating throughout Europe, so Italy's occupation of Albania produced similar reports. Tunis, Corfu, Egypt and Gibraltar were places the French feared would be attacked. The British were sceptical, though prepared to believe the worst.

In a dramatic midnight meeting, the Greek Prime Minister, General Ioannis Metaxas, gave secret information to the British Minister, Sir Sydney Waterlow. The Italians intended to attack Corfu within the next four days. They "have taken the bit between their teeth." Greece would resist at all costs. Metaxas made no direct appeal, but he obviously wished Britain to declare her intentions.

If, as a spearhead for further Italian penetration into the Balkans, Albania was important, the Greek island of Corfu was a strategic jewel. As a potential naval base, the British hoped to use it for operations in the eastern Mediterranean. The threat of an Italian attack here was sufficient to concern every Englishman. In a letter to Chamberlain on April 9th, Winston Churchill strongly urged a British occupation of the island in order to forestall an Italian move.[22]

The same day, the Italian Chargé d'Affaires, Guido Crolla, was called before Halifax. Let there be no misunderstanding, Halifax sternly warned him, action against Corfu meant an Anglo-Italian war. If Italy had no hostile intentions against Corfu, let Mussolini give formal reassurances to both London and Athens. Pocketing his pride, Mussolini acted as Halifax had suggested. The Duce had no immediate plans against Greece and needed time to digest the latest addition to Italy's new empire. The Greeks received Mussolini's "distinctly flowery message" with suspicion. While it seemed reassuring, it could equally be "intended to chloroform them". Chamberlain needed Mussolini's assurance for parliamentary purposes. It also seemed to him as evidence of the Duce's future good intentions.

The French government was more worried about the security of the Mediterranean. Any British help for Greece to resist Italy, Edouard Daladier, the French Prime Minister, assured the British Ambassador, Sir Eric Phipps, would receive French support. The democracies were dealing "with gangsters" was Daladier's blunt appraisal.[23]

The initiative for further action now rested with the Cabinet, which met on April 10th. Ministers' holidays were interrupted once more by the dictators. With Chamberlain back in the presiding seat, the effect of possible British action on Mussolini's susceptibilities inevitably became a sensitive issue. But the voice of Sir Samuel Hoare was again the firmest of all his colleagues. He favoured Britain making unilateral declarations supporting Greek and Turkish independence. This was done in the case of Poland and the situation had been steadied. Sir John Simon surprisingly agreed with such outspoken plans. His reasons were more practical. It "would make it easier to defend acquiescence in what had happened in Albania." The principal of reinforcing Greece and Turkey against Italy received warm approval.

Chamberlain had remained unusually silent. He was surprised at the strength of Cabinet feeling against Mussolini. He intervened only to close the discussion and leave further decisions to the Foreign Policy Committee. He no doubt needed time to think.

Chamberlain had no better luck, unfortunately, in the Foreign Policy Committee later that afternoon. Supported by such loyal colleagues as William Morrison, Chancellor of the Duchy of Lancaster, and Sir Thomas Inskip, he wanted to take a soft line with Italy. Mussolini was withdrawing his troops from Spain as part of the Anglo-Italian Agreement. Nothing must be done to stop these withdrawals. Besides, as he quoted approvingly from a letter sent him by the absent Lord Chancellor, Lord Maugham: "The Greeks are a tricky people."

At once the critics in the Committee, Chatfield, Hoare and Stanley reacted. They had lost all their faith in the promises and pledges of dictators. A "warning in unmistakable terms" to prevent further acts of aggression must be issued from London, they pleaded. "The man in the street regarded this Albanian affair as an insult directed personally against the Prime Minister." There would be uproar and division in the Commons, and a disastrous effect on American public opinion, if definite action was not taken. The plainest speaking came from Chatfield:

> If we had felt bound to guarantee the independence of Poland, a country in regard to which we had little direct interest, ought we not in practice to adopt a similar line in the case of countries like Greece and Turkey, the maintenance of the independence and integrity of which was of direct interest to us? If so, would it not be better to say so now, rather than to wait until an attack had actually been launched upon these two countries, or upon Roumania?

Chatfield had again spoken without any military illusions. As with the Polish guarantee, he knew a guarantee to Greece was a gesture. "Our objective would not be to save Greece from being overrun but to smash Italy."

With such a clash of opinions compromise was inevitable: a solution Chamberlain was learning to accept. During the discussions the necessity to accord different treatment to Greece and Turkey slowly emerged. The Chiefs of Staff had favoured having Greece neutral in war. Her long frontier with a hostile Bulgaria was impossible to defend. A unilateral declaration of

British support for Greece seemed best calculated to warn Italy and bolster Greece. As the step least likely to infuriate Mussolini, who was already aware of British concern for Corfu, Chamberlain offered no objection.

Turkey, however, was what Chatfield called the "key to the situation in the Eastern Mediterranean". Without her help the Balkan powers "might all collapse like a pack of cards". A reciprocal bilateral agreement, similar to the Anglo-Polish agreement, would alone suffice. But this meant consulting the Turks as to their plans to resist aggression in the Balkans.

It was time to attune policy and strategy. Chatfield decided to sound out the Chiefs of Staff. The Strategic Appreciation Sub-committee, which included the Chiefs of Staff, was conveniently sitting, considering other business. Their advice was simple and consistent: ensure Turkish assistance for the Allies even if this meant an alliance with Greece; and offer British political and military support to a Balkan bloc – even if it "proved impossible or fickle and unreliable" – of Turkey, Greece, Rumania and Bulgaria.

As with all their advice, the Chiefs of Staff were blunt on fundamentals. Britain, they added, "could not, in the very early stages of hostilities, give the Balkan countries direct military assistance (a fact which they must be well aware)." Instead, Britain must help to pay for the rearmament of south-east Europe.[24]

Bluntness did not always imply practicality. A Balkan bloc was desirable but would need time to negotiate. A depleted British treasury meant little money could be handed out for rearmament. More ominously, the Turkish government was now becoming cautious. Britain had neither yet publicly condemned Italy nor announced its support for Greece. The British Ambassador in Ankara, Sir Hughe Knatchbull-Hugessen, pleaded for a "categorical statement" to be issued from London.

It was this fear of losing the Turks which convinced the Foreign Policy Committee on April 11th to give Greece a straightforward guarantee of British support. It was not a panic decision; for the moment Mussolini seemed content with

Albania. Chamberlain himself still hankered after a less outspoken declaration, but he reluctantly conceded. The sudden wavering in Ankara also convinced Halifax to make the daring suggestion to guarantee Turkey itself, as the "one Power round which the other Balkan countries could rally".

A guarantee of Turkey, Chamberlain thought, was going too far. He argued that British help could only be effective if the Balkan countries themselves were prepared to resist. Firstly it was necessary to ask the Turks if they would help the Greeks and the Rumanians. Only then could proposals be advanced for Anglo-Turkish mutual assistance.

Here was the diplomacy of March being re-enacted. Again a potential ally was first being asked to make a commitment. The Turks refused to play. Their reply contained the usual assurances of friendship and sympathy. But they also wanted cast-iron guarantees of their own security, before they publicly committed themselves to the democracies in face of the Axis Powers.[25] The British and French governments were again isolated; this time to guarantee Greece unilaterally.

What had happened meanwhile about Rumania: the object of such publicity in March, abandoned later as Poland was guaranteed, and then left to the care of Colonel Beck? Situated in the heart of the Balkans, her security had been as equally threatened as that of Greece. While Italy's occupation of Albania led to action as regards Greece and Turkey, Rumania appeared once again to be deserted. This left out of account, however, both Rumania's determination to have the protection of a British guarantee, the diplomatic efforts of Viorel Virgil Tilea, and the friends Rumania had in the British Cabinet, outside it, and in France.

During the hectic Cabinet and Foreign Policy Committee meetings which followed Beck's visit to London, Rumania was not forgotten. Oliver Stanley and Lord Chatfield again and again urged their colleagues to help protect Rumania. Her rich resources were a temptation irresistible to Hitler. Britain must define her position in case of aggression. The Italian occupation of Albania added further urgency to their pleas. To all these arguments Chamberlain returned the same answer: any British action on Rumania had to await the results of Beck's private talks with Bucharest. He also hoped, by holding back, to force Rumania to reconcile its frontier differences with Bulgaria. In this way, efforts to form a Balkan bloc would be considerably advanced.

The Secretary General of the Rumanian Ministry for Foreign Affairs, Alexandre Cretzianu, slipped quietly into London on April 9th. He had come on a secret mission that not even his Minister had been informed of in advance. Tilea arranged an appointment for the next day at the Foreign Office. They first saw Cadogan and then quickly found themselves escorted into Lord Halifax's office. Cretzianu revealed the object of his mission. Communications from Bucharest to London, he explained, passed through Germany and Italy. It was safer, therefore, for him to talk directly in London.

"The Rumanian Government were anxious," he stated, coming immediately to the point, "that His Majesty's Government should make a declaration of their willingness to assist in the defence of the Rumanian frontier, if attacked, even before the negotiations with Colonel Beck were completed." Halifax listened patiently as Cretzianu elaborated why he preferred to bypass Beck and directly approach Britain. "I understood the point clearly," Halifax replied, "but I could not go further at present." He neither refused nor agreed.

Tilea understood this point when he discussed the interview with Cretzianu on the pavement outside the Foreign Office. Cretzianu, however, left London dejected and disappointed.[26] He underestimated the lobbying skill of his London Minister.

Had Tilea heard the discussions in the Foreign Policy Committee later that afternoon, he might have shared Cretzianu's chagrin. Chamberlain did not want to guarantee Rumania unilaterally. He thought this would encourage the Poles to help their southern neighbour. It might also similarly prod the Turks. Lord Chatfield implied "that Poland was not directly interested in preventing Germany from driving through to the Black Sea." It was a correct estimate. An unnamed colleague then reminded the Committee that, only three weeks ago, the Cabinet had specifically met to consider a possible attack on Rumania. There was no response. Rumania would just have to wait. Sir John Simon once again provided the excuse for procrastination. If Rumania was meanwhile invaded, he pointed out, the Government could at least say that they were in consultation with Poland.[27]

Ignorant of these details, but conscious of the growing isolation of his country, Tilea used the only weapon left to him: discreet pressure on the Government. He indirectly contacted Winston Churchill and had a private interview with Hugh Dalton at the Rumanian Legation. He briefed the diplomatic correspondent of the *Daily Telegraph*, Victor Gordon-Lennox, and once again turned to his friend Lord Lloyd, President of the British Council. To all, his message was similar. If Chamberlain guaranteed Greece and Turkey and left out Rumania, it would have the "most disintegrating effect" in Bucharest. The Rumanians "will feel that they must make terms with Berlin at all costs, and the will to resist may disappear." Speed was essential. The British must guarantee Rumania.

The message was urgently conveyed to Chamberlain himself by Churchill and Dalton. Chamberlain was polite but unmoved. Lord Lloyd took the liberty of calling, uninvited, at the home of Sir Alexander Cadogan. Finding Lloyd on his "doorstep", Cadogan listened and then abruptly "turned him out."

Whilst private pleas could easily be rejected, official ones had to be considered seriously. On April 12th Tilea put through an urgent telephone call to the Foreign Office. As Cadogan was at 10 Downing Street, his Private Secretary, Gladwyn Jebb, took the message. Beck had so far given "no sign whatever" that he intended to co-operate with Rumania. Grigore Gafencu had just asked Tilea on the telephone, therefore, "most strongly to press" for a guarantee. "I do not know whether we should be prepared to do this", was Cadogan's minute in reply.[28]

Later that day, the Foreign Office was thrown into confusion. The French government had always proved a difficult and annoying ally. The Quai d'Orsay could never hold a secret; documents were always leaked. Its officials alternated between moods of panic-stricken defeatism and postures of aggressive confidence. Since March it was the latter which had predominated. On April 12th the French Council of Ministers decided to unilaterally guarantee Rumania also, besides Greece, whatever Britain decided.

The anger of the Foreign Office, when informed, was veiled in diplomatic niceties and political argument. The Poles and the Turks must first declare themselves; Rumania was in no immediate danger; and Greece was the main cause for concern. The French Prime Minister, Edouard Daladier, replied adamantly, answering politics with strategic common sense. To leave Rumania exposed would be to invite German aggression within a matter of hours: "silence would be interpreted as a sign of disinterestedness." Above all Daladier emphasised what the British seem to have forgotten. Without Rumanian oil, the German war machine could not engage in lengthy hostilities.

The next day, April 13th, Gladwyn Jebb handed a crucial document to Cadogan. From the latest industrial intelligence reports came confirmation of Daladier's assessment. Germany could fight for no longer than three to six months without Rumanian oil.

The Cabinet was meanwhile sitting, gloomily discussing the dilemma posed by the French. For every British objection the French had a reply. Their case seemed unanswerable. It was Halifax who reminded the Cabinet that to lose Rumania meant a gain to Germany of valuable wheat and oil. There must be no "loss of morale in the Balkans or in the United States".

Even while this debate was in progress, a telephone message from Grigore Gafencu reached the Foreign Office. In support of the request already made by Tilea, Gafencu begged the British government to guarantee Rumania.

Chamberlain realised that "he could not afford to differ publicly from the French at this stage." It was only to avoid what Halifax called the "evils of divergence between France and Great Britain" that Chamberlain consented to announce in Parliament that same afternoon the unilateral guarantees to Rumania and Greece.[29] The French government made a simultaneous declaration.

The Turkish government was only temporarily ignored. On May 12th similar announcements were made by the British and Turkish Prime Ministers in the parliaments of London and Ankara. Both countries declared that, pending the completion of a definitive agreement, they would co-operate and fully support each other "in the event of an act of aggression leading to war in the Mediterranean area", and would continue to work towards the "establishment of security in the Balkans". This general formula disguised serious disagreements on many issues which delayed until October 19th the signature of an Anglo-French-Turkish Treaty of Mutual Assistance.

Two further measures of the determination of the British government to reinforce its general strategy had also been made public before the end of April. The approval of plans for a substantial continental army, the enlargement of the Territorial Army, and the need to man almost continuously the air raid defences of the country raised major problems of ensuring sufficient manpower with adequate equipment. Until 1939 the demands for the creation of a Ministry of Supply had always been turned down by the Government. It was argued that only conditions of actual war would enable it to impose powers of compulsion to ensure adequate production. On April 9th, however, Sir Horace Wilson at last added his authoritative opinion in favour of the Ministry. He believed it would be advisable to give it a "trial run under peace conditions as it wld. certainly be wanted in time of war". The question was discussed by the Cabinet on April 19th and the decision to set up the Ministry of Supply was announced in the House of Commons the next day.

Simultaneously, the question of conscription had been under discussion. Pressure from the French government to adopt some form of compulsory national service had been a theme of many communications from Paris to London since the beginning of 1939. Both the Foreign Office and the War Office had for weeks strongly advocated the move. When the American government joined in the chorus, there was little Chamberlain could do but give way.

On April 26th, before announcing the decision in the Commons, Chamberlain met members of the General Council of the Trades Union Congress at 10 Downing Street. He explained how the policy of guarantees "plunged the country into Central European affairs and in certain circumstances, over which this country might have no control, would mean war". Referring then to criticism from "our friends abroad" that Britain was still not prepared to mobilise her manpower in support of her assurances of assistance, the Prime Minister acknowledged that he had indeed pledged never to introduce conscription in peacetime. But when "everyone knew that we might pass into war in a matter of hours, no one could pretend that this was peace time in any sense in which the term could be used."[30] That afternoon Chamberlain told Parliament of his Government's intention to introduce a limited measure of military conscription. It became law on May 18th.

In a mere twenty-nine days the British and French governments had redrawn the diplomatic map of Europe. On March 15th eastern Europe, from the Baltic to the Black Sea, appeared on the point of crumbling, surrendering to the powerful pressure of German expansionism. Then the British had no obligations east of the Rhine. They seemed determined to preserve that freedom. The French were entangled in a whole network of commitments. They were equally determined to fulfil none of these. By April 13th the British and French were committed to come to the defence of three governments east and south-east of Germany: Poland, Greece and Rumania. By May 12th a fourth, Turkey, was added. A line of defensive outposts now dotted the map of eastern Europe.

What was in the minds of the Allied governments in this new policy has always remained a mystery. Were the guarantees a manifestation of suicidal tendencies in the capitals of western Europe? Had heroism and bravado replaced caution and appeasement? Was this a disguised military strategy to force Germany to fight a war on two fronts? Or were the guaranteed states to be sacrificial lambs, symbols of Allied determination to deter Hitler from absorbing his eastern neighbours?

British and French politicians issued their guarantees as a gesture of deterrence. They were giving Hitler a warning and a last chance. They silently prayed he would not accept their challenge. Privately and under their breaths, they admitted that he could easily destroy any of Germany's eastern neighbours.

Anglo-French military planners, however, were quick to perceive the new strategic prize opening before them. Instead of fighting the one-front war they had already planned, there was now a prospect of confronting Germany simultaneously on its eastern and western fronts. To realise this, additional plans had to be elaborated. A supreme effort was to be made to add a military backbone to the deterrent front the politicians had assembled in eastern Europe.

A superlative opportunity to align politics and strategy occurred at the very moment the guarantees were given. For these coincided with the Anglo-French staff conversations which were proceeding at the War Office in London. The talks, the direct result of the January war scares, had opened on March 29th in greatest secrecy. The French delegation had been asked to travel to London inconspicuously and to wear plain clothes at all times to avoid publicity. If any leakage did occur, it was agreed to tell the press that the talks were a routine continuation of the contacts which had been going on for the last three years.[31]

During the first stage of the Anglo-French talks, planning had proceeded on normal lines without taking into account what was to be called the "new political hypothesis in Europe". There was an immediate and remarkable coincidence of views. The delegations agreed that Anglo-French strategy must be "adapted to a long war, implying – (1) A defensive strategy at the outset, at least on the continent, while executing the greatest measure of economic pressure. (2) The building up of our military strength to a point at which we can adopt an offensive strategy."

The war the delegations contemplated fighting would cover three phases. The principal aim at the outset would be to defend Anglo-French territorial integrity, their empires and vital interests against attack. The blockade, upon which "ultimate success" would depend, must begin to bite at once. The second phase would be directed "to holding Germany and to dealing decisively with Italy." Meanwhile, the Allies would build up their military strength in preparation for an offensive major strategy. "The final object of the Allies is to defeat Germany."

This strategy was approved by the Chiefs of Staff on April 12th. It contained no provision to fulfil the guarantees or to make use of a second, eastern, front.

It is hardly surprising, therefore, that both delegations agreed on March 30th that if war broke out in eastern Europe, neither Britain nor France "could render direct assistance to a victim of German aggression, though we could make a diversion by attacking Germany in the West, and applying pressure by naval action."[32]

Alerted on March 31st that Poland might become an ally, both the British and the French delegations prepared appreciations of the new situation. The British view was that neither ally "could afford Poland and Rumania direct support by sea, on land or in the air to help them to resist a German invasion." The French concluded: "The entry of Poland into a war on the side of Great Britain and France can only assume its full value if it brings about the constitution in the East of a *long, solid and durable front.*" Both the British and the French appreciations emphasised the supreme importance of the USSR as a source of military supplies for Poland.[33]

The subject of a second front in eastern Europe and the problem of fulfilling the Anglo-French guarantees was discussed at meetings on April 26th and May 3rd. Both delegations found themselves at once in agreement. "It would . . . only be a matter of time before Poland was eliminated from the war." On the problem of the USSR supplying Poland with material there was some disagreement. The British delegation admitted their ignorance of the practical problems involved and warned that the

Soviets were incapable of operating from outside their frontier. General Lélong, the Military Attaché in London, acting as the leader of the French delegation, "did not believe that the Russian Army was incapable of operating from outside Russia." The real problem was whether its neighbours would invite the Red Army to collaborate on their territory.

As to the southern end of the front, both delegations agreed on the value of Turkey in operations against Italy, but differed on Rumania. The British estimate of the value of the Rumanian army was very low, "human material being poor, and the armaments of varying types". The French disagreed with this assessment and thought it vital that Rumania "should prolong the front in the East". Its thirty-five divisions, combined with the fifty Polish ones, "would constitute a reasonably strong front". That matter was left for future discussion. The British delegation was given the task of preparing a joint paper on the problems arising out of the eastern European theatre of action and the new political situation in Europe.

The meeting of May 3rd proved to be the final one before the staff talks were hurriedly resumed on August 28th in the shadow of impending war. The most important aspect of the paper the two delegations had to consider that day was their agreed conclusion on the action the two allies could take if, as seemed likely, Germany stood on the defensive in the west and attacked Poland in the east. If at the same time Italy remained neutral at the outset of hostilities and deprived the Allies of being able to take action against her to relieve the Poles, the dilemma would be even more acute. How could the Allies then fulfil their guarantee to Poland? When the Chiefs of Staff had examined this paper two days earlier they were alarmed. They found it too "vague" and wanted the problem to be raised again with the French.

It was put to General Lélong on May 3rd. He said "that if Germany decided to remain strictly on the defensive, and if Italy remained neutral, a very thorny problem would be presented to the French and British." There was no question of a "hurried attack" on the Siegfried Line. While an advance into Germany through Belgium and Holland required the consent of these

countries. This was most unlikely. The problem returned to the
need to establish a solid eastern front, comprising Greece,
Turkey, Rumania, Poland and possibly the USSR. If successful,
and if Germany then attacked eastwards, "it might be possible to
spare forces to go to the assistance of the eastern front, in the
form of specialist troops and material."

A member of the British delegation, Group-Captain Slessor,
then provided an obvious though difficult solution. He "suggested
that some air assistance might be rendered to Poland. The object
of the Allies would be to ensure for Germany the disadvantages
of a two-front war. They would not effectively achieve this object
unless they took some action in the west." General Lélong
promised to refer the problem to Paris and obtain the views of
the French general staff.

The second stage of the Anglo-French conversations ended
without agreement. The French counted on the eastern front,
once established, to fight its own battle. Without an adequate
land army, the British looked to the French to provide a solution
on the western front. Both sides maintained that without Soviet
military assistance the "consolidation of a long and durable front
in Eastern Europe would be problematical".[34]

Could the British provide the answer on the lines suggested by
Group-Captain Slessor? The Chiefs of Staff tackled the problem
on May 10th. It had an added poignant urgency. On April 19th
they had very reluctantly agreed to open staff talks with Poland.
How could these be undertaken if Britain and France had not
agreed as to their own plans of action? The Chiefs of Staff put on
record the "grave view" they took of what seemed like the
French decision to take no effective action in the west to assist
Poland, and "of the conception that the Franco-British forces
should make no real effort to compel Germany to fight on two
fronts from the outset." The Cabinet was to be informed. The
Chief of Air Staff, Air Chief Marshal Sir Cyril Newall, was to
examine what the British air force could do "to make it a 'two
front' war for Germany".[35]

Despite strenuous efforts to obtain a definitive answer as to
how they intended to help Poland, the French refused to reveal

the form and extent of the operations they intended to launch against Germany.

Meanwhile, the British government went ahead with its staff conversations in Warsaw on 23rd–25th and 30th May. The delegates were specifically instructed to leave no doubt that any Anglo-French aid to Poland would be indirect. They returned from Warsaw in a state of shock. They had discovered that the Poles suffered from "light-hearted optimism". They had also learned that Poland and Rumania had no mutual plans for military co-operation against Germany, and Poland had "no conception of a common stable eastern front". They estimated that without outside assistance, Poland would be out of the war in six months, and strongly recommended that negotiations between the Poles and Russians should begin "without delay" to ensure adequate military supplies. For their part, the Poles asked the Allies for an attack by land forces and intensive air action on the western front to draw off German forces from the east. On neither account did the British delegation give them much encouragement.[36]

Following these talks, staff conversations with the Turks began in Ankara. These were undertaken with considerably more enthusiasm and hope for practical results. "Next to France, we consider Turkey potentially as our most valuable military ally in Europe," was the view of British military planners. As Poland was regarded as the key to the second front to the north, so Turkey was given the role of key to the south-east European front. But the staff conversations went badly from the start. The British hoped Turkey would be satisfied with encouraging words. The Turkish general staff insisted on concrete financial credits to pay for their massive rearmament programme. Without this they did not intend to invite German anger or play the role cast for them in Anglo-French strategy. The hard bargain they were driving was a prerequisite to the signature of any political agreement.

The negotiations with the Turks dragged on week after week. On August 3rd the Deputy Chiefs of Staff heard the view that the "Franco-British defensive front in the Balkan region was not yet firmly built up, and would be a source of anxiety if war were to break out in the near future . . . it would not be easy to carry out our guarantees to Greece and Roumania." On August 24th the Deputy Chiefs of Staff warned that without arms credits for Turkey "we were in danger of losing her as an ally".[37] The heavy financial price for the Turkish alliance was only paid after war broke out.

———

The problem of how to relieve German pressure against Poland in case of war continued intensely to preoccupy British strategic planners. A heated discussion between the Chiefs of Staff on June 1st produced agreement on just one point: dissatisfaction with the obligations imposed on British strategy because of the guarantees. The Chief of Air Staff, Air Chief Marshal Sir Cyril Newall, and the Deputy Chief of the Imperial General Staff, Lieutenant-General Sir Ronald Adam, agreed that "we *must* do something to assist Poland". Air action was the only means available, despite the risks of inviting massive German retaliation. The Deputy Chief of Naval Staff, Rear-Admiral Tom Phillips, put the cautious view.

"For the sake of 'doing something' to help Poland, we should be running a grave risk of heavy and immediate retaliation on England, without at the same time imposing severe pressure on Germany or of relieving pressure on Poland." Having reached a deadlock and having pointed out that the decision was really a political one, the Chiefs of Staff decided to summarise their views and information in a new report.

The problem at last reached top level when it was discussed at the Committee of Imperial Defence on June 22nd. The Chiefs of Staff had by then come to the conclusion "that the only possible way in which we could support Poland would be by air action in one form or another." From the discussion which followed, "it became clear that some action to support Poland, were she being overrun by Germany, would be essential." No one seemed to like the idea of unilateral British air action. Suddenly, Sir Samuel Hoare suggested that the best chance of diverting Germany from her attack against Poland was for operations to be started against Italy. German troops would be diverted to help Italy and the pressure on Poland relieved.

What if Italy were not in the war from the start? Neville Chamberlain pointedly asked. Was a neutral or hostile Italy more preferable? The answers were left to the Chiefs of Staff to decide.[38]

The moment of vital decision had arrived. It took no less than four meetings of the Chiefs of Staff to hammer out their reply. They advised that Italian neutrality "would be decidedly preferable" to her active hostility. In the event of Italy being allied with Germany, "no action that we can take on sea, on land, or in the air would materially relieve the pressure of a German attack on Poland." There were in fact no grounds for believing that Italy could be knocked out of the war in its early stages. The only solution remained the one previously envisaged: air action against Germany. *

"As a general point," the Chiefs of Staff observed, "we would emphasise that the fate of Poland will depend upon the ultimate outcome of the war, and that this, in turn, will depend upon our ability to bring about the eventual defeat of Germany, and not on our ability to relieve pressure on Poland at the outset. This must therefore be the over-riding consideration which governs our choice of action."

This advice amounted to an obituary notice for Poland. It was not easy for the Ministers attending the Committee of Imperial Defence on July 24th to accept. For the first time they were brought face to face with the total failure of Allied strategy to provide the military planning needed to take advantage of the guarantees and the prospect of forcing Germany to fight on two fronts. It was a harsh truth to digest. Neville Chamberlain

---

* There were four possibilities – named courses "A–D": to take all necessary preparatory measure on land, sea and air, but not to initiate any offensive air action, except at sea; to attack purely military objectives; to extend air action to include installations related to military establishments; or finally, to "take the gloves off" from the outset and ignore the possibility of civilian casualties. (COS Paper 939, July 7th, CAB53/51.)

lamented the lack of a co-ordinated Allied strategy. Sir Robert Vansittart was worried by the unfavourable effects in the Balkans and the United States. Leslie Hore-Belisha was totally disconcerted. "There appeared little we could do", he observed in disbelief, and moaned: "If this was to be our position, it appeared we should lose the war from the start."

Anger and frustration were vented on the French. The Committee called for the earliest possible continuation of talks with them to resolve the "indeterminate" state of inter-allied strategy. Specifically included were instructions to reach a decision on the course of air action to be taken to relieve the Poles.[39]

By the time war broke out on September 3rd the situation had suddenly become simplified for Allied grand strategy. Any hope of relieving German pressure on Poland by attacking Italy, the weaker end of the Axis, vanished. On August 24th the Chiefs of Staff repeated that, in the event of war, a neutral Italy was preferable. Within days, Benito Mussolini, on his own initiative, luckily obliged.

The question of what air action could be taken to distract Germany from any onslaught on Poland was also resolved in an indirect way. On August 21st Lord Halifax approved a paper by the Chiefs of Staff which set out the instructions governing Allied bombardment policy at the outset of war. It recommended that the Allies must not initiate air action against any but purely military objectives and which would not involve loss of civilian life. It was preferable that Germany should be first to launch the air war and that she should "incur the stigma" of unrestricted bombing.[40]

The decisive event, however, took place in Moscow. The signature of the German-Soviet Non-aggression Pact on August 23rd completely transformed the strategic situation. The Allied powers virtually abandoned hope of any significant and prolonged Polish resistance to a German attack without the material assistance of the USSR. This helped solve the vexatious problem of what air action to take against Germany to relieve pressure on Poland.

The fate of Poland was sealed on August 28th by virtue of a

recommendation from the Joint Planning Sub-committee. "It is clear that our initial action, from the military point of view, should be dictated from the outset by considerations of how best to contribute to the ultimate defeat of Germany, and not by those of how we can afford immediate relief to Poland which in fact we cannot do." British reserves of warplanes and personnel were limited. Therefore, "we should conserve our resources at the outset with a view to the ultimate defeat of Germany." From the purely military point of view course "A" was advised: to prepare fully but to initiate no offensive action in the air, except against warships at sea.[41] General Lord Gort himself was to describe this derogatorily as doing "little other than the execution of reconnaissance and the dropping of propaganda leaflets".

Later that day and again during meetings on the following three days – up to the eve of the German attack on Poland – the Chiefs of Staff engaged in bitter debate. After months of discussion and consultation with the French it seemed to all unbelievable that no decision had ever been taken. There was enough feeling displayed to prove that the desire to help the isolated Poles was not lacking. The ability to do so was precluded by British unpreparedness, the dictates of long-term strategy and a terror of inviting German air retaliation. On September 3rd the War Cabinet approved the decision not to dissipate Britain's limited air power in the futile defence of Poland. Allied grand strategy returned to the defensive planning adopted before it was disturbed by the policy of the guarantees.

The German-Soviet agreement also furnished the conclusive and sad answer to a hope entertained ever since the guarantees had been given. The view of Britain's military planners was that with the Moscow bombshell, "the possibility of organising a 'long, solid and durable front' in the east has now vanished."[42]

How had the Allies lost Russia?

CHAPTER SIX

Enter the Russians

On January 28th, 1939 a Soviet owned Rolls-Royce drove through the gates of the Kremlin and stopped before the offices of Mikhail Kalinin, Chairman of the Presidium of the Supreme Soviet. Sir William Seeds stepped out, accompanied by the Soviet chief of protocol, and was received moments later by Kalinin and the Soviet Foreign Minister, Maxim Litvinov. The Russians wore lounge suits to greet their guest dressed in full uniform.

Seeds handed Kalinin letters accrediting him as British Ambassador in succession to Viscount Chilston, and then "produced a visible sensation". He spoke in Russian, saying how pleased he was to return to Moscow after a lapse of forty years. Further conversation followed, in a "spirit of cordiality verging on goodfellowship".[1] He had been given a half hour of Kalinin's time, three times longer than usual for this formal ceremony. He had clearly made a good start on his third stay in Russia.

In 1899, at the age of 17, Seeds had gone to St Petersburg where he stayed for a year and a half, living with several Russian families. He studied the language and culture, and during a summer spent on an estate in the country grew to love what he afterwards described as the "real old Russia like a story or play by Chekhov, complete with landowners, sinister Chiefs of Police, Orthodox priests, and above all the childishly cunning peasants – all rather alcoholic and my very good friends." Two years later Seeds briefly revisited the estate, and then in 1904 entered the Foreign Office. He hoped one day to return to Russia as a member of the British diplomatic corps. As the years passed, his ambition seemed destined never to be fulfilled. Various diplomatic postings carried him as far as China and Brazil. In 1935 he went into semi-retirement, his career seemingly ended.

News that Viscount Chilston was to retire in 1938 as British Ambassador in Moscow suddenly gave Seeds a glimmer of hope. He arranged an interview at the Foreign Office and asked to be appointed in succession. The job was given him at once. Moscow in the 1930s was an isolated, bleak capital, offering diplomats innumerable problems and few rewards. Enthusiasm or a desire for obscurity were the only two possible incentives. Sir William Seeds was exceptionally enthusiastic. "He is the only Englishman I have met who really wanted to live in Moscow," Lord Halifax later remarked.[2]

Sir William Seeds could have congratulated himself on arriving in Moscow at what promised to be an auspicious time in Anglo-Soviet relations. The winter of 1938–39 witnessed a thaw in the relations between London and Moscow. During the whole of the previous year, while Hitler had concentrated world attention on the Sudeten-German minority in Czechoslovakia, the Russians had been snubbed and cold-shouldered. After the Munich conference, the British and French governments treated the Russians with reserve but not hostility. As long as secret intelligence indicated that Hitler's next move would be eastwards, it was considered best in London and Paris to ignore the Soviets, and leave Hitler to deal with them as he saw fit.

The Russians for their part assumed an outward pose of sulky isolation. Ivan Maisky, the Soviet Ambassador, told his parliamentary acquaintance, Robert Boothby, that after the Munich conference his government had decided "to retire into a well-protected isolation".[3] In actual fact, the USSR was very worried at being cast as the pariah of European diplomacy. Wherever possible the Russians clutched at the few hands of friendship extended to them. On November 26th, 1938 they reaffirmed their non-aggression treaty with Poland and announced that they intended to settle peacefully their outstanding frontier differences and to increase trade. Commerce likewise served as the façade to reopen quietly relations between Moscow and Berlin. In early January 1939 the Russians pressed for a visit from a German trade delegation. The official chosen got as far as Warsaw when press publicity forced him to return.

The war scares of January 1939 helped to change the diplomatic map of Europe. They also initiated the thaw in Britain's relations with the USSR. As soon as intelligence reports switched and suggested Hitler was intent on attacking westwards, feeling in the Foreign Office began to turn in favour of improving relations with the Russians. It was not an easy nor smooth transition. "Russia is no friend of ours," was the common opinion. Many still felt that Anglo-Soviet relations, "based on a mutual and inevitable antipathy", were best left in limbo. Others, however, pointed out the importance of the USSR as a "very important makeweight in the uncertain balance of Europe". When Lord Halifax added his authoritative opinion that "there is much to be said for improving our relations with Russia if we can", the doors were suddenly flung open.

Sir Robert Vansittart provided an acceptable plan. As a gesture of goodwill, Robert Spear Hudson, Secretary of the Department of Overseas Trade, and a former diplomat who had served in Russia, was chosen to head a trade delegation to Moscow. The visit was to be a gesture of general goodwill and, it was hoped, would have a deterrent effect on Germany.[4]

Lord Halifax gave the new enterprise his full support. He even seemed to have had second thoughts on Soviet military strength which had previously been debunked. "Best way to describe Russia now is something between the 1914 attitude of 'the unconquerable steam roller' and looking at her as entirely useless militarily. We cannot ignore a population of 180,000,000 people", Halifax told a private meeting of the Conservative Party on February 16th. He apparently even regretted Britain having been so "rude" to the Russians. While, at Cabinet level, he warned against doing anything to further alienate Moscow.

Such opinions and sentiments were not shared by Neville Chamberlain. In a letter to his sister on January 8th, he wrote that he had been advised to "make a grand alliance [with the USSR] against Germany. In other words better abandon my policy & adopt Winston's! Fortunately my nature is as Ll[oyd]

G[eorge] says extremely 'obstinate', & I refuse to change."[5] This
was not a happy portent for improved Anglo-Soviet relations.

At the same time, Field-Marshal Göring was pressing in
Berlin for improved economic relations with the USSR, in order
to ensure German access to Soviet raw materials in case of war.
This became known to the British government. The junior
members of the German Embassy in Moscow were on friendly
terms with their British opposite numbers. On this occasion, if
not on others, they supplied the secret information. The Foreign
Office itself had other intelligence about German moves for a
rapprochement with the USSR. This was considered "too vague
and too secret" to be sent even to the British Embassy in Moscow. It was considered serious enough to warrant getting into the
good graces of the Russians.[6]

Trying to soften the Russians was the tricky task entrusted to
Sir William Seeds. In his first interview with Maxim Litvinov,
Seeds explained that the British government was not trying to
cold-shoulder the USSR. Lord Halifax had particularly instructed
him, Seeds continued, to try and dissipate any such impression.
Remembering past experiences, Litvinov showed he still retained
his suspicions.[7]

Meanwhile, in London, Ivan Maisky was as busy as ever,
inviting sympathisers to the Soviet Embassy, offering opinions
and eliciting advice. The frequency of his recorded comments,
and their bewildering contradictions, show that Maisky's
suspicion reflected both his, and his government's sheer surprise
at the turn Anglo-Soviet relations had suddenly taken. He
alternated between sombre threats of isolation and assurances to
the contrary. On February 3rd Maisky warned R. A. Butler that
"upon Anglo-Soviet relations would depend the future peace of
the world". Butler gained the impression that the Soviets
intended to pursue an isolationist policy.

While entertaining guests at the Soviet Embassy on February
9th, and after the vodka had begun to circulate freely, Maisky
admitted that his government "was obviously much wounded by
Munich", and Britain could "expect no advances" from Moscow.
An approach from London, however, might be reciprocated. At

about the same time, when addressing the Anglo-Russian Parliamentary Committee, Maisky warned that "there might be a change of policy".[8]

Ivan Maisky remained decidedly suspicious of the limp hand of friendship being extended in London. The USSR "would judge the seriousness of [British] intentions by the degree Anglo-Soviet relations were improved not by words but by deeds", he told Robert Hudson. Speaking again to R. A. Butler, Maisky was more blunt. "He could not believe that friendship with Russia formed part of the Prime Minister's policy of appeasement." As for the offers of friendship, Maisky believed the British government was anticipating trouble and therefore was seeking Russian help.

What the Soviets feared most was being snubbed again. Should the spectre of an Anglo-Soviet rapprochement convince Hitler to be more compromising, they suspected Chamberlain might throw Russia overboard. "We are dealing with gestures and tactical manœuvres," was how Litvinov summed up his government's reaction.[9]

Reassuring words from British officials, the prospects of a trade mission to Moscow, and a much publicised visit by Neville Chamberlain to a Soviet Embassy reception – a heroic gesture from a Tory Prime Minister – were evidence of how the USSR lay on the conscience of the British government during the early months of 1939. It was a calculated exercise in having a "bogey up your sleeve". The Russians accurately gauged the intention. On March 10th Joseph Stalin warned that he would never allow his country "to be drawn into conflicts by warmongers who are accustomed to have others pull the chestnuts out of the fire for them."[10] Russian suspicion of British motives and distrust of Chamberlain, balanced by equally strong distrust of Bolshevism in British government circles were to haunt every effort soon to be made to enlist the USSR against Germany.

In the British Embassy in Moscow, meanwhile, Sir William Seeds felt very excited by the prospects of his new appointment. Barely had he time to settle down and explore with wide eyes the changes brought by the Bolshevik revolution, than he found to his consternation that he had chosen the European capital on which millions placed their hopes to avoid war.

———

After the German occupation of Prague, the British and French governments made every effort to include the USSR in their plans. Lord Halifax promised the Cabinet on several occasions that he would "take whatever steps were possible" to keep in with Moscow. Even Neville Chamberlain showed himself to be open to the most daring proposals. He temporarily considered having a secret Anglo-Soviet agreement. This would have been separate from any arrangements with Colonel Beck and have ensured Soviet aid to Poland. Fears of leakages and of offending Beck destroyed this plan.[11]

In the last week of March, however, events developed so as to exclude the Russians. Because their participation in the projected four-power declaration annoyed Poland and raised a chorus of protest from Portugal, Spain, Japan, South America and Canada, the proposal was dropped. Because the British Ambassador in Rome, Lord Perth, reported that Italian propaganda was accusing the Western Powers of trying to create a "democratic Bolshevik front" to encircle the Axis, Chamberlain denied in Parliament that he intended to split Europe into contending ideological blocs.[12] Because Chamberlain exhibited an almost paranoic fear of being accused of anti-Russian prejudice, his government tried to associate the USSR with the guarantee to Poland. Because vocal public opinion and the trade union movement clamoured for an agreement with the USSR, the British government was forced to propitiate Maisky without being able to offer any concrete proposals. And finally, because of Beck's skilful diplomacy and the urgency of the reported threat to Poland, the Soviet government was again excluded from European affairs.

"Expediency and not . . . any ideological consideration," was how Chamberlain explained his action towards the Russians.[13] But there was a basic clash between Soviet and Anglo-French conceptions of security: the former sought a "grand alliance" against Hitler, the latter pinned its hopes on a deterrent front. This conflict was never resolved. Nor was this for any lack of effort as was soon to be revealed.

The British Cabinet, accepting the advice of the Chiefs of Staff, recognised the Soviet Union's usefulness as an emergency arsenal for the beleaguered Poles. The need for an alliance to ensure this, also urged by the Chiefs of Staff, was only slowly perceived. Within two months of the guarantee to Poland, the Cabinet decided to conclude the alliance. This decision, a long struggle for the heart and mind of Neville Chamberlain, caused a dramatic split in the Cabinet and was resolved only by his humiliating concession.

There was no jubilation in Moscow when the guarantee to Poland was announced. Sir William Seeds was ordered to appear before Maxim Litvinov and was told that the Soviet government had not been kept informed. They "had had enough and would henceforth stand apart free of any commitments." Seeds failed to move Litvinov. It was clear British action had been "misunderstood and not at all appreciated."

Criticism from Moscow was not tolerated in the Foreign Office. A "typical Soviet manoeuvre" and "wilfully misunderstanding our motives" were the pained comments of officials. "The Soviet Government have attacked H.M.G. in the past for their failure to take up a definite attitude towards German aggression", William Strang noted on Seeds' telegram. "Now that H.M.G. have done so, the Soviet Government sit back and wash their hands of the whole affair." Strang seemed unconcerned. He doubted whether the Russians would intervene against Germany short of a direct threat to their own security. "It would not be at all contrary to their desires to see Great Britain and France at grips with Germany and in process of destroying each other."

Feeling guilty at the way events had tended to exclude the USSR, Lord Halifax agreed to see Ivan Maisky, try to mollify him, and keep him better informed. Halifax asked his subordinates for "guidance as to what to say to him"! Thankfully his interview with Maisky on April 6th was friendly, despite the Ambassador's "inquisitorial persistence" in trying to discover whether Britain was making an "honest attempt" at resistance to Germany.[14]

At the same time, pressure from all sides was exerted in favour of a policy of Anglo-Soviet collaboration. Sir William Seeds later apologised for Maxim Litvinov's annoyance with the British government. His "*amour-propre* had been wounded", the Ambassador explained, and he urged the Foreign Office to invite Soviet views on future co-operation.[15] In the House of Commons, following the guarantee to Poland, the eloquent voices of Winston Churchill, David Lloyd George and Anthony Eden, among others, had pleaded for the Government to back their action by an alliance with the USSR. They had pointed out Poland's obvious inability to withstand a German attack without Soviet military support.

Such pointed criticisms must have caused uncomfortable squirming on the Government front benches. For it was also on April 3rd that the Chiefs of Staff memorandum on the guarantees to Poland and Rumania had been circulated. They had advised precisely the policy being urged by the parliamentary critics.

Ivan Maisky was meanwhile sulking as usual behind the scenes and briefing his sympathisers. One of these interviews had a dramatic effect. Maisky had excellent contacts with the British left-wing press, and especially with W. N. Ewer, diplomatic correspondent of the *Daily Herald*. Despite his association with the Soviet Ambassador, Ewer was considered to be "very levelheaded and well disposed" to the Foreign Office: an ideal situation for his reports to be treated seriously.

On April 4th Ewer had a long talk with Maisky. At first Maisky expanded on his government's continued suspicion that Chamberlain "does not mean business". The absence of consultation with Moscow, and continued flirtations with Italy, were perturbing signs. So too was Chamberlain's refusal to bow to widespread pressure to broaden the basis of his government by including such critics as Churchill and Eden. Ewer's record continued:

After listening patiently I asked him in effect "so what".

What should be done to convince Moscow we were in earnest and to start cooperation. At first he took the line that it was not his business to make suggestions. So I began making them. I suggested first that Moscow should put up proposals. But he brushed this aside. Then I suggested that we should ask *them* what they thought ought to be done? This he tried at first to evade . . . finally he thought it a good suggestion. . . . Then suddenly he had a brain-wave. . . . Why, he said, did not His Majesty's Government invite Litvinov to London?

Ewer put this plan to the Foreign Office. Soviet pride, he pointed out, "has been wounded and needs repair. I suspect that a lunch at Windsor to Litvinov would work wonders."

A meeting between British royalty, whose distant relation Tsar Nicholas II had been murdered by the Bolsheviks only twenty-two years before, and the Soviet Foreign Minister was a hazardous proposition. "I hope we will not allow Maisky's fictitious grievances and Litvinov's assumed sulks to push us into action against our better judgement," was Sir Orme Sargent's immediate word of caution. Yet on consideration, he added an afterthought. It changed a journalist's off-hand proposal into a major diplomatic event. "Personally I should have thought that the best way of calling the Soviet bluff was by asking them point blank to make us a definite and detailed scheme showing the extent to which & the manner in which they are prepared to cooperate."

Sargent's scheme received Sir Alexander Cadogan's enthusiastic support. Although he regarded "associating with the Soviet as more of a liability than an asset", Cadogan also wanted to call the Soviet bluff, "indicating that we don't want a lecture on 'moral issues', but some practical indication of what they propose should be *done*." The concurrence of Halifax allowed the plan to proceed.[16]

During the next few days, enthusiasm for calling the Soviet bluff died down. In a conversation on April 11th with Halifax, Maisky shied away from a suggestion that it was time for the USSR "to play their part". He patiently explained that his government "would always be ready to consider with sympathy any concrete proposals that might be put to them." But this would have to be closer to a "system of real collective security" than Britain was pursuing. "On March 31st we made a step, which is a genuine revolution in our foreign policy", Halifax retorted. Maisky was quite unimpressed. The Soviet Ambassador in Paris, Yakov Suritz, spoke similarly to the French government.[17]

It seemed that the USSR would take no initiative. Calling the Soviet bluff in a grand manner suddenly seemed less attractive and doomed to failure. Yet an approach to Moscow had to be made. Sir William Seeds pointed out on April 13th, the day the guarantees to Greece and Rumania were given, that an obvious temptation to the Kremlin would now be "to sit back and do nothing". An even greater danger existed if Germany proposed to the USSR to jointly carve up Poland, Rumania and the Baltic states. Could something be done to prevail on Poland and Rumania to accept Soviet aid?

Seeds' warning, always present in Foreign Office thinking, was well taken. His advice, once the guarantees had been given, was impractical in the form he proposed, but suggested another possible approach. Why not ask the Soviet government to make a unilateral public declaration, pledging their assistance, *if requested*, to any country bordering on the USSR and which was attacked?

If the Russians "wished to be helpful", Lord Halifax told the Cabinet on April 13th, "they should stop talking in general terms" and act as suggested. Several Ministers objected, pointing out that the Soviet Union had already made such declarations. There is no recorded reply. The plan was to be put to Moscow.[18]

The next day, April 14th, bluff clashed with bluff at the Foreign Office. Despite what Ivan Maisky had told W. N. Ewer and Lord Halifax, the Soviet government decided to make a gesture. Before Halifax had a chance to present the British scheme, Maisky blurted out his instructions. In view of British interest in the security of Rumania and Greece, the USSR wished to take part in helping Rumania. How did Britain envisage this assistance being given? Unprepared for this gesture, which he himself had allegedly requested on April 11th, Halifax could only offer his thanks, and describe the proposal Seeds was to explain to Maxim Litvinov.[19]

The diplomatic wires between London, Paris and Moscow had become overheated by April 14th. The British had asked the Russians to play their part. They had responded and were now being asked to make a unilateral declaration.

The Soviet government had become confused. Within the previous three weeks, the diplomatic map of eastern Europe had changed as significantly as in any year since the end of the First World War. It was taking time for the fact to sink in that Britain was now pledged to the hilt on the Soviet Union's borders. The British guarantees had left the Russians breathless and still suspicious. Ivan Maisky was clearly out of touch. A report he had sent to Moscow on April 9th still maintained that Chamberlain had not given up hope of inciting Germany to attack the Soviet Ukraine. He was merely responding to public opinion and would return to appeasement as soon as circumstances permitted.[20]

At the same time, the French were causing the British further headaches. After forcing them to guarantee Rumania, the Quai d'Orsay took another controversial step. Without consulting the British Foreign Office, Georges Bonnet told the Soviet Ambassador on April 14th that he was prepared to sign a bilateral mutual assistance agreement, supplemented by concrete military arrangements.[21] On that day, in receipt of two such opposing proposals, the Kremlin decided to recall Maisky to attend a top-level conference. The acid test of Anglo-French intentions was about to be launched.

Incredulity, embarrassment and anxiety gripped the Foreign Office on April 18th. A telegram had arrived early that morning from Sir William Seeds, containing the combined Soviet reply both to the British declaration and the French mutual assistance proposals. The eight clauses of this, telegram no. 69, contained two basic propositions: Britain, France and the USSR should sign a mutual assistance agreement in case of direct attack, and pledge to assist against aggression all the east European countries bordering on the USSR from the Baltic to the Black Seas; and secondly, Britain, France and the USSR should conclude a military convention to complement the political agreement and to enter into force simultaneously. *

Lord Halifax took a brief look at the Russian proposals and sent for Sir Alexander Cadogan. "Mischievous" and "embarrassing" was their mutually agreed response. Cadogan was instructed to prepare an analysis on which to base Cabinet discussions. The Foreign Office sensed at once that great care would have to be taken in handling this telegram. They agreed with the French that a "flat rejection would enable the Russians to cause . . . considerable embarrassment".[22]

The Russians intended neither mischief nor embarrassment. Their sweeping gesture was designed to fathom precisely Anglo-French thinking and intentions. Would the Western Allies accept a "grand coalition" against the Axis, which would split Europe into contending ideological blocs; a coalition which was visible, strong, with equal obligations, equal risks and which provided an automatic system of sanctions against aggression?[23] It meant giving Moscow and not Warsaw the position of senior partner in east European security. Chamberlain had repeatedly told the Cabinet that "Poland was the key". The USSR had in effect replied, as Maisky wrote to Litvinov, that only in Soviet hands "rested the key to any system of European security".[24] While the British searched for a Soviet contract to supply arms, the Russians countered with a blatant partnership agreement. They intended to make sure Britain and France did not rat in case of a German attack against the USSR itself: this possibility was not covered by the British proposal.

This first exchange illustrated the wide gulf separating Soviet and British conceptions of European security. The USSR stated

* With the assistance of a reliable, and obviously very well placed, informant in the Foreign Office itself, the German government received almost immediately the full details of this and all subsequent exchanges between London and Moscow. The identity of the informant was never established and his actions only came to light in January 1940. (Dilks, *Cadogan Diaries, 1938–1945*, p. 249.)

its terms and waited stubbornly for these to be accepted. When the Cabinet finally agreed to ally with Bolshevik Russia, after five weeks of bitter controversy, it was not out of conviction as to the merit of their scheme. It is now clear that only fear of a German-Soviet rapprochement tipped the scales.

Reflecting on these events many years later, Sir William Seeds wrote: "The negotiations began in that spirit of gingerly apprehension felt by a traveller who has been lured into playing with 3-card-trick operators in a railway carriage, and the Russians did nothing during the talks to remove the suspicion. . . . Of course the Russians were suspicious too."[25]

Meanwhile, determined to reject the Soviet alliance proposals, the British government marshalled its best debating points. These were not difficult to find. The note that Sir Alexander Cadogan had prepared on telegram no. 69, and which was read to the Foreign Policy Committee on April 19th, contained no less than twenty-two negative observations. Both from the political and military points of view, Cadogan's note argued against accepting the Soviet offer. A triple alliance, he concluded, "may alienate our friends and reinforce the propaganda of our enemies without bringing in exchange any real material contribution to the strength of our Front."

In the discussion which followed, there was no disagreement with Sir Samuel Hoare's emphasis on Polish military weakness and, therefore, the need to supply her with Soviet armaments. For this purpose it was hardly necessary to conclude an alliance, Chamberlain wryly observed. A triple alliance "might be expected to sting Germany into aggressive action. That was an unnecessary provocation to offer to Germany, and one which ought to be avoided." Poland was the state "next to the wolf" and had to be strengthened. She was the first barrier against aggression. "While, therefore, not turning down the Russian proposal", Chamberlain declared, "we should endeavour to convey the impression that the time for a military alliance was not yet ripe." The Foreign Office were to make sure the French took no unilateral action on the Soviet proposals, which they were inclined generally to accept.

The political arguments for turning down an alliance seemed watertight; it was the military considerations which needed clarification. The Committee agreed, therefore, to ask the Chiefs of Staff to report urgently on the "present military value and capacity for performance of the Soviet Army, Navy and Air Force". They were deliberately excluded, by the Prime Minister himself, from giving an opinion on the political desirability of an alliance with the USSR. Chamberlain no doubt sensed that the answer might not be entirely to his liking.

Chamberlain's distrust of military advice was more than instinct or even prejudice. During March the Chiefs of Staff had twice pointed out that Poland could not withstand a German attack without Soviet military assistance. On April 22nd, in a paper analysing the military implications of the new Anglo-French guarantees, the Chiefs of Staff went a step further. The "participation of Russia as an ally would result in containing considerable German land and air forces on the German Eastern front and might afford direct assistance to Roumania if she were attacked."[26]

The report of the Chiefs of Staff, requested by the Foreign Policy Committee, was ready when it met again on April 25th. This brief meeting proved a triumph for Chamberlain's approach. In reply to his instructions, the Chiefs of Staff stated that the armed services of the USSR had been weakened by the purges. The forces she could maintain in the field were considerably smaller than her advertised strength of 130 divisions, and the assistance which she might give to Poland, Rumania and Turkey was "not so great as might be generally supposed". This Chamberlain took as decisive support for his policy of strengthening the first line of defence – Poland and Rumania. And in view of their reluctance to accept Soviet aid, nothing must be done to impair their confidence. The military arguments now appeared to decisively strengthen the political ones for rejecting an alliance with the USSR.

Only one member of the Committee seems to have carefully, and unselectively, read the Chiefs of Staff analysis. "We should perhaps draw attention", the report had stated, "to the very grave military dangers inherent in the possibility of any agreement between Germany and Russia." The co-operation of the USSR could deny raw materials to Germany. Malcolm MacDonald, Secretary of State for the Colonies, pointed out that, if Russia were neutral or siding with Germany, Anglo-French economic warfare would be "gravely embarrassed". There is no recorded reply. The mood of the Committee accorded with Chamberlain's approach. "We ought to play for time", Halifax advised. It seemed best to once again ask the Russians for a unilateral declaration.[27]

The wisdom of this approach seemed confirmed as soon as rumours of Litvinov's offer began to circulate. The Polish government was quick to reiterate its opposition to accepting Soviet aid. The Italians and Germans hinted that soliciting Moscow's assistance was proof of a British encirclement campaign. The Finns, who considered the Russians more in need of military help than themselves, made vigorous protests. The Latvians and Estonians did likewise, but with less brashness.

The Rumanians had the advantage of making known their views during the visit to London from April 23rd–26th of their Foreign Minister, Grigore Gafencu. He was in the middle of a tour which took him to several European capitals. Whether in Warsaw, Berlin, London or Rome, his nimble diplomacy managed to satisfy the wishes and assuage the fears of all his disparate listeners.

In Berlin, Gafencu held out to Joachim von Ribbentrop the prospect of a German-Rumanian rapprochement. A guarantee from Germany would be as welcome as the British one, he said. Rumania did not want a pact with Russia. He spoke likewise to Hitler: "one could not engage in European politics with Russia". Gafencu left Berlin assured of Hitler's peaceful intentions, but frightened of the provocative effects a pledge of Soviet assistance would have in Germany.[28]

In London, Gafencu turned on all his charm.* He impressed

---

* After meeting Gafencu, Sir Howard Kennard had written: "I was surprised that Roumania could produce anyone with so much simplicity and intelligence. Perhaps he owes something to his Scottish blood." (*Documents on British Foreign Policy*, IV, no. 187.)

Cadogan as "very nice – forthright, good looking, sincere . . . and a good talker." The important question of the negotiations with the USSR was raised by Neville Chamberlain himself. "An agreement with Russia might lead Roumania where she did not want to go", Gafencu stated. "If there were a 5 per cent chance of peace, he did not wish to jeopardise it by associating with a country in whom he had no confidence." No words could have better expressed Chamberlain's own thoughts. He asked whether open association with the USSR would introduce a dangerous element into the situation and precipitate action by Germany? Gafencu replied that this was what he feared. The best thing was not to trust the Russians. He then promised to make these views known both to the Labour Opposition and the Quai d'Orsay.

Lord Halifax's conclusion, that "it was desirable not to estrange Russia, but always to keep her in play" summed up the current mood and indicated future policy.[29]

The Cabinet on April 26th gave rubber stamp approval to the decision to reject a triple alliance. In case of war, Halifax told his colleagues, it would be desirable for Russia to remain neutral or then join the allied side. The "value of Russia was by no means as high as seemed to be believed by prominent members of the Labour Party."[30]

To have reached this conclusion in light of other news Gafencu brought was foolhardy. During his talks with Colonel Beck in Warsaw a week before, Gafencu had agreed not to tamper with the existing interpretation of the Polish-Rumanian treaty. The British had counted on these two guaranteed countries to work out technical arrangements for the case of a German attack on either. Instead, Beck and Gafencu agreed this was unnecessary. Thus died the hope of creating a solid second front by unifying eastern and south-eastern Europe.

The Foreign Office, in trying to dampen French sympathy for a triple alliance, outlined its main arguments on April 28th. To reconcile various considerations – the necessity for Soviet help in wartime, respect for the susceptibilities of Poland and Rumania, the importance of not provoking Hitler into violent action, nor allowing him to use the anti-Comintern propaganda – a revised declaration proposal was worked out. In deference to the French and to allay Russian suspicion, it was thought that making Soviet assistance dependent on a prior Anglo-French involvement would give Maxim Litvinov the assurance of reciprocity he desired.[31]

"Contrary to what often happens in the West, individual Ministers in the Soviet Union do not conduct their own policy. Every Minister puts into effect the general policy of the Government as a whole. Therefore, although M. M. Litvinov has resigned as People's Commissar for Foreign Affairs, the foreign policy of the Soviet Union remains the same. Consequently the proposals we made on April 17th remain in force."

With this statement, Ivan Maisky tried to reassure Lord Halifax that all was well in Moscow. The sensational news of the dismissal of Litvinov, for years the voluble, and well-known Soviet Foreign Minister and leading publicist of collective security, appeared in the western press on the morning of May 4th. The first rumours of this change reached the Foreign Office a day earlier. In the USSR the news was relegated to an inconspicuous four-line notice on back pages of the press.[32]

The talk throughout the western world was on the significance of Joseph Stalin changing his Foreign Minister in the middle of delicate three-power negotiations and while his deputy Foreign Minister was touring the Balkans. Was it merely a personal quarrel between Litvinov and Stalin, as Maisky privately stated;[33] or was it a dispute on major policy issues? If it was a top-level Kremlin disagreement, it could only have one sinister meaning. Stalin had decided to get rid of his Foreign Minister in preparation for a possible agreement with Hitler. Maxim Litvinov was Jewish and a veteran spokesman of resistance to Germany. If some arrangement was possible with Hitler, the tough, dour and uncompromising Vyacheslav Molotov was more suitable.

Litvinov's dismissal culminated several vital weeks of deliberations in the Kremlin. Maisky had been suddenly recalled to

Moscow just prior to the Soviet proposal for a triple alliance. The timing suggests that a quick British response was not anticipated. Alexei Merekalov, appointed Ambassador by Litvinov to Berlin just nine months earlier, was also recalled. On April 17th Merekalov had succeeded in opening a window to Berlin. In his first ever conversation with the German State Secretary, Ernst von Weizsäcker, the Ambassador had cautiously suggested that Germany and the USSR could have normal and, eventually, improved relations. The significance of these remarks had not escaped Weizsäcker.[34]

If Alexei Merekalov could bring this news to Moscow, Ivan Maisky's reports on Britain must have been depressing. He was recalled specifically, as he himself revealed, to discuss the prospects for a triple alliance. At a secret conference in the Kremlin, he "told the truth and only the truth – and the picture in consequence was not a very consoling one". That picture Maisky did not describe. Yet from his telegrams to Moscow, and his private conversations, it is obvious he believed that, while Neville Chamberlain remained Prime Minister, Britain would never sign a treaty with the USSR.[35] According to Maisky, however, the Soviet government decided to continue the negotiations in good faith.

While both Soviet Ambassadors were in Moscow, Vladimir Potemkin, the Deputy Foreign Minister, set out on a fact-finding mission in south-east Europe. He was trying to discover the extent of Balkan cohesion, the strength of resistance to Germany, possibilities of Soviet assistance and progress in the Anglo-Turkish negotiations. He found nothing favourable from the Soviet point of view. There was little unity, less military capability, and in Ankara the Turkish government was on the verge of committing itself to the Allies.

Potemkin's diplomatic tour was the second part of a two-pronged offensive. In late March the tiny Baltic states of Latvia and Estonia had already been warned not to flirt with the Germans. Then the Finns had been given a note expressing Russia's interest in several Finnish islands as protection for Leningrad.[36] Potemkin's mission was designed to complete

Litvinov's sounding of all the USSR's western neighbours. The assessment reached in Moscow, even before Potemkin returned, probably indicated that the border states could not be relied upon. When added to Maisky's doubts about Britain's interest in a triple alliance, Litvinov's dismissal seemed inevitable.

The Soviet Union decided, therefore, to place no impediments in the path of exploring sound relations with Berlin. Molotov was not identified with the policy of collective security. Unlike Litvinov, he was a member of the Soviet Politbureau. He was also, reputedly, the intimate of Stalin, and since 1935 had favoured collaboration with Germany. The stage was now set for Berlin to lurk ominously in the shadows of the tripartite negotiations.

Hitler was later to claim that "readiness on the part of the Kremlin to reshape its relations with Germany" became apparent with Molotov's appointment. American and Italian diplomats in Moscow, and the outspoken French Ambassador in Berlin, Robert Coulondre, strongly suspected the same.[37]

The possible implications of Molotov's appointment for German-Soviet relations could hardly, and did not, escape the Foreign Office. Caution in analysis, awareness of danger, and accuracy of intelligence characterised its thinking. The news was immediately seized upon as a move towards isolation, which in practice would work to the advantage of Germany. Foreign Office minutes analysed this and other possible implications in great detail and were forwarded to Lord Halifax for his information. "The outlook is dark whatever may be the exact explanation" was one observation which summed up the grim news from Moscow.[38]

In the following days there was a flood of wild rumours and reports into London, suggesting that either the Germans and Russians were already negotiating or had concluded an alliance. Rome was a particularly fertile source. Despite ideological differences, Italy enjoyed surprisingly good relations with the USSR. She was reported to be acting as mediator between Moscow and Berlin.[39]

Nor was Berlin itself immune as a source for similar speculations. The ever-present Dr Karl Goerdeler sent a message on May 6th to Frank Ashton-Gwatkin, the Economic Counsellor at the Foreign Office, warning that the German generals had received a "new and unexpected offer" from the Soviet Union which might entirely change the situation. General Bodenschatz, aide-de-camp to Field-Marshal Göring, began to gossip, no doubt intentionally, of a coming change in German-Soviet relations.[40] For military and economic reasons the German generals wanted a rapprochement with the USSR. Their point of view was gradually winning acceptance. Meanwhile, other reports merely pointed a warning finger at the absence of any anti-Bolshevik diatribe in Hitler's April 28th speech in the Reichstag. Berlin press comment on Molotov's appointment, it was also noticed, had been friendly.

Foreign Office experts, avidly reading the reports from Rome and Berlin of advanced negotiations or Italian mediation, dismissed them as "wishful thinking" and "rash assumptions". The balance of evidence available in London was quite accurately against these rumours being well founded. The Secret Intelligence Service had specific evidence negating Goerdeler's news.[41]

Indeed, by the first week of May nothing more sensational had occurred in German-Soviet relations than the rather innocuous conversation between Alexei Merekalov and Ernst von Weizsäcker on April 17th. This had been followed on May 5th by another desultory talk between Soviet and German officials on possibly resuming economic negotiations.[42] The Germans were to find the road to Moscow as tough as the current British and French travellers.

In contrast to the rumour grapevine, leading Soviet spokesmen gave binding assurances of continuity in Soviet foreign policy and the validity of the triple alliance proposals. They were not lying. A pro-German policy in early May was more a threat than a reality. Consequently, these assurances were accepted in London. When Sir William Seeds submitted his considered judgement of Litvinov's dismissal, the Foreign Office seemed reassured as to its decision to keep negotiating. The evidence,

Seeds wrote, indicated neither a retreat into isolation nor any immediate change in Soviet policy. "So, for the moment, I see no option but to continue to take them at their word and to believe that they are not manoeuvring to let us down with a sudden bump."[43]

That sudden bump finally came on August 24th. In May, however, the British and French governments had no choice. To have cut off the negotiations with Moscow would have left the field open to the Germans. To continue gave the Russians all the trump cards. As Ivone Kirkpatrick later explained to the Labour MP, Hugh Dalton:

> At the beginning our Government thought they were inviting the Russians to join the Turf Club and that they would fall over themselves with delight. The Russians, on the other hand, felt that they had a valuable oriental carpet to sell and were dissatisfied with the price offered.[44]

Fear and anxiety, doubt and frustration forced the British and French governments to raise humiliatingly their price in a bid to buy an alliance with the USSR.

———

When the negotiations with the Soviet Union were discussed at the Cabinet on May 3rd, Lord Halifax was already sounding the alarm bells. The dilemma, as he put it, was agonizing: a triple alliance would make war inevitable. If Britain rejected the proposal, "Russia would sulk. There was also always the bare possibility that a refusal of Russia's offer might even throw her into Germany's arms." Leslie Hore-Belisha added "that although the idea might seem fantastic at the moment the natural orientation suggested an arrangement between Germany and Russia." But the anti-alliance faction still predominated. When Halifax introduced a long letter from Cardinal Hinsley, Archbishop of Westminster, expressing anxiety at an alliance with Russia, the arguments seemed clinched.

Neville Chamberlain cut short the discussion. He preferred to ask the Soviet Union once again to make a public declaration.

To his mind, this had the advantage of keeping the negotiations simmering.[45]

What the French gave with one hand they took back with the other. The Foreign Office was pleased when the Quai d'Orsay, which was proving too sympathetic to the Russians, agreed to support the British reply. Outrage and embarrassment prevailed, however, when on the same day, May 3rd, news arrived of Georges Bonnet's latest gaffe. In a fit of temper he had shown the Soviet Ambassador the text of the French proposals, held in reserve in deference to the British. These closely accorded with the triple alliance idea.

It is not surprising that Lord Halifax opened the Foreign Policy Committee meeting on May 5th in a depressed mood. He candidly admitted he did not anticipate the Russians agreeing to a modified public declaration. Georges Bonnet had made this certain.

In the discussion which followed the subsidiary proposal of a "no separate peace" clause, advanced by the Russians on April 17th, provoked a sharp clash of opinion. Neville Chamberlain wanted to keep his hands free in any final agreement with the USSR. "It would be impossible to foresee every contingency that might arise", he stated. "For example, we might wish to make a separate peace by reason of some intervention on the part of President Roosevelt." He overlooked that this was precisely what the USSR feared: being left to face Germany alone. Malcolm MacDonald, Oliver Stanley and Sir Samuel Hoare considered the Soviet view "not at all unreasonable".

Chamberlain partly rejected the "no separate peace" clause because of his suspicion that Molotov's appointment signified a possible change in Soviet policy. It was the meaning of the upheaval at the Narkomindel* which recurred during the discussion. The Ministers anxious to conciliate the Soviet Union dreaded a breakdown in the negotiations which might follow if a hard line was taken. It was again Malcolm MacDonald who repeated the ominous warning from the Chiefs of Staff "on the

* People's Commissariat for Foreign Affairs.

very real danger of Russia remaining neutral in a war and supplying Germany with foodstuffs and other raw materials". Reminded of this, Lord Chatfield and even the Chancellor of the Duchy of Lancaster, William Morrison, one of the bitterest of anti-Soviet Ministers, recognised there was a strong isolationist or even pro-German faction in the Soviet Union. However, fears of "risking the alienation of our friends" weighed more heavily than possible changes in Soviet policy.[46]

On May 8th Sir William Seeds handed Molotov the revised proposal for a Soviet declaration. Seeds himself had wanted the Foreign Office to be more accommodating to the Russians. His worst fears were realised. Molotov lashed out with undisguised anger and subjected him to a relentless cross-examination. Bonnet's gaffe cost the Ambassador a "most unpleasant ten minutes". Only his quick wits and diplomatic experience carried him through.

"I am very sad at Litvinov's disappearance", Seeds wrote more than a week later to Sir Lancelot Oliphant at the Foreign Office. "Talks with him were always stimulating. . . . We had got to understand each other well, whereas Molotov is still an enigma and I shall have to walk warily." His only words of anger were reserved for Bonnet who had acted with the "foolish amateurishness of a politician".[47]

Seeds' interview "did not sound too promising", Lord Halifax told the Cabinet on May 10th. Nor did a Tass communiqué, published in the press that morning, make matters any easier. The communiqué criticised the latest Anglo-French proposals for again hesitating to conclude a triple alliance. The Foreign Office feared the effects this information would have in the United States. It had been noticed that the American press was absorbed in the whole question of these negotiations. Plans were made at once, therefore, to publicise in the New York afternoon papers the precise position of the British government.[48]

The discussion of this communiqué in the Cabinet showed again that Soviet fears of being involved alone in a war with Germany were understood only by a few Ministers. Neville Chamberlain and Lord Halifax felt the guarantees to Poland and

Rumania gave the Soviet Union abundant security. They felt little sympathy with Soviet fears that to omit protecting the Baltic states would invite a German attack through that corridor.

Why should the Foreign Secretary not invite Molotov to a meeting at Geneva? Sir Samuel Hoare suddenly asked. "He was more and more impressed by the serious consequences which would ensue from a breakdown of the negotiations." Halifax understood what Hoare was hinting at. However, "he had no information bearing on the likelihood of some secret agreement being concluded between Herr Hitler and M. Stalin. He found it difficult to attach much credence to these reports, which might be spread by persons who desired to drive us into making a pact with Russia." He agreed the negotiations must not break down.

During the meeting of the Foreign Policy Committee on May 5th Lord Chatfield had expressed the surprising view that, in strategic terms, the friendship of Spain was of more importance than that of the USSR. He now summarised the advance report of the Chiefs of Staff on this subject. A hostile Spain would weaken the position in the western Mediterranean and threaten Atlantic communications. Spanish friendship, however, would only be worth retaining on the assumption the USSR would be benevolently neutral. "On the other hand, the greatest danger we had to face would be a combination of Russia and the Axis Powers."

Neville Chamberlain, who could turn a blind eye to advice he found unpalatable, wanted this report circulated to the Cabinet.[49] He probably hoped the first part of the Chiefs of Staff advice would impress his colleagues more than the concluding warning.

Faced with the divergent Anglo-French proposals, the reply from Moscow was predictable. "Only the fool (which the Russian is not)", Sir William Seeds later wrote, "will not go all out for the more advantageous." On May 14th Molotov rejected the request for a unilateral declaration. It was unsuitable "as a basis for organisation of a front of resistance" against further aggression in Europe. He repeated the Soviet Union's previous comprehensive demands, and this time explicitly demanded guarantees to Finland, Estonia and Latvia. In Molotov's opinion, the essence of the Soviet reply was a "request for reciprocity".

When this dismal news reached the Foreign Office at 9.30 a.m. on May 15th, everyone understood the moment of truth was near. Nor was Molotov's reaction to the proposals entirely unexpected. In a briefing on May 10th to W. N. Ewer, which as usual he sent to the Foreign Office, Ivan Maisky had been especially blunt. Unless the British government was "prepared to go further than pious declarations there would be no agreement".[50] Contingency plans, going much further than previously envisaged, were prepared in the Foreign Office with the help and approval of the Prime Minister. On the afternoon of May 15th a departmental meeting drafted a possible Anglo-French-Soviet agreement which came closer to the Soviet view. After repeating the request for a unilateral declaration, it added that Britain, France and the USSR would assist each other should war break out as a result. Sir Orme Sargent sent this draft to Lord Chatfield with instructions to ask for the views of the Chiefs of Staff.

Neville Chamberlain bitterly complained the next day that his military advisers had changed their minds. This was not so. The Chiefs of Staff had never been asked previously to advise on a military alliance with the USSR. Having sensed the drift of opinion in the Foreign Office towards an alliance, they immediately took advantage of an invitation to air their views for the first time. Their report, signed after a full day of discussion on May 16th, proved to be a bombshell. It completely unnerved the Prime Minister. On April 24th and May 10th his military advisers had produced opinions which buttressed his political objections to an alliance with the USSR. Suddenly, he found the military arguments cut out from under him. Within a week he was to give in, but not before a last desperate battle.

"From the broad point of view, it is felt that a full-blown guarantee of mutual assistance between Great Britain and France and the Soviet . . . would present a solid front of formidable proportions against aggression". With these words the Chiefs of Staff opened their military advice to the politicians, and continued:

If we fail to achieve any agreement with the Soviet, it might be regarded as a diplomatic defeat which would have serious military repercussions, in that it would have the immediate effect of encouraging Germany to further acts of aggression and of ultimately throwing the U.S.S.R. into her arms. Even if this did not occur, we certainly want something better than the bare neutrality of Russia, not only from the point of view of being able to draw on her resources, but also to enable assistance to be rendered to Poland and Roumania. Furthermore, it would leave her in a dominating position at the end of hostilities.

Conscious of their previous advice on Spain, the Chiefs of Staff added that a solid eastern front was more important than antagonising Spain.

For more than two hours, the Foreign Policy Committee discussed this report on the evening of May 16th. Lord Chatfield admitted that "we had much to gain and very little to lose by adopting the policy favoured by the Chiefs of Staff." They had been very much influenced by the fear that Russia might decide on a policy of neutrality and isolation, and were very anxious to avoid a German-Soviet alliance. He himself was worried by Poland's military weakness. "Issues of great strategical importance were involved," Chatfield continued, "and his colleagues would realise how distasteful it was to him personally to contemplate an alliance with the Soviet." Nevertheless, he felt bound to support the Chiefs of Staff. If, by baulking at an alliance, Britain drove Russia into the German camp, "we should have made a mistake of vital and far-reaching importance."

Sir Samuel Hoare and Oliver Stanley strongly approved this eloquent exposition. After five weeks of negotiations, Stanley pithily summed up, "we seemed to have reached the position when we must choose between a Three Power Pact or no arrangement of any kind with Russia." He wanted to tie Russia up and so ensure her help to the Allies.

Lord Halifax seemed troubled by conscience. He agreed with

these views, yet he felt deep bonds of loyalty to the Prime Minister, and therefore stood by his side. Chamberlain himself was disorientated. He frankly admitted the Chiefs of Staff had "alarmed" him and he clutched at any argument to support his reluctance to ally Britain with the USSR. He refused to believe there was no alternative. "As against the military advantages of Russian assistance must be weighed the political objections", he noted. These were now becoming stale. When he referred again to "serious difficulties with certain of the Dominions", no one replied.

Sensing Chamberlain's growing isolation, the less influential members in the Committee, R. A. Butler, William Morrison, and Leslie Burgin, attending his first meeting and enjoying it, as he wrote privately, like "undiluted jam", rallied to his side. They tried to argue the case for postponing a decision on an alliance. One more effort should be made. They had a plan. Sir Robert Vansittart had just had a conversation over lunch with Ivan Maisky. Why not let Vansittart again try some unofficial haggling? In exchange for agreeing to the British plan, and omitting the inclusion of the Baltic states, Britain and France would agree to open staff conversations.[51]

Sir Robert Vansittart, for so long denied an active role, was an appropriate emissary. He was on very friendly terms with Ivan Maisky. For nearly two weeks he had also been writing urgent minutes to Lord Halifax pleading that all considerations were irrelevant besides the one goal – an alliance with the USSR.[52]

The Cabinet which heard developments on May 17th was almost the victim of a desperate ploy. Lord Halifax opened the discussion with a long exposition designed to emphasise the political objections to a triple alliance. The difficulties which had arisen during the past month, he stated, could have been avoided if Russia had simply agreed to Britain's proposals. "He also thought that the conclusion of an alliance with Russia might be held to make war more likely."

At this point an unnamed Cabinet Minister mentioned the latest Chiefs of Staff report, which Halifax had ignored. Lord Chatfield then summarised it. "In further discussion, the view was expressed that it was desirable that the Cabinet should see the Report of the Chiefs of Staff." The Prime Minister agreed.[53]

Was this deliberate deception? Once before Chamberlain had apparently suppressed the advice of his military advisers when they disagreed with the guarantee to Poland. Later he had circulated two of their reports which confirmed his attitude to the USSR. This time he failed in a similar plan. He had lost the support of most of the Foreign Policy Committee the previous day. Once the latest Chiefs of Staff report was circulated, he was to lose the Cabinet as well.

Vansittart's second meeting with Maisky on May 17th was described to the Foreign Policy Committee two days later. The position was simple and desperate. The Soviet government was not prepared to continue negotiations unless the principle of a triple alliance was accepted. Further delay was impossible, Lord Halifax said. The time had come to accept or reject the Soviet terms, though the final decision would be taken by the Cabinet.

Another blow was unexpectedly struck at Neville Chamberlain's snowballing isolation. Halifax now conceded that "there was very great force in the arguments" advanced by Lord Chatfield "that we might as well enter into a full-blown alliance with Russia". At the same time, Halifax expressed his strongest "distaste for a policy which meant our acquiescing in Soviet blackmail and bluff".

The Prime Minister then pulled out his last debating points. What about the supposed objections of Poland and Rumania to being associated with a triple alliance? Sir Samuel Hoare replied with considerable sympathy for the USSR's suspicion of the Poles. They feared either Poland or Rumania succumbing to German blackmail and thus being left without allies and at Hitler's mercy. The Poles were, in Hoare's opinion, "politically unstable and unreliable".

Chamberlain next tried the more delicate issue of encirclement: the most devastating product of the German propaganda machine. Taking his cue from Halifax, he tried to argue that a triple alliance would unite all Germans behind Hitler, particularly the "important moderate elements", whom it was

179

desirable to foster and encourage. Hoare again was unsatisfied. He replied that the German government would only be deterred by fear. When the emergency arrived the moderate elements would disappear. Chamberlain was exhausted. Even his most loyal supporters were showing signs of deserting him. It was time to close the discussion and ask the Polish and Rumanian governments for their reaction to a triple alliance.[54]

Neville Chamberlain's growing isolation in the Cabinet reflected pressures from all directions to ally with the USSR. An ever widening circle of press and parliamentary opinion was moving in the same direction. The House of Commons debate on May 19th was stormy but almost unanimous. Winston Churchill, having been briefed the previous day by Ivan Maisky, insisted that the objections of Poland and the Baltic states should be overridden. "Without Russia there can be no effective Eastern front", he reminded Chamberlain. If the government "now reject and cast away the indispensable aid of Russia", they will "so lead us in the worst of all ways into the worst of all wars."

The Anglo-Soviet negotiations had become so complex that Chamberlain had asked for Foreign Office notes to guide him in the debate. His final words, however, were personal. What was being aimed at was not alliances, he explained, rather a "peace front against aggression". Unfortunately, a "sort of veil, a sort of wall" prevented agreement. He strenuously denied that ideological mistrust was influencing his policy. However, it was the critics who eventually carried the day. Chamberlain ruefully commented several weeks later that the Commons "had pushed him further than he wished to go."[55]

The joint Anglo-Turkish temporary declaration on mutual assistance in the Mediterranean area, announced on May 12th, also helped to influence the British government. It was appreciated in London that, in view of Turkey's close relations with the USSR, the negotiation of a permanent and, strategically vital, treaty with Turkey would be facilitated by an Anglo-Soviet agreement.[56]

The French government continued, as previously, to apply firm pressure for a pact along Soviet lines. After Czechoslovakia had been destroyed and Poland, Rumania and Greece guaranteed, the French realised they were dangerously overextended. It was the French and not the British army which would have to bear the brunt of the land war in western Europe. They were frantic, therefore, to enlist Soviet help against Germany. They were also frightened of recurrent rumours of a German-Soviet rapprochement.[57]

The spectre of Hitler and Stalin shaking hands and becoming friends haunted London, as it did Paris. It decisively moved the Cabinet towards allying with the USSR. The most persistent rumours on German-Soviet contacts involved the German generals. On May 17th Sir Robert Vansittart submitted one of his neatly typed foolscap minutes to Lord Halifax. It was marked "secret". The urgent information which it contained came from the German general staff, and alleged that "Hitler has been negotiating with Stalin through the Czech General Sirovy".* Hitler had decided to throw away the "mask of Europe's protector against Bolshevism" and had delivered, through Sirovy, proposals designed to carve up Poland, help the USSR retake Bessarabia, dominate the Dardanelles and support a Soviet invasion of India. Vansittart advised: *"there is no time to be lost in this Russian business."* The next day a letter from Sir Nevile Henderson arrived in the Foreign Office, also referring to the Sirovy mission. Sir Alexander Cadogan minuted: "This is important."[58]

The circumstances which temporarily removed the Anglo-Soviet negotiations from London to Geneva were bizarre and significant. Having to attend the League of Nations Council meeting

---

* General Jan Sirovy, a former Prime Minister and President of Czechoslovakia, was Minister of Defence when Prague was occupied. He was sentenced in 1947 to 20 years' imprisonment on charges of collaboration with Germany. J. M. Troutbeck, the former Secretary of the British Legation in Prague, described the Sirovy mission as "pure myth". (FO371/23020, C8660/54/18.)

at Geneva in May, Lord Halifax hoped to meet a top Soviet leader there for intimate discussions. The Foreign Office welcomed the idea, and Sir William Seeds was instructed to sound out the Kremlin. After the League Council meeting was delayed to allow Vladimir Potemkin to attend, his visit was unexpectedly cancelled. The reason was obvious. The Soviet government had nothing to discuss so long as the British baulked at a full triple alliance. Ivan Maisky was sent instead as a substitute.

On May 20th Lord Halifax stopped briefly in Paris, en route to Geneva, to explain British objections to a triple alliance. Edouard Daladier, the French Prime Minister, was unconvinced and spoke frankly. Since Litvinov's departure, the Soviet attitude had stiffened. They "were now on their dignity and would accept nothing less than complete equality and reciprocity."

"I asked the French Ministers", Halifax recorded the next day, "whether they thought that there was serious danger of an accommodation between Germany and Russia if we failed to close with the Russians now. They replied that this danger could not be ignored. . . . Russian policy was quite incalculable and was liable to sudden changes."

Lord Halifax was impressed. On the boat train to Paris he had admitted to his Foreign Office entourage that a full alliance would probably not drive Hitler off the deep end. William Strang and Oliver Harvey, Halifax's Private Secretary, also thought that "we ought to go the whole hog" and avoid being slowly dragged along.[59]

The atmosphere in Geneva where the Foreign Office delegation and Ivan Maisky arrived on May 21st was "friendly, futile, fantastic, like a Hollywood scenario of Ruritania." Here Halifax and Maisky met to discuss the Anglo-Soviet negotiations. The Soviet Ambassador found Halifax "much 'freer' " and a useful exchange of views took place. Maisky at once criticised the weakness of Britain's proposals. They were based on the guarantees to Poland and Rumania and were dangerous in practice. The two border states could conceivably make friends with Hitler. The USSR would then be left to fight Germany alone. Only a triple alliance would prevent war. Otherwise the Soviet Union could "take care of herself and . . . preserve her own liberty of action".

Lord Halifax tried every argument to shake the Soviet Ambassador; a difficult enough task in normal circumstances. But he was speaking without conviction, in a conciliatory tone, and gradually revealed the full extent of concessions which would be made. His telegram reporting this conversation stoically concluded that the choice facing Britain was "disagreeably plain": a breakdown in negotiations or a triple alliance. For his part, Maisky cabled to Moscow that the "British Government is avoiding a three-power pact purely from a desire not to burn its bridges to Hitler and Mussolini."[60]

A message which reached Sir Robert Vansittart at his country home on May 21st made certain there would be no breakdown. A "secret German source" informed him that Julius Schnurre, an official of the Economic Policy Department in the German Foreign Ministry, was leaving Berlin for Moscow the next day. He was to negotiate a commercial agreement with the Soviet government. Vansittart who telephoned this message to Cadogan at the Foreign Office was "in a flap". Cadogan remained cool.

The information given Sir Robert Vansittart had only a grain of truth. The German Foreign Ministry was prepared to send Schnurre to Moscow. On May 20th Molotov had refused, however, to have anything to do with such a visit. The "necessary 'political basis' " had first to be constructed, he told the German Ambassador, Count Friedrich von der Schulenburg.

The "secret German source", which Cadogan confided to his diary to have been Helmut Wohlthat, economic adviser to the German four-year plan, is astonishing. He was to feature two months later in a public and more sensational affair. That he was also the source of this, and perhaps other, information on the secret German-Soviet feelers may have a simple explanation. He hoped his news would possibly stimulate the British government to sign an agreement with the USSR. Hopefully this alliance would deter Hitler, and then leave the way open for a genuine and final settlement of Anglo-German differences.

Helmut Wohlthat's information was sent to Lord Halifax at Geneva and to Sir William Seeds in Moscow. Not surprisingly,

Vladimir Potemkin denied there was any truth in the report. No request from Schnurre for a visa had been received, he calmly told the British Ambassador.[61]

At Le Bourget airport, on his way to London, Lord Halifax was handed a letter from Sir Alexander Cadogan, written the previous day, May 23rd. It spared Halifax the painful task of trying to convert Neville Chamberlain.

> The Prime Minister sent for me this afternoon to discuss the Soviet negotiation. He has, I think, come to the view that it may be necessary to accept the Soviet principle of a triple pact, but has come to this view reluctantly and is very disturbed at all that it implies.

In his diary, Cadogan wrote: "P.M. apparently resigned to idea of Soviet alliance, but depressed."[62]

Neville Chamberlain knew that he had been defeated and he resented it. He had not changed his personal attitudes and estimates of the Soviet Union. To his sister he had written on April 9th: "I regard Russia as a very unreliable friend", incapable of offering effective help, "but with an enormous irritative power on others." When his advisers had produced reports supporting his views, he had been self-satisfied. If an Anglo-Soviet alliance, he had written on May 14th, echoing the Chiefs of Staff, alienated Spain and drove her into the arms of the Axis, more would be lost in the west than could be gained on the eastern front. The Russians "have no understanding of other countries' mentality or conditions & no manners, & they are working hand in hand with our Opposition."

When his advisers deserted him, Chamberlain grew depressed and irritable. The worst aspects of his complex character surfaced. Sir Alexander Cadogan, who witnessed this change from day to day, felt Chamberlain "was a man of prejudices which were not easily eradicated". His "instinctive contempt for the Americans" was matched by "what amounted to a hatred of the Russians . . . he was, in a sense, a man of a one-track mind."

It was not after all distrust based on political and military considerations which motivated Chamberlain's attitude to the

Soviet Union. It was, on the contrary, pure ideological antipathy. He was driven to absurd lengths to keep the Russians out of Europe. His final gesture of naivety and petulance was recorded by Cadogan on May 20th: "P.M. says he will resign rather than sign alliance with Soviet."[63] This was pure bluff: a cry of despair and a rhetorical threat. He intended yet to cushion the blow to his ego of agreeing to ally his government with Bolshevik Russia.

The heavy file of Cabinet papers* each Minister had received before the Cabinet meeting on May 24th contained the story of Neville Chamberlain's defeat. The first to speak to the assembled Ministers was Lord Halifax. He was blunt and precise. Sifting through all the available evidence, he thought the idea of a German-Soviet rapprochement "was not one which could be altogether disregarded". Warsaw and Bucharest no longer appeared to object to a triple alliance provided they were not committed or mentioned in the agreement. Consequently, he was now ready to sign an alliance with the USSR.

Having had the ground prepared for him, Neville Chamberlain then began his painful speech.

> THE PRIME MINISTER said that as his colleagues would be aware from the attitude which he had hitherto adopted in this matter, he viewed anything in the nature of an alliance with Russia with considerable misgiving. He had some distrust of Russia's reliability and some doubt of her capacity to help us in the event of war. Further, an alliance with Russia would arouse considerable opposition and objection in many quarters. . . .

He realised the dangers of a breakdown in the negotiations.

> In these circumstances, the Prime Minister thought it was impossible to stand out against the conclusion of an agreement

---

* These included the Chiefs of Staff report of May 16th, the minutes of the two previous meetings of the Foreign Policy Committee, a report by Sir Thomas Inskip, showing the Dominions now recognised the need for an alliance with the USSR, and a Foreign Office memorandum weighing the advantages and disadvantages of an Anglo-Soviet alliance.

on the lines proposed. The question of presentation, however, was of the utmost importance and his . . . difficulties would be greatly decreased if . . . the arrangement could be presented as an interpretation . . . of the principles of the Covenant. . . .

This would not be a "mere *façade*", Chamberlain continued, yet he confessed that linking the alliance to Article XVI of the League covenant,* "introduced an element of a temporary character into the arrangement".

According to a plan, prearranged with Sir Alexander Cadogan, Sir Samuel Hoare spoke in support of the scheme. Having differed so violently with Chamberlain for weeks, it was a touching gesture of loyalty.[64]

Neville Chamberlain was pleased with his clever stratagem and confident the Russians would accept. He felt that he had turned a humiliating defeat into a personal victory. The full story of this desperate invention he revealed to his sister on May 25th. "At the present time I am in a happier mood", he wrote. "The worst times for me & the only ones which really cause me worry are when I have to take a decision & don't clearly see how it is to come out. Such a time was the early part of last week." He then set out the issues as they appeared after Halifax's return from Geneva. He pointed out that the press was in favour of an alliance and it was clear that to refuse would cause enormous problems in the House of Commons, even if he could carry the Cabinet.

Chamberlain went on to repeat his unrepentant distrust of Soviet aims and doubts as to their military abilities. But this was secondary to his real motives for opposing an alliance. It "would definitely be a lining up of opposing blocs & an association which would make any negotiation or discussion with the Totalitarians difficult if not impossible." No one except R. A. Butler, a supporter without influence, would back him. In these circumstances, he sent for Sir Horace Wilson, and together they concocted the scheme which

---

* Since September 1938, reform of this article, which dealt with sanctions, had been discussed at Geneva. This would have made sanctions voluntary.

gives the Russians what they want, but in form & presentation it avoids the idea of an Alliance & substitutes a declaration of *intentions* in certain circumstances in fulfilment of our
obligation under Article XVI of the Covenant. It is really a
most ingenious idea for it is calculated to catch all the mug-
wumps & at the same time by tying the thing up to Article
XVI we give it a temporary character.

Chamberlain had no doubt that Article XVI would one day be
amended or repealed and that the alliance with Russia could then
be reviewed. Having clearly worked this out, he concluded with
a flourish, "I recovered my equanimity".[65]

The Prime Minister was confident the Russians would agree.
He was mistaken. Two years of carefully observing Neville
Chamberlain had left the Kremlin with no illusions about him.
His every ploy evoked suspicion; his stubbornness was matched
by greater persistence. Despite the optimism and cheerfulness
displayed in his letter to his sister, he was not yet finished with
the Russians.

CHAPTER SEVEN

Danzig or Poland?

THE British and French had refused to die for Czechoslovakia in 1938. But for Danzig, a remote Baltic port at the northern tip of the Polish Corridor, guaranteed by the League of Nations, with various rights reserved to the Polish government, and inhabited mainly by Germans, they were pledged to offer their lives. During five tense months prior to the outbreak of the Second World War, the question debated in public and private, in the mass media and in foreign offices was whether it was worth dying for Danzig. By September 3rd, 1939, however, Danzig no longer represented a place but a principle.[1]

For the British and French governments the debate was not academic. The guarantee to Poland of March 31st, 1939, was a public pledge and a warning to Hitler. A freely negotiated settlement, satisfying all interested powers, would be welcomed. A resort to force would be met by force. The issues were simple; the outcome in doubt and feared; the challenge, eventually accepted.

The tragedy of the guarantee to Poland was that the British Foreign Office realised Danzig was an "artificial structure, the maintenance of which is a bad *casus belli*."[2] The independence of Poland, however, was essential to the success of the Anglo-French deterrent front. To separate the two issues became the aim of those, both in London and Paris, still interested in a settlement with Germany. Those hoping to deter Hitler tenaciously fought to weld the two issues – Danzig and Poland – into an inseparable whole.

The Poles were no particular friends of the British. The cynical way in which Poland had helped herself to the rich industrial area surrounding Teschen at the height of the Czechoslovak crisis in September 1938 created an impression of opportunism and distrust which lasted months afterwards.

The negotiations carried on intermittently between the German and Polish governments at this time were carefully followed in London. It was hoped their differences could be settled, helping the general cause of European appeasement. But the Polish government had a passion for secret diplomacy. Decades of conspiratorial activity under foreign domination was a habit not easily lost. All British efforts to determine what had passed between Warsaw and Berlin failed.

These negotiations reached top-level with a meeting between Hitler and Colonel Jozef Beck at Berchtesgaden on January 5th, 1939. The encounter was friendly, but tough. As Danzig was a German city, Hitler declared, "sooner or later it must return to the Reich." To which Beck rather lamely replied: the "Danzig question was a very difficult problem." To soothe the Polish Foreign Minister, Hitler added that "there would be no *faits accomplis* in Danzig". What he feared to say to Hitler, Beck told Joachim von Ribbentrop the next day at Munich. He was "in a pessimistic mood" and "saw no possibility whatever of agreement."[3]

The Foreign Office was bursting with curiosity about this meeting. Secret intelligence proved barren. Journalistic sources in Berlin, the usual stand-by, were wide of the mark. Beck himself, when later confronted by the British Ambassador, Sir Howard Kennard, was "extremely evasive". Yet intelligent guesses by Foreign Office officials produced fairly accurate conclusions. It was assumed the interview was amicable and that Hitler was in one of his calm moods. Further information, gleaned from Polish diplomats at the League meetings later in January, confirmed that Hitler was "pursuing his usual 'gin and gun' policy, i.e., lulling the victim until the moment has arrived to strike."[4]

Hitler's speech on January 30th confirmed what is now known. German military planning was, at this stage, not concerned with Poland. Hitler still hoped for a peaceful settlement with Beck.

Friction between Polish and German students in Danzig and anti-German demonstrations in late February received little coverage in the German press and were obviously being played down. "The Germans quite clearly do not want to precipitate the Danzig question", Roger Makins minuted on March 3rd after reading these reports. "The effect of the firm front being shown by the Poles is worth remembering." The Foreign Office never forgot. They were dazzled by Beck's diplomacy. It remained for Sir Howard Kennard to sound on March 7th a realistic note. Danzig was Beck's "Achilles heel" and "at any moment Germany may put on the screw with painful or even disastrous results".[5]

In late March the British and French governments feared that moment had arrived. They protectively took Poland and her problems under their wings. There could hardly have ever been a more momentous decision taken in such a precipitate manner.

When it was decided on March 18th that Poland must be a British ally in the eastern containment front, all of Poland's differences with Germany landed in the British lap. A day later Neville Chamberlain made his position clear on the Danzig issue. He was not concerned with the "violation of frontiers", he told a small meeting of Ministers, but "what we were interested in was the maintenance of the integrity and independence of Poland. If Poland thought it necessary to fight on the Danzig issue then we were at once interested." On March 20th the Cabinet endorsed this view.

Lord Halifax immediately revealed to the Polish Ambassador, Count Edward Raczynski, British thinking about the Polish trouble spot. A settlement of the dispute by direct negotiation was desirable. A German threat to the Free City would be of the "gravest concern". Halifax emphasised that "it would have to be a threat to Polish independence and not merely the outbreak of disturbances in Danzig." Raczynski appreciated this and gave an assurance that Colonel Beck could be counted upon to avoid trouble with Germany over Danzig.[6]

Raczynski's assurance seemed dangerously fragile. Almost simultaneously rumours of German preparations for either a quick coup in Danzig or an attack against Poland raced through Europe. The crisis Cabinets which met on March 30th and 31st were no longer dealing with hypothetical situations. The most vital decisions taken concerned two questions: Was there a distinction between a seizure of Danzig and an attack against Poland? Who decided if a Danzig coup threatened Polish independence?

Neville Chamberlain was always at his worst when unsure of himself or his policy. On March 30th he initially appeared impressed by the opinion of his ageing and nervous Lord Chancellor, Lord Maugham, that Britain "should not encourage Poland to go to war with Germany about Danzig." But Chamberlain felt inclined to leave the decision of a response to a Danzig coup to the Polish government.

As Chamberlain pondered this problem, he had second thoughts. The guarantee he planned to give Poland, he told the Cabinet at noon on March 31st, must be subject to conditions. The most important was that action taken by Germany "must clearly threaten Polish independence. It would, of course, be for us to determine what action threatened Polish independence and this left us some freedom for manoeuvre." He did not want to become "embroiled as a result of a mere frontier incident".[7]

The guarantee announced that afternoon was a firm warning to Hitler. It was also one of the most ambiguous statements ever uttered by a British Prime Minister. In his own mind, Chamberlain felt he had reserved to himself the ultimate sanction against Poland. That was why the guarantee pledged support for Poland's independence and not her territorial integrity. This left ample room for frontier adjustments with Germany.

"It is we who will judge whether her independence is threatened or not", Chamberlain wrote to his sister on April 3rd.[8] Unfortunately, the words of the declaration used in the House of Commons gave the British government no explicit sanction against Poland. Not surprisingly, many were confounded at what appeared to be a blank cheque given to a distant east European nation. Never before had a British government handed over to a foreign power the ultimate decision of war or peace.

On April 1st *The Times* argued in a leading article that the British government had not guaranteed "every inch of the present frontiers of Poland. The key word in the declaration is not integrity but 'independence'." This aroused a storm of public protest and violent objections from the Poles. The Foreign Office hastened to issue a mollifying statement, reaffirming the guarantee. Nevertheless, *The Times* leader accurately reflected the true position.* After reading it on April 1st, Chamberlain said to Halifax: " That's just what I meant." Halifax agreed that it was just about right.[9]

There seemed to be only one safeguard against the Polish government cashing their blank cheque, and that ironically was the personality of the Polish Foreign Minister. Wild stories circulated by Ian Colvin that Colonel Beck was in German pay and "sordid rumours" about Madame Beck, "bandied to and fro in every tram in Warsaw", were dismissed as "ridiculous" by Sir Howard Kennard. The Foreign Office agreed with the Ambassador that Beck was about the only genuinely non-anti-German element in Poland. He became a positive "safety factor" which could control anti-German feeling and not unreasonably provoke Hitler.[10]

The Foreign Office did not trust Beck, yet realised that in him lay the last hope of peace. For the man who had successfully held off the Germans all winter could be relied upon to negotiate successfully with Hitler, if such a possibility still existed. Beck's obvious desire to avoid war became the basis for the confidence shown in him. His distasteful habits of evasiveness and his penchant for secret diplomacy suddenly had their attractions.

* The controversial leader was actually written by A. L. Kennedy, "entirely on the lines" of a talk with Sir Alexander Cadogan on March 30th. It was apparently the Foreign Office which preferred to limit the guarantee to the independence of Poland. But it was Geoffrey Dawson, the Editor of *The Times*, who inserted the phrase "not integrity". Kennedy conceded that the leader had placed too much emphasis on the limitations and not the implications of the British declaration. (Entry of April 4th, A. L. Kennedy Diaries.)

The topic which occupied least attention during Beck's visit to London in early April was Danzig. The Foreign Office had prepared briefs on the subject which assumed Neville Chamberlain had indeed offered the Polish government full and unconditional support, even in the case of a threat to Danzig. If the British government was encouraging a firm stand by the Poles, then "we may be forced to support Polish rights in Danzig". But any sort of "corrupt bargain" on this issue between Beck and Hitler would rebound against the western democracies, shake Polish morale and destroy the eastern containment front. "It would not therefore be to our interest to suggest that the Poles should abandon their rights in Danzig."

This advice, given to Neville Chamberlain and Lord Halifax, was well taken. The Danzig question was only briefly touched on during the four sessions of intensive conversations. Beck's dogmatic assertion that the "local Danzig affair . . . was not yet in negotiable shape" surprised Halifax but was not pursued.

"Danzig had become a kind of symbol", Beck told Chamberlain on April 4th. Any sort of German *fait accompli* would be resisted by Poland "as a matter of principle". Chamberlain did not object. He had a more urgent problem on his conscience. Had the British guarantee interrupted delicate negotiations between Poland and Germany which could have been successful? Second-hand reports of these contacts had reached London, but had left too many questions unanswered. Beck had already stated he never thought the Germans intended aggressive action in March. Had the British government been stampeded by false intelligence?

Insistent probing on these problems by both the Prime Minister and the Foreign Secretary stimulated Beck to greater evasiveness. He refused to give his new ally the benefit of exact knowledge of the state of German-Polish contacts, namely, a stalemate. In a clever manoeuvre, he admitted "conversations" about Danzig had been going on, but "that no negotiations were in progress".[11]

The British government ended its talks with Colonel Beck no wiser, yet deeply impressed. He seemed a worthy creditor to have handed over a blank cheque.

Any loose ends as to the exact meaning of the guarantee were effectively tied up at a final meeting on April 6th. No minutes were taken. William Strang later recalled "that both sides agreed that the occupation of Danzig by German armed forces would be a clear threat to Polish independence" and would bring the British guarantee into operation. It was for this reason that the "Summary of Conclusions", a confidential document communicated only to the Dominions and the United States, discreetly referred to "other action" which threatened Poland and which the Polish government considered it necessary to resist.[12]

Faith in what was hoped would be the deterrent effect of the guarantee upon Hitler was instrumental in giving the British government the courage to make the decision. Hitler reacted by preparing for possible war. He retired to Berchtesgaden, leaving instructions in Berlin that the Polish question was to be reserved to himself. On April 3rd, on his instructions, General Keitel, Chief of the High Command of the *Wehrmacht*, issued the orders for "Operation White": the code name for the plans of a possible attack against Poland. These orders were signed by Hitler on April 11th.

Although Germany would continue trying to avoid a conflict with Poland, the preamble to "Operation White" stated that Poland would be destroyed if she changed her policy. Military preparations had to be complete and plans ready for action by September 1st, 1939. The task of diplomacy was to isolate Poland. The British, the French, and even the Russians, might yet conceivably abandon their new ally. Meanwhile, independently of "Operation White", a "surprise occupation" of Danzig might prove possible "by exploiting a favourable political situation". Military preparations, employing only peacetime units, were to go ahead in all branches of the armed forces.[13]

Exact details of these directives were among the few, but best kept, secrets of the German high command. The usual crop of rumours, however, kept the foreign offices and intelligence services of the Western Allies working feverishly. A direct German attack against Poland was not thought likely as yet and there were fewer rumours to this effect. In any case, the Anglo-French guarantee made the result of such action quite clear. A quick German coup, limited to the return of Danzig to the Reich, was the main headache. Reports of such action, planned for various dates, circulated freely within a week of the guarantee. On April 8th it was reported from Berlin that the walls and tables of the general staff's office were covered with maps exclusively of Poland.[14]

The first test of British nerves came on April 14th. From Berlin Sir George Ogilvie-Forbes reported that the German government intended to unite Danzig with the Reich by April 20th, Hitler's birthday. Failing an amicable settlement with the Poles, an internal revolt followed by a German military occupation would be staged in Danzig.

Similar information had reached the Foreign Office from other sources and could not be disregarded. The return of Danzig would have been a most suitable birthday present for Hitler. On receipt of Ogilvie-Forbes' news, the Foreign Office temporarily panicked. After a meeting with Lord Halifax, Sir Orme Sargent was asked to draft a telegram to Warsaw. He did not like it at all, and minuted on April 17th: "Beck, I am afraid, would interpret it as being an attempt to treat him to a repetition of Munich." The advice finally telegraphed to the Polish government only suggested they "cut the ground from under the feet of the German Government by showing their disposition to negotiate."

Had the Foreign Office known, what was later revealed, that a stalemate had been reached in negotiations between Poland and Germany, this telegram would never have been sent. Colonel Beck at once replied that he did not believe a Danzig coup was likely at that time. Nor did he feel it opportune to reopen talks with the Germans.

This reply was difficult to accept in London, but there was no alternative. Beck was asked to keep the Foreign Office informed of any new developments and let no chance of a peaceful settlement slip by. Nothing must be done which could allow Germany to complain that British support for Poland was making a settlement difficult.[15]

The British government were smarting at the success of the latest German propaganda campaign. Officials in Berlin were insisting that the guarantee had made the Poles obstinate and a solution impossible. Beck had to be advised, therefore, not to be intransigent. But such advice was gratuitous. The Foreign Office believed the Poles did not want a war "any more than we do, for they know that we can lend them no direct help." On the other hand, the stench of the Munich conference still hung at least in the corridors of the Foreign Office. "If we press them [the Poles] to be conciliatory, they will think that we are preparing another Munich at their expense, with utterly disastrous results," was the opinion of Ivone Kirkpatrick.[16] The Poles richly harvested the humiliation of the Czechs.

Herr Hitler's birthday was celebrated on April 20th. Danzig was still a Free City. Once again Colonel Beck, in refusing to be panicked, had demonstrated his skill in handling the Germans. Once again the Foreign Office was impressed. "My feeling is that it would be better to let the Poles play their own hand in this question," Roger Makins minuted on April 20th, "and not put pressure on them which could be interpreted as a desire on our part that they should give way."[17]

Another round of the Danzig war of nerves had passed; but the fear of a German coup remained. Lord Halifax voiced his anxieties about this "danger point" at the Cabinet on May 3rd. The issues of war and peace, he argued, should not depend solely on Polish judgement. One of the conditions of the guarantee had been that Polish independence must be clearly threatened. This "gave us some right to exercise our own judgement on the matter." But no British action or words should ever suggest "that we were trying to whittle away" the March 31st undertaking.

Where his Foreign Secretary had been cautious, Neville Chamberlain did not mince his words: "It was very difficult to be sure whether the inclusion of Danzig in the Reich would constitute a threat to Polish independence. The answer to that question really depended on Germany's intentions." The Cabinet agreed to telegraph to Colonel Beck, asking him to be more frank in the future as to any German demands and his own intentions. The telegram also emphasised that, while Poland was the "ultimate judge" of a threat to her independence, the British government expected to be consulted before action was taken in response to a German threat. Beck calmly replied on May 4th that he "would generally bear in mind these considerations".[18]

The Cabinet had raised the question of Hitler's "ultimate intentions" towards Poland. No such wavering on details haunted the Foreign Office. "From what we know of German intentions", Ivone Kirkpatrick minuted on May 5th, "it is quite clear that German ambitions and aspirations do not stop with the incorporation of Danzig in the Reich. The goal is the elimination of Poland from the number of independent states in Europe only as a stage in the realisation of vaster aims."

The danger to European peace still lay in the possibility of a quick German military coup at Danzig. It was with a cynical frankness that Ivone Kirkpatrick impatiently asked his Foreign Office superiors for clarification. It was vital to decide either that a Danzig coup would be covered by the guarantee or else "save the situation by another Munich, this time at the expense of Poland".

Kirkpatrick's minute reached almost every desk in the Central Department. Sir Alexander Cadogan was getting bored with details and hypothetical analyses. He thought Kirkpatrick was too cynical. He also felt that the only advance preparations necessary were for war with Germany should Poland herself decide her independence was threatened. "We are, I suppose – or should hope – preparing for war to the best of our ability."

The implication of these comments, that German intentions and not Danzig was the issue, was ignored by Halifax. He wanted to know what form of a coup was possible in the Free City, and to ensure Beck would discuss in advance his probable response. On May 10th Sir Howard Kennard was asked to find out what Poland intended to do if the Danzig Senate declared its union with Germany, unaccompanied by any military action. "You will realise, as I am sure he does," Halifax telegraphed, "that it is important that Poland should take no step which will give Germany an excuse for putting her in the wrong with general world opinion."[19]

The Polish Foreign Minister showed no signs of being either bored or annoyed with the constant enquiries from London. On May 10th he patiently explained to Kennard that it was unlikely the Danzig Senate would act on its own. If it did, his government would "react in an energetic manner" and would treat German military action there as an act of war. Of course, the British government would be kept informed, but Beck "could not at this moment state what definite action Polish Government would take in any hypothetical case until he was aware of how this case was likely to present itself." However, Poland "would not blindly precipitate a crisis which might lead to war."

"Have we got an undertaking from Beck to consult us before taking action that might lead to war?" was Lord Halifax's note on this telegram. Of course there was none. But the situation, as Sir Orme Sargent pointed out, had built-in safeguards. Any rash action by Beck leading to war would be fought initially on Polish soil. This the British guarantee could not prevent. Furthermore, a German style *blitzkrieg* would hardly leave time for consultations. Consequently, Beck would keep in his own hands the question of what constituted a threat to Poland. Sargent concluded: "with the precedent of Munich before him he is not prepared, by consulting H.M. Government beforehand, to allow them to have a voice in deciding if and when Polish independence is or is not threatened." Halifax was unhappy with this advice, though he only asked that Kennard "keeps very close to M. Beck".[20]

———

Endless British inquiries to Warsaw to try and elucidate the meaning of the guarantee was not an exercise indulged in for the benefit of Foreign Office legal experts. The peaceful celebration of Hitler's birthday brought no end to the stream of war scares. In a truculent and uncompromising speech to the Reichstag on

April 28th, Hitler denounced the German-Polish Non-aggression Pact of 1934. For the first time he publicly revealed the proposals for a settlement which he had put to the Polish government in March. These were no longer valid and would not be repeated. In menacing tones, he declared that Danzig would have to return to Germany, and on this he was still willing to negotiate.[21] Ironically, this was the first time the British government had the details of Hitler's proposals, which they had never succeeded in eliciting from Beck.

The full blast of the Nazi propaganda machine was at once turned on Poland. Europe reacted nervously and another war scare followed. On May 2nd Sir Nevile Henderson learned "that all preparations were being made for an invasion of Poland . . . within the next 14 days". The "possibility of an early coup cannot be excluded," he telegraphed. The man with the coolest temper and hottest diplomatic post in Europe, Consul-General Gerald Shepherd in Danzig, described on May 4th the "increasing nervousness" of the population, most of whom expected to be soon welcoming German troops.

While worried by this information, the Foreign Office at first tried to influence the weaker side of the dispute. But squeezing the Poles was not a popular activity in the Foreign Office. Nothing had been done since the guarantee to caution the Germans. British intelligence was dismayed by the fact that leading Nazis, such as Ribbentrop, were convinced Chamberlain would rat on the Poles in case of a conflict. Something had to be done in Berlin to dispel this conviction.

Several Secret Intelligence Service reports on May 8th made it imperative to give a clear warning to the Germans. Intelligence showed that plans had been made for a coup in Danzig and a solution of the Polish problem if Hitler was not otherwise satisfied soon. The danger period was to be from May 14th–20th. How were the Germans to be warned? Ivone Kirkpatrick, always ready with slapdash advice, wanted immediate mobilisation to show Hitler "that we meant business".

Gladwyn Jebb, responsible for liaison with the intelligence services, had another scheme. The German general staff was known in London to despise the Nazi Party. Why not let Sir Nevile Henderson frankly tell Generals Keitel and Halder that, if Hitler provoked a war over Danzig, Britain and France would come in and eventually the Nazi Party and the German Reich would both be destroyed. Jebb doubted whether the general staff would have any influence on Hitler "at the real moment of crisis". Keitel he considered "rather a lightweight and a time-server". Halder was "alleged to have views of his own". Still, Jebb thought a warning to the general staff might do good, especially if supplemented by a similar warning to circles connected with the court and army in Rome. "It is not the faintest use talking any more either to Herr von Ribbentrop or to Count Ciano. Both are stupid, both are vain, and both are irrevocably committed."

To this plan, Sir Orme Sargent added another on May 8th:

I doubt whether it is any good telling Sir N. Henderson to talk to the German Generals & on the whole I should prefer not to do so. On the other hand could we not "plant" a warning on suitable Nazi agents (in the same way as we suspect them of planting news on us). But our "plantings" have not been over-done like theirs & are not therefore discredited. Such a warning is more likely to reach & to impress the few people who really matter in Germany than any number of warnings given to the Generals whom Hitler considers as we know to be "cowards".[22]

Telegrams were accordingly despatched on May 9th to Sir Nevile Henderson (no. 150) and to Sir Percy Loraine. The intelligence services arranged to plant a warning on known Nazi agents. But Henderson, who thought he knew best how to conduct diplomacy in Berlin, was unhappy with his instructions. He decided to let his Military Attaché talk to the German military authorities and in a way which greatly weakened the warning.

When it occurred to both the Foreign Office and Henderson that a favourable opportunity to approach either Keitel or Halder might just not occur, Henderson suggested sending telegram no. 150 "as if by error" in a cipher which the Germans were known to have decoded. "R" code* was chosen, therefore, and on May 11th the warning was again telegraphed to Berlin.[23] Two days later Lord Halifax angrily ordered Henderson to obey his instructions exactly. The German generals, however, proved elusive, refusing invitations to lunch. Henderson did have a pleasant chat with Ernst von Weizsäcker, the German Secretary of State, and weeks later finally saw Halder. To both Henderson gave the warning.[24]

No one had been particularly happy about the scheme to direct a warning to the German generals. From the information coming out of Berlin it seemed that the only advice Hitler received from his Foreign Minister was that Britain would never fight if Germany attacked Danzig. The problem, therefore, was "how to counter Ribbentrop's obnoxious advice". The other Foreign Ministry officials could not go behind Ribbentrop's back. Field-Marshal Göring, who was thought to be more sensible, was supposed to have lost favour with Hitler. There were only left the German generals in order, as William Strang put it, "to try and get it across to Hitler that we really mean business."[25] The scheme was never again attempted.

———

By the end of May, Berlin and Warsaw had each had its share of representations. But even further behind the scenes a crucial, sometimes bitter, though always polite, battle of wits was taking place.

Sir Nevile Henderson had returned to Berlin on April 24th. He carried a heavy burden. The cancer, which eventually killed him three years later, had not improved. But he described it as "getting less uncomfortable". Equally troubling was that he knew that the Foreign Office and the Prime Minister had both lost confidence in him. Lord Halifax had hinted to him that his days

---

* "R" code, though known to have been deciphered by the Germans, had been in use until this time and even subsequently for communication with the British Embassies both in Berlin and Warsaw. The explanation was that "R" code was an unconfidential code. It was simply cheaper to send telegrams in this code rather than *en clair*.

in Berlin were numbered. A search was already being made for a successor. The crushing weight of these two burdens only spurred Henderson on to greater efforts. "War is such an appalling adventure", he wrote to Halifax on May 17th, "that I have always felt, and still feel, that everything else must first be tried."[26] He was determined to spare no effort to realise the goal he had set for himself two years earlier on being appointed Ambassador – peace with Nazi Germany.

In the weeks following his return to Germany, Henderson sent back to London "streams of hysterical telegrams and letters".[27] He never considered that Hitler's appetite for territorial expansion was unlimited. Austria and the Sudetenland belonged to Germany. The occupation of Prague was inevitable and due to the uncooperativeness of the Czechs. Memel was German; and so too, in his view, was Danzig. Its return to Germany, along with some concessions in the Polish Corridor, was inevitable. He was frankly "appalled" that Danzig could become a cause for war. The Poles were heroic, but foolhardy, untrustworthy, and "dangerous allies". They must be coerced into making concessions. Satisfy Germany's legitimate grievances, he argued again and again, and she would return to the respectable fold of nations. A racially unified Germany would eventually prefer butter to guns. "I am neither pro-Polish nor pro-German", Henderson explained, but "whereas Germany is a menace all the time Poland is only a menace as an ally."[28]

Such outspoken views, which ignored the crisis of confidence created by the occupation of Prague, made no impression. By May 1939 Henderson did not have a single sympathetic friend in the Foreign Office. His letters and telegrams were filed away, decorated with biting marginal comments, and outspoken minutes.

Where the Foreign Office violently disagreed with Henderson was in their estimate of the real issues involved and in Hitler's ultimate intentions. To Henderson's belief that Hitler's ambitions were limited and Danzig capable of a lasting solution, Roger Makins, for example, questioned: "How can we ensure that a settlement of the Danzig question will in fact be the end, and not a prelude to further demands?" Danzig could not be considered in isolation, Makins minuted on another despatch from Henderson. "Danzig is a very small part of the general problem confronting us and has to be considered in perspective." A solution which offered a "final and lasting settlement" of Polish-German relations seemed unattainable. On other occasions, Henderson's telegrams were criticised as "weighted in favour of the German case". According to Sir Robert Vansittart, the Ambassador was pro-German, anti-Polish, and biased towards the dictators.[29]

In the Polish capital, Sir Howard Kennard, an experienced diplomat, had been Ambassador since 1934. He knew the Poles and Poland. He also carefully read Henderson's telegrams and sensed he had a fight on his hands. In a calm and reasoned despatch on June 13th, he firmly answered Henderson. Poland had accepted the role of a bulwark against further German aggression in east Europe. It was essential that nothing be done to weaken her materially or morally. "For Poland's strength is our strength and her necessities are our necessities."

Given the state of European tension and Hitler's ambitions, concessions to Germany would be used as a lever to weaken Poland. The Munich agreement had only delayed for six months Czechoslovakia's dismemberment and "ultimate slavery". This was a lesson the Poles could not forget. It was for this reason that Kennard advised against any "attempts at surgical operations even of a minor character". Only a reduction of European tension, and the re-establishment of mutual confidence and goodwill could lay the foundations for a permanent settlement.

"I think Sir H. Kennard more nearly reflects the views of this department than Sir N. Henderson"; "I am in entire agreement"; "An excellent telegram" were the conclusive comments of Makins, Sargent and Cadogan respectively.[30]

This exuberant support was the result of more than just Kennard's persuasive arguments. Gladwyn Jebb had returned on June 9th from a secret visit to Poland. He was on an unofficial mission to gain first-hand experience of the Polish situation. Everywhere he found the same confidence in Poland's ability to handle the Germans and to ultimately prevail in battle.

"I came to the conclusion", Jebb wrote, "that our guarantee to Poland was, on the whole, less hazardous than I had previously thought . . . . that, once having given it, we have no option . . . but to help the Poles to resist by force any 'solution' of the Danzig question." If Britain should try to wriggle out of the guarantee, a fourth partition of Poland by Germany and the USSR was likely. "If this occurred, the effects on our own position in the world would be apparent to the meanest intelligence."

Jebb sent his report to the intelligence services. They replied with a very rare and revealing political judgement. Polish confidence was a dangerous sign, an intelligence official wrote, "that is, if there is any valid basis for settling the Danzig issue without war. But perhaps there is not, for even if Hitler were to give undertakings regarding non-militarisation, Polish trade facilities, etc. his word is so utterly valueless and his ulterior motives regarding Poland so sinister. . . . If we have to honour our guarantee, we will no doubt get a loyal and brave return from the Poles. Your conclusions seem unanswerable. We would not be fighting only for Danzig, any more than Hitler would be."[31]

To stand quietly and firmly by the guarantee to Poland, the policy so desperately urged by the Foreign Office, required patience and an iron will. The Foreign Office had both and they were usually successful in conveying these virtues to 10 Downing Street. The impasse reached in relations between Poland and Germany, however, was a cause of daily anxiety. The reopening of direct negotiations appeared unlikely. During April and May, Sir Nevile Henderson often suggested Britain might try to mediate. The ill-fated mission of Lord Runciman to Czechoslovakia in 1938 was not a happy precedent for British mediatory efforts.

Neville Chamberlain suddenly became intrigued by the idea of enlisting the help of the Scandinavian states. He was very anxious to prevent a local clash at Danzig degenerating into war. If the Scandinavian states could be available to mediate, this could provide all parties concerned with a breathing space to arrange a truce. He never intended to suggest mediation in the larger problem of Polish-German relations. But so tense was the situation, and so sensitive were the Foreign Office and Kennard to signs of weakness, that Chamberlain's plan was pounced upon and derided. Sir Alexander Cadogan thought it "silly" and he intended to prove it so. Kennard, flatly refusing to even approach Colonel Beck, misinterpreted the Prime Minister's limited proposal, and argued that it would be unacceptable to the Poles "as suggestive of weakness".[32]

Neville Chamberlain first told the Cabinet on May 24th about his Scandinavian mediation scheme. It had not been happily received. Sir Samuel Hoare, increasingly playing the gadfly among his colleagues, preferred the Government to concentrate on military rather than political measures in order to secure a breathing space in case of a sudden emergency in Danzig. The next day, Lord Halifax told a special meeting of the three Service Ministers that it was necessary to prepare a series of defence measures, working up by degrees to mobilisation of the fleet. The object of such measures would be to support diplomatic efforts to cool tempers in case of a crisis in Danzig. The Service Ministers agreed to gather this information.[33]

At the same time, Ambassador Kennard was asked yet once more, despite Cadogan's strong reservations, to advise Colonel Beck not to respond violently to a peaceful coup in Danzig. Such restraint would give an opportunity to warn Hitler of British support for Poland and enable "certain preparatory military measures" to be taken.

Colonel Beck replied on May 31st with his usual moderation, saying his government would act prudently and take no precipitate action. Having been pressed so repeatedly, Beck then jumped at the chance to tie the British down. Could the British and, indeed, the French governments state exactly what preparatory measures they envisaged to reinforce any *démarche* at Berlin?[34]

The Foreign Office was embarrassed by Beck's reply. It had been caught at its own game. In a minute which might have been composed in the Polish Foreign Ministry, Sir Alexander Cadogan wrote: "we can say nothing definite as to what we shd. do in a variety of hypothetical situations." This was only part of the explanation. Major-General Hastings Ismay, Secretary of the

Committee of Imperial Defence, suggested on June 8th that progressive mobilisation of all three services would be an adequate reply to Beck. Nothing could be said as to joint measures with the French. The Anglo-French military conversations had never discussed allied reaction to a local Danzig coup. They had concentrated on assistance in the event of war with Germany. And even in the latter case, Ismay noted, the French "have been a little sticky . . . and we have yet to obtain a really satisfactory line as to how we could jointly relieve the pressure on Poland if she were attacked."[35]

Once more muddle resulted from good intentions. On June 5th Sir Orme Sargent asked for the whole matter of mediation to be dropped. "I don't think anything very practical or useful wd. come of this", Cadogan minuted in agreement. "I think that the suggestion never had enough hope in it to warrant risking the creation of suspicion in the minds of the Poles." By June 17th, Sir Horace Wilson was also urging the Prime Minister to abandon the project. "If Danzig does blow up", he wrote, "it will probably be necessary for us to deal direct with Germany & Poland." Chamberlain noted his agreement and bowed to Cabinet and Foreign Office advice.[36] The idea of third party mediation was shelved.

Kennard had reminded Sargent on June 11th that he still had no instructions to give Beck the information requested. "Mutual confidence is all-important", Kennard sternly advised. The reply, sent on June 16th, followed the suggestion made by Ismay. The absence of firm Anglo-French war plans to help Poland was mentioned only for Kennard's information. He was not to reveal to Beck that, two and a half months after the guarantee, Poland remained the sacrificial lamb.[37]

"Danzig is again full of rumours of an impending coup", Gerald Shepherd, the British Consul-General, telegraphed to Lord Halifax on June 24th. Another test of British and French nerves was about to begin.

Although minor Polish-German incidents had erupted since

May, these had been localised and settled. Towards the end of June tension again increased. Sir Nevile Henderson was quick to bring to the attention of the Foreign Office the reported castration of a German in Poland. Gerald Shepherd described on June 28th the increasing militarisation of Danzig: members of the SA were preparing defences around the Free City; cars, lorries and horses were being registered; ss men from East Prussia and Germany were arriving; and the formation of *Freikorps* was proceeding quickly. Heinrich Himmler, head of the ss, also paid a brief incognito visit to the city.

With such an explosive situation in the making, Gerald Shepherd asked if his leave could be postponed. The Foreign Office agreed to his request until his "substitute and namesake" – Francis Michie Shepherd, due to arrive in Danzig on June 28th – felt "sufficiently acquainted with local conditions to take charge". Gerald Shepherd finally took his leave on July 10th and never returned. The Foreign Office believed his reports of military preparations in Danzig had been exaggerated and too alarmist.[38]

Gerald Shepherd's "very disquieting" information in June was supported by similar news from the French Embassy in Berlin. This was forwarded to London on June 29th and brought to Chamberlain's attention. Hitler's plans, it was stated, included the saturation of Danzig with German soldiers disguised as "tourists" arriving on the *Kraft durch Freude* (Strength Through Joy) liners. On July 20th, during a two days' visit, the return of Danzig to the Reich would be announced. Afterwards, Field-Marshal Göring would visit Danzig, aboard the cruiser *Königsberg*, and seal the fate of the city. The western democracies were expected to accept this *fait accompli*.[39]

Sir Nevile Henderson suspected anything with a date. This latest rumour, of which he was well aware, left him unmoved. He did not believe Hitler had yet made up his mind. His practice was "to take his decision at last possible moment and then to act like lightning". Henderson regarded the militarisation of Danzig as a form of German insurance against any Polish provocation.[40] Before these soothing words could be digested, a new "week-end crisis" erupted.

On Friday, June 30th, the Foreign Office received urgent news from Paris. The French Prime Minister, Edouard Daladier, had heard "from a first-rate source" that Hitler planned "to settle Danzig" during the week-end. Hitler was certain neither Britain nor France would react. Would the Foreign Office be prepared to announce immediately its knowledge of the coup and its "inflexible determination to fulfil all their obligations towards Poland?" he asked. He added that Otto Abetz, Paris representative of Ribbentrop's private bureau, had the effrontery to telephone various people, announcing the impending coup in Danzig. Daladier had therefore asked that Abetz be persuaded to leave France, which he did on July 2nd.[41]

In contrast to Daladier's panic reaction, the British took this latest crisis of nerves very coolly. They now had the benefit of experience. As Sir Alexander Cadogan had remarked several days earlier, Europe seethed with many "conflicting stories. It was quite impossible to tell whether these were deliberately put about to confuse and alarm us or whether there was any truth in them". In the news from Paris, the British smelled a rat. They suspected Daladier had overreacted, having been personally incensed at Otto Abetz's activities and wished to get rid of him. Finally, Sir Eric Phipps the British Ambassador in Paris, had discovered the source: contact made in Switzerland – this time by a Frenchman – with someone connected with the Reichswehr.[42]

From no capital other than Paris had come similar news. From Warsaw itself came assurances of complete indifference. On Saturday, July 1st, Colonel Beck described this latest rumour to Clifford Norton, the British Embassy Counsellor, as the "forty-ninth of its kind". He had decided not to move a single Polish soldier and "had gone to bed and slept peacefully". He intended to be absent from Warsaw for the week-end.

Despite their doubts and suspicions, the Foreign Office decided to be on the safe side. The press was given a "certain amount of inspired direction". It was hoped that such publicity on July 1st for Hitler's rumoured week-end plans would embarrass and deter him. Lord Halifax then spent the day with Geoffrey Dawson, Editor of *The Times*, watching the cricket at Eton.[43]

The French, however, persisted in apparent alarm. On July 1st the German Ambassador, Count Johannes von Welczeck, was summoned to the Quai d'Orsay to receive a stiff warning from Bonnet. In case of a conflict between Germany and Poland, he was told, France would at once assist her ally. Bonnet asked the Foreign Office to speak similarly to the German Ambassador in London.[44]

Pressure from their ally across the Channel was always distasteful to the British. But Sir Howard Kennard, at the time on leave in London, was desperate for a firm and immediate warning to the Germans. He favoured a parliamentary statement as the appropriate method and embodied his suggestions in a Foreign Office minute on July 1st. Sir Orme Sargent lent his enthusiastic support.

On Monday, July 3rd, Kennard, Chamberlain and Halifax agreed that the latter should make a statement in Parliament, reviewing the whole situation in Danzig and defining Britain's attitude. Halifax and Chamberlain "emphasised the importance of leaving the door open to any possible negotiations between Germany and Poland". Kennard replied that he "did not think that there could be any question of any such negotiations until the present atmosphere had radically altered." On the same day the Foreign Office also prepared a draft of a possible statement to the German Ambassador, as requested by the French government. It concluded by reiterating the March 31st guarantee of Poland. Halifax gave his approval to both statements on July 4th.[45]

News of the planned week-end coup had circulated in America as well as Europe. So distressed was President Roosevelt by the prospects of imminent war that he had telephoned on July 1st to Ambassador Bullitt in Paris. The American public was completely ignorant of the issues surrounding the Danzig crisis, Roosevelt said. Britain, France and Poland should at once try "to enlighten the Americans by means of supplying the necessary information and material to the American Press without delay."

Sir Eric Phipps telegraphed this information to London. From experience the Foreign Office knew how easily the Americans could suspect enlightenment as a disguise for propaganda. They were also surprised to find that the American press needed such guidance. "It is largely run by Jews who can surely be relied on to get the facts and the anti-German view on any outstanding question of the day. Library shelves groan under the unending volumes of American press reporters." The News Department decided to do their best, in the most discreet way.[46]

The Foreign Policy Committee met on Tuesday morning, July 4th. The French request for a warning to the German Ambassador in London was still unfulfilled. Danzig remained a free city. The week-end had passed peacefully.

The suggestion for a parliamentary statement – "to leave open the possibility of some revision of the existing arrangements at Danzig without any implication of weakness or surrender" – was at once approved. The ignorance of American public opinion as to the Danzig situation had obviously shocked Halifax and he wanted to remedy this. The question of a warning to the German Ambassador excited no one. Neville Chamberlain pointed out that Dirksen would only reply that Britain's position was well known in Germany. Nevertheless, he agreed to let Halifax go ahead.

The presence of Sir Howard Kennard at the meeting gave the Ministers an opportunity to discover, at first hand, what chances existed for a peaceful settlement of the Danzig question. The Ambassador spoke forcefully and honestly. His views cast a deep shadow.

The "gap was so wide between the points of view of Poland and Germany that in the present state of tension no useful purpose would be served by suggesting that conversations should take place between the two countries in regard to Danzig", Kennard stated. Ideas were advanced for a possible solution. The Ambassador countered by referring to the tense atmosphere as the barrier. The one assurance he did give was that the Poles had taken heed of the warnings not to indulge "in any rash or foolish action". While they "were generally an excitable race they had shown themselves able to remain calm and restrained through recent crises."[47]

The Foreign Policy Committee then approved the Prime

Minister's plan to address another communication to Mussolini. This was intended to give him a warning of the issues involved in the Danzig dispute and of the consequences if war ensued. At moments of crisis, Chamberlain's thoughts always turned to the weaker end of the Axis to put a brake on Hitler. As usual, the Italian government and press misinterpreted the latest warning "as evidence of weakness and fear".[48]

After friendly consultations with the Polish government, Neville Chamberlain made a parliamentary statement on July 10th, reaffirming the guarantee. It was the only direct warning given Germany. Lord Halifax had three days earlier decided against speaking to the German Ambassador. The French suggestion was always disliked and a parliamentary warning was considered adequate. "Enough has been *said* . . . only deeds would henceforth count", Sir Robert Vansittart advised Halifax.[49] Meanwhile, the Polish-German dispute festered and remained unsolved.

During the week-end of July 1st–2nd Europe had successfully weathered another crisis of nerves. How long would it be before a new crisis would finally spark off war? Faced with the growing number of scare reports that Hitler was planning a coup in Danzig, the British government on June 30th had asked Beck if he·had "any ideas" on how to meet such a situation. A sudden coup might force the Poles to react with violence, making them appear the aggressors. It was imperative for Britain, France and Poland to consult and co-ordinate their plans.

Time and again Beck had been asked how his government would react to such a situation at Danzig. His answer had invariably been vague: Poland's response would be proportionate to the provocation offered. To this latest inquiry, Beck stated that he preferred to think it over for a few days. When his reply came, it was as usual reassuring and unhelpful.[50]

A combination of frustration and a realisation that the problem was as much military as political provided an alternative approach. On July 1st Sir Howard Kennard had suggested that the Foreign

Office would never get a "clear and frank answer" from Beck. The "time has come to address ourselves direct to Marshal Smigly-Rydz." The best way of approaching the Marshal, according to Kennard, was for Britain and France to send a distinguished serving General to Poland to discuss the situation. Such a visit "would steady the Poles while giving us an opportunity of controlling Polish plans and urging caution if necessary in present circumstances." It was also hoped to discover Poland's military plans in case of trouble in Danzig. Sir Orme Sargent advised that the visit of the General should be made public. This "would serve as salutary warning to Hitler that we meant business."[51]

The man chosen by the War Office to meet the distinguished Polish Commander-in-Chief, Marshal Smigly-Rydz, was General Sir W. Edmund Ironside. Known as "Tiny" because of his six feet four inches height, Ironside was an accomplished linguist, and in May had been appointed Inspector-General of Overseas Forces. He had arrived in London on July 1st from his previous position as Governor of Gibraltar, and was told on the 4th of his difficult mission.

The "Poles have a plan for dealing with Danzig", he noted in his diary, "but they won't divulge it. I and a French General are to go and deal direct with Smigly-Rydz and find out what it is."[52] As the French already had a general in Warsaw, Ironside made the journey alone.

The Cabinet approved the mission on July 5th and seemed determined Ironside should receive precise instructions, preferably avoiding political subjects. Sir Orme Sargent objected. He wanted to give Ironside complete freedom to probe the Poles and discuss everything. During meetings with Neville Chamberlain and Lord Halifax on July 10th and 11th, Ironside made a favourable impression. In turn, he found both men convinced war was "almost inevitable", with Chamberlain completely distrustful of Hitler.

Ironside's final instructions, approved by the Prime Minister, were to discover Poland's precise plans for dealing with the current military activity in Danzig. He was also to discover Polish reaction to a possible proclamation from the Danzig

Senate of union with the Reich, in circumstances ranging from the peaceful to the entrance of German arms and troops. Finally, he was to deliver the usual cautionary advice to the Poles.[53]

During his brief four-day visit to Poland, Ironside's "forceful character and clarity of purpose" made a deep impression. He was cheered in the streets of Warsaw, received full and favourable press coverage, and faithfully carried out his instructions. His conversations with both Colonel Beck and Marshal Smigly-Rydz, a "simple and charming person . . . of peasant stock but cultured" were frank and friendly. The mutual goodwill was abundant; the results, meagre.[54]

"I impressed upon the two men the great responsibility which fell on their shoulders", Ironside wrote in his final report. "We have practically given them an open cheque, and we wanted to be sure that this cheque would not be presented unless there was every reason for it. They both appreciated this and assured me that the British Government would be kept in closest touch with events."

Neither Smigly-Rydz nor Beck, however, would bind themselves to consult London before taking military action. They admitted to Ironside, as the Foreign Office noticed with satisfaction, that they would only attack Germany if Poland itself was invaded. In case of war, they did not intend to squander Polish soldiers in defence of Danzig. A crisis in the Free City would merit nothing stronger than firm protests both there and in Berlin.[55] The one assurance everyone in London wanted from Ironside's visit – that Poland would not act alone – was never given.

Crumbs of comfort from the Ironside mission seemed to provide temporary satisfaction. For even while he was in Warsaw, being wined and dined, the atmosphere in Europe suddenly changed. Weeks of nervous tension gave way in mid-July to another lull. "Germany was 'soft pedalling' in regard to Danzig", Lord Halifax informed the Cabinet on July 19th.

The European weathercock was always turning; sometimes with reason, sometimes not. Hitler, having made his plans, kept his own counsel and spoke rarely. From his entourage leaked a continuous flow of reports, and in mid-July these messages were uniformly hopeful. Hitler had no aggressive intentions. Problems such as Danzig and the return of former German colonies would be settled by negotiation. According to Walter Hewel, liaison officer between Hitler and Ribbentrop, the Führer "is determined not to run any risk and definitely does not want war. He is playing with Danzig but keeps his head very cool." Dr Meissner of the German Propaganda Ministry stated that Hitler was "seriously contemplating in the near future to make a big peace gesture"; he intended to propose holding a conference. Sir Robert Vansittart was very sceptical of this information. Nevertheless, it was brought to the attention of the Prime Minister.[56]

As the hot summer days of July ticked by, even more evidence came into London. An official of the Secret Intelligence Service later described what happened: "We reported 'faltering' in mid-July, and MI5 information, mentioning 'cold feet', tended to confirm; it was a faltering which was apparently to be kept from the knowledge of all but a few at the top."[57]

The German Gauleiter in Danzig, Albert Forster, provided what seemed like authoritative proof of Hitler's new reasonableness. He informed the League of Nations High Commissioner in Danzig, Professor Carl Burckhardt, that Hitler had stated he would do nothing to provoke a conflict. The Danzig dispute could wait until next year or even longer. This information, given in strictest confidence to the British, French and American governments, was described by Lord Halifax on July 26th to the Cabinet.

As these reports arrived at the Foreign Office, officials expressed no surprise. Every piece of written advice had for weeks advocated that only a firm front would impress Hitler. These efforts were now showing results. British and French action during the week-end crisis, Royal Air Force flights to France, the calling up of naval reserves, and the Prime Minister's speech in the Commons on July 10th had at last impressed Hitler. Even the Americans seemed convinced that Britain was prepared to resist any new German aggression.

The Foreign Office in 1939, however, had few illusions about

Hitler. The "notes of appeasement" coming from Berlin were described by Ivone Kirkpatrick as "an encouraging portent"; but he also warned that past experience showed Hitler was "cunning and we must be on our guard. . . . He will not willingly become a good European."[58]

Two senior and experienced Foreign Office officials were also cautious. "All is not yet necessarily plane [*sic*] sailing", Sir Lancelot Oliphant minuted, and asked Lord Halifax to so advise the Cabinet, which was done. Neither could Sir Orme Sargent credit Hitler with a new reasonableness. The "Danzig agitation was a completely artificial one", Sargent minuted. If Hitler intended to damp it down, he was certain to "continue to keep the whole of Europe on tenterhooks and in a state of tension, since this is the only policy open to him in present circumstances. He will see to it, in fact, that the war of nerves continues . . . to see whether we can stand the strain."

It must have been a sense of prophecy which also forced Sargent on July 18th to issue a strong warning:

> . . . there are certain indications that Hitler's mood may be changing. If so, I think we can flatter ourselves that this change is due to our firm attitude and our close cooperation with the Poles. But the change has not gone far enough for us to foresee as yet the possibility of negotiations being opened – and any sign of weakness on our part at this stage might well check this change altogether.[59]

There were others, in the British government and civil service, who thought differently. For them, "notes of appeasement" from Berlin invited, not caution, but sensational gestures.

CHAPTER EIGHT

The "Menacing Silence"

APPEASEMENT became a dirty word on March 15th, 1939. On that day a proud public policy went underground. Never again would any member of the British government speak from a platform in support of unilaterally redressing Germany's grievances.

The cartoonists' portrayals of an ageing Prime Minister with winged collar and furled umbrella, devoted to a hazardous peace mission, had become overnight a cruel caricature. The humiliation suffered by Neville Chamberlain led him to admit to the Cabinet on March 18th that

> he had now come definitely to the conclusion that Herr Hitler's attitude made it impossible to continue to negotiate on the old basis with the Nazi regime. This did not mean that negotiations with the German people were impossible. No reliance could be placed on any of the assurances given by the Nazi leaders. On the occasions when he had met Herr Hitler, he had thought that while Herr Hitler might mean what he said, it was always possible that he would find reasons to change his views later.[1]

In these careful sentences Chamberlain laid the basis for the astonishing acts of policy he approved in the next month: guarantees in eastern Europe, negotiations with Soviet Russia, and the introduction of conscription.

The "old basis" for negotiation which Chamberlain referred to were the bonds of trust, confidence and the generosity of concessions. Appeasement prior to March 1939 believed in the sanctity of the pledged word and the honoured signature. If statesmen meant what they said and acted as they promised, a settlement of outstanding European differences was possible. This was Chamberlain's faith. On March 15th Hitler destroyed this and created a crisis of confidence.

During the next five and a half months prior to the outbreak of war, never once did Chamberlain weaken in his distrust of Hitler. He repeatedly stated that "no undertakings by Hitler would be any use".[2] Hitler would have to prove in some concrete way, therefore, that he had finally abandoned the use of force·

At the same time, Chamberlain was a realist. Ultimately European "peace cannot be achieved without an understanding between this country and Germany", he wrote.[3] Until then, other more urgent tasks had to be accomplished: the British must become strong. In the privacy of his frequent and intimate letters to his sisters, Chamberlain explained:

> We should just have to go on rearming & collecting what help we could from outside in the hope that something would happen to break the spell, either Hitler's death or a realisation that the defence was too strong to make attack possible.
>
> . . . the longer the war is put off the less likely it is to come at all as we go on perfecting our defences, and building up the defences of our allies. . . . You don't need offensive forces sufficient to win a smashing victory. What you want are defensive forces sufficiently strong to make it impossible for the other side to win except at such a cost as to make it not worth while.[4]

Chamberlain himself never weakened in his resolve to see his delicate tight-rope policy through to the end.

On every possible occasion Chamberlain carefully reiterated his new approach to European problems. The message was always similar: Britain and France had no intention to encircle Germany; legitimate economic and trade expansion by Germany was in everyone's interest; economic negotiations could be resumed; raw materials could be equitably distributed; and ideological blocs would be avoided – so long and as soon as Germany proved concretely she could behave.

From the German capital came no encouragement, only criticism. Gestures of Britain's good intentions were ignored and derided. Allied guarantees and war preparations were instead publicised as proof of Anglo-French perfidy and belligerence. Behind the propaganda and speeches of both sides, an iron wall divided Europe.

In both Berlin and London there were few who shared Chamberlain's and Hitler's patience. When both leaders had spoken and fallen silent, there were others who wanted to carry on the dialogue. Such a situation offered the reward of heroism or the obscurity of humiliation. In the Europe of 1939 there were many on both sides prepared to take this risk. The well-connected businessmen, the well-intentioned nonentity, the impatient civil servant, and the election-conscious politician now had a field day. They were prepared to step into the gap left by the leaders of Britain and Germany.

It took less than three weeks from the day Poland received her guarantee, for the first British official to crack under the already unbearable strain. R. A. Butler, Parliamentary Under-Secretary of State for Foreign Affairs, was in a difficult situation. With the Foreign Secretary in the House of Lords, he was regularly called upon to answer questions on foreign policy in the Commons. His performance there was savagely criticised by Lloyd George, in a private letter on May 15th, as that of the "imperturbable dunce who says nothing with an air of conviction". Butler's problem was his conflict between sympathy and duty. He admired Chamberlain and fervently supported appeasement. Yet, whether the Foreign Office distrusted him or not, at least in 1939 telegrams were not regularly shown him. His devotion to the Foreign Office strong line must have been suspect. "I consider that the Parliamentary Under-Secretary should be very carefully fed in future", Butler complained on March 22nd.[5] But the situation hardly improved. On several occasions he found himself misinformed or uninformed.

On April 19th, a day after the Soviet Union's proposals for a triple alliance arrived in the Foreign Office, Butler was listening to the views of the 8th Duke of Buccleuch. The Duke, Lord

Steward of the King's Household, had just returned from abroad, full of impressions from "his friends in Germany". Britain could improve the atmosphere, he suggested, by encouraging talks between the Poles and Germans, resuming trade negotiations, not meddling in eastern Europe and, above all, not allying with the USSR "if we desired to retain any sort of moderation in Herr Hitler's outlook".

Butler at once grasped this opportunity to reveal his thoughts to Lord Halifax. "We have had a certain success in our 'offensive diplomacy', that is in active diplomacy, and now there is great room for healing diplomacy to follow." Talks between Germany and Poland on Danzig, and between Italy and France on the Mediterranean crisis should be encouraged, Butler wrote in his minute of the conversation. "A dual system of offensive and healing diplomacy may well relieve tension without sacrificing our vital interests."

After reading Butler's minute, Halifax himself then met the Duke of Buccleuch. Apparently not satisfied, the Duke then wrote to Sir Horace Wilson a letter which was anti-Polish and openly sympathetic to the German cause. When the letter was sent to the Foreign Office, Sir Alexander Cadogan filled its margins with acute criticisms. "Not much in this, I think." was his laconic final comment. "He has been well filled up!" was Sir Robert Vansittart's brief minute.[6]

The wall of silence separating the main protagonists of Europe proved too great a temptation to others. At an official level, Pole did not speak to German, or Frenchman to Italian. Only Chamberlain and Mussolini seemed to share a direct line. Sir Francis Fremantle, a distinguished doctor and Conservative MP, had a "brain and heart-wave" which came to him in church on May 1st. Why not ask the former Prime Minister, Stanley Baldwin, to "go for a cure or holiday, say, to the Black Forest, and on to friends in or near Berlin and let it be known that he would like to meet Hitler as a private individual."

The drama of the Munich conference in 1938, with its meeting of heads of state, had created the myth. Direct contact at high level seemed a positive prescription for appeasement. This was impossible after the German seizure of Prague. Instead, there slowly percolated the idea of a meeting at slightly lower levels. Sir Francis Fremantle's suggestion for a Baldwin-Hitler confrontation was possibly the first.

Lord Halifax was not enthusiastic, but took the opportunity, in replying, to reveal much about the nature of appeasement after Prague. "I quite agree with you," he wrote on May 8th, "that we must try to drive into Hitler the conviction that he can satisfy every German aspiration by peaceful means and that we are more than ready to forget the past and co-operate with him in this task." A private interview between Hitler and some prominent Englishman could be useful. "At the moment unfortunately Hitler shows no disposition to receive an Englishman or even to discuss outstanding questions with us."[7]

It was Hitler's tragedy that he failed to realise how much Britain was still willing to concede in order to secure peace. As Halifax admitted, Germany could have been satisfied on all points, providing Hitler gave up his habit of triumphal entries into foreign capitals.

Few of the concessions supposedly needed to satisfy Hitler could come from London. Danzig and the Corridor were Polish. German exploitation of the economic wealth of south-east Europe was being resisted by the countries concerned. And both these aims were on the top of Hitler's agenda.

The one tangible concession Britain could have made to Germany in 1939, Neville Chamberlain still resisted. After the First World War, Germany's colonial possessions had been taken from her. As part of the peace treaty of 1919, the British had received as mandates Tanganyika and parts of Togoland and the Cameroons. The return of these, or other colonies, was not a pressing issue with Hitler and he never officially put forward his exact claims. Chamberlain realised, however, it was the one definite incentive he could hold out to Hitler.

Replying to a letter from Lieutenant-Colonel Lord Francis Scott, uncle of the Duchess of Gloucester, Chamberlain revealingly wrote on June 12th:

. . . a permanent peace between this country and Germany . . . involves the return to Germany of the colonies which she possessed before the War without any conditions other than certain restrictions upon the military use of these territories. I could never consent to the satisfaction of German claims on such a basis. The recent action of Hitler in Czechoslovakia has destroyed confidence in his assurances, and it is difficult to see how, after his recent action, he could give such evidence of his reliability in future as would carry conviction.

Chamberlain refused to give a binding obligation, requested by Lord Francis Scott, never to negotiate the colonial question with Germany. The time was simply not ripe: "it would be impossible even to discuss the colonial question with Germany in the present atmosphere of resentment over her past action, and over Hitler's breach of faith and of suspicion as to her intentions in the future."[8] The opportunity was destined never to occur.

———

The most startling, dramatic and least effective attempt to break the European stalemate came in a surprise move from President Roosevelt. American intervention in European affairs was so rare as to evoke instant attention. Roosevelt strongly believed that it was essential for the United States to support the Anglo-French deterrent front. His efforts to revise the neutrality laws were bogged down in Congress. How else, other than materially, could he help the democracies in their fight to deter Hitler? In early April Roosevelt made up his mind to speak out.

During his Pan American Day address on April 14th Roosevelt appealed to the states of Europe to adopt a policy of pledges against aggression, and to engage in the "open doors of trade and intercourse". The Foreign Office was immediately enthusiastic about these comments and planned to let Roosevelt know how much his address was appreciated.[9] No sooner had the draft telegram been prepared than it was cut across by the President's "Saturday surprise".

In a letter addressed to Hitler and published on April 15th – "because no troops are at this moment on the march" – Roosevelt proposed a method to do away with the "constant fear of a new war" shared by millions of people. He firstly admonished both Germany and Italy, in terms which Neville Chamberlain could himself have written up to a month before. "In conference rooms, as in courts, it is necessary that both sides enter upon the discussion in good faith, assuming that substantial justice will accrue to both; and it is customary and necessary that they leave their arms outside the room where they confer."

Roosevelt then went on to ask the Axis Powers to give an assurance that for at least ten years they would not attack any one of a list of thirty independent nations in Europe and the Middle East. If given, Roosevelt offered to participate in discussions on disarmament and increasing international trade. During this time, governments other than the United States would have the choice to discuss their political differences free from the threat of force or fear of war.

Within a half hour of the announcement of Roosevelt's message, secret orders went out to the US fleet. In response to a plea from Lord Halifax on March 21st, the fleet was ordered to return from the Atlantic to its regular base at San Diego. This move, intended to impress the Japanese, enabled the British navy to concentrate its attention on the Mediterranean.[10]

The British Foreign Office had the benefit, entirely by accident, of several hours' prior notice of Roosevelt's appeal. During the morning of April 15th, Herschel Johnson, Counsellor of the American Embassy, visited E. M. B. Ingram of the Southern Department on other business. Johnson brought with him a copy of the Roosevelt appeal. Seeing its importance, Ingram asked him to send copies to Sir Orme Sargent and 10 Downing Street "without delay".

What attitude could possibly be taken towards the President's initiative? The Foreign Office News Department thought it best to say that "any initiative by the President of the United States in the cause of peace . . . is warmly to be welcomed". But any conclusion must await the German and Italian replies. The communiqué issued to the press on April 15th, approved by both Chamberlain and Halifax, followed this line and added that Roosevelt's appeal offered a "real opportunity" to avert a European catastrophe.

The press communiqué gave no hint of the utter cynicism Roosevelt's message had evoked among officials in the News Department. They considered the message had "obvious shortcomings". After the events of March 1939 "how can we accept Hitler's promises of non-aggression; and (2) even if we did, is it sufficient for Hitler to promise not to invade independent countries, seeing that experience shows that he can destroy their independence by other means?" To Neville Chamberlain the whole episode must have confirmed his opinions expressed in 1937: "it is always best and safest to count on nothing from the Americans but words".[11]

The German Foreign Ministry took only two days to conceive of an ingenious and brilliant way of dealing with Roosevelt's message. On April 17th instructions went out to most of the countries mentioned in the President's telegram, asking them to indicate whether they felt threatened in any way by Germany. Out of fear and intimidation, most countries could only reply in the negative. Few had the courage of the Rumanian government to state that Germany herself was in the best position to judge if any menace existed. Still, the burden of the replies was a brilliant counter-propaganda stroke, ostensibly showing Roosevelt there was no need for the guarantees he suggested.

The Italian government never bothered with the diplomatic nicety of an official reply. The Roosevelt telegram was considered in Rome "as a comic document of mental aberration" and dismissed by Mussolini, privately, as "A result of infantile paralysis"; publicly as typical of "messages of the messianic type".[12]

Hitler finally delivered his expected reply when addressing the Reichstag on April 28th. Using the replies of most of the governments mentioned by Roosevelt, he stated he would give the assurances provided these governments requested it. But there was enough in Hitler's speech to make State Department officials wonder whether he had left the door open to discussion.

The same uncertainty plagued officials in London.[13] For Hitler's speech, besides replying to President Roosevelt and denouncing both the German-Polish Non-aggression Pact of 1934 and the Anglo-German Naval Agreement of 1935,* contained many friendly references to Britain. Hitler again repeated that he had no quarrel with the British, provided they would recognise German interests and not interfere in her affairs.

Did Hitler's speech prove "that the recent alignment of Powers had had a sobering effect"? Lord Halifax, when giving the Cabinet his impressions on May 3rd, thought this might be so. He pointed out that the speech "included a studied effort to conciliate British public opinion by rather clumsy flattery." The discussion which followed proved there were few prepared to succumb to this sort of flattery.

Lord Halifax wanted to limit any British reply to answering Hitler's denunciation of the Anglo-German Naval Agreement. But Hitler had also spoken of his readiness for a clear and practical understanding with Britain. "It might be considered whether we should ask him what proposals he had in mind."

It was Neville Chamberlain who spoke with greatest authority in doubting the wisdom of negotiating with Hitler. The return of German colonies, trade negotiations and a "free hand" for Germany in eastern Europe were three areas of possible appeasement. Chamberlain was painfully aware that for propaganda purposes Hitler would argue that Britain wanted war with Germany, was refusing his generous offers, and aiming at encirclement. Yet the Prime Minister steadied any wavering in his Cabinet. He would and must stand firm.

"It was quite impossible to discuss with Germany any question of the return of her Colonies at the present time," he stated, and "nothing should be said which would imply that we were prepared to do so". As for the trade negotiations, broken off by

---

* This agreement recognised the priority of Britain's interest at sea by limiting the strength of the German fleet to a fixed proportion – a ratio of 35:100 – of the naval forces of the entire British Empire. Its denunciation had been expected for weeks and the consequences for Britain not regarded as serious for another two years. (FO371/22995, C3682,3541,3746/19/18.)

Germany's occupation of Czechoslovakia, "within a reasonable time, if there was no further disturbance in international affairs" these "might be resumed".

Finally, this Cabinet meeting effectively destroyed the myth that Britain had ever implicitly promised Hitler a "free hand" in eastern Europe. Lord Chatfield pointed out that Hitler was now taking the view, or had persuaded himself, that the Anglo-German Naval Agreement had been concluded in the expectation that Britain had given Germany a "free hand". This assumption was false, and nor did Hitler indicate at the time the Naval Agreement was signed that it was based on such a crude bargain.

The "first time the idea of a free hand in Eastern Europe had been mentioned", Chamberlain added, was at his interview with Hitler at Bechtesgaden on September 15th, 1938. He did not think another naval agreement with Hitler would be useful. "There was no assurance that the Agreement would be kept."[14]

It took the Foreign Office almost three months to prepare the British reply to the denunciation. The final discussion was at the Foreign Policy Committee on June 13th. The Prime Minister repeated that he had nothing to say to Hitler "on wider and more general lines". He could not accept Hitler's understanding that a "free hand" in eastern Europe had been given in exchange for a "free hand on the sea". The reply cabled to Berlin on June 23rd stated that the original agreement was only concerned with the "problem of naval limitation". But it also contained evidence of a slight back-pedalling. If Germany contemplated negotiating another agreement, the British government was prepared to receive proposals.[15] On the main issue, a renewed bout of appeasement with Germany, the Cabinet had stood firm. Hitler's latest offer had been rejected.

On May 3rd, 1939, Oliver Harvey, Private Secretary to Lord Halifax, wrote in his diary:

"Appeasement" is raising its ugly head again. I keep hearing indirect reports that No. 10 is at it again behind our backs. There is the usual *Times* leader striking the defeatist note – "Danzig is not worth a war" and a letter from Lord Rushcliffe whom nobody supposes could have written a letter himself and the paternity of which is attributed to Horace Wilson.

The same day, Sir Alexander Cadogan wrote similarly:

> Went to see H. J. W[ilson] about a telephone intercept, which looks as if No. 10 were talking "appeasement" again. He put up all sorts of denials, to which I don't pay much attention. But it's a good thing to show we have our eye on them.

On May 8th Harold Nicolson, a National Labour MP, recorded in his diary:

> Gladwyn Jebb . . . is now wholly anti-appeasement and his sole fear is that Chamberlain may rat again. The influence of Horace Wilson is being revived with bad results. The Foreign Office call him "Father Joseph".[16]

So sensitive was the Foreign Office and so dirty a word had appeasement become that the slightest apparent wavering from the Prime Minister's office was enough to outrage the officials across the street.

What 10 Downing Street was doing to rouse such anger is a mystery; what Sir Horace Wilson was up to remains an enigma. What is clear is that there was no wavering at No. 10 on fundamentals. On May 12th Sir Horace Wilson sent a letter to Sir Nevile Henderson in Berlin. "It was, of course, inevitable that we should have 'firmed up' during the last two or three months", Wilson wrote "and all my information goes to show that it has proved wise to have done so. At the same time, you will have noticed that the Prime Minister and the Foreign Secretary have been careful in all their public utterances to make it perfectly plain to everybody that our policy is a balanced one."[17] There was no heresy in these comments.

Neville Chamberlain and Lord Halifax were indeed being most careful in public speeches. On April 26th the Prime Minister told the House of Commons that he was always willing to consider constructive proposals from Berlin. In a speech at the Albert Hall in London on May 11th, he returned to the same theme. It was his public answer to Hitler's Reichstag speech of April 28th. He told his audience that Britain would fully support Poland. He also made it equally plain that, while his government remained receptive to whatever proposals Hitler cared to advance, they were "determined not to submit to dictation."[18]

The European silence unfortunately only grew deadlier. Hitler made no reply to these public declarations, and he offered no easy solution. Out of desperation Lord Halifax finally asked the German Ambassador, Herbert von Dirksen, to come to the Foreign Office on May 18th. He tried to emphasise how shocked English opinion was by the destruction of Czechoslovakia. If Hitler ever threatened any of the guaranteed states "that would mean war". The Ambassador merely retorted that Hitler "was a very sensible man" and would never challenge the deterrent front.

Lord Halifax was not satisfied with this assurance. He asked Dirksen whether the German government "might be able themselves to show some evidence of intention that would bring a measure of reassurance to the world". Could not Hitler just once speak publicly, without insulting the democracies, and state that he had given up "forcible solutions" and would instead act on "free and *bona fide* methods of negotiation"? Such a step "would immediately evoke a favourable response in official quarters" in Britain. An even more emphatic assurance was added by Halifax. He did not record this in his official note of the conversation. British policy, he told Dirksen, "might seem to resemble putting a notice on a plot of grass warning others from treading on it and of the results if this was done." It is not certain whether Halifax spelled out the details.

Halifax suspected Dirksen's reports were never read by Hitler. He asked the Ambassador, therefore, to convey his remarks to the "highest quarter". Privately, Halifax doubted whether the conversation would have "any practical result of value".[19]

Neville Chamberlain's determination to seek a settlement with Germany continued to occupy his thoughts. "The dominating purpose of what remains to me of political life", he wrote, "is to re-establish peace and a sense of security in the world."[20] But the time was still not ripe. The door to Berlin remained tightly shut. Chamberlain was not prepared to risk a snub from Hitler, possible personal humiliation and public anger, by himself advancing peace proposals to Berlin. The pressures he had to resist were strong.

The circle of Dominion High Commissioners in London was a hotbed of appeasement. They had not been consulted about the guarantee to Poland. They did not like it and were frightened of possible consequences. Vincent Massey and Charles te Water, High Commissioners from Canada and the Union of South Africa respectively, were agreed that Germany "had a genuine claim to Danzig" which in their opinion was an "extremely bad reason" to go to war. They were puzzled as to why Britain had felt it necessary to draw the line at Danzig.

In late May, when an Anglo-Soviet agreement appeared on the verge of success, the High Commissioners returned to the charge. During a meeting at the Dominions Office on May 23rd, Charles te Water asked Sir Thomas Inskip "to consider the possibility of some bold action on the part of the United Kingdom in the direction of conciliation towards Germany." A non-aggression pact with Germany and an offer to revise the Versailles Treaty was what he had in mind.[21]

On May 24th after a long discussion in the Cabinet, Neville Chamberlain had finally agreed to ally Britain, France and the USSR. At this point, Sir Thomas Inskip mentioned his meeting with the High Commissioners and threw his whole weight behind their recommendations.

The suggestion was that, when we had strengthened our position by making an agreement with the Russian Government, we should take the initiative in a renewal of the search for appeasement. . . . An approach . . . might be rejected, but if it was accepted it would constitute an important step towards appeasement. The Foreign Secretary in speaking to the German Ambassador had suggested that Herr Hitler should take the initiative, but he (the Dominions Secretary) doubted whether Herr Hitler could do so. Once we were in a sufficiently strong position, we could afford to take the initiative ourselves.

Oliver Stanley could not restrain himself on such delicate issues. Even before Chamberlain could reply, he put his finger on the crux of the problem. The great difficulty, he astutely pointed out, was that many of Germany's grievances "involved concessions not by us but by other countries". At once Chamberlain intervened to authoritatively declare:

> . . . while he did not reject the suggestion put forward by the Dominions Secretary, he thought that it was premature to adopt it. It was necessary not merely that we should be strong, but that others should realise the fact. Further, public opinion in this country was not ready for such a move at this juncture.

There is no record that appeasement was ever again discussed so frankly at Cabinet level. In fact, Chamberlain went as far as to almost ban the word "appeasement" in political speeches because of the "considerable misconstruction" it evoked.[22]

The Dominion governments were told the next day that the time was not yet ripe for a "statement of positive proposals for removing causes of disagreement between the Powers". When the South African government repeated its suggestion in a personal message from the Prime Minister, General Hertzog, to Lord Halifax, a massive document was sent in reply, almost a month later. This illustrated with examples taken from no less than ten speeches in two months by government Ministers that they still intended to secure a lasting peace in Europe. But meanwhile they "have . . . thought it essential to insist upon some concrete sign showing that the German Government are in fact prepared to co-operate in a peaceful solution of the problems confronting Europe. They are . . . watching for some such sign to put forward constructive proposals."[23]

Patience and an iron-will were needed while waiting for a sign from Hitler. Determination was also needed to resist a growing movement in England "for making our aims clear in advance of war".[24] But the strangest source for some such declaration proved astonishingly to be the German moderates. Although better known for their advice to the democracies to stand up to Hitler, they too had a more positive, less known, side to their activities.

Dr Karl Goerdeler secretly journeyed to London in May. This was his first visit since he had outlined to his contact, Arthur Young, a "positive plan of action" on March 16th, involving a conference between Hitler and the democracies.[25] On that occasion, as with his previous proposals for a European settlement, Goerdeler had been unsuccessful. His ideas, communicated through Young in November and December 1938, were rejected outright as leading to the moribund policy of British concessions in exchange for vague assurances and promises of change within Germany. Sir Alexander Cadogan had minuted on December 10th, 1938: "we are expected to deliver goods, and Germany gives us I.O.U.'s."

After paying calls on Winston Churchill and Sir Robert Vansittart, Goerdeler had three long conversations between May 25th–30th with Frank Ashton-Gwatkin, Economic Counsellor to the Foreign Office. He was one of Goerdeler's regular contacts and most enthusiastic supporters. "G[oerdeler] is a palpably honest man. He is a German patriot. He is not an agent provoacateur," was how Ashton-Gwatkin later described him. This was not an opinion shared by Vansittart, to whom Goerdeler was "merely a stalking-horse for German *military* expansion . . . although Dr Goerdeler may from time to time be able to furnish interesting pieces of information on the internal situation in Germany, he is not only worthless but suspect as an intermediary for 'settlement'."[26]

Ashton-Gwatkin readily listened as Goerdeler gave him the usual predictions on the inevitable economic collapse of the Third Reich. According to Goerdeler, the German army "still have it in their power to overthrow the régime; but the decision is a question of timing." He himself "was ready to strike now". But the "leader of the whole movement", whose name he refused to divulge, considered it still too early.

To all of this Ashton-Gwatkin replied that the British government should not be expected to make a revolution in Germany for the German people. Goerdeler agreed, but pointed out that the Germans needed prior assurances of outside support. Therefore, he wished to see Britain and France issue a plan for the construction of a better Europe, based on a halt to the armaments race and a permanent solid peace. On May 30th Goerdeler gave Ashton-Gwatkin a seven-page document, entitled "A Plan for Peace Partnership in Europe". It included ideas for freedom of trade, guarantees for the "rule of right" in internal and international affairs, and a new organisation, the "New Society of Nations" to replace the League of Nations.[27]

The Foreign Office had no objection in principle to a "peace initiative". In fact some of the best brains, including Sir Frederick Leith-Ross, Chief Economic Adviser to the Foreign Office, had already been put to work secretly on a " 'Peace Aims' idea". Not surprisingly, little progress had been made. The difficulties of this, as of Goerdeler's proposals, were immense. Hitler's speeches at the time were no encouragement to think he would be receptive. It was doubtful whether such an offer would lead to an army revolt in Germany. And to devise such a plan seemed impossible. The real dilemma was pointedly analysed by Sir Orme Sargent:

> Either our plan goes so far to meet the German demands that Hitler is able to accept it, in which case he obtains a further bloodless victory and secures Danzig, the Colonies, raw materials etc. in return for promises of future good behaviour, which nobody will believe; his position in Germany is thus immediately strengthened, and Dr Goerdeler's friends will have no pretext and no inclination to start a revolution.
>
> Or else our plan is so vague and indefinite that Hitler can wriggle out of giving any definite reply, just as he did in the case of President Roosevelt's proposal without actually

putting himself so definitely in the wrong as to enable Herr Goerdeler's friends to intervene. The very fact that, for instance, they did not intervene when President Roosevelt made his proposal is, I think, a warning to us not to put too much trust in Dr Goerdeler's assurances as to their intentions, their ability & their courage.

Sargent was being too hard on the German moderates and too dogmatic on a peace plan. The more methodical Sir Alexander Cadogan, equally distrustful of the moderates, doubted their ability to do anything against the Nazi régime. But he gave careful thought to the peace plan idea. "Hitler has rather publicly burnt his boats over Danzig," he minuted. Unless a Danzig settlement could be found which was quite different from Hitler's proposals, he would stand firm. "Therefore, if Danzig could be embedded in a much wider 'plan', there might be a hope of settlement." And if that plan was reasonable and ignored by Hitler, his position in Germany might be undermined.

"But all this is begging the question – which is," Cadogan sadly added, "to find the 'plan' . . . I confess it is beyond my powers of imagination."[28]

————

During June, Europe settled down briefly to one of its periods of strange calm. Hitler's final diplomatic and military offensive was expected when the harvest had been gathered in.[29] Lord Halifax, very unwisely, decided to test the mood in Berlin. He acted on the advice of Sir Nevile Henderson. After visiting Karinhall, Field-Marshal Göring's private residence, Henderson came away convinced that Hitler was "feeling sore". His favourable references during his Reichstag speech had been ignored. Therefore, he could not make the sort of speech Halifax had asked for during his private conversation with Dirksen on May 18th. "If this is so", Henderson advised on May 30th, "might he not be helped to do it by something you or the Prime Minister might say first?"

Lord Halifax decided he would help Hitler along. He consulted Sir Alexander Cadogan as to "whether with some stiffer stuff I could put anything in to my speech next week to acknowledge Hitler's remarks about British Empire." The result appeared on June 8th in a very conciliatory speech he delivered in the House of Lords. He did not refer to Hitler's Reichstag address. Instead, he described the "staggering blow that was levelled at confidence and at the value of the pledged word in international relationships" by Hitler's lightning occupation of Czechoslovakia. But if confidence could be re-established and the independence of nations recognised, "any of Germany's claims are open to consideration round a table".

The reaction from the German press was predictably disparaging and critical. "Nothing doing I think at present," was Halifax's laconic assessment on June 13th. Yet that day he received a confidential letter from R. A. Butler, anxious to influence foreign policy once again in the direction of unilateral appeasement. Butler wrote that the time was indeed ripe for considering what he called "forward moves". Britain herself must reopen the dialogue with Germany by offering discussions on trade, raw materials and colonies. Halifax's reaction, while not recorded, was abundantly clear from an observation he made three days later to the German Ambassador, Herbert von Dirksen. Hitler "had broken the china in Europe", Halifax said, "and it was only he who could put it together again."[30]

It was in this mood that Halifax next spoke on foreign affairs. With a carefully prepared speech, privately circulated beforehand for comments, Halifax addressed an audience at Chatham House on June 29th. He clearly and unmistakably summed up the new basis of government thinking:

British policy rests on twin foundations of purpose. One is determined to resist force. The other is our recognition of the world's desire to get on with the constructive work of building peace. If we could once be satisfied that the intentions of others were the same as our own, and that we all really wanted peaceful solutions – then, I say here definitely, we could discuss the problems that are today causing the world anxiety. In

such a new atmosphere we could examine the colonial problem, the questions of raw materials, trade barriers, the issue of
Lebensraum, the limitation of armaments, and any other issue
that affects the lives of all European citizens.

But that is not the position which we face today. The threat
of military force is holding the world to ransom, and our immediate task is . . . to resist aggression. . . . And if we are ever
to succeed in removing misunderstanding and reaching a
settlement which the world can trust, it must be upon some
basis more substantial than verbal undertakings. It has been
said that deeds, not words, are necessary. This is also our
view. . . .[31]

It was the German Secretary of State, Ernst von Weizsäcker, who
ironically was to coin the phrase which so accurately described
what the British were attempting. On June 11th Roger Makins
had secretly met at Bâle the League of Nations High Commissioner in Danzig, Professor Carl Burckhardt. He had been testing opinion in Berlin, Warsaw and Danzig and was making a
secret report to Makins. Burckhardt stated that Weizsäcker "considered that the best chance for peace was that England should
maintain a solid front, '*un silence menaçant*'. Otherwise Herr von
Ribbentrop would again succeed with his thesis that the British
would not march. He thought that the door to negotiations
should be kept ajar, but only just."[32] The Foreign Office adopted
Weizsäcker's phrase as their watchword. The slightest weakening
was henceforth to arouse the warning to preserve the "menacing
silence".

Once more, where open diplomacy had so miserably failed,
there were others with varying motives prepared to jump into
the breach. The door to negotiations, being kept slightly ajar,
had many prepared to test it. Some preferred to fling the door
wide open. Others wanted it firmly shut.

General von Reichenau, the "most Nazi of the German
Generals", was sent to London as a personal emissary by Hitler
to report on British opinion. Although in what Gladwyn Jebb
described on June 8th as the "throes of a move" which impaired

its efficiency, MI5 was asked by the Foreign Office to follow Reichenau to "ensure . . . that he obtains the right impression" while in Britain. Reichenau's message was that Hitler was prepared to take risks, but would not be provoked by the Poles.[33]

Visitors from the German military resistance brought a different story. Fabian von Schlabrendorff had been to England in May on a visit arranged by Admiral Canaris, head of the *Abwehr*, the German military intelligence staff. In conversations with Winston Churchill and Lord Lloyd, he warned that war was imminent. Hitler was determined to attack Poland and would soon come to an agreement with the Soviet Union. The only "slim chance" to prevent war was for Britain to act quickly in impressing Hitler that action against Poland would mean full-scale war.[34]

Schlabrendorff was followed by another, perhaps more important, military figure whose visit had significant results. Lieutenant-Colonel Count Gerhard von Schwerin, head of the English section of the Intelligence Department at the German War Ministry, arrived in London on June 14th, took a flat in Piccadilly, had visiting cards printed and made himself generally available. He was already well known to the Prime Minister and the Foreign Office as "one of our sources of information". On March 28th he had warned the British Embassy in Berlin that Hitler had decided to push his eastern expansion policy in 1939. His visit in June on behalf of the general staff was not secret but not publicised. On May 23rd Hitler had told a meeting of senior officers of the *Wehrmacht* of his determination "to attack Poland at the first suitable opportunity". "It is not Danzig that is at stake", he declared. "For us it is a matter of expanding our living space in the East and making food supplies secure."[35]

The German general staff sent Schwerin to warn the English. He was wisely chosen. Admiral Godfrey, Director of Naval Intelligence and responsible for seeing that Schwerin was "properly fed", considered him a "very acceptable type of German" who "had charming manners, spoke English perfectly, was unobtrusive and receptive, and a good mixer". Under Godfrey's management, Schwerin met a careful selection of

Foreign Office and intelligence officials and MPs. To all he carried the same message. Hitler had definitely decided to attack Poland in the summer. The "only one hope for peace" was for Britain to impress Hitler both with its strength and determination to fight. Hitler underrated both of these. He "took no account of words, only of deeds." Schwerin urged, therefore, a naval demonstration or mobilisation, an invitation to German air officers to see Britain's growing air strength and the co-operation of Anglo-French forces on French aerodromes, and the immediate conclusion of the Anglo-Soviet negotiations.

Schwerin's final suggestion was very delicate: "Take Winston Churchill into the Cabinet. Churchill is the only Englishman Hitler is afraid of. He does not take the Prime Minister and Lord Halifax seriously, but he places Churchill in the same category as Roosevelt."[36]

Such a mixed bag of suggestions had a surprisingly positive effect. Schwerin himself was "shown something impressive in the air". On July 13th, after an impassioned plea from Vansittart to Halifax,[37] reserve fleet exercises were announced. Royal Air Force flights to France were undertaken. Success in the Anglo-Soviet negotiations, however, depended also on the Soviet Union and they were bogged down. And taking Churchill out of the wilderness was repugnant to the Prime Minister. He was aware since early April, from information given him by the Conservative Chief Whip, Captain David Margesson, that Churchill strongly wished to enter the Cabinet. But Chamberlain "had no intention of being bounced into taking back Winston". It would have symbolised to him an admission of personal failure. He always considered Churchill as one of those irresponsible men, prepared immediately to run the risk of war. He intended to resist them for as long as possible.

Nor did the suggestion to take back Churchill particularly recommend itself to Sir Alexander Cadogan:

... we have guaranteed Poland, Roumania, Turkey & Greece: we have gone beyond the wildest dreams of our friends and introduced conscription. We are told that this is not enough:

we must take the larger and bolder step of introducing Mr Churchill into the Govt. It may be that that would be a very good thing to do, but I shouldn't hope that it would do the trick.[38]

The dissident group of MPs gathered around the former Foreign Secretary, Anthony Eden, thought otherwise. On June 29th they found out about Schwerin's visit and his various suggestions. At once they decided that Churchill must be taken into the Cabinet. Such a step "would show to the whole world that there can be no further Munichs". The group approached, among others, Lord Camrose, proprietor and Chief Editor of the *Daily Telegraph*, to support Churchill's return to the Government. He agreed immediately and launched in early July a major press campaign.

Chamberlain was infuriated. He tried unsuccessfully to discover from Lord Camrose the source for the campaign. He personally suspected Ivan Maisky and Randolph Churchill as the principal conspirators. But this was one incident in which neither *bête noire* was involved. The campaign, though prolonged and vociferous, proved futile. There were limits beyond which a reluctant Chamberlain could not be prodded. On July 20th he unburdened himself, as was often his habit, to the American Ambassador, Joseph Kennedy. Later that day Kennedy wrote to President Roosevelt, describing the conversation:

> He told me he is unwilling to admit Churchill, because he does not believe in the first place that he could deliver nearly one-tenth as much as people think he could; he has developed into a fine two-handed drinker and his judgement has never been proven to be good. Chamberlain is also convinced that if Churchill had been in the Cabinet, England would have been at war before this.[39]

Schwerin was deeply impressed by what he heard and saw in Britain. Before returning to Berlin, he told Admiral Godfrey that he would do his best to inform everyone that the British "were in earnest". But he also warned that "unwelcome intelligence" was very difficult to get to the heads of the army and state. After war had been declared, Godfrey received an "anonymous message of unmistakable origin" via Switzerland: the information "had been delivered but not believed".

The German government could hardly be blamed for treating Schwerin's and similar reports with disbelief. For the field of private visits and secret contacts was not held only by the German military resistance or others assessing British intentions and strength. Simultaneously, the door to negotiations, being held slightly ajar, attracted many determined to see how far it could be opened. Their activities convinced Hitler that the British were not serious. It was the dilemma of Chamberlain's policy, intent on exploring all negotiating possibilities, however tenuous, which destroyed his credibility as an implacable opponent. Schwerin had implicitly given a warning about this, when talking to Admiral Godfrey. "As long as Chamberlain is Prime Minister, most Germans will continue to think that we [the British] shall pursue a policy of appeasement whatever we say."[40]

In early June, Adam von Trott zu Solz, a former Rhodes scholar and later a member of the "Kreisau circle" of the German resistance, travelled to England. His excellent connections there, including friendship with the Astor family, ensured him access to government officials and influencial circles. During a dinner on June 4th at Cliveden, the Astors' country house near Maidenhead, Trott heard from Lord Astor and Lord Lothian, the future Ambassador to the United States, regrets as to their inability to continue publicly voicing the need for concessions to Germany. Both still believed in giving Germany her rightful dominant position on the continent. Lord Halifax, who was also present, admitted to Trott that, after the Munich conference, he was prepared to see Germany preponderant in central and south-east Europe. But after the occupation of Prague, the expedient of self-defence had forced the Government to issue guarantees and negotiate alliances. Britain "would not shrink from a necessary war", Halifax warned, though she was still "prepared to take any really reasonable peaceful way out."

Trott absorbed these views but realised that only Neville Chamberlain retained the "decisive say". It was indeed fortunate that he had a conversation with the Prime Minister himself on June 8th.

"Do you believe that I enter into these obligations gladly? Herr Hitler forces me to it", Chamberlain told Trott. Hitler's occupation of Prague had destroyed confidence. If Hitler could furnish proof of his intention to respect his neighbours, an Anglo-German settlement, the one key to European peace, could still be achieved. Chamberlain sadly admitted "that he personally tended to regard such proof as practically impossible."

A careful reading by Hitler of Trott's report, which was submitted to him, could have brought only limited comfort. The German Ambassador in London, Herbert von Dirksen, rightly observed that "leading British personalities . . . were tending towards a discussion with Germany on burning problems." Unfortunately, these were not the people who made ultimate decisions, as the German Foreign Ministry realised. So far there was nothing which "can be regarded as constructive" was Weizsäcker's assessment on June 28th.[41]

Meanwhile, the hopeful and the well-placed had continued and still insisted on offering their services. On June 6th Axel L. Wenner-Gren had been received by Neville Chamberlain. Recommended by the Crown Prince of Sweden, the future King Gustav Adolf VI, Wenner-Gren, an influential, rich and philanthropic Swedish businessman, had easy access to Field-Marshal Göring. In commenting to Wenner-Gren on his record of a talk with Göring, Chamberlain clarified his attitude to Hitler. He was finished with the policy of "all give on our side and all take on his". It was impossible to trust any fresh assurances from Hitler. Chamberlain continued:

. . . I was as anxious as ever for a satisfactory understanding with Germany and a relaxation of the existing state of tension. As a practical man, however, I felt that, for the present, Hitler himself had made it out of the question for me to think of entering into any discussions with this end in view. Somehow or other confidence must be restored before conversations could be thought of. I did not myself see how this was going to be done but, in my view, it was for Herr Hitler to undo the mischief he had done.[42]

Wenner-Gren had two further conversations with Göring in Berlin, but advanced matters no further. Chamberlain's prerequisite for negotiation, the restoration of confidence, was an insuperable barrier.

Almost at the same time, another Swede, Birger Dahlerus, appeared who was to play a more active role. Like Wenner-Gren, he was also an industrialist but with even easier access to Field-Marshal Göring. He employed Göring's stepson on his staff. Not recommended by royalty, Dahlerus began his peace efforts with the assistance of his contacts among British industrial circles. He had lived in England during the 1920s when he was a managing director of several companies, including for a time Electrolux Limited,* founded by Wenner-Gren. With qualities of confidence, aggressiveness and egotism – rather like a cock-sparrow, his former associates recall – Dahlerus was nevertheless found wanting, eventually sacked, and returned to Sweden.

The Foreign Office first heard of Dahlerus on June 30th when it was informed that he had proposed holding a secret conference where British industrialists would meet with Göring. Dahlerus' motives remain obscure, his methods, though characteristic, were highly questionable, and his efforts proved ultimately fruitless. His main inspiration appears to have been the belief that if a German like Göring could see "how really human" Englishmen were, peace could easily be achieved. Göring, the object of so many peace-minded probers, unfortunately did not control policy. Even more, he regarded such

* Wenner-Gren was then a member of the board, whose chairman was Sir Harold Wernher. It was he who later, on July 24th, wrote a letter of introduction to Lord Halifax, on behalf of Dahlerus, attesting to his integrity and urged the Foreign Secretary to finally meet the Swede. (FO371/22990, C10951/16/18.)

approaches by third parties which could be traced to England as a "sign of weakness".

The Foreign Office remained sceptical of Dahlerus' first private meetings with Göring and the plans for a Baltic Sea rendezvous with British industrialists. "Göring is always interesting," Ivone Kirkpatrick minuted on July 13th, "but these whole proceedings seem very amateurish."[43] Nevertheless, Halifax, Chamberlain and Sir Horace Wilson were kept informed. They were not yet involved. Soon they were to have more sensational events to busy themselves with.

Waiting for Hitler to behave, mend his ways and advance concrete proposals of repentance was the official line of the British government. As the weeks passed, there was no move from Berlin. The situation was getting desperate. Sir Nevile Henderson began to crack under the strain. In early June his German doctor recommended he return to London for medical treatment. On June 29th Henderson wrote to Sir Alexander Cadogan suggesting that if Britain made a "constructive effort for peace", Hitler "may well be prepared to talk." As a prerequisite it was imperative to recognise *de jure* the changed map of Europe. Then, if Hitler would agree to substitute negotiation for force, Britain should be prepared to sit down and discuss economics, raw materials, disarmament and even colonies.

Sir Nevile Henderson made no mention of the Polish-German problem. Ignoring this omission, Cadogan and Halifax saw nothing to dispute in his letter. Sir Orme Sargent's minute of July 4th, however, barely disguised his annoyance and anger:

> Until Hitler is ready to make a proposal *to us* there will I fear be no possible ground for negotiation and until such time "le silence menaçant" recommended by Weizsäcker is I am sure in all that concerns Anglo-German negotiations the only safe and indeed fruitful policy and the only one moreover which will not be distorted by Hitler and turned against us.[44]

When in London, Henderson's doctor permitted him to continue his work. To his colleagues, the Ambassador appeared "in a very nervous and overwrought state". While anxious to see him voluntarily retire, the Foreign Office and 10 Downing Street, nevertheless, agreed to his returning to Berlin. In a letter to Lord Halifax on July 9th Henderson returned to his "idea of a constructive effort for peace" and enclosed a draft letter from Chamberlain to Hitler. This, he suggested, should be sent as soon as the negotiations with the USSR had been concluded, one way or the other.

Lord Halifax thanked the Ambassador on July 11th for his effort and said he would keep the suggestion in mind. But that same day Halifax gave the Dominion High Commissioners a fuller guide to his thinking. He said "that if we were careful to shut no doors to negotiations, probably the best course now would be to observe a 'silence menaçant'."[45] Could these two policies be pursued simultaneously without an explosion?

CHAPTER NINE

Appeasement Cremated

THE lull which suddenly followed the Danzig "weekend crisis" of July 1st–2nd proved a disaster. The Foreign Office stood firm and unflinching. Neville Chamberlain quietly raised hopes of eventual negotiation, but publicly maintained his silence, waiting for a sign from Berlin. Suddenly the nerves of Whitehall seemed to crack wide open. Proposals in a more concrete form than ever appeared to come from the British side. Hitler's signal could not be awaited any longer.

The "menacing silence" burst during the most unlikely event of 1939 – a whaling conference. It was scheduled for June 13th, backdated to June 6th and then postponed to July 17th, a date found acceptable to the participants: Norway, the United States, Japan, Great Britain and Germany.[1]

The man who was perversely determined to put a whaling conference into headlines was Robert Spear Hudson, Secretary of the Department of Overseas Trade, and the son of a wealthy soap king. He was ambitious, volatile, a notoriously indiscreet politician and, significantly, a former diplomat. Desperately anxious to leave his mark on political events, he disregarded both consistency and scrupulousness in his activities.

In December 1938 Robert Hudson led a revolt of junior Ministers against the slow pace of rearmament. Summoned by Chamberlain to explain his actions, Hudson declared his "wholehearted and complete support of the policy of appeasement." For months he had been "formulating plans for an economic agreement with Germany, believing that this was the best prelude to political agreement." Nevertheless, he was "seriously disquieted about armaments".[2] The revolt fizzled out. Hudson also temporarily shelved at the Department of Overseas Trade his plans for economic appeasement. He held them ready to be dusted off at the first opportunity.

In February 1939 Hudson was chosen to accompany Oliver Stanley to Berlin for trade talks and then personally to lead a delegation on a tour of northern European capitals. News of these plans leaked out before the official announcement. Cadogan suspected the indiscreet Hudson of being responsible.

Hitler's occupation of Prague forced the cancellation of the Stanley-Hudson visit to Germany. Hudson pleaded in vain with Halifax for the visit to be allowed to go ahead. He had to settle for the lesser limelight of the northern capitals' tour. Disregarding instructions to limit himself to economic issues, Hudson fished in Moscow for a large-scale political agreement. Foreign Office instructions forced him to stick to economic issues. Although only a junior Minister, Hudson also angled for a personal interview with Joseph Stalin. This request was politely turned down by Maxim Litvinov.

Still Hudson persisted in seeking the limelight. In April he tried to accompany Sir Frederick Leith-Ross, who was leading a commercial mission to Rumania. Cadogan succeeded in stymieing this attempt.[3]

For the whaling conference, Hudson had especially grandiose ideas. Having heard that the Norwegian delegate, Professor Bergersen, was very pro-German, Hudson asked the Air Ministry to organise a demonstration of Britain's air strength. The Foreign Office considered that "whaling experts were perhaps not ideal subjects for air propaganda" but had no objections to the plan. The Ministry of Agriculture and Fisheries, sponsors of the conference, succeeded in stopping Hudson's latest brainwave.[4]

On July 17th the whaling conference met in London. The German delegation was led by the economic adviser to Göring's four-year plan, the brisk, efficient Helmut Wohlthat.* His knowledge of, and role in, secret diplomacy far exceeded his expertise

* Despite the evidence now available that Wohlthat was in secret contact with Sir Robert Vansittart, the Foreign Office files relating to his selection to attend the whaling conference are still closed until 2015. (FO371/23661.)

on whales. But the conference provided Wohlthat with a perfect cover story for yet another visit to London.

On June 6th and 7th, Wohlthat had, in connection with refugee questions, discussed Anglo-German relations with Sir Horace Wilson and Sir Joseph Ball, Director of the Conservative Party research department. During lunch with Frank Ashton-Gwatkin, Wohlthat developed an idea for an economic settlement between England and Germany. His scheme was as simple as it was unrealistic. Britain had only to "recognise Germany's sphere of economic interest in South-Eastern and Eastern Europe". In return, Germany would abandon some of her restrictive currency policies. Ashton-Gwatkin was not impressed. Political questions had to be settled before a return to economic appeasement. Meanwhile, a suitable "symbol for peace", he suggested, would be for Hitler to sack some of his Cabinet. Wohlthat hinted he would be back for the whaling conference, but he was not to see Ashton-Gwatkin, who was by now quite disillusioned with all schemes for the economic appeasement of Germany. Britain could not, and should not, help Germany out of her economic difficulties "until her whole policy and her politicians have changed", he warned Lord Halifax that same day. The Germans would interpret any overtures "as weakness signs".[5]

As soon as he returned to London, Wohlthat asked for a meeting with Sir Horace Wilson. According to the record made by Wilson the next day, July 19th, the conversation, lasting just over an hour, was unremarkable and hopeless. Göring had not yet reacted to their June discussions. Nor had Wohlthat done any homework to prepare a "framework" which was to have included topics of mutual interest. Wilson may have been annoyed but was outwardly cautious. "I did not press him to do this, as I was most anxious to maintain the position that had been adopted in the June conversation, namely that we were not unduly apprehensive about things and that the initiative must come from the German side." Wilson's parting message to Wohlthat was that Anglo-German co-operation was still possible, as soon as favourable conditions had been created.[6]

There was no encouragement to Wohlthat from this source.

Neville Chamberlain saw Wilson's record of the conversation on July 19th and added his initials without comment. He was satisfied with Wilson's conduct of the discussion.

Robert Hudson had failed to get his air display to impress the Norwegian whaling expert. Instead, he used this delegate to arrange an interview for July 20th with Wohlthat. Hudson was acting on his own initiative, playing a solitary and dangerous hand.

The record Hudson made of his conversation with Wohlthat is astonishing both for its egotism and flights of fantasy. Two minor officials, without power and with little influence, sat discussing plans for the capital and industrial development of whole areas of the globe – including Russia, China and the colonies.* Hudson believed, as a result of his recent visit to the United States, that the Americans would help. On the problem of the colonies, he envisaged an Africa administered jointly and economically exploited by the European powers. Finally, he proposed that if Hitler was prepared to disarm, Britain could help Germany to be economically strong, thereby permanently preserving the "benefits" the Führer had conferred on the German people.

Although Hudson got carried away with visions of economic grandeur, Wohlthat was able to interject a warning. Economic considerations, he stated "to his sorrow . . . played very little part in the Führer's mind." That was why he had to work through Field-Marshal Göring.[7]

Wohlthat's warning also explains the most controversial aspect of his talks in London. After having returned to Berlin, he wrote Göring a memorandum on July 24th. This combined the conversations with both Wilson and Hudson and reveal some discrepancy with the records made by the two Englishmen. For according to Wohlthat, on July 18th Wilson had his secretary

---

* An even lesser official than Hudson had in fact acted earlier, on his own initiative, with a similarly grandiose scheme. On June 3rd Eric Cable, Consul-General in Cologne, had outlined for that city's Gauleiter an "international five years' plan to meet . . . German requirements". Cable was reprimanded. A copy of his scheme was sent to Hudson on June 24th. (FO371/23020, C8572/54/18.)

bring in a prepared memorandum approved by Chamberlain, outlining points to be negotiated between Britain and Germany. The Wilson "Programme for German-British Co-operation" covered political and military questions. It was to include a declaration renouncing the use of aggression, thereby making Britain's guarantees "superfluous"; a declaration of non-interference in respective spheres of influence: the British Empire and greater Germany; and a declaration on arms limitation.

Hudson's proposals, dealing with economic and colonial questions, were described immediately after the Wilson "programme" and closely followed, only in greater detail, the record Hudson himself made. Taken together in the form presented to Göring,[8] Wohlthat gave the impression of having carried off a major diplomatic success. Without awaiting the sign from Hitler, concrete peace proposals had come from London, apparently approved by the Prime Minister himself.

The orderly records of conversations made by officials with ulterior motives, fencing for position, disguise many curious and entangled aspects of this puzzling story. Helmut Wohlthat was possibly as ambitious as Robert Hudson, and he was desperate for success in his secret economic negotiations in London. Göring was not taking him seriously enough; Hitler was inaccessible and deaf to economic considerations. How better to gain attention than to weld hints, suggestions and various proposals into an orderly programme of wide-ranging appeasement. And this is what Wohlthat did in Berlin.

Sir Horace Wilson never acted without Chamberlain's express approval. He could not possibly have given any memorandum to Wohlthat. The files of 10 Downing Street would not have contained such specific material. Nor is it likely Wilson saw Wohlthat on July 21st, as the latter claimed in his report to Göring.

"I have no recollection of such a meeting and doubt if it took place", Wilson explained years later in reply to an inquiry from the Cabinet Office. "My book shows seven appointments on that day and there is no mention of Wohlthat. I had seen him three days earlier . . . and had told him enough to make the position clear to him: I don't think he would have wanted to come again and it is extremely unlikely that, if he did, I gave him a 'memorandum' such as is described."

Wilson also explained how the contact with Wohlthat arose: "I suggest that it is unnecessary to pay much attention to Wohlthat. He was not an accredited diplomatic representative and the only reason for explaining to him the British policy (determined re-armament but willingness to live at peace if Germany ceased to misbehave) was that Goering was his chief and that Goering was at that time thought to have a little influence with Hitler and to be perhaps a counter-weight to Ribbentrop."[9]

If Sir Horace Wilson's role becomes less dramatic as a result, that of Robert Hudson becomes explosive. For it is clear that Hudson used his meeting with Wohlthat to dust off the files on economic appeasement he had encouraged his department to develop. It was he who might even have given Wohlthat a written memorandum. And it was he who was partly responsible for the dangerous publicity about Wohlthat which appeared in the press on July 22nd.

Secrecy was the essence of this diplomacy. Yet suddenly the "menacing silence" burst into a deafening embarrassed roar.

On July 22nd the *News Chronicle* scored a journalistic scoop by reporting a "new and very sensational attempt" at appeasement put forward by "at least one member of the Government" to the Germans. The details were totally inaccurate. It was to have included the offer of a £1,000,000 loan in exchange for Germany's voluntary disarmament. Unfortunately, such money was simply not available in the depleted British Treasury.

As rumours multiplied and the size of the loan mushroomed to £1,000 million, Robert Hudson spoke out. " 'I Planned the Peace Loan to Germany', Minister tells of his talks with Wohlthat" blared the headlines of the *Daily Express* on July 24th. Hudson had decided to give an exclusive interview. He wanted to deny the garbled versions of his plans which had spread throughout the world and went on to describe the substance of his talk with Wohlthat.

Hudson could not reveal the source of the leakage. For sometime during July 20th or 21st he had indulged in his usual indiscretion. As Neville Chamberlain soon discovered, Hudson himself had leaked the information about his talk with Wohlthat.[10] But he also had an unknown companion in indiscretion. To the well connected politician or diplomat, eager for information, the London grapevine could hold few secrets. The Spanish Ambassador, the Duke of Alba, suddenly found himself by accident the most knowledgeable diplomat in London. He heard about the plan for economic appeasement first from Hudson and later from the German Ambassador. The Duke then went to the French Embassy, where he revealed all he knew. Anxious about the effect such a peace plan would have on the new Anglo-French allies in eastern Europe, the French Embassy – as the Germans in London suspected at the time – leaked the story to the press.[11]

Chamberlain was enraged. He personally interviewed Hudson and then ordered him to make a note of his conversation. This was finally sent to him on July 24th. At the same time, the Treasury and the Board of Trade worked feverishly, throughout July 21st–23rd, collecting information on people's contacts with Wohlthat.[12] An obviously inspired notice was put in *The Times* on July 22nd, denying the "fantastic rumours" surrounding Wohlthat's visit, and stating "only routine matters" were discussed.

The storm broke in the press and Parliament on July 24th. Chamberlain's critics howled against what they considered to be evidence of a return to appeasement. The German Ambassador, Herbert von Dirksen, telephoned at once to both Sir Horace Wilson and Sir Orme Sargent. He denied the wilder press statements and emphasised that the German Embassy was innocent of leakages. Wilson, according to Dirksen, "was very circumspect" and made no reply, but immediately informed the Prime Minister.

Sir Orme Sargent's brief minute of his conversation with Dirksen cleverly disguised his curiosity and, doubtless, suppressed anger. For the Foreign Office had been deliberately excluded from any contact with Wohlthat and had been denied initially any details. Halifax at once complained to Chamberlain. He wanted to be shown the exact records of the conversations. Hudson's note was sent to the Foreign Office on July 24th. Wilson sent his, on Chamberlain's instructions, a day later. Sargent asked to retain a copy for his files.

Sir Robert Vansittart seemed to sum up the feelings in the Foreign Office. In a minute to Halifax on July 26th he mentioned that he knew who was responsible for the leakage, but he felt the less said the better. "It has been an unhappy and damaging affair. . . . We can only hope that nothing of the sort will occur again." "The Secretary of State agrees", Oliver Harvey replied.[13]

In the House of Commons, Chamberlain loyally defended his talkative junior Minister. He stoically shouldered the wave of public criticism. Privately he revealed his true feelings. In a letter to his sister on July 23rd, he described how convinced he was that Hudson had not told him the entire truth about his talk with Wohlthat. He accused Hudson of plagiarising, as usual, other people's views and publicising them. Economic appeasement, for example, had been a subject of discussion in government departments for the past year. In his final comment, dissociating himself completely from Hudson's actions, Chamberlain wrote that it was still too early to reopen negotiations with the Germans. They had not yet given up the use of force. That was why he regretted Hudson's ill-timed revelations.

A week later Chamberlain returned to the subject in another letter to his sister. Hudson's tactless blunder had been very harmful, he wrote. Nevertheless, he wished to continue discreet contacts with Germany, which must be convinced

> that the chances of winning a war without getting thoroughly exhausted in the process are too remote to make it worth while. But the corollary to that must be that she has a chance of getting fair and reasonable consideration and treatment from us and others if she will give up the idea that she can force it from us and convince us that she has given it up.

The publicity given to Hudson's activities had one advantage. It hid the more significant contact established between Wilson and Wohlthat. In Parliament, Chamberlain admitted the two men had met, but the details remained unknown outside the two governments concerned and every effort was made to protect Wilson.[14]

In Berlin, Field-Marshal Göring seemed this time excited enough by what Wohlthat had brought him from his British contacts. He sent the report to Ribbentrop who, probably not believing his own eyes, telegraphed to Dirksen for more details. Dirksen immediately replied, confirming Wohlthat's account, and excitedly predicted that during the coming weeks a "programme of negotiations" could be expected.[15]

The German Ambassador's enthusiasm appeared, at least to himself, well based. Support for a constructive peace initiative towards Germany came from another quarter. Charles Roden Buxton, a prominent, though very individual Labour Party spokesman on foreign affairs, and a passionate activist for an Anglo-German settlement, could not ignore all this appeasement publicity. Since late 1937 he had privately written, discussed and then submitted memoranda to the Labour Party's Advisory Committee on International Questions pleading for a programme of "peaceful change".[16] On July 19th the Committee agreed to pass the memorandum to the National Executive Committee of the Party. The memorandum argued that the "Party's Peace Policy" should have aims beyond mere support of the deterrent front being created in Europe. Its object should also be to "remove the legitimate grievances of the 'have-not' powers". Colonial questions, treaty revision, trade liberalisation and access to raw materials, and rescinding of the "war guilt" clause of the Versailles Treaty were some of the many aspects on which it was felt negotiation was desirable.[17]

As a contribution to world-wide appeasement, this would not have surprised the Chamberlain government. Public opinion might very well have been, in view of the virulent opposition voiced by the Parliamentary Labour Party to Chamberlain's views on appeasement.

Charles Roden Buxton decided he could not wait for the Party machinery to thrash out a document so dear to his way of thinking. On July 29th he had a private talk with Theo Kordt,

Counsellor of the German Embassy. Buxton's choice was deliberate. He was aware from his own pipelines to Germany, mainly via membership of the Quaker "Society of Friends" and friendship with Professor Conwell Evans, of Kordt's secret contacts with the British. Buxton proposed "to revert to a sort of secret diplomacy" in order to avoid a conflagration. He then put forward a plan for a "reasonable understanding" with Germany. In inspiration it was based on the Labour party memorandum. But he also went dangerously further in advocating an Anglo-German "delimitation of spheres of interest". Germany would promise not to interfere in British Empire affairs, in return for an Anglo-French withdrawal from eastern Europe.

Buxton emphasised that he was speaking neither on behalf of the Labour Party nor the Government. Kordt preferred to draw other conclusions. Buxton's ideas, he assumed, had been either discussed with or inspired by talks with Sir Horace Wilson and Neville Chamberlain.* Likewise, Dirksen thought the plan was of sufficient interest to be sent to the German Foreign Ministry.[18]

Like Robert Hudson, Buxton was playing a lonely and dangerous hand. He was adding to the growing German impression that the British were faltering, having second thoughts, and weakening in their support of the guaranteed states.

Neville Chamberlain did in fact want to continue contacts with Germany. Thus with his approval Halifax encouraged Birger Dahlerus to go ahead in late July with the secret meeting between Göring and a group of British industrialists. Typical, too, was the encouragement Chamberlain gave to the Canadian Prime Minister, William Lyon Mackenzie King, to accept an invitation extended by Hitler on July 21st for a group of students and army officers to visit Germany as personal guests of the Führer. Mackenzie King, who had been favourably impressed when he

---

* In actual fact, Buxton saw Halifax on July 13th, cryptically spoke of a "method of communication ... altogether outside the Foreign Office machinery", and showed Halifax a memorandum which broadly followed the proposals made to Kordt. Whether Buxton's meeting with Halifax was a preliminary to his talks with Kordt, or to his visit to Berlin in mid-August is difficult to ascertain. (FO800/316, H/xv/230; *Documents on German Foreign Policy*, VI, no. 87.)

had met Hitler in June 1937, was certain that the invitation was an "approach . . . towards conciliation". Chamberlain replied that he generally did not like to let any friendly gesture from Hitler pass without response. "But at the same time it would be well not to build too great hopes on substantial results ensuing."[19]

Similar encouragement was given to the secret, and little known, visit to Berlin of another businessman, Ernest W. D. Tennant, a self-admitted "amateur in politics". His qualifications included the experience of no less than 180 visits to Germany since 1919, the honorary secretaryship of the Anglo-German Fellowship, and an intimate friendship with Ribbentrop whom he had met in 1932. Tennant's motive was simply a sincere belief in Ribbentrop's good intentions. In July he could no longer resist the temptation to settle Anglo-German differences. On July 22nd he managed to receive an invitation to see Ribbentrop at his castle, Schloss Fuschl, near Salzburg.

Two days later, July 24th, while the exaggerated publicity of the Hudson-Wohlthat talks dominated the press, Tennant was received by Sir Horace Wilson. Neville Chamberlain had been informed and approved. Wilson left on record the minute of his briefing to Tennant. It gives an accurate picture of his thinking.

"Mr. Tennant has clearly in mind that the two phases of policy are: (a) Determination; and (b) Willingness to reason with reasonable people as soon as confidence is restored." Ribbentrop must not be given the impression that Britain had any proposals in mind. Then Wilson added:

> . . . it was useless to talk about a credit or a loan or anything of that kind in present circumstances. I thought that the essential thing was to see whether the German Govt. were prepared to create the conditions in wh. international confidence cld. be restored.

The message Tennant brought back from Ribbentrop, and sent to the Foreign Office on July 31st, was unoriginal and quite hopeless. Peace depended on a division of the world into British and German spheres of influence. Ribbentrop had no other proposals.[20]

The pathetic but brave search for proposals emanating from the German side continued in earnest, even desperation. Simultaneously with the disappointing Tennant visit came a sudden ray of hope. Lord Kemsley, owner of Allied Newspapers, another strong believer in Anglo-German reconciliation, and a fervent supporter of Chamberlain's policies, had been invited to Berlin by Otto Dietrich, the Reich Press Chief. This visit was to discuss the exchange of press articles on German and British opinion. It served as a convenient façade for more important events. On July 20th Sir Horace Wilson briefed Kemsley on what to say if received by high-ranking Nazis.

On July 27th Kemsley had more than an hour's talk with Hitler in the Wagner House at Bayreuth, after both had attended a performance of *Parsifal*. Hitler contemptuously dismissed the contents of the Hudson–Wohlthat talks: "these did not interest him because Germany was not after money." But in response to Kemsley's question "as to whether Herr Hitler had any proposals to make for a better understanding, he [Hitler] suggested that each country should put its demands on paper, and that this might lead to a discussion." Hitler mentioned he was after colonies and the cancellation of the Versailles Treaty.

Was this the sign which Chamberlain had been waiting for, coming directly from Hitler? Had he not been cordial, reasonable and forthcoming? Had he actually cracked under the strain of the crisis of nerves?

During the evening of July 31st, after Lord Kemsley had seen the Prime Minister earlier and then handed in the written notes of his discussion with Hitler, Chamberlain, Halifax and Wilson sat discussing the question. They were obviously excited, but aware of the need to act cautiously and in the greatest secrecy. Besides Sir Alexander Cadogan, no one in the Foreign Office was to be let in on the plan. "Harmless" and "useless' was Cadogan's opinion when he was informed. His experienced assessment proved precise.

Chamberlain and Halifax decided to take Hitler up. They thought the "best step" was "to put questions to see what exactly is meant by the suggestions" about each country putting its demands on paper. "It is recognised", Sir Horace Wilson wrote in his minute of the conversation, "that care would have to be taken to make it clear that we were not ourselves in any way anxious to start discussions, that we regarded the suggestion as indicating a German initiative and that all we were doing at the moment was to try and ascertain what that initiative denoted".[21] The next day, August 1st, Wilson prepared the appropriate draft letter. He showed it that afternoon to Lord Kemsley who "was quite ready to adopt it and to send it".

"I urged upon Lord Kemsley again the importance of secrecy", Wilson recorded. "He said he would have the letter typed in his private office and, at my suggestion, he agreed to send his secretary . . . to see Dietrich and to give him the letter by hand."

The "Kemsley letter" put Hitler on the spot. It asked Dietrich to secure from Hitler a written statement, showing precisely what he wished to be discussed and what proposals he had in mind. On this basis, British opinion could be convinced that confidence in his intentions could be re-established. "Simply in my private capacity as a newspaper proprietor", Kemsley concluded, "I can take the next step."

Otto Dietrich needed an interpreter to help with his poor English when reading the "Kemsley letter" on August 3rd. He also had difficulty of another kind – with the core of the letter. For it "contained a reference to the Führer saying that 'if we put down on paper' our views, it might lead to a better understanding. He thought there must have been some misunderstanding about this, as he was sure the Führer did not use those words 'put down'."

Had Kemsley really misunderstood Hitler? Or had Hitler meanwhile changed his mind? Was Dietrich wary of approaching Hitler? Such questions must have occurred to both Chamberlain and Wilson as they read, on August 4th, the note of the conversation made by Kemsley's secretary. On August 17th they discovered the answer. Hitler let Kemsley know via Dietrich that, until confidence had been restored, there was "no object in preparing for conversations".[22] The reply was as clever as it was baffling.

Before Hitler's message had been received, however, preparations were going ahead in 10 Downing Street for what was considered a major breakthrough. Kemsley's report of his conversation with Hitler had seemingly prepared the ground and the mood. The German Embassy in London also seemed even more forthcoming than usual.

During the early evening of August 2nd, R. A. Butler received a visit at his home from Theo Kordt. He had been asked by Ernst von Weizsäcker to return to Berlin. But first he wanted to see "some very authoritative person". Alternatively, Chamberlain or Sir Horace Wilson should immediately receive Dirksen. Kordt had "questions of major policy" on his mind, Butler wrote to Wilson that same evening. Would Britain recognise German *Lebensraum* in eastern Europe if Hitler gave an assurance of "quietude by some concrete act". Kordt also asked: "were they to regard your & Rob's [Robert Hudson] conversation with Wohlthat as meaning anything?" According to Kordt, Hitler "had shown interest" in these conversations.

Disregarding what Hitler had already told Lord Kemsley – that Wohlthat's report did not interest him – Chamberlain plunged ahead. He preferred to stay in the background himself and delegated Wilson to see either Kordt or the German Ambassador. Lord Halifax was kept informed by Butler.

On August 3rd it was Dirksen and not Kordt who appeared on the doorstep of Sir Horace Wilson's home. Wilson was not surprised: "I concluded that it had been thought wiser for Number One to come rather than Number Two."

For nearly two hours, Wilson and Dirksen discussed political issues and exchanged ideas. Afterwards, both men wrote records of the conversation. Once again the discrepancy is glaring and revealing. According to Wilson's record, it was Dirksen who was anxious to know where the British government stood after the talks with Wohlthat. Wilson replied that he had told Wohlthat nothing which had not previously been stated publicly by Chamberlain and Halifax. A new round of appeasement "was dependent entirely upon the pre-restoration of the confidence that had been shattered in March." A relaxation of mobilisation, toning down the German press and public speeches, patience over Danzig, or even a declaration of eventual autonomy or home rule for Bohemia and Moravia were the sort of concrete gestures Wilson said Britain was looking for.

Dirksen replied, according to Wilson, that Hitler wanted something from the British side. He had no confidence in British intentions.

"We were in a vicious circle", Wilson commented. But Dirksen put forward a suggestion – revealing what he was after. "Was it possible to frame an agenda and a programme that would include points that interested him [Hitler] and was it possible, without of course trying to get an actual agreement, to show that there were reasonable prospects of progress being made?"

Wilson firmly stood his ground. So long as "German troops were marching up and down the Polish frontier" it was useless to arrange an agenda or bother about Wohlthat's "framework". The next step depended entirely on Hitler. What had he in mind to follow up Wohlthat's report? Can he be sure to prevent an explosion in the coming weeks? And what sign can he give as a precondition to successful negotiations?[23]

On the other hand, the German Ambassador sat down and produced a different record, which has wrongly indicted Sir Horace Wilson ever since. According to Dirksen, Wilson confirmed in detail the programme of negotiations he had originally suggested to Wohlthat. In fact, it was for this very reason that Dirksen claimed Wilson himself asked for the interview.* For the rest, Dirksen's record closely followed that made by Wilson, except for the warning that "Chamberlain would probably be forced to resign" if details of future Anglo-German negotiations were to leak out.

Before parting from Dirksen, Wilson hinted he was unenthusiastic about having any further talks with Theo Kordt. But if, as

---

* There is no evidence for Dirksen's allegation in the letter written to Wilson by Butler on August 3rd. Therefore, Dirksen presumably feared to give his Berlin superiors the impression that he was chasing after the British and stated Wilson had asked for the interview. It is significant that a new security man from the Gestapo was attached during July to Dirksen's Embassy to keep an eye on him. (FO371/22975, C10611/15/18.)

a result of Kordt's visit to Berlin, "his instructions were such as to indicate that his Government wished to make any move," Wilson said he would be available.

The next move in this delicate game of positions was dependent, in the British view, on Germany. Wilson reported that evening to the Prime Minister and they discussed strategy. Chamberlain felt, subject to Lord Halifax's concurrence, that the "wise course would be to keep the movement alive if the Germans wished that to be the case. This process might include a discussion as to what items should make up the agenda." On August 4th Halifax told Wilson he was satisfied: "the aim would be to discuss a hypothetical agenda and programme for possible use in hypothetical circumstances."[24]

———

In the unpredictable summer of 1939, "hypothetical circumstances" were the most dangerous to plan for. On August 9th Dirksen saw Halifax to say goodbye before going on leave. Not a word was said about the conversation with Sir Horace Wilson. Kordt had paid an obviously fruitless visit to Berlin. Dirksen only hinted "that the possibility of resolving antagonisms by means of negotiation was blocked on all sides." Halifax later replied that the "signal" from Hitler would be awaited. Then, given a period of calm, the British government would still be interested "to discuss appeasement questions".

The German Ambassador arrived in Berlin on August 14th. He never returned to London. Ribbentrop refused to see him. Dirksen discovered that his conversation with Wilson had been interpreted by officials in Berlin as a "further sign of Britain's weakness". Anglo-German negotiations for a settlement of all outstanding issues did not have priority on the Nazi agenda.

On August 20th Hitler sent a secret message to Sir Horace Wilson via the press adviser to the German Embassy, Fritz Hesse. Hitler had seen the reports of Wohlthat and Dirksen. However, "if they were proceeded with the effect would be so to obscure the Danzig question as to lead to its abandonment." This question must be settled directly between Germany and

Poland. Only then Hitler intended to put forward his proposals for a general settlement, including an Anglo-German alliance.[25]

Hitler obviously intended to have Danzig. The British had hoped to defuse this issue by burying it within the prospects of a general settlement. Hitler refused to bite. The break in the menacing silence had miserably failed. The publicity encouraged Hitler to believe he would get Danzig. It also helped to convince the Russians that their security could best be bought in Berlin rather than London.

CHAPTER TEN

Moscow Morass

THE members of the Cabinet leaving 10 Downing Street after their meeting on May 24th were pleased, though for different reasons. Following weeks of stubborn resistance, Neville Chamberlain had finally consented to ally with the USSR on terms he personally could swallow. His closest sympathisers fully shared his relief. The pro-alliance faction were content, despite some misgivings, that they had actually persuaded the Prime Minister to concede as much as he did.

After lunch Chamberlain went to the House of Commons. As a result of proposals about to be telegraphed to Moscow, "full agreement at an early date" could be expected, he told Parliament. Despite some outstanding points, "I do not anticipate that these are likely to give rise to any serious difficulty."[1] Chamberlain then travelled to Chequers for a rest, and later went fishing in Wales. When he returned to London, he was shocked to discover how much he had underestimated possible Soviet objections to the proposals he had himself largely concocted.

The first sign of trouble came on May 25th. Sir William Seeds informed the Deputy Commissar for Foreign Affairs, Vladimir Potemkin, that the British and French governments accepted a triple alliance, "based on a system of mutual guarantees in general conformity with the principles of the League of Nations." What precisely was implied by this reference to the League? Potemkin asked. Seeds had no clue. The Narkomindel was really in no doubt. The precise reasons and motives which had inspired Chamberlain's manoeuvre were known. The Russians had no intention to sign what, in their view, would be a "scrap of paper".[2]

Fortified with three detailed telegrams explaining the Anglo-French proposals and a first draft treaty, Sir William Seeds and the French Chargé d'Affaires, Jean Payart, were received in the Kremlin on May 27th. The Foreign Commissar, Vyacheslav Molotov, sat at a large desk on a seemingly raised dais, with the Anglo-French representatives and the interpreter before him. The draft treaty was translated orally into Russian. Seeds afterwards described how astounded he and Payart were by Molotov's reaction. Neither could believe their ears.

The Anglo-French proposals were unacceptable and rejected, Molotov decisively said. They were "calculated to ensure the maximum of talk and the minimum of results." The British and the French "were prepared to visualise Moscow being bombed by the aggressor while Bolivia was busy blocking all action in Geneva." Besides, nothing definite was said as to the conclusion of a military treaty and too much regard was being paid to the susceptibilities of other powers.

Sir William Seeds produced in vain his best debating points. He found argument was futile, and even feared Molotov's brutal attitude was a manoeuvre to close the negotiations. He advised Lord Halifax to concede to the Russians the point of simultaneously negotiating a military treaty.

Another tedious meeting, "on sadly familiar lines", followed on May 29th. Seeds was afterwards left with the definite impression that the Soviet Union would stubbornly insist on a guarantee of the Baltic states. He was also apprehensive: "My impression of these two long conversations is that it is my fate to deal with a man totally ignorant of foreign affairs and to whom the idea of negotiation . . . is utterly alien."[3]

Any lingering doubt about the tough Soviet position was effectively destroyed by a remarkable speech which Molotov delivered on May 31st to the Supreme Soviet of the USSR. He offered no hope of any arrangement except on Soviet terms. For the careful listener, he also hinted at the alternative. Political negotiations with Britain and France, he stated, did not preclude commercial negotiations with Germany. Talks about a new German credit to the USSR were interrupted earlier in the year.

"Now there are certain indications that negotiations may be resumed."

This was Molotov's first public speech as the new Soviet Foreign Commissar. It was also the first and last public mention by a Soviet statesman of the secret negotiations which led, on August 23rd, to the German-Soviet pact. In a telegram to London on June 1st, Seeds stated that he regarded a German-Soviet political agreement as "just a possibility". Further commercial negotiations, however, should be expected. "A good telegram (in parts)" is the only Foreign Office minute on Seeds' assessment.

On June 2nd Molotov handed Seeds and the French Ambassador, Paul Émile Naggiar, a document which he described as the Anglo-French draft treaty, modified to meet Soviet views. It contained two controversial issues. Belgium, Greece, Turkey, Rumania, Poland, Latvia, Estonia and Finland were specifically listed. Aggression against any would automatically invoke the treaty. Reservations as to their "rights and position" – a British suggestion – were considered unnecessary. The Soviets also now proposed the simultaneous entry into force of the political and military agreements.[4] Molotov was to soft-pedal on this last proposal – Article Six. Explicit guarantees to the border states was to be next on his methodical agenda. This the British and French finally conceded on June 26th. Article Six took weeks of complicated haggling before that, too, was settled on July 23rd to Molotov's satisfaction.

A feeling of depression had already seized London long before Molotov handed over the first Soviet draft treaty. On May 24th the excitement of the chase appeared to be over. A week later it was evident that the hunt for agreement had only begun. There seemed few prepared for such a long haul. Sir Alexander Cadogan was downhearted at how "tiresome and contemptuous" Molotov had been towards the proposals. For the lonely struggle of the Ambassador in Moscow, Cadogan had praise and sympathy. "I am sorry for Sir W. Seeds, who did his best in difficult circumstances." He "kept his end up fairly well."

Neville Chamberlain could spare little time for sympathy,

except possibly for himself. He found the whole situation, as he told Joseph Kennedy on June 9th, "most annoying". If the USSR rejected Britain's proposals, he was tempted to call the whole thing off.[5] His disappointment was understandable. He had counted on a quick conclusion of a treaty. Had he not conceded the main Soviet demand for reciprocal mutual assistance? Had not a British government actually guaranteed Bolshevik Russia against attack?

The fact that the Prime Minister's concession had not been made earlier, when it could have been used as a valuable bargaining point, only vitiated the drama of the British gesture. The manner in which Chamberlain clothed his concession aroused Soviet suspicions of his intentions. From early June the whole character of the Anglo-French-Soviet negotiations changed. Mutual mistrust festered and increased as the weeks passed. The debate in the Cabinet and the exchange of notes and telegrams between London and Moscow degenerated into a legal charade. Tempers were frayed, threats were voiced but not carried out, and perspective seemed drowned. The hopes of millions were starved by the snail's pace of progress.

Why then continue such seemingly farcical negotiations? The British, of course, hoped to ensure Soviet military support for the isolated Poles: the original inspiration of the talks. But the fundamental reason remained that British intelligence knew Berlin and Moscow were in secret contact. The information was imperfect, though serious. To forestall any Nazi-Soviet agreement, negotiations with Moscow had to continue. Frustration and humiliation were the price for keeping Hitler away from Stalin's door.

The Russians, for their part, were threatened by spasmodic fighting with the Japanese in Mongolia, suspicious to the point of paranoia about the "appeasing" Neville Chamberlain, unsure of Hitler's ultimate intentions, and wary of his discreet feelers. They had no choice but to persevere out of a desperate hunger for security. Meanwhile, they would continue squeezing concessions from the British government. The clamour of British parliamentary and public opinion for an alliance would prevent a breakdown. At the same time, the Russians also waited for Hitler to advance concrete offers.

The telegram containing the Soviet draft treaty of June 2nd was circulated the next day. Looking at it, the Prime Minister commented: "I should be disposed to refuse to guarantee the Baltic States." The most he would concede was for consultations to take place if these states were threatened.[6] When the Foreign Policy Committee met on June 5th, Neville Chamberlain had little difficulty in convincing his colleagues of the wisdom of his views. Agreement on a new reply was quickly reached.

What proved to be a more thorny problem was how to speed up the negotiations. An obviously "bad effect" was being created by the continued exchange of cabled proposals and counter-proposals. Lord Halifax told the Committee that some kind of mission to Moscow was bad tactics. It would "give the impression that we were running after the Russians." The only alternative was to recall Seeds, brief him fully, and then let him go ahead on his own with Molotov.

One unnamed member of the Committee used this opportunity to criticise Seeds. He was not using "any close or sustained argument" and merely exchanged notes. What was needed was an "expert adviser . . . to reinforce" him and explain British proposals to Molotov. Another Minister then suggested that the Foreign Office legal expert, Sir William Malkin, might make the trip. The idea met with general assent. Lord Halifax, however, was unhappy at this prospect. Without Malkin, there was no one in the Foreign Office who could make sense of the negotiations and draft the ingenious replies necessary. Halifax and Chamberlain agreed afterwards, in a private tête-à-tête, that Malkin could not be spared. They decided the Ambassador should be recalled for consultation.

Sir William Seeds read the telegram ordering his recall while confined to bed with influenza. He hoped his doctor would allow him to travel in two or three days' time. A hasty discussion of this setback on the morning of June 7th led to one of the most controversial decisions of these negotiations. Seeds was ordered to remain in Moscow. "I have decided instead", Halifax cabled to him, "to send someone to Moscow with full instructions in order to assist you in the further negotiations with M. Molotov."[7] The official chosen was William Strang, head of the Central Department of the Foreign Office, who had served at the British Embassy in Moscow from 1930–33. Such were the precise origins of Strang's mission.

Speed had seemed essential. The intentions were honourable; the plan dictated by circumstance. Yet the decision was made not to await Seeds' recovery. Should a more dramatic gesture have been made?

There were some who were prepared to try and close the breach between Britain and the USSR. A former American Ambassador to Moscow, Joseph E. Davies, still a keen observer of the Russian scene, was anxious to be of service. His dominating fear was a German-Soviet alliance. On April 18th he had asked the State Department to be permitted to undertake a special mission to Moscow. President Roosevelt himself wisely turned down this offer. Davies would have spoken in Moscow with no authority other than his own.

In early June, Anthony Eden stepped forward. He had kept in close touch with his successor as Foreign Secretary, Lord Halifax. Frequent meetings with him gave Eden the benefit of full inside information on the negotiations. He suggested that, as the only British Minister ever to have been received by Stalin (in 1935), he be allowed to visit Moscow and speed up the negotiations. "Halifax pondered the proposition and seemed to like it." However, Chamberlain preferred to deny Eden any possible glory.[8]

Lord Halifax himself toyed with the idea of trying his hand with the Russians. On June 8th, he told the Soviet Ambassador, Ivan Maisky, that he had been advised himself to go to Moscow. Rather modestly, he had concluded that "this kind of business was better handled by Ambassadors". Within two days Maisky received instructions to inform Halifax that "his coming would be welcomed in Moscow". This invitation Halifax politely declined.

The announcement of a visit by Chamberlain or Halifax doubtless would have been greeted with enthusiasm from all sides. It

would have flattered Russian dignity, assuaged their susceptibilities, and convinced them the British were genuinely anxious
for a pact, a point on which there was considerable doubt in
Moscow. Maisky was privately saying that the British government "was at bottom opposed to a pact and was reluctantly and
gradually being pushed against its will into making one." That
impression was a chief reason for Soviet suspicions and stiff
attitudes. Although Strang's mission officially evoked no adverse
Soviet reaction, Maisky was again, privately, unenthusiastic:
"Strang was not 'big enough'."[9]

Strang was adequate, however, to continue the haggling in
Moscow. There were still basic areas of dispute which Chamberlain was not yet prepared to concede. Nevertheless, a serious
error of tactics was committed. This was more than just a
"routine assignment" as Strang later contended. It would have
been better not to have sent anyone. Alternatively, Maisky's
invitation, which he later alleged was designed "to probe the
genuine intentions" of the British government,[10] should have
been accepted. *

William Strang, at the time on a fact finding tour of Poland,
hurried back to London where he arrived on June 8th. He
immediately threw himself into the hectic work at the Foreign
Office preparing for his visit to Moscow. A foretaste of obstacles
he was to face was given him when attending the Foreign Policy
Committee on June 9th. The discussions he witnessed were
tedious and more suited to legal rather than political minds.

The Foreign Office had drawn up a series of memoranda laying
down the lines of various possible approaches to each article of
the draft treaty. It was hoped that this would enable Sir William
Seeds, with the help of Strang, to build up a triple alliance article
by article. The Foreign Policy Committee spent a long time

* Sir William Seeds still holds very strong views about this episode. He
emphasises that Strang's mission was simply to brief him on various
aspects of Britain's diplomatic commitments which Molotov queried and
on which he had little information. Seeds believes it was a mistake to
have sent Strang. He is quite convinced, however, that a visit by any of the
"politicians" would have proved futile. (Author's interview with Sir
William Seeds, September 18th, 1968.)

debating these memoranda, particularly on how to tackle the Russian demand for a guarantee of the Baltic states.

Almost as much debate centred on the question of tactics. Lord Halifax forcefully put the case for carrying on despite all obstacles. He admitted to "considerable distrust of Bolshevik guarantees and undertakings" and was sure the Russians would act entirely in their own interests. Nevertheless, by an agreement with Russia "we should have safeguarded ourselves for the time being against what might be the most serious danger, namely, an agreement between Germany and Russia and we should also have gone far to safeguard the position of Poland. It seemed clear that Russia was anxious to secure the maintenance of Poland's independence and had no wish to see Poland destroyed." For someone who had just expressed distrust of Soviet undertakings, this last belief was extremely naive.

The Prime Minister was himself aware of the "psychological value at the present time" of an agreement. But he was more interested in dealing with the Russians as he felt they had handled him. He wanted "to drive a hard bargain", and "did not think that Russia could now afford to break off negotiations". The Government should take a fairly stiff line.[11]

The man responsible for reinforcing Chamberlain's decision to drive a hard bargain was William C. Bullitt, the American Ambassador in Paris. Before returning to Washington to consult with President Roosevelt, he had spoken to Sir Eric Phipps. Bullitt was clear on the need for an agreement with the USSR. But he was "still more convinced that we shall never reach it if we give them the impression that we are running after them."

Bullitt spoke with the authority of personal experience as a former Ambassador to the Soviet Union. His advice also had the advantage of coinciding with Chamberlain's own inclinations. Not surprisingly, therefore, Bullitt's views were approvingly described to the Cabinet on June 7th and to the Foreign Policy Committee two days later. On the former occasion, Halifax explained that it was also a "good reason against sending a Minister to Russia".[12]

William Strang, accompanied by another Foreign Office official,

Frank Roberts, arrived in Moscow on June 14th. Above all the other instructions they carried, one brief sentence stood out. Conclude a treaty "as short and simple in its terms as possible", the Foreign Office had instructed. "It is better that agreement should be quickly reached than that time should be spent in trying to cover every contingency." Increasingly suspicious, the Soviets intended to cover every contingency, to leave no loopholes in the text which the British could exploit.

Inside the Kremlin, from behind a desk which appeared mistakenly to be on a raised dais, Vyacheslav Molotov saw a new face on the afternoon of June 15th. It was William Strang having his first Moscow experience of the negotiations. Molotov immediately launched into an "irritating" interrogation of Anglo-French commitments. Strang was able to handle this with skill and discretion. Having satisfied his curiosity and expressed his disappointment at the latest Anglo-French proposals, Molotov retired to consult his superiors.

The next day the Foreign Commissar let loose at the Anglo-French negotiators. Sir William Seeds described how "M. Molotov was most emphatic in his anxiety to make us understand that, in his view, the British and French governments were treating the Russians as simpletons (*naivny*) and fools (*duraki*). It became necessary for M. Potemkin [acting as interpreter] to assure him that he had well and truly rendered the word *duraki* as *imbéciles*." A way must be found to guarantee the Baltic states, Molotov insisted. Otherwise, the Soviet government was prepared to sign instead a simple triple alliance, guaranteeing mutual assistance only in case of direct attack against Britain, France or the USSR. In a telegram to his Ambassadors in London and Paris, Molotov accused the British and French governments of not seeking a "serious treaty in line with the principle of reciprocity and equality of obligations".[13]

Was Molotov issuing an ultimatum by this suggestion? Lord Halifax preferred to take it as proof that Molotov "was not seeking an excuse to break off the negotiations". The suggestion itself was quickly rejected in the Foreign Office. Halifax admitted it "would be a plain confession of defeat, [and] would encourage

Hitler". It also negated the object of the negotiations – protection for Poland and other states.

Once again concessions seemed the only solution. Neville Chamberlain, in a humiliating about face, agreed to drop the reference to the League. On June 19th, Halifax informed Seeds that this and the other previously cherished stipulation as to the "rights and position of other Powers" could be omitted. Staff conversations could begin as soon as the political agreement was signed. "I attach the greatest importance to early and rapid progress", Halifax exhorted his Ambassador.[14] And in this desire for speed, the Baltic states were slowly being abandoned.

The meeting of the Foreign Policy Committee on June 20th added further to the list of concessions. Despite strong distaste, it was agreed that the treaty should include a no separate peace clause as Molotov had demanded. The Committee also confirmed the decision against falling back on a triple pact of mutual assistance.

THE PRIME MINISTER thought that . . . the disadvantage was not only that public opinion would think that the negotiations had, in fact, failed but that Russia would be left in a very dissatisfied and sulky state.

THE SECRETARY OF STATE FOR FOREIGN AFFAIRS warned the Committee that information from many different sources pointed to the necessity, after we had gone so far, of reaching an agreement with Russia, as otherwise Hitler might well be encouraged to take some violent action.

THE PRIME MINISTER thought that the Russians had every intention of reaching an agreement but wished to get the best possible terms by bargaining.

The haggling in the Kremlin was to continue.

With their new instructions, the Anglo-French representatives made two more visits to the Kremlin on June 21st and 22nd. The discussions ended in deadlock. In Molotov's view no progress had been made. The two meetings only confirmed the total rejection by the Soviet government of all Anglo-French efforts at compromise. "Argumentation and skilful formulae" were exhausted, Seeds telegraphed to London on June 23rd. Either accept Soviet demands to guarantee the Baltic states and list them by name, he advised, or fall back on a simple triple pact of mutual assistance.[15]

Neville Chamberlain did not like Seeds' analysis of the choice. The Baltic states must not be listed by name in the treaty "for the good reason that all of them strongly objected to this procedure", he told the Foreign Policy Committee on June 26th. The British government "had made concession after concession". He seemed determined to draw the line, though he had to admit that "we were nothing like as expert in this bazaar haggling".

Such a dogmatic stance invited argument. There were many Ministers determined to secure an agreement at any price. Lord Halifax was among them. He tried firstly to explain Russian psychology to the Prime Minister, pointing out that they were a suspicious people who feared a British trap. "They suffered acutely from inferiority complex and considered that ever since the Great War the Western Powers had treated Russia with haughtiness and contempt."

When Chamberlain proved unimpressed by this, Halifax talked common sense. The British guarantee to Poland had given Russia considerable security, and had strengthened Molotov's bargaining position. His government was perfectly "free to decide on the day whether Russia should collaborate with the Western Powers or not." Chamberlain disagreed.

Halifax pointed out finally that the difference between agreeing to Molotov's demand to name the Baltic states in the treaty itself or listing them in a secret protocol, which would leak out, was not substantial enough to justify a collapse of the negotiations. Besides, Halifax added, it was still vital "to block the door to any agreement between Germany and Soviet Russia".

Against such argument, supported by most of the Committee, Chamberlain was forced to retreat. Never one to do so without exacting a price, he now demanded that Switzerland and Holland be added to the list of guaranteed states. Halifax hated to see Chamberlain admitting defeat, and declared his support for the idea. He described it as the "acid test of Soviet sincerity and good faith". In his only recorded contribution to the discussion, Leslie Burgin, the designate Minister of Supply, summed up the prospects: the "importance of securing an agreement with Russia was much greater than the risk of offending the smaller states."

This latest batch of concessions, along with others urged by Sir William Seeds and the French government, were telegraphed to Moscow during the following few days. Britain had tried to avoid driving the Baltic states into the arms of Germany, Halifax explained to the Ambassador. "In the last resort we are prepared to take this risk in order to get the treaty." These instructions were accompanied by a strongly implied warning that no further "obstacles" from the Russians would be tolerated. "We must dig our toes in" even if that led to a breakdown, Sir Alexander Cadogan commented.[16]

This mood was shared by Neville Chamberlain. On June 28th, in his room at the House of Commons, he faced a highly critical deputation from the National Council of Labour. Among the problems discussed was the danger of a breakdown in the negotiations. When pressed as to his opinion of the consequences, the Prime Minister replied, "in his flat, obstinate way, 'Well, I don't think that would be the end of the world'."[17]

Negotiating with Molotov always held surprises. On July 1st he added a refreshing touch of compliance to his usual obstinacy. The British and French Ambassadors had arrived at the Kremlin prepared to see a list of guaranteed states included in the published treaty. Without argument, Molotov indicated his government was willing to have the list embodied in a secret annex.

Then came the surprises. To include the Netherlands, Switzerland and Luxembourg, the latter added at French insistence, was out of the question, Molotov said in his familiar peremptory tone. The first two states did not even have diplomatic relations with the USSR. Almost casually he raised another point. Germany had been successful in undermining the independence of Czechoslovakia without a violent clash. The Anglo-French-Soviet treaty, therefore, should apply equally in cases of both direct and "indirect" aggression. A definition of indirect aggression, by which Molotov explained he meant an "internal *coup d'état* or a reversal of policy in the interests of the aggressor", must appear in the secret annex. Seeds was quick-witted enough to retort that all this was not mentioned in the Soviet draft treaty advanced on June 2nd. Molotov was unimpressed. He had his right to raise new points during discussions.

On July 4th the British government received the full reports of the latest encounters in the Kremlin. The negotiations had reached crisis point. Lord Halifax asked the Foreign Policy Committee, meeting that day, whether the Government should either break off the negotiations or conclude a limited triple alliance? He personally favoured struggling on: "as our *main object* in the negotiations was to prevent Russia from engaging herself with Germany."[18]

Despite the formidable obstacles and perpetual hurdles to be overcome, Lord Halifax had remained a convinced supporter of an Anglo-Soviet alliance. He regarded the negotiations as the "most important factor in the situation". With public opinion everywhere waiting to see if they were concluded, the British government could not risk a breakdown. He was unmoved by criticism that an agreement with the USSR would provoke Hitler and destroy any chance for peace. "It would be folly for us not to conclude an agreement with Russia at the present time in view of our commitments in Eastern Europe," he observed, "and the Nazis themselves would be the first to despise us for omitting so obvious a precaution." He also rejected the German argument that the negotiations were an "insuperable obstacle to any conciliatory initiative on Hitler's part". On the contrary, they were being pursued because of the "sobering influence" they would have in Berlin.[19] After an agreement with the USSR had been reached, the Allied Powers could approach Berlin from greater strength. That would be the moment to renew Anglo-German contacts.

Neville Chamberlain had remained an interested though bemused spectator of these dealings with Moscow, forced to suppress his strong distaste and suspicion of the Russians. He let

Halifax lead the running, and patiently waited for what he considered to be the inevitable breakdown. Describing the negotiations with Russia to his sister on July 2nd, Chamberlain emphasised his ever increasing suspicions of Soviet intentions. In view of the Cabinet's anxiety to achieve an alliance and their fears of the results of a breakdown, he had to tread carefully. However, "I am so sceptical of the value of Russian help", he wrote, "that I should not feel our position was greatly worsened if we had to do without them." He was impatient with the time being absorbed by the negotiations. If he had his way, they would have been terminated, successful or not, weeks ago.[20]

These discussions could not be peremptorily closed, as Chamberlain himself must have realised. The British and French were already too deeply involved. Besides, the talking had to continue if an agreement between Stalin and Hitler was to be stymied.

Early in June, Paris received reports of a conversation Hitler was supposed to have had with Generals Keitel and Brauchitsch, who emphasised the importance of Russia's attitude. Brauchitsch warned that if Russia marched against Germany a war would be lost. The French Prime Minister, Edouard Daladier, used this report to warn the Foreign Office of the dangers of further delay.

Information of any sort was always suspect in London if it came from the French; particularly when they had a vested interest. So it was with caution that Frank Roberts commented on June 10th: "It is of course plainly in the German interest to put such confident stories about, just as it is in the Russian interest to frighten us with the bogy of an agreement with Germany." Besides, there was a conflict of evidence as to the truth of the whole story.[21]

Yet the sheer persistence of intelligence that Germany was working for a rapprochement with the USSR and that the two countries were in contact could not be, and was not, ignored. On June 2nd, agents of the Director of Naval Intelligence, Admiral Godfrey, reported that Ribbentrop had sent three of his best assistants to Moscow to help in the negotiations. Direct contact between Berlin and Moscow had been resumed, Stafford

Cripps, a Labour MP, warned Halifax a week later. In Berlin people were asking "when will comrade Stalin be paying his visit to the Führer?" On June 13th Sir Nevile Henderson wrote: "I feel intuitively that the Germans are getting at Stalin." Field-Marshal Göring had boasted to him: "Germany and Russia will not always be enemies."[22]

The most accurate information curiously came not from secret intelligence, but rather from the Soviet Embassy in Berlin. Replying to an inquiry from the British Press Attaché, the Soviet Counsellor, Georgi Astakhov, confirmed that "commercial conversations" between Moscow and Berlin were proceeding. They "were of an informatory character only", no definite proposals had yet been made, and the initiative had been taken by Germany. Astakhov was never again to speak with such honesty and frankness.

Moscow itself was the most difficult place to gather intelligence. Nevertheless, Sir William Seeds carefully observed the activity at the German Embassy. He noted the arrival and departure of its officials and drew the conclusions – accurate for the time – that only commercial negotiations were in progress.[23]

Sir Robert Vansittart's "diminishing band of German moderates" also kept him informed. He sent Halifax their most recent news on June 16th. "The military are delighted to have got Hitler on the path to an arrangement with Soviet Russia and assure him that this prospect has frightened the British statesmen and made them again uncertain." Hitler planned "to connive with Russia and build up a big bloc of friendly or vassal states . . . around the Reich". This report was circulated in the Foreign Office and carefully studied. It exactly coincided with another disturbing account.

"Herr Kordt stated definitely that Germans and Russians are in contact as the result of an approach made by Herr von Ribbentrop to the Soviet Ambassador in Berlin. The German aim appeared to be to neutralise Russia. . . . Herr Kordt's conclusion is that if we want an agreement with Russia we had better be quick about it!"

This was the message Dr Erich Kordt, Senior Counsellor in

Ribbentrop's office and the brother of Theo Kordt, had travelled to London to deliver. At great personal risk and under the guise of wishing to holiday in Scotland, Kordt had brought on June 16th an unmistakable warning. An Anglo-Soviet pact, in his opinion, would be a strong deterrent to war. It was unfortunate, however, that Sir Alexander Cadogan had recorded the view that he did not "trust either of the Kordts".[24]

Throughout June almost daily reports came into the Foreign Office. European military attachés dropped hints to their British counterparts. Well-informed ambassadors in London and on the continent told the same story. An agreement between Germany and the USSR would soon be completed. The object was the cynical division of eastern Europe between the two great powers.[25] Each item of news, gossip or intelligence, however incidental, was forwarded to Lord Halifax for his personal attention.

The Intelligence Department of the War Office was meanwhile also assessing developments. On July 4th a report, provoked by the "unusually large number of rumours" of a German-Soviet rapprochement, was drawn up. Secret intelligence did not unfortunately add up to a uniform picture.

At the end of June, Admiral Canaris, head of the *Abwehr*, "was reported to have said that negotiations were in progress, that the USSR would not support Poland in war, and that they would supply Germany with raw materials." There was however contradictory evidence, including

> at least one most secret report indicating that the Germans held the view that the elimination of Stalin was essential for their plans. Another most secret report from a reliable source on the Russian side stated that Stalin was very bitter on account of German intrigues in the Ukraine and that, so long as he remained, no question of a rapprochement was possible. A further report early in June stated that although certain sections of influential Soviet opinion might be against active co-operation with the Western Powers, yet the feeling against Germany was still very bitter.

What conclusion therefore could be drawn? The War Office

experts justifiably settled for caution. They emphasised there was "no real circumstantial evidence to show that any such rapprochement is in fact in progress of negotiation". On the other hand "there is every possibility that Germany and Russia may reach a commercial agreement". If this succeeded, there would be created

> an atmosphere which, in spite of the personal antagonisms of Stalin and Hitler, may be conducive to the possibility of a future rapprochement, for there is much economic logic to recommend it and there are leading personages in both countries, but particularly in Germany, who desire to bring it about. Although there seems immense ideological difficulties, no opportunist change of policy is impossible to Stalin, and Hitler might well excuse himself by coming to an agreement with Soviet Russia while maintaining his antagonism to the world-revolution policy of the Comintern. The danger of such a rapprochement cannot therefore be discounted, and it is still wise to watch the situation very carefully.[26]

The War Office report, crucial both for its candour and accurate guesswork, reveals that the British government had no accurate intelligence as to the precise details of the secret German-Soviet conversations. They knew contacts were in progress. They also understood German motives in pursuing Stalin and vice versa. But the possibility of a German-Soviet rapprochement was common talk in the Europe of 1939.

In its estimate that a commercial agreement was the talking point between Berlin and Moscow, War Office intelligence was accurate. For June was not an especially fruitful month for advances towards a German-Soviet agreement. Political topics had surfaced briefly from time to time, and had then been submerged under the mutual mistrust. It was still the opening of commercial negotiations which was proving the major stumbling block.

The German government entrusted Gustav Hilger, the Economic Counsellor at the Moscow Embassy, with the task of softening the Russians. After a thorough briefing in Berlin at the end of May, he returned to Moscow and discussed economic questions with Anastas Mikoyan, the Soviet Trade Commissar. A visit by Julius Schurre was tentatively agreed upon. On June 17th Mikoyan was informed that Schurre would be coming with full powers to negotiate a commercial treaty. This enabled Molotov to resist stubbornly any concessions to the British and French Ambassadors during their meetings of June 21st and 22nd.

Then the Russians had a sudden change of mind. Perhaps they were worried about the publicity that might attend the appearance of a German official, coming so soon after William Strang's arrival. They also continued to distrust German motives. Was Berlin not playing a "political game"? Mikoyan pointedly asked Hilger. Before Schurre's visit existing differences should first be ironed out. "We must not lose patience", was Ernst von Weizsäcker's advice in Berlin.[27]

An attempt by Count Friedrich von der Schulenburg, the German Ambassador, to conciliate Molotov on June 29th failed. Mikoyan had obviously spoken under strict orders. There was only one glimmer of hope which Schulenburg carefully noted. Molotov had not mentioned his May 20th demand for the prior construction of a political basis before resuming economic negotiations.

Hitler could be as easily annoyed with the Russians as Neville Chamberlain. As the Führer read the latest telegrams from Moscow, he decided he had had enough. On June 29th he ordered economic discussions to be discontinued and any further political overtures temporarily suspended.[28] An eleven-day pause followed before talks were to resume.

———

The Foreign Policy Committee met on July 4th to consider the Moscow morass. Fatigue, annoyance and cynicism flavoured every remark made by the Committee members. It seemed generally agreed that to continue the negotiations meant interminable discussions. The idea of handing the Russians an ultimatum began to find favour.

Virtually all the Ministers condemned the newest sticking point of the negotiations – Molotov's definition of indirect aggression. "Open to objection", "difficult to swallow" and "obnoxious" were common epithets. Only Oliver Stanley, President of the Board of Trade, doubted whether it was as dangerous as everyone suggested. "If we cared to be cynical we might safely accept it with a mental reservation that if it ever came within sight of having to be implemented we could differ from Soviet Russia on every point of its interpretation."

Lord Halifax added what he called his own "very cynical appreciation". The Soviet government "would act as suited them best at the time, and without the slightest regard to any prior undertakings written or otherwise." They would either support Poland, or alternatively, join with Germany in a new partition of Poland "without a qualm". Neville Chamberlain was not prepared for deviousness on either side. It was "most dangerous and contrary to the public interest" to accept Molotov's definition.

Firmness on this question was equally balanced by conciliation on another. No one was particularly disappointed that Russia had boggled over guaranteeing the Netherlands and Switzerland. It was one debating point the Committee seemed relieved to graciously concede. However, where were the negotiations leading? Even concession on this point, Halifax pointed out, might still involve "interminable arguments . . . and any other novelties M. Molotoff might think fit to produce".

One solution, suggested by Halifax, was after all to fall back on a simple tripartite pact, even though it "would be a ridiculously small mouse for the mountains to have produced". It did have the advantage of destroying the bargaining power of the Soviet government vis-à-vis Germany. Neville Chamberlain plucked up his courage sufficiently to suggest the time for an ultimatum had arrived. He personally would have preferred a simple triple pact, though he realised the disadvantages. He suggested therefore proposing two alternatives to the Russians – to select one or the other "without further ado".

Such a step needed a Cabinet decision. On July 5th, during a lengthy Cabinet debate, Chamberlain received support for the plan he had himself largely devised. Not all Cabinet Ministers were happy with such tough tactics. They seemed reassured by Halifax's opinion that the Soviets would not break off the negotiations. "If this happened, it would, he thought, show that Russia had never seriously intended to conclude a treaty with us." The Cabinet agreed with the new tough policy towards the Russians.[29]

Three strongly worded telegrams of instructions were cabled on July 6th to Sir William Seeds. The British government was prepared to forget about the Netherlands, Switzerland and Luxembourg, provided Molotov abandoned his "completely unacceptable" definition of indirect aggression. The formula the Foreign Office was willing to sanction postulated two prerequisites. There had to be a clear threat of force by another power against the guaranteed state and the obvious abandonment of its independence or neutrality. If agreement could not be reached on these terms, Seeds was informed, a simple triple alliance was the only alternative. "We attach great importance to showing, in the near future, some result of our protracted negotiations." A threat to break off the negotiations was not mentioned!

It took the Anglo-French negotiators in Moscow two days of hard bargaining with Molotov, on July 8th and 9th, to carry out the latest instructions. The conversations were inconclusive. Molotov stood out adamantly against a guarantee to the Netherlands, Switzerland and Luxembourg. Then, perhaps having himself sensed how repulsive was his earlier definition of indirect aggression, he proposed an alternative. * This point was destined never to be settled. Various definitions were telegraphed back and forth between London and Moscow during the next month.

---

* This defined indirect aggression as action accepted, by any of the states in the secret annex "under threat of force by another Power, or without any such threat, involving the use of territory and forces of the State in question for purposes of aggression against that State or against one of the contracting parties, and consequently involving the loss of, by that State, its independence or violation of its neutrality."

The French quickly accepted Molotov's new definition. The British, always last to compromise, took much longer. When they finally agreed it was too late.

The newest surprise which came from Molotov carried the negotiations into fresh fields of dispute and debate. As the treaty neared completion the question of military talks began to lurk ominously in the background. "You realise of course that we cannot agree to make entry into force of Agreement dependent on conclusion of military conversations", Lord Halifax had telegraphed to Sir William Seeds on July 6th. Three days later Halifax had his first hint of real trouble. The details were fully spelled out on July 9th to the astonishment of the Anglo-French negotiators in Moscow.

"There were differences of opinion amongst members of the Soviet Government on some points connected with the Agreement but on this point they were unanimous." Molotov had just expanded Soviet views on Article Six. Besides wishing the political and military agreements to enter into force simultaneously, he now insisted they be signed at the same time. Prior to this, the political agreement, although initialled, would not even exist as a valid document.

"I think we can carry the negotiations no further without further instructions", Sir William Seeds wearily concluded his record of this conversation at 3.25 in the morning.[30]

CHAPTER ELEVEN

Exit the Russians

"THE Prime Minister said that he could not bring himself to believe that a real alliance between Russia and Germany was possible." This opinion Neville Chamberlain revealed to the Cabinet on July 19th. In February he had confided to the American Ambassador, Joseph Kennedy, that he could not take this possibility seriously. When the subject had been raised at the Committee of Imperial Defence, at the same time, Chamberlain asserted that a German-Soviet rapprochement "was a possible contingency in the future, but was still too remote to necessitate serious consideration at the present time."[1] Almost five months later he was still not worried. While his Cabinet colleagues brooded gloomily over this danger, the Prime Minister was complacent. On the sole authority of Sir Nevile Henderson, he commented, in the Foreign Policy Committee on July 10th, that "it would be quite impossible in present circumstances for Germany and Soviet Russia to come together." It was the question of holding military conversations with the Soviet Union that had evoked Chamberlain's comment.

What several days earlier had been a matter of high principle suddenly became another bargaining point in the Moscow bazaar. Lord Halifax must have startled most of the Committee members by his opening remarks. "Subject to the Soviet Government agreeing to our proposals regarding indirect aggression", he said, "we might try and meet them on the point that staff conversations should be concluded before the political agreement was officially signed." The "best course would be to try to bargain a concession in the matter."

In opposition to the generally tough mood prevailing in

London, the Foreign Secretary nonchalantly proposed making this vital concession. The reasons he gave show that politics and not grand strategy sent an Anglo-French military mission to Moscow. Firstly, "so long as the military conversations were taking place we should be preventing Soviet Russia from entering the German camp", Halifax said. Secondly, it was unlikely any progress would be made during these conversations. They "would drag on and ultimately each side would accept a general undertaking from the other. In this way, we should have gained time and made the best of a situation from which we could not escape."

Even more surprising was the ready assent Chamberlain gave this plan. He admitted he greatly disliked opening military conversations with the Russians. To stand out against it would only cause endless trouble. In any case, he personally "did not attach any great importance to it".

Such frivolities angered Lord Chatfield, the Minister for Co-ordination of Defence. Military conversations were serious matters to him, requiring careful planning, under expert hands. They were not to be undertaken lightly. He told the politicians sitting round the Cabinet table that it would be very difficult to conclude an agreement with the Soviets. They attached great importance to these staff conversations because they wanted a detailed agreement.

"Up to the present we had never made a military agreement with another country and it was a grave matter to decide in advance what particular action in the naval, military or air sphere we, and the French, would be prepared to take in different contingencies and in the case of various countries." Chatfield anticipated that the discussions would be "very prolonged". He preferred them to be conducted on the level of the Deputy Chiefs of Staff, and to take place in London or Paris, but not in Moscow.[2] His instinct about the Russian attitude to military talks was exact.

Chatfield's remarks, however, seemed wasted on the Committee; not least on the Prime Minister. Chamberlain by now regarded these whole proceedings with remarkable equanimity.

He could not see an Anglo-Soviet alliance as a victory, he wrote privately on July 15th. He believed he shared with the Germans a low regard for the Soviet Union's military abilities, and was convinced the Russians could not be trusted. The negotiations had already caused difficulties with otherwise friendly powers. "I would like to have taken a much stronger line with them all through, but I could not have carried my colleagues with me."[3]

For several days the Foreign Office debated and consulted with the French government over the main conclusion reached by the Foreign Policy Committee: to trade Soviet acceptance of the British definition of indirect aggression in return for the opening of staff talks and the simultaneous entry into force of the political and military agreements.

On July 17th the Anglo-French negotiators once again faced Vyacheslav Molotov. Sir William Seeds was acting under strict instructions, approved by the Prime Minister, not to concede, as yet, the opening of immediate staff talks, despite French wishes to do so. Molotov reacted even more curtly than usual. Unless Britain and France "could agree that [the] political and military parts of the agreement between the three countries should form one organic and inseparable whole there was no point in pursuing the present conversations." He then proposed that further discussion should be adjourned until agreement on this point had been reached.

The British and French Ambassadors returned to their Embassies to telegraph their usual early morning reports to London and Paris. Molotov retreated to his office to brief his Ambassadors in the same capitals. The Western Allies, "swindlers and cheats", he telegraphed on July 17th, were resorting to "all kinds of sharp practices and unworthy subterfuges". Without a military agreement, the whole treaty would become an "empty declaration".[4]

Molotov had never before issued an ultimatum to the British and French. Why had he made such an audacious and potentially dangerous gesture? He was aware that the British and French were getting fed up with the negotiations. The answer lay in Berlin.

After having ordered all contact broken off with the Russians at the end of June, Hitler changed his mind. On July 10th Anastas Mikoyan, the Soviet Trade Commissar, was given important news. Gustav Hilger described to him, in full and satisfactory detail, a possible German-Soviet economic agreement. The next step was up to the Russians. Mikoyan listened, according to Hilger's impression, "with obvious interest". The terms were tantalising and hinted at greater adjustments to come.

The Narkomindel ordered E. Babarin, the deputy trade representative in Berlin, to return at once for consultations. More details were needed of what the Germans had in mind. By July 14th Babarin was back in Berlin, instructed to make contact with Julius Schnurre, "in order to discuss with him direct the points that were still not clear". The Soviet government hoped for "final clarification" before committing itself. It had obviously been decided that serious commercial negotiations would provide the testing ground for German intentions. It could pave the way for a political settlement. The Russians now felt free to adopt shock tactics with the British and French. The Germans were to be coaxed and encouraged, the Western Allies prodded into greater concessions. On July 17th, therefore, Molotov issued his ultimatum.

Babarin carried out his instructions on July 18th. The Germans had been previously informed of his return. But they had not been fully forewarned. Babarin had other news which he revealed to Schnurre. "If our discussions resulted in a clarification, he was empowered to sign the treaty here in Berlin." Did the German government agree?

Schnurre reserved his attitude towards what he described as "this astonishing statement". He was puzzled as to why the Russians had decided to shift the negotiations away from their own capital. He rightly concluded that unobtrusive negotiations in Berlin were preferable to damaging publicity in Moscow.[5]

While the Germans pondered their next step, the British debated Molotov's ultimatum. A full day of intensive discussions on July 19th began with a Cabinet meeting. Lord Halifax, as usual, was the main speaker. The unusual aspect of his performance that morning was his cynicism about a possible breakdown. "If the negotiations should, after all, fail," he said, "this would not cause him very great anxiety." For whatever form an agreement finally took, he believed the Russians would ultimately act in their own interests.

Fatigue with the interminable wrangle in Moscow was not the only problem worrying the Foreign Secretary. Secret intelligence was showing that the British and French were being very roughly handled. Halifax stated that

> there was some evidence that Germany was trying to make matters as difficult for us as they could in our negotiations with the Soviet Union. It seemed that some discussions of some kind were proceeding between the German Government and the Soviet Government. It was impossible to assess their real value, but it seemed likely that these discussions related to industrial matters.

For all the rumours circulating of political talks between the Germans and Russians, this was a remarkably accurate assessment. The one Minister who did not share Halifax's worries was Neville Chamberlain. Even to the intelligence at hand, he was turning a wilfully blind eye. He was convinced, as he told Joseph Kennedy the following day, that the Russians had "made up their minds probably not to make a deal with anybody but to watch them all tear themselves apart."[6]

The members of the Foreign Policy Committee then stayed behind in the Cabinet room for their own meeting at 12 noon. It proved an acrimonious gathering. The irritation of all present strikingly intrudes into the minutes of the discussion. Talk of meeting Molotov's ultimatum with a British counter-threat was common, but not shared by all. Sir Samuel Hoare, still enthusiastic for an agreement, pointed out the advantage of keeping the talks alive during the dangerous months of August and September. When he described the disastrous effects a breakdown would have on Britain's allies in eastern Europe, Chamberlain snapped back: must Britain agree to all of Molotov's demands simply to keep these allies "sweet and happy"?

Such irritation inevitably led into a degrading search for scapegoats. Hoare criticised Sir William Seeds for not arguing exhaustively the British case. Chamberlain joined in this witch-hunt by adding that Seeds' records of his conversations gave the impression the British "had been feeble and weak-kneed" when confronting Molotov.

To attack Seeds in this way was short-sighted. He had done his best "in most difficult and disagreeable circumstances", Halifax hotly retorted. Others in the Committee sprang to Seeds' defence. Criticism, they pointed out, should be levelled at the Cabinet not at the Ambassador. His position had been made impossible because he had never been given instructions to stand fast on any particular point. Furthermore, the manner in which Molotov discussed – he "sat aloft enthroned with the two Ambassadors on a much lower level" – added to the difficulties of rational negotiation and sustained argument.

It was then suggested that William Strang should return to London. No, replied Chamberlain, that would be humiliating. Should the Chiefs of Staff begin their preparatory work for the military talks? Lord Chatfield asked. Absolutely not was Chamberlain's peremptory ruling. "He understood that the Sub-Committee had other and even more urgent important questions before it."

After all the acrimony a decision had still to be reached. Chamberlain was in favour of calling the Soviet "bluff by laying down once and for all our final conditions". The Committee agreed to accept Soviet thinking on Article Six, on the condition that the political agreement was first concluded with the British definition of indirect aggression fully accepted. Military talks could then begin at once. Only on this basis could the negotiations continue.[7]

Within two days of having taken this decision contradictory instructions were cabled to Seeds. Such a startling about-face was yet another concession to French prodding. On July 18th in a series of letters and notes from their Embassy in London and in a direct impassioned plea from Georges Bonnet to Lord Halifax, the French urged immediate acceptance of Molotov's views on

Article Six. "M. Bonnet does not think we can afford to fail now", the British Chargé d'Affaires in Paris wrote on July 19th. Even the most humiliating concession, in French opinion, was preferable to a disastrous rupture in the negotiations.[8]

Disregarding the conclusions of the Foreign Policy Committee two days earlier, a telegram was sent to Sir William Seeds on July 21st. The British government was prepared fully to meet Molotov on Article Six, rather than risk a breakdown. Military talks could even begin before the political agreement, including the definition of indirect aggression, was settled.

"I do not like this", Halifax wrote to Seeds and added: "This compromise would avoid a definite break and would afford evidence in other quarters of practical co-operation between Russia, France and ourselves."[9]

This concession was timed, coincidently, with remarkable astuteness. On the evening of July 21st Moscow Radio carried a startling announcement, printed the next morning in the Soviet press. It was a terse statement issued by the Commissariat of Foreign Trade:

> During the last few days negotiations with regard to trade and credit have been renewed between Germany and the USSR. Comrade Babarin, Deputy Trade Representative at Berlin, is conducting negotiations on behalf of the People's Commissariat of Foreign Trade, and Herr Schnurre on behalf of Germany.

Had the Russians gone mad? Just four days earlier Babarin had given Schnurre the distinct impression of wishing to avoid publicity. Why had the Soviet government so blatantly announced what they were doing?

The message to the British government should have been clear. Between July 18th and 21st Helmut Wohlthat was busy in London with his secret conversations for an Anglo-German settlement. Ivan Maisky, the Soviet Ambassador, might have been doing his usually adept homework. His network of informants reached deeply inside all branches of the government. He just might have got wind of these talks and warned the Narkomindel.

Even without such intelligence, Maisky was already sending back assessments which were damaging to the success of the negotiations. On July 14th he had reported the views of Lloyd George that the "Chamberlain clique" was manoeuvring to reach an agreement with Germany. After the parliamentary recess on August 4th, and without the harassment of the Opposition, Chamberlain intended "either to break off the Anglo-Soviet negotiations altogether, or at least to freeze them for an extended period". On July 24th, when Maisky first officially telegraphed the Narkomindel about Wohlthat's talks with Hudson, he jubilantly proclaimed them as a complete vindication of Lloyd George's analysis. The Soviet Ambassador in Paris, Yakov Suritz, reporting on French opinion, had come to the same conclusion as Maisky. "We must expose this game", Suritz had advised his Foreign Commissar on July 19th.[10]

By publicising the German-Soviet commercial negotiations the Russians hoped to warn the British and French that Moscow too could play its German card. The announcement might also have been intended to hasten agreement on Article Six. A breakdown, whatever Molotov had threatened, would have been disastrous. It would have destroyed the leverage necessary to extract concessions from Berlin, and would have isolated the USSR in a hostile Europe. Publicity encouraged the German government to act in a forthcoming manner, and served as protection against a sudden change of mind in Berlin. The announcement seemingly brought satisfactory results from both London and Berlin.

Molotov could not receive Sir William Seeds and Paul Émile Naggiar until July 23rd. He greeted the news that the Soviet version of Article Six was acceptable with "keen satisfaction". The definition of indirect aggression – the focus of such bitter dispute for three weeks – would no longer "raise insuperable difficulties", he unexpectedly said. Why "waste time upon points of detail"? The international situation was threatening. Military conversations should begin at once. The two Ambassadors were taken aback.

On July 25th Lord Halifax telegraphed another concession to Moscow. Although the political agreement was incomplete, the

British government was, he informed Seeds, "ready to agree to immediate initiation of military conversations at Moscow". Molotov received this news on July 27th as a matter of course.[11]

Excitement in the Kremlin was running high. Very soon Molotov's curiosity as to "how many divisions each party would contribute to the common cause" would be satisfied. That was the test of Anglo-French sincerity. At the same time developments in Berlin were proving tantalising.

With the help of its "reliable source" within the Foreign Office itself, the German government was being kept accurately informed of every twist and turn of the triple negotiations. On July 21st, the same day that Seeds was being told of British agreement on Article Six, Herbert von Dirksen was cabling this "top secret" intelligence to Berlin. The sudden British rush forward had to be matched. The next morning the German Foreign Ministry decided to "act in a markedly forthcoming manner". The Ambassador in Moscow, Count von der Schulenburg, was ordered "to pick up the threads" of the political discussions suspended in late June. An agreement with the USSR was now necessary at the earliest possible date.[12]

The British decision to open military conversations with the USSR had followed the familiar pattern of concessions on issues of principle. Harassment in Moscow, Paris and London led to a reluctant decision, accompanied by serious reservations, and then rationalised without conviction. Lord Halifax told the Cabinet on July 26th that the military conversations were regarded by the Russians "as a test of our good faith. He thought that the opening of these conversations would have a good effect on world opinion, although he did not disguise his view that the conversations would take a long time."

How was it possible to discuss military strategy and secrets with the Soviet Union? A political agreement was not yet concluded. There was no assurance the Russians would after all become allies. They could still choose isolation or an agreement with Germany. The Cabinet agreed, therefore, that the military representatives "should be instructed to proceed very slowly with the conversations until a political pact had been concluded." The Russians must not be allowed to discover Allied plans or secrets. Instead they should be probed from the outset as to their military plans and intentions.[13] This was a fatal decision.

The attitude with which the military mission was approached was reflected in the choice of personnel, the instructions given them, and the method of transporting the mission to Moscow. This created the distorted legend of a party of "military, naval and air Strangs",[14] invested with inadequate powers, and conveyed on a slow boat to Moscow. But each decision taken and every arrangement made had behind it the logic of the entire negotiations.

William Strang had advised on July 20th that at least one officer of high rank should be sent to Moscow. The Ironside mission to Poland had been widely publicised in the Soviet press, and any less senior officer would offend the Russians. Ivan Maisky used his contacts in the Labour Party to get the same message through to Chamberlain.

The British were in a muddle. Ironside was actually considered for a time, but as Commander-in-Chief of the Allied intervention forces in Archangel in 1919, it was recognised he might not be welcome in Moscow. Other top-ranking officers were needed in London during the European summer crisis. They could not be spared to languish in the USSR, especially if the talks, as seemed likely, were to be lengthy.[15]

"It is for consideration whether we should not make an admiral the leader of our delegation," Ivone Kirkpatrick minuted on July 25th. Lord Chatfield was strongly opposed. It would falsely raise Soviet hopes as to the role which the British fleet would play in the Baltic. He preferred a senior army or air officer as head.[16] He was overruled.

On July 27th a telephone call was made to the home of Admiral Sir Reginald Aylmer Ranfurly Plunkett-Ernle-Erle-Drax. He was instructed to go to London to see the new Chief of Naval Staff, Admiral of the Fleet Sir Dudley Pound. The next morning Drax was informed that he was to head a military mission to Moscow. Air Marshal Sir Charles Burnett, a former Director of Operations and Intelligence at the Air Ministry and Deputy Chief of Air Staff from 1931–33, and Major-General Thomas G. G. Heywood – "John Bull with a monocle" – a distinguished soldier-diplomat, intelligence officer, and Military Attaché in Paris from 1932–36, were to represent the other two forces.

Admiral Drax had more to recommend him than the amusement his name was to give to the Russians. He was an experienced and aggressive naval officer, the inventor of various mechanical devices employed in the navy, and the first Director of the Royal Naval Staff College at Greenwich. During the 1930s he was an outspoken critic of appeasement and a firm advocate of conscription. He continuously bombarded the Admiralty with bold naval plans to wage offensive war against Germany and Italy. On October 15th, 1938, barely two weeks after the Munich conference, he was invited to serve at the Admiralty in an independent capacity to develop his ideas more fully. There he helped to draft the Admiralty contribution on future naval strategy which was embodied in the important "European Appreciation" paper of February 1939. Still on the Admiralty active list, he was appointed on April 1st, 1939, first and principal Naval Aide-de-Camp to King George VI. During the Second World War he served as Commander-in-Chief, the Nore, and later as Commodore of Ocean Convoys. A "very bluff naval man" was how Brigadier Firebrace, the Military Attaché in Moscow, fondly remembered him years later.[17]

After being informed of the composition of the British and French delegations,* Ivan Maisky and Yakov Suritz cabled their respective appreciations. Maisky was "suspicious" that because of the posts they held, the "members of the delegation will be

---

* General Doumenc, commander of the Lille military region, an unofficial member of the Supreme War Council and designated to command an army in wartime, headed the French delegation. He was a specialist in the problems of a motorised army. General Valin, commander of the 3rd Air Force Division, and Captain Willaume of the French Naval Academy represented the other two services.

able to stay in Moscow indefinitely. This does not promise any particular speed in the conduct of the military negotiations." Suritz was struck by the predominantly "narrow specialists" chosen by the French, "also witness to the inspection aims of the delegation – to their intention to find out, above all else, the condition of our army."[18] Had either Ambassador known of the instructions given to the military mission, they could well have been pleased with their accurate observations.

Even before officers had been chosen for despatch to Moscow, instructions were being prepared. On July 19th Lord Chatfield's advice to begin planning had been turned down by the Prime Minister. Chatfield renewed his plea on July 25th. He estimated that this detailed work would take about ten days and time was pressing. On this occasion his advice was accepted and promptly executed.

On the morning of July 26th instructions went out to the members of the Joint Planning Sub-committee to begin a preliminary examination of what was expected of the Russians on land, sea and air; whom should they supply with war materials; and how much should they be told of allied war plans. The preliminary report was ready and approved by the Deputy Chiefs of Staff the next day. It strongly recommended that "there must be no delay in the initiation of the Staff Conversations" if the political atmosphere was to be cleared to allow a treaty to be concluded.[19]

At midday on July 29th the Joint Planning Sub-committee completed the final memorandum for the guidance of the British delegation. It received the approval of the Deputy Chiefs of Staff on the morning of July 31st. Later that day the Deputy Chiefs of Staff met the military mission. Lord Chatfield was present to welcome them and "expressed the hope that the difficulties in front of the Delegation would not be too great". He implored them to "understand the political background on which their instructions had been framed." Lieutenant-General Sir Ronald Adam, Deputy Chief of the Imperial General Staff, was more precise: "The Delegation was being sent to Russia largely to assist in the conclusion of the political negotiations."[20]

The delegation spent the next two days closeted in a room at Gwydyr House in Whitehall, carefully examining their very detailed instructions.[21] Its first part dealt with general policy. In accordance with Cabinet instructions, the delegation was ordered to go very slowly with the conversations and to treat the Russians with reserve, until the political agreement was concluded. Confidential information was to be carefully imparted.

"We warn the Delegation that there is danger of leakage of information to Germany", the memorandum pointed out, "since there may be contacts between the Russian and German General Staffs, and it is probable that the Delegates will be closely watched and attempts made to obtain copies of papers."

When the political agreement was concluded, the delegation could pass to the second stage, negotiating a military convention. Even this, when signed, should be confined to the broadest possible terms. Major issues of policy, if raised by the Russians, were to be referred to London.

The strategic note, part two of the memorandum, was a desperate plea for help. The sad story of how Britain and France could not directly assist Poland and Rumania, and how dependent these countries would have to be on Soviet material help to maintain an eastern front, was again described for the benefit of the delegation. It was starkly underlined that the "economic help that Russia can render to our Eastern allies may well prove to be the vital factor upon which the maintenance of Polish and Roumanian resistance will depend." The memorandum then outlined the strictly limited tasks which Anglo-French strategy wished the Russians to undertake.

Getting from the Russians information which the British themselves were not prepared to reveal was the final task of the military delegation. Since rearmament had been stepped up, the British had lost their shyness about engaging in military conversations. They were now interested "to know what the Russians had and what they were prepared to do."[22]

The restraints of political circumstance and the limited military demands on Soviet assistance restricted the scope of the mission. The role still being cast for the USSR in eastern Europe was that of a supplier of arms and materials. The Russians had more ambitious plans which were soon to be revealed.

The privilege of attending a meeting of the Committee of Imperial Defence was given on August 2nd to the three leaders of the military mission. This was their final briefing. Admiral Drax was already suffering from what he later described as "mental indigestion". He found the documents, memoranda and intelligence reports thrust before him neither pithy nor precise.

When invited by Lord Chatfield, therefore, to make any comments, Drax asked for some "enlightenment". It was assumed that the object of his mission was to get a military agreement and help achieve a political one. Yet his instructions ordered him to proceed cautiously until a political agreement was reached. "There might be some difficulty in this," he said, as the Russians would probably search for some tangible results from his mission before committing themselves politically. Lord Halifax appreciated the difficulty. He hoped that the mission "would do something to encourage and expedite" the political agreement. From his own hurried perusal of the instructions, it was clear they "would create a good deal of suspicion in the Russian mind". If the Committee considered the instructions too rigid, now was the time to make any corrections, Lord Chatfield heatedly interjected.

Drax did not rise to the occasion. He refused to press home his obvious dissatisfaction. He spoke next only to say that he was content with the instructions and did not advocate any major alterations. The Committee spent its remaining time discussing the cloak and dagger aspects of the mission. Leslie Hore-Belisha urged that every precaution should be taken. "There was no doubt that every possible device would be used to spy upon the members", he said. "Dictaphones might be installed, baggage would be examined, waste paper would be collected and scrutinised." The instructions for the mission were then approved.

Drax was very disturbed when he left the meeting. No one seemed hopeful or enthusiastic about his mission. From a private talk with the head of the Secret Intelligence Service,

Admiral Sir Hugh Sinclair, he received no encouragement. Sinclair was not optimistic as to the outcome, and said: "It's an infernal shame that they should send you out to Moscow to try and clear up the mess that has been made there by the politicians."

The politicians were themselves unhelpful. In case the discussions failed, Drax asked Lord Halifax, should the proceedings be drawn out as long as possible? Snow in October would make a German campaign in Poland impossible. There followed a "short but impressive silence", until Halifax expressed his agreement to what Drax described as this "uninviting prospect". During an interview on August 4th with Chamberlain, Drax found himself faced by a "worried and uneasy" man. The Prime Minister "felt some doubt" about a successful outcome to the military talks.[23] The mission was now ready to depart.

Sea, air or rail? The method of transporting the Anglo-French military mission to Moscow, including more than thirty officers, secondary officials and cipher clerks, had engrossed Whitehall since July 25th.

R. C. Skrine Stevenson, the Secretary of the Situation Report Centre, responsible for assessing and issuing daily co-ordinated intelligence summaries, had discussed the thorny transportation question with his Committee on July 25th. The suggestion then advanced to the Foreign Office was dramatic. "The best and most spectacular way" of impressing world opinion and the Axis Powers "that we really mean business by these conversations" was to send the mission with an escort of cruisers and destroyers.

This scheme to show the British flag in the Baltic went straight to Lord Halifax's desk. He turned it down against the advice of Lord Chatfield and the Deputy Chiefs of Staff. Halifax felt "it might be regarded as rather provocative to send a cruiser into the Baltic at the present time." The prospect of much needed naval vessels lingering there was not inviting, when war was a daily possibility.

It proved likewise difficult to find appropriate aircraft. Commercial planes were unsuitable. The Royal Air Force had no planes of sufficient capacity and range to spare. Besides, the

German Air Attaché in London had let it be known that his government was sensitive to British service planes flying over Germany.[24]

The same objection was raised to a journey by rail via Germany. Prime Minister Daladier and General Doumenc liked this scheme. The latter shrugged off criticism by saying that there were a "lot of 'tourists' travelling about these days." However, Sir Nevile Henderson advised against this "unnecessarily provocative" method of travel and the Foreign Office agreed.[25]

Having exhausted most of the possibilities someone suggested the mission "might bicycle" to Moscow. When that point was reached a "less ostentatious method of travel" was adopted on August 1st. A merchant ship of the Ellerman Lines, *City of Exeter*, was chartered. She was roomy, comfortable, and also old.[26]

The choice of sea transport forced the French delegation to come to London. A joint briefing took place on August 4th. The instructions to both missions coincided, at least on paper. But the French were up to their old tricks. Unknown to the British government, Daladier had seen Doumenc privately on July 31st and warned him: "Bring us back an agreement at all costs."[27]

On August 5th the mission left London by a special train for Tilbury landing stage. Once on board, Admiral Drax was horrified to find that the ship could only steam at thirteen knots. Her hasty selection had made it impossible to carry out essential repairs needed for maximum speed. It was a depressing prospect in contrast to the twenty-seven or twenty-eight knots which might have been expected from a large cruiser. Arrival in Moscow would not occur before August 11th – seventeen days after the decision to open immediate talks had been communicated to Molotov. This was not too long a period to prepare for such a unique and complex venture. But the secret German-Soviet negotiations were very shortly to make a successful outcome of the military talks quite improbable.

———

In the unlikely setting of Ewest's, a small but luxurious Berlin

restaurant, Julius Schnurre had decided on July 26th to enter-
tain the two top-ranking Soviet diplomats, Georgi Astakhov, the
Chargé d'Affaires and E. Babarin, the head of the trade delegation. The conversation, frank and unrestrained, continued past
midnight, with politics emerging as of greater interest than
economics. Acting according to his instructions, Schnurre
dangled in front of the two Russians the hope of a settlement of
all outstanding German-Soviet differences. By firstly establishing
economic collaboration, good political relations would follow.
"German policy was aimed against Britain", Schnurre confided.
While from the Baltic to the Black Sea, where German-Soviet
interests did not clash, a "new arrangement" satisfactory to both
governments could be made.

Astakhov reacted cautiously. He was obviously taken aback by
such frank, off the record haggling. "Moscow could not quite
believe in a shift in German policy towards the Soviet Union."

"What could Britain offer Russia?" Schnurre retorted. "At
best participation in a European war and the hostility of Germany, hardly a desirable end for Russia." Germany had more to
offer. "Neutrality and keeping out of a possible European conflict, and, if Moscow wished, a German-Russian understanding
on mutual interests which, just as in former times, would work
out to the advantage of both countries."

Astakhov promised to report these remarks to the Narkomindel. Otherwise he maintained his reserved attitude. Schnurre
was not hopeful and suspected the Russians would continue their
delaying tactics.[28] He underestimated his own debating skills.
The picture he had painted for the Russians, enjoying Berlin's
nightlife, was that which undoubtedly influenced the final Soviet
decision to ally with Germany.

The German Foreign Ministry stepped up its pressure. The
plunge from dull economics to glittering politics had been taken
at Ewest's. The opening had to be widened. The urgency of the
situation was heightened by secret information, this time from
Paris, of the imminent despatch of the Anglo-French mission to
Moscow. It was first vital to gauge the reaction to Schnurre's
bold proposals. On July 29th Schulenburg was ordered to

arrange an interview with Molotov. If the Foreign Commissar was receptive, he was to be given further details of the territorial concessions Berlin was prepared to make.[29]

Ribbentrop abandoned his aloofness. He personally stepped into the negotiations, kept in constant touch with Schnurre, and continually exchanged views with Hitler. The Russian problem was of *"extreme urgency"*. Ribbentrop aimed, on the negative side, to disrupt the Anglo-French Soviet negotiations; on the positive side, to get a German-Soviet agreement.

Almost daily Hitler himself was growing more optimistic. He was convinced, he told the Hungarian Foreign Minister, Count Istvan Csaky, that the "Soviets would not repeat the Czar's mistake and bleed to death for Britain." He accurately forecast that, without becoming militarily involved, they would help themselves to the Baltic states and part of Poland.

Impatient and feeling very heady, Ribbentrop invited Astakhov to a meeting at the Foreign Ministry on August 2nd. Delicacy was not Ribbentrop's forte. At once he blurted out the possibility of Germany "coming to an understanding with Russia on the fate of Poland". The choice lay with Moscow. Almost in the same breath, and doubtless conscious that the Soviets had not yet committed themselves, Ribbentrop delivered a brief warning on the need for discretion in handling his remarks.[30]

In his desire for speed and concrete results, did Ribbentrop go much further than his own record indicates? According to the telegram Astakhov sent to Moscow, Ribbentrop had actually suggested signing a secret German-Soviet protocol to delimit the interests of the two powers "all along the line from the Black to the Baltic Sea". It is not surprising this premature offer was rejected. The Anglo-French military mission was about to depart for Moscow. The Germans did not intend "to observe sincerely or for long any eventual commitments", Astakhov advised the Narkomindel.[31]

Meanwhile, Schulenburg's important confrontation with Molotov was being eagerly awaited. Astakhov himself had already given some encouragement. His conversation with Ribbentrop on August 2nd "had created great interest" in the

Kremlin, he told Schnurre a day later. Astakhov added that "absolute discretion" would be observed.

On August 3rd Schulenburg spent an hour and a half with Molotov. He could hardly have been encouraged by the results of the conversation. For the first time Molotov did abandon his habitual reserve. He spoke frankly and with unusual cordiality. The economic negotiations were proceeding well. But "proofs" that Germany had ceased to be hostile to the USSR were still lacking. Faced with such mistrust, Schulenburg was not free to continue dangling the bait of a carve-up of eastern Europe as Ribbentrop had hoped would be possible. The Soviet government, Schulenburg cabled to Berlin, was still determined to sign an agreement with the British and French.[32]

Some time during the next forty-eight hours, a historic decision was taken in the Kremlin. There was a clear danger the German government would tire of Russia's insistence on "proofs" of future good behaviour. It was time to commit the Soviet government to concrete political talks with Nazi Germany. In early August, too, the negotiations with Britain and France had reached a new low point. Neville Chamberlain announced, on July 31st in the House of Commons, the names of the heads of the military mission. The omission of any leading military figures, either from London or Paris, made the Kremlin doubt allied enthusiasm for the next stage of the negotiations.

This was followed by a major disaster. While preparing for the military talks, work was going ahead in the Foreign Office on the definition of indirect aggression. A new proposal was presented to Molotov on August 2nd. Not only was he uninterested, but he had nothing new to offer. Seeds telegraphed to London: "M. Molotov was a different man from what he had been at our last interview and I feel our negotiations have received severe setback."

It was in fact much worse. The political negotiations never resumed. On August 4th William Strang was instructed to return to London. His presence in Moscow was no longer necessary. The Russians would have assumed that no new concessions would emanate from London. The tortuous marathon in the Kremlin had ended – painfully close to full agreement. Ironically, eight days later, on August 12th, a new formula on "indirect aggression" received Chamberlain's personal approval. It almost completely coincided with the Soviet definition, but never saw the light of day in Moscow.[33]

The results of the Soviet decision could be implied from the strange story Astakhov brought to Schnurre on August 5th. The political questions affecting German-Soviet relations, Astakhov blurted out, were "urgent and serious". Molotov had for the first time discussed these matters and felt his last conversation with Schulenburg "had ended on a positive note".

This was definitely not Schulenburg's impression. Rather it was Soviet bait to the Germans. This exciting opening was pressed home on August 10th. Again facing Astakhov, Schnurre laid his cards on the table. He knew the military time-table. A conflict arising from "megalomaniac Polish aspirations" was any day possible, he said. There would be valuable benefits to the Soviet government if an agreement with Germany were previously reached.[34] The effect of these words in Moscow was electric. Important new instructions were telegraphed to Astakhov. On August 12th he communicated them to Schnurre. The Soviet government was now ready for a systematic discussion of all outstanding issues, including the Polish question and previous German-Soviet treaties. This should take place only "by degrees" and preferably in Moscow.

The news was given at once to Hitler. He was overjoyed; his confidence, flatteringly bolstered. "Russia would not be prepared to pull the Western Powers' chestnuts out of the fire", he boasted first to the Italian Foreign Minister, Count Galeazzo Ciano, and then to a meeting of his top generals.[35]

Life aboard the *City of Exeter*, carrying the British and French officers to Moscow, was a mixture of work and pleasure. Three days were spent, in what had been the children's playroom of the ship, amiably discussing strategy for the forthcoming talks and outlining a draft military agreement. Most of these papers and notes were then burned. Spare time was occupied with a deck tennis tournament, won by Admiral Drax, and long copious meals of curry served by Indian stewards in turbans. In the early morning of August 10th the *City of Exeter* reached Leningrad. The delegation was met by an official Soviet reception, speeches and photographers. Having missed the midnight "Red Arrow" to Moscow, the delegation spent the day sightseeing, shepherded by Soviet officials.

The delegation finally reached Moscow on the morning of August 11th. During an afternoon courtesy call on Molotov and the Soviet Defence Commissar, Marshal Klement Voroshilov, it was agreed to hold the first session on the following day. A banquet and concert rounded off the day's events.

These social preliminaries increased the optimism of the Anglo-French delegatation. The first genial twenty-four hours in the USSR seemed to indicate the Russians were genuinely interested in a military agreement. Only Admiral Drax was not taken in by the display of Soviet hospitality. He later recorded: "to me the atmosphere always seemed to savour faintly of the Iron hand in a velvet glove."[36]

The first session of the military talks,[37] in the lavish Spiridonyevka Palace, began with an amicable discussion on procedure. Then Marshal Voroshilov rose from his seat at the large round table and solemnly produced a document empowering him to negotiate and sign a military convention.* What credentials and powers did the British and French delegations possess? he asked.

General Doumenc quickly exhibited satisfactory credentials. Admiral Drax was in trouble. He had nothing on paper which he could show Voroshilov. His instructions, which gave him power to negotiate, was a secret document. In vain he explained that no precedent existed for granting full plenipotentiary powers to a military delegation. Nevertheless, he agreed to send for

---

* Besides Voroshilov, the Soviet delegation consisted of B. M. Shaposhnikov, Chief of the General Staff of the Red Army, N. G. Kuznetsov, Commissar for the Navy, A. D. Loktionov, Chief of the Air Force, and I. V. Smorodinov, Deputy Chief of the General Staff.

written credentials, and immediately telegraphed accordingly to London.[38]

As this first session of the military talks was drawing to a close, Astakhov was telling Schnurre of Moscow's readiness to begin political negotations. The mission was now unlikely to deflect the Kremlin from the more attractive alternative available from Berlin.

In the first play for position, Voroshilov had already secured an important psychological victory. He emerged even more clearly as a powerful, confident adversary later that day. Drax and Doumenc asked the Soviet Marshal to expound his ideas on mutual military co-operation. With Germany ready for hostilities, it was necessary to agree "on general principles of common action".

Principles were of no interest, they were self-evident, Voroshilov tartly replied. He wanted to discuss plans of action. Let the British and French delegations firstly describe what they were prepared to do in case of aggression in Europe.

Not surprisingly, Voroshilov had his way. The Allied mission wished "to show confidence" in their possible future ally. On August 13th the French delegation was given the thankless task of speaking first. In the process they divulged some highly secret figures of the strength and equipment of their armed forces. The British delegation then followed with a partial exposé of British plans. After endless probing questions, Voroshilov declared he would be willing the next day to discuss Soviet plans for the eastern front. He then embarked on a painful lesson in arm-twisting and geography:

What part do these Missions or the General Staffs of France and Britain consider the Soviet Union should take in a war against the aggressor if he attacks France and Britain, or if he attacks Poland or Roumania, or if he attacks them together, and also if he attacks Turkey? In brief, how do the British and French Missions conceive our joint action against the aggressor or the aggressive bloc in the event of an aggression against us . . . I wish to make it clear. The Soviet Union, as you know, has no common border either with Britain or with

France. We can, therefore, only take part in the war on the
territory of neighbouring states, particularly Poland and
Roumania.

This exposition proved a gentle hint of more explicit demands
which were to follow. Its meaning was clear to both Drax and
Doumenc. Their ability to deal with the problem was unfortunately precluded.

The third day of the Anglo-French-Soviet military talks,
August 14th, proved decisive. Marshal Voroshilov was taking
his turn as chairman. At once he asked for a reply to his question.
Neither Drax nor Doumenc could produce a satisfactory answer.
Both patiently explained that assistance to Germany's eastern
neighbours should only be rendered if requested. The initial
eastern front would rest on Polish and Rumanian armed forces.
Soviet troops, therefore, should be concentrated on the western
frontier of the USSR, and intervene only when considered desirable and convenient.

Voroshilov found this all annoying and vague. "I regret my
bluntness," he stated, "but we soldiers must be forthright in
what we say. This scheme is not clear. . . . Do the French and
British General Staffs think that the Soviet land forces will be
admitted to Polish territory in order to make direct contact with
the enemy in case Poland is attacked?" Furthermore: "Is it
proposed to allow Soviet troops across Roumanian territory if the
aggressor attacks Roumania?"

"Without an exact and unequivocal answer to these questions", Voroshilov concluded, "further conversations will not
have any real meaning." His delegation could not "in all conscience recommend to its Government that it take part in an
undertaking obviously destined to fail." It was up to Britain and
France to approach their east European allies. However, pending
the receipt of a reply, Voroshilov magnanimously agreed to
continue the talks.

"I think our mission is finished," Admiral Drax said afterwards to his colleagues in the garden of the Spiridonyevka
Palace. There was general agreement.[39]

The heads of the military mission and the Ambassadors then held an emergency conference. A crisis point had been reached. On August 12th Sir William Seeds had sent an urgent telegram to London to which there was still no reply. He had forcefully argued the case for abandoning the reserved attitude towards the military negotiations. Otherwise Russian fears would be confirmed that the British were neither serious nor interested in a concrete agreement. Seeds had asked for information on whether London still intended merely "vague generalities" until the prior solution of the indirect aggression problem. "I should deeply regret if that were the actual decision of His Majesty's Government, as all indications so far go to show that Soviet military negotiators are really out for businesss."[40]

Sir William Seeds' plea had a profound impact in London. He was not to discover this until three days later. His telegram convinced Lord Halifax on August 14th that Admiral Drax's instructions were too rigid. If the Soviets were really out for business, the British must respond. That afternoon the telegram was sent to the Deputy Chiefs of Staff for their "urgent consideration". They reacted enthusiastically, never having liked the shackles imposed on the military mission. By the following morning they had drafted a new telegram. It was approved personally by Lord Halifax and Lord Chatfield, recalled hastily to London for this purpose. At 5 p.m. on August 15th it was sent to Moscow. Sir William Seeds' advice had been fully accepted. Drax was now ordered to ignore the progress of the political negotiations. He was to conclude the military conversations "as soon as possible".[41]

No sooner had work been completed on these new instructions for the military mission, when another telegram from Moscow arrived on August 15th. It described the demands made by Marshal Voroshilov the previous day. The Ambassadors and the heads of the military mission advised that, as the organisers of the deterrent front, Britain and France must now approach Poland and Rumania. Without passage rights for the Red Army, the negotiations would break down. The military mission was impressed with Voroshilov's "apparent sincerity". He seemed genuinely anxious to conduct operations outside Soviet territory.[42]

The question of Soviet passage rights through its reluctant neighbours had been at the root of many of the difficulties of the tripartite negotiations. It was familiar and embarrassing to all concerned. Yet a solution had been deliberately avoided. The Foreign Office had preferred to pretend the problem did not exist and to hope it would not be raised in Moscow.[43] The French government had similarly buried its head in the ground.[44] What was wanted from the USSR was the military output from its factories, not the assistance of the marching hordes of the Red Army. In a regrettable *faux-pas*, Admiral Drax had admitted, during the meeting of August 14th, that without the help of the Red Army, Poland and Rumania could be expected quickly to become "German provinces". The significance of this was not lost on Voroshilov.

Once again the machinery of Whitehall and the Quai d'Orsay went into action, with a desperation rare in peace time. The French made the first moves. They pressed the need for co-operation with the USSR with the Polish Ambassador in Paris, Juliusz Lukasiewicz, and with the Foreign Ministry in Warsaw. A member of the French military mission in Moscow was rushed to Warsaw to influence the Polish general staff.[45]

The Foreign Office put the problem to the Deputy Chiefs of Staff on August 16th. They were asked to advise on the military aspects. It had long been recognised that Soviet military supplies were essential to prolong Polish resistance against a German attack. The Chiefs of Staff had also repeatedly advised a diplomatic offensive to initiate some form of Polish-Soviet co-operation. It had so far never been suggested that Soviet armed forces should operate from Polish territory. That was the astonishing conclusion the Deputy Chiefs of Staff returned the same day. It expressed all the anger and frustration of those responsible for British strategy in a war which might be fought because of guarantee commitments they were incapable of fulfilling.

We feel that this is no time for half-measures and that every effort should be made to persuade Poland and Roumania to agree to the use of their territory by Russian forces.

In our opinion it is only logical that the Russians should be given every facility for rendering assistance and putting their maximum weight into the scale on the side of the anti-aggression Powers. We consider it so important to meet the Russians in this matter that, if necessary, the strongest pressure should be exerted on Poland and Roumania to persuade them to adopt a helpful attitude.

It is perfectly clear that without early and effective Russian assistance, the Poles cannot hope to stand up to a German attack on land or in the air for more than a limited time. . . . The supply of arms and war material is not enough. If the Russians are to collaborate in resisting German aggression against Poland or Roumania they can only do so effectively on Polish or Roumanian soil; and . . . if permission for this were withheld till war breaks out, it would then be too late. The most the Allies could then hope for would be to avenge Poland and Roumania and perhaps restore their independence as a result of the defeat of Germany in a long war.

We suggest that it is now necessary to present this unpalatable truth with absolute frankness both to the Poles and to the Roumanians. To the Poles especially it ought to be pointed out that they have obligations to us as well as we to them; and that it is unreasonable for them to expect us blindly to implement our guarantee to them if, at the same time, they will not co-operate in measures designed for a common purpose.

The conclusion of a treaty with Russia appears to us to be the best way of preventing a war. . . . At the worst if the negotiations with Russia break down, a Russo-German rapprochement may take place of which the probable consequence will be that Russia and Germany decide to share the spoils and concert in a new partition of the Eastern European States.

This report from the Deputy Chiefs of Staff was incorporated, almost verbatim, in a stiff telegram sent to Ambassador Kennard on August 17th. The Rumanian government was to be temporarily ignored. Kennard was asked to support his French colleague, Léon Noël, in a joint effort to convince Colonel Beck that the passage of Soviet troops was "vital for European security". Otherwise, he would be responsible for the military talks in Moscow breaking down.

The Poles could not be intimidated. Political and military circles in Warsaw, Kennard telegraphed, remained "absolutely obdurate". He could still not persuade Beck to agree to any form of Polish-Soviet collaboration prior to the outbreak of war. If Poland agreed to the passage of Soviet troops, Beck warned, Hitler "would see red and not hesitate to precipitate a war".[46]

Hitler did "see red", as Beck had warned, but for reasons which Beck had not envisaged. On August 12th the Soviet government had agreed to open political negotiations. The search for a pact was nearing its end. Desperate Anglo-French efforts to force the Poles into a last minute change of mind would have come too late.

On August 14th further instructions were sent to Schulenburg to be used during an interview arranged with Molotov the next day. Ribbentrop asked for a "speedy clarification" of relations in view of the crisis in German-Polish relations. He proposed to bypass the usual diplomatic channels and visit Moscow to give Stalin the benefit of Hitler's views. The German-Soviet negotiations were now too important to be left to anybody but the highest officials.

Molotov listened to the German Ambassador "with greatest interest". Russia now believed in Germany's sincere intentions and Stalin would be kept informed, Molotov stated. He hedged, however, at a visit from Ribbentrop and instead asked: Was the German government interested in three proposals: a non-aggression pact, help in improving Soviet-Japanese relations, and a joint guarantee of the Baltic states?

This sudden confidence may have been derived from Georgi Astakhov's abrupt change of mind. After having repeatedly warned the Narkomindel that the German government could not be trusted, he had telegraphed that they were now "prepared . . . to make declarations and gestures which, half a year ago, would have appeared completely out of the question."[47] For the first time Molotov dared to reveal the hidden aims of his government. A non-aggression pact would leave the USSR undisturbed when Poland was attacked. German influence with Japan could help end the running border dispute in Manchuria where fighting was again in progress. Finally, Germany, unlike Britain and France, could satisfy Russian fears as to the security of their Baltic frontiers.

The moderation of Molotov's demands surprised the German Ambassador. He was at long last hopeful of success in Moscow. His optimism was well-based: August 15th was the day Marshal Voroshilov had insisted on the need for Soviet transit rights through Poland and Rumania.

Hitler and the German Foreign Ministry immediately responded to Schulenburg's latest telegram. All three points raised by Molotov could be satisfied, Ribbentrop telegraphed on August 16th. He was now ready to visit Moscow any time after August 18th and sign the appropriate treaties.

Such unseemly haste "gratified" Molotov when he faced Schulenburg again on August 17th. What a contrast to William Strang, an "official of second-class rank", sent as Britain's emissary, Molotov jovially remarked. But a visit from the German Foreign Minister required thorough preparation. Meanwhile, the Foreign Commissar suggested both governments should firstly sign a trade and credit agreement and draft a non-aggression pact. He wanted the latter to contain a "special protocol" for the purpose of, he euphemistically described, "defining the interests of the contracting parties in this or that question of foreign policy".[48] The carve up of eastern Europe was on the agenda.

———

While Vyacheslav Molotov jockeyed for position with Count Friedrich von der Schulenburg, Marshal Klement Voroshilov was left discussing military issues with the Anglo-French mission at the Spiridonyevka Palace. It was almost time to close these proceedings. While awaiting the replies to his question on passage rights for the Red Army, Voroshilov had agreed to continue the talks. On August 15th the Soviet delegates gave a rosy picture of Soviet military strength and plans of action. The Anglo-French mission then outlined allied naval plans and, the following day, offered an exposition of their air strength.

Voroshilov was getting bored. The information given him was useless and known to every intelligence service in Europe. The insistence of Admiral Drax and General Doumenc on signing a declaration of agreed principles was annoying him. He wanted a "concrete military convention fixing the number of divisions, guns, tanks, aircraft, naval squadrons, etc., to act jointly in the defence of the contracting Powers." He did not intend to "waste time on meaningless declarations". Unless an answer from London and Paris had arrived soon, he warned, the conversations could not proceed. The meeting broke up in acrimony and disarray. That night the British delegation agreed that, if Poland and Rumania withheld permission, the talks would collapse.

At the end of the morning session of August 17th, Marshal Voroshilov suddenly rose from his seat and declared: "The Soviet Mission considers that we shall have to end the work of our conference until we get a reply to our questions. Until receipt of this reply I recommend our dear guests to rest, see the sights of Moscow, visit the [annual Air] Exhibition, and make themselves at home."

Admiral Drax and General Doumenc did not fancy playing tourists. After they had vigorously protested, Voroshilov agreed to reconvene the talks on August 21st. Drax was outraged and suspicious when he left the meeting. He detected backstage intrigues. Next time he faced the Soviet delegation, he planned to ask them outright "what they were playing at". His colleagues managed to dissuade him.[49]

On the evening of August 17th, with the military discussions just suspended, Molotov had received the German Ambassador and suggested drafting a non-aggression pact. The German government again pressed forward, prepared neither to wait nor countenance any further Soviet hesitation. The imminence of action against Poland made it imperative to conclude a final agreement with the USSR and thereby avoid a war on two fronts. On August 19th, after urgent instructions had been sent to Moscow, Schulenburg was twice received by Molotov. At the second of these interviews, and presumably with Stalin's approval, Molotov relented. The German Foreign Minister was welcome to arrive in Moscow on 26th or 27th August.

Hitler was growing more impatient and tense as he read Schulenburg's latest telegrams. He disliked Molotov's delaying tactics and decided to intervene personally. The price he had to pay was humiliating, though necessary for his military preparations. On August 20th the Nazi Hitler sent a personal telegram to his previously irreconcilable enemy, the Bolshevik Stalin, asking for a favour.

"The tension between Germany and Poland has become intolerable . . . a crisis may arise any day." It was vital not to lose time, Hitler wrote. Could Ribbentrop not be received on August 23rd at the latest? At 7.55 on August 21st the tense wait in Berlin ended with the first report of Hitler's success. Less than two hours later the text of Stalin's reply arrived; marked "MOST URGENT" and "SECRET". Ribbentrop could make his journey on August 23rd to sign the non-aggression pact.[50] Hitler was at once informed. The same day a German-Soviet trade and credit agreement was announced in the press.

Several hours before Schulenburg was handed the text of Stalin's reply, the military conference was engaged in what proved to be its last session. Admiral Drax excitedly read to Marshal Voroshilov the English text of his official credentials which had arrived via airmail from London. Voroshilov was not interested and asked that the talks be indefinitely postponed. If the reply to the questions put on August 14th was not received, there would be no need to reconvene.

The Anglo-French delegation agreed with reluctance. Before parting they put on record their incomprehension as to the reasons which had compelled the Soviet mission to raise "difficult political questions", involving considerable delay. The parting words of the Russians were equally blunt. They could not envisage how Britain and France had despatched negotiators to Moscow without "precise and positive instructions on such an elementary matter" as the passage of Soviet troops. The meeting then broke up.

Meanwhile, the British and French governments were making desperate attempts to break the deadlock over Poland's refusal to sanction the passage of Soviet armed forces. Against a background of growing war scares, the imminent failure of the military conversations, and reports of a Soviet-German deal, Lord Halifax again telegraphed on August 20th to Sir Howard Kennard. Gone forever were the favourite arguments about the secondary role of the USSR in the peace front. Instead, Halifax emphasised the "very serious situation" if the talks broke down because Beck refused Soviet co-operation. "I am convinced that such failure must encourage Herr Hitler to resort to war, in which Poland would bear the brunt of the first attack. On the other hand," Halifax continued, "I fully believe that the conclusion of a politico-military agreement with the Soviet Union would be calculated to deter him from war." The risks of allowing Soviet troops on Polish soil were preferable to the destruction of Polish independence.

The Ambassador did not consider it useful to press these further arguments on Colonel Beck. The answer of August 18th had been emphatically negative. Kennard sympathised with the Polish government. "Passage of Russian forces", he pointedly recalled, "has been the rock on which every proposal for a collective alliance in Eastern Europe has . . . foundered." The most recent attempt appeared similarly doomed.

The French, although more desperate than the British and more pervasive in their efforts, could report little progress. On August 19th Beck replied with *"un 'non' catégorique"*.[51] His suspicion of Russian motives and scepticism as to their good faith were too deeply rooted. More important, the Polish government doubted that the USSR could mount an effective offensive and that a German-Soviet alliance was possible.

On August 21st the French took drastic measures. They approved a scheme which originated with their diplomatic and military representatives in Moscow. It was decided to disregard Polish objections and give Marshal Voroshilov an "affirmative answer in principle". The approach failed. On August 22nd Voroshilov told Doumenc that he was still unsatisfied. In any case, he continued, discussions could not be resumed until "everything has been cleared up". The British and French had "allowed the political and military discussions to drag on too long. That is why we must not exclude the possibility, during this time, of certain political events."[52]

Marshal Voroshilov had in mind the expected developments resulting from a sensational press report of the same day. A Soviet communiqué announced the impending arrival of Ribbentrop. In order "to avert the danger of war", the communiqué stated, Germany and the USSR had decided to conclude a non-aggression pact.

"Calm and reserve" was how the French and British quickly agreed to treat this bombshell. The outcome of Ribbentrop's visit to Moscow was still unknown. Could he not be expected to suffer the same delaying tactics Molotov had used during the tripartite negotiations? Any pact might even contain an "escape clause", making it inoperative if one of the two signatories attacked a third state. Soviet sources encouraged such thinking, while Ivan Maisky insisted the negotiations with Germany were "purely a peace move". Sir William Seeds who, according to the American Ambassador, Laurence Steinhardt, was "apparently oblivious to the gravity and portent" of the new situation, felt the military talks might yet resume. Admiral Drax himself requested permission to remain in Moscow and await developments.[53]

The British and French governments considered that latitude for further efforts in Warsaw still remained. Kennard was instructed, therefore, to support the French Ambassador, Léon Noël, in a final appeal. At last Beck relented and on August 23rd agreed to a compromise. This would have sanctioned Polish-Soviet military collaboration in case of German aggression under certain conditions.[54] The Polish concession came too late. Nor did it contain the conditions which would have satisfied Voroshilov.

At noon on August 23rd two planes carrying the German Foreign Minister and his entourage of thirty officials landed at Moscow's airport. They took off twenty-four hours later. In two long conversations with Stalin and Molotov, Ribbentrop settled the few outstanding differences between Europe's most improbable allies. A pact of non-aggression was signed on previously agreed lines. To this document was appended a secret protocol. It contained the German bribe for Soviet friendship. The two governments agreed to divide eastern Europe into spheres of influence. Russia's interest in Finland, Estonia, Latvia and the Rumanian province of Bessarabia; and Germany's interest in Lithuania and Vilna were recognised. Poland was divided along the Pissa, Narev, Vistula and San rivers. The question of whether Poland was to remain an independent state, and in what form, was left to be "determined in the course of further political developments." The evening ended with innumerable toasts being drunk to Stalin, Hitler and the non-aggression pact. "How we did blackguard each other in the past", were Stalin's parting words to Ribbentrop.[55]

The terms of the German-Soviet Non-aggression Pact, but not the secret protocol, were known to the world on August 24th. Marshal Voroshilov spent the day duck shooting. On August 25th he received Admiral Drax and General Doumenc for the last time to confirm the termination of the military discussions. In a genuine outburst of Russian hatred for the Poles, Voroshilov said: "Were we to have to conquer Poland in order to offer her our help, or were we to go on our knees and offer our help to Poland?" He later explained to the French military attaché: "We could not wait until the Germans smashed the Polish army and attacked us, beating us piecemeal while you stood on your frontier and contained some 10 German divisions."

Sir William Seeds had already seen Molotov on August 22nd. He then accused the Foreign Commissar of "an act of bad faith". In diplomatic language this was hardly a compliment, but Seeds was delighted with the chance to express his true feelings. On August 25th Seeds and Naggiar were received by Molotov. They heard the final pronouncement that the Anglo-French-Soviet negotiations, in view of the "changed political situation", were terminated.[56]

———

The one capital which had spoken least but knew most of the secret German-Soviet negotiations was Washington. In Europe, rumour and conjecture circulated freely and abundantly. At the State Department precise and accurate reports of every stage of the German-Soviet negotiations flowed in as soon as they were enacted in either Berlin or Moscow. The information was thoroughly reliable. It came from "certain members" of the German Embassy in Moscow.[57]

For many months President Roosevelt and the State Department nervously hoarded this astonishing intelligence windfall. To have prematurely warned the British and French governments might have resulted in an indiscretion. This could have choked off the flow at its source. In any case, at least until July, the Germans and Russians were still jockeying for position.

Nevertheless, broad hints of what was going on behind their back were given to the British. On April 28th, when Hitler delivered his major speech to the Reichstag, he had omitted his usual abuse of Bolshevik Russia. A State Department official, in conversation with a member of the British Embassy in Washington, made a point of drawing attention to this omission.

During April and May 1939 the American press had splashed sensational disclosures made by W. G. Krivitsky, a former chief of Soviet military intelligence in western Europe who had defected in October 1937. Krivitsky gave details, later proved accurate, of Stalin's attempts since 1934 to do a deal with Hitler. Despite continued rebuffs and in order to keep the USSR out of a war, Krivitsky claimed, Stalin was still searching for terms which Hitler could accept.[58]

The Northern Department of the Foreign Office was mystified. First reactions were to dismiss Krivitsky's revelations and speculations as "mostly twaddle", and "rigmarole". The main stumbling block was Krivitsky himself. Neither the British intelligence services nor the foreign diplomatic community in Moscow had any file on him or any knowledge of his previous career.

As the weeks passed the Krivitsky revelations began to be seriously examined, particularly when his name was found to be a pseudonym. The "chaff may contain a few grains worth gleaning", Laurence Collier, the head of the Northern Department wrote on June 27th.

A little nudge from the State Department also helped. Sensing that the British were being dim-witted, another hint was dropped. On July 14th the British Embassy in Washington wrote to the Foreign Office: "From a chance conversation with a member of the division concerned we gather that the State Department's opinion of these articles is that they are not to be ignored but not to be taken literally either." Officials of the Northern Department, dealing with Krivitsky's revelations, took special note of this hint. By early August, they no longer disputed his facts on Russian appeasement of Germany. They still doubted, however, his interpretation that a German-Soviet pact was inevitable.[59]

On August 4th President Roosevelt himself decided to make a discreet intervention. The mounting intelligence at his disposal of German-Soviet contacts was distressing. He remembered a conversation which he had had on June 30th with the Soviet Ambassador, Constantine Oumansky, who was returning to Moscow on leave. "Tell Stalin that if his Government joined up with Hitler", Roosevelt had warned the Ambassador, "it was as certain as night followed day that as soon as Hitler had conquered France, he would turn on Russia and that it would be the Soviet's turn next."

This message, Roosevelt conjectured, had either not been delivered or had been ignored. The Russians had continued to negotiate with the Germans. Oumansky actually reported on July 2nd as follows: "For the British and French, there can be no doubt of his, Roosevelt's, personal interest in a favourable conclusion of the Moscow negotiations." Roosevelt decided to repeat the substance of his warning in a telegram to Ambassador Steinhardt. For security reasons a copy was also carried by special courier from Paris to Moscow. On August 16th Steinhardt delivered the warning. It was cagily side-stepped by Molotov.[60]

Intelligence regarding the crucial conversation between Schulenburg and Molotov on August 15th convinced the State Department that a German-Soviet pact was imminent. War would inevitably result. The long period of discretion and guarded hints was at last ended. A direct warning had to be given to the British of what was happening behind their backs in Moscow.

Sumner Welles, the Under-Secretary of State, summoned the British Ambassador, Sir Ronald Lindsay, on August 17th. Welles at once described what had transpired between Schulenburg and Molotov two days earlier.

"Under-Secretary of State assured me", Lindsay telegraphed to London that evening, "that this information came from a source which in the past had proved very reliable. He made me promise not to disclose its identity to you by telegram as he distrusted security of all cyphers. I am sending it by air mail due in England August 20th." Lindsay's second communication read: "Source of information is the United States Ambassador at Moscow who is most anxious that this fact shall not be known as it would give away his informant." Nevertheless, Steinhardt could not resist on August 23rd giving Sir William Seeds precisely the same information, without mentioning his source.[61]

Here was intelligence more accurate than anything ever available to the British government and from an impeccable source. If disclosed at an earlier date it might have frustrated a German-Soviet pact. It would have forced a triple alliance at whatever price the ussr demanded. It would also have deflated Neville Chamberlain's confidence that Europe's two most bitterly opposed dictatorships could never ally.

The American intelligence disclosure came too late. It was also mysteriously processed. Although telegraphed by Sir Ronald Lindsay at 9 p.m. on August 17th and received in the Foreign

Office Communications Department at 9.30 the following morning, it was not immediately deciphered!* Only on August 22nd did the telegram finally reach the Central Department. It was mentioned during the Cabinet which met that afternoon at 3 p.m. The minutes are strikingly silent as to any reaction or recrimination.

"It is a great pity that this tel. was not decyphered until 4 days after receipt, with the result that we were taken by surprise this morning", Frank Roberts of the Central Department minuted in the best laconic and professional manner. Sir William Seeds did register his resentment as to why, considering the friendly relations between the British and American Embassies in Moscow, the "Americans never told us here about it until late in the day". As late as October 20th, Sir Orme Sargent explained that "unfortunately there was a bad oversight in the Communications Department".[62]

The most sought after man in the House of Commons on the night of August 24th was R. A. Butler. As the Foreign Office representative, MPs naturally approached him with the one burning question after the German-Soviet pact had been announced that day. They all asked "what 'our intelligence was up to?' " Butler did not have the answer. He turned to the Foreign Office.

There the very same question was being asked. A "paper of secret intelligence on the subject of German-Russian intrigues"

---

* Was there anything more sinister? On September 27th, 1939 Captain John Herbert King, a cipher clerk in the Communications Department of the Foreign Office, was arrested and on October 18th he was sentenced to ten years' imprisonment on charges of spying for the USSR. He may have been responsible. (Dilks, *Cadogan Diaries, 1938–1945,* 207–8; *The Times,* June 8th, 1956; *The Daily Express,* June 9th, 1956.) But August 1939 was a month of intense European crisis. The volume of telegraphic traffic through the Foreign Office was increasing to the extent of causing "serious delays" to occur. Telegrams from Washington would not have had the highest priority. On the authority of Sir Alexander Cadogan, additional staff was hired. With the exposure of King, there was a total dismissal of officials and a reorganisation of the Communications Department. (FO366/1062, X4714/448/504; FO366/1063, X10631, 12904/448/504.)

was hastily assembled. That paper has remained secret; but the Foreign Office archives contain Laurence Collier's memorandum, written on August 25th, which examined these intelligence reports in some detail. It is sufficiently revealing to answer that mystifying question put to Butler and never since publicly known.

British intelligence on German-Soviet relations, Collier wrote, came through four channels: either direct German or Soviet sources, or third parties in touch with German or Soviet sources. Information direct from Soviet sources was scarce and "notoriously difficult" to obtain. Much more plentiful, though "contradictory", was information from direct German sources. While reports from third parties "usually came from persons of questionable reliability".

> In general, we find ourselves, when attempting to assess the value of these secret reports, somewhat in the position of the Captain of the Forty Thieves when, having put a chalk mark on Ali Baba's door, he found that Morgiana had put similar marks on all the other doors in the street and had no indication to show which mark was the true one. In this case there were passages in many of our reports which told against the probability of a German-Soviet rapprochement. We had no indications that these statements were in general any less reliable than those in a contrary sense.

British intelligence had failed to penetrate the veil of secrecy surrounding the German-Soviet negotiations. The precise details of meetings and conversations between German and Soviet officials which were known in Washington eluded London. "The fact remains that we were never told that the Germans & Russians had started negotiations with one another – which was the only thing that mattered," Sir Orme Sargent angrily minuted on September 3rd.[63] It was a costly intelligence failure.

During the night of August 25th the Anglo-French military mission left Moscow. Admiral Drax returned via train to Finland and then plane from Helsinki to London. He was back in his home on August 28th in time for his 59th birthday. General Doumenc returned to France to take up his command. Sir William Seeds was a heart-broken man. The German-Soviet pact hit him like a bombshell. He was always aware that Moscow might seek an agreement with Berlin. His enthusiasm for an alliance with the USSR compelled him to hope the catastrophe might be averted. Many years later he recalled how he had been "left holding the beastly baby!"[64] In January 1940 he departed from the USSR and retired from diplomatic life.

CHAPTER TWELVE

Crisis

HERRINGS and margarine, customs inspectors and frontier guards, were the mixture of mundane and politically explosive issues which ended the last peace lull before the outbreak of war. On August 4th a long-simmering customs dispute between Poland and the Danzig authorities suddenly erupted. Until that day such disputes had always been the "daily bread of Danzig-Polish intercourse", as the British Consul-General, F. M. Shepherd wrote to Lord Halifax.

A report that the Danzig authorities no longer intended to recognise the Polish customs inspectors and that even the frontier with east Prussia would be opened reached the Polish government on August 4th. The response was immediate. Such a direct challenge to Polish treaty rights invited a stiffly worded warning. Any such action, the President of the Danzig Senate, Arthur Greiser, was told that night, would be met with immediate reprisals and would be considered a *casus belli*. The orders must be countermanded within twenty-four hours.[1]

Had Hitler opened his final campaign to solve the Danzig dispute? The Poles took no chances. Their ally, the British government, was frightened. This crisis seemed the fulfilment of a long-standing nightmare: a local Danzig squabble, escalating into a full-scale confrontation. A telegram was hastily sent to Clifford Norton, the Chargé d'Affaires in Warsaw, late in the evening of August 4th.

"Do you consider that any intervention on our part would contribute to a settlement of the points now in dispute?" Lord Halifax asked. The inquiry came too late. The Polish government, contrary to repeated assurances, had already acted without consulting London. Whatever anger or apprehension the Foreign Office felt, there was initially official silence. Sir Howard Kennard, the Ambassador in Warsaw, delivered on his own initiative a mild reprimand to Colonel Jozef Beck. Britain ought to be informed in advance of any action contemplated in any similar situation. Beck, as usual, dutifully agreed.

The Polish government had been precipitate, but also fortunate. On August 5th Greiser replied by telephone that no action had ever been planned. The Poles wanted written confirmation. They got this too; all as a result of what proved to be an order issued by a subordinate customs official and a "baseless rumour".

What changed a Polish-Danzig dispute into a crisis was publicity. An official Polish press communiqué released details of the exchange of notes. The British and French press, despite government advice to the contrary, took up the story – dramatising it as a "climb down" by the Danzig Senate and a victory for Beck's foreign policy.[2] It proved a most regrettable development.

Hitler was infuriated. He would not suffer a public humiliation. He ordered an immediate militant press campaign to be launched against Poland. The next time the Poles dared to send an "ultimatum" to Danzig there would be an appropriate German reply, he told the Hungarian Foreign Minister, Count Istvan Csaky, on August 8th. What that might be Hitler presumably revealed in confidence to Gauleiter Forster with whom he was at that time also conferring. The next day Ernst von Weizsäcker, acting on instructions from Joachim von Ribbentrop, let loose. A repetition of any ultimatum-type demands made to Danzig, he told the Polish Chargé d'Affaires, Prince Lubomirski, would aggravate German-Polish relations. It would also invite "consequences" for which Poland would be responsible. Lubomirski's attempts to explain were cut short.

"Now it begins", Beck said as he read the report of Weizsäcker's remarks. He returned at once to Warsaw from a country retreat. In anger, contrary to advice, though with dashing courage, he sent a reply. It amounted to a curt warning to the Germans to mind their own business.[3]

Beck had got in the last word and was still worried. This "was the first time that the Reich had directly intervened in the dispute between Poland and [the] Danzig Senate", he told Sir Howard Kennard on August 10th. Would the British government consider taking "any useful action in Berlin to reinforce Polish attitude"? Ambassador Raczynski repeated this plan for a "preventive démarche" when he saw Sir Alexander Cadogan at the Foreign Office the same day. Raczynski then revealed a more important message. Beck was now anxious to replace the existing reciprocal guarantees with an Anglo-Polish alliance.

It was the wrong moment to ask the British government to confront Hitler with a preventive démarche. Beck's action against the Danzig Senate was of course supported at the time by Kennard and regarded in the Foreign Office as a reasonable reaction to a dangerous threat. However, as Hitler's anger became known and as the anti-Polish press campaign intensified, British confidence in the Poles waned. They had reacted "too precipitately and vigorously", Roger Makins minuted later.[4] His harsher judgement reflected the growing anxiety at the European situation which had worsened after the customs dispute.

"The conditions of our guarantee to Poland are not such as to bear indefinite extensions", Lord Halifax minuted on August 10th, "we must (however we do it!) make it plain that our guarantee was not a blank cheque. Therefore consultation *before* instead of *after*." A warning in suitable terms was sent to Beck.

It is not surprising that the Foreign Office preferred to ignore Beck's suggestion of a preventive démarche. Sir Alexander Cadogan wanted to wait because the Germans would probably tell the British to mind their own business. There was also a more important consideration. On August 10th news had reached the Foreign Office that Professor Carl Burckhardt, the League High Commissioner in Danzig, had accepted an invitation to visit Hitler at Berchtesgaden for a discussion of the Danzig situation. Until the results of this visit were known, Cadogan felt "it would be dangerous to take any action which might tip the scale if Herr Hitler's intentions in summoning him are pacific rather than the reverse."[5]

Parliament had risen on August 4th. Neville Chamberlain had advised his relatives to take their holidays. He did the same and went fishing in the north of Scotland. But the affairs of state rudely intruded into his favourite pastime. Neither gave any comfort. "Everything is going wrong here from the fishing point of view," he wrote on August 13th to Cecil Syers, his Principal Private Secretary at 10 Downing Street. Chamberlain was confident Cadogan was right to await the result of the Burckhardt-Hitler conversation: "It would seem likely that this will give us the best indication of the probable course of events during this month." The letter concluded: "I am sending you a salmon (not caught by me) and will be glad if you will distribute such of it as you don't want yourself to any of the staff who are on duty. . . . The cook or the kitchen maid at No. 10 will cut up the fish."[6]

An invitation to a conference with Hitler contained an element of high drama. Professor Burckhardt's departure from Danzig, aboard Hitler's own Condor aircraft, was cloaked in strictest secrecy. He was received by Hitler on August 11th at Berchtesgaden.

"Herr Hitler looked . . . much older and whiter. He gave the impression of fear, and seemed nervous, pathetic and almost shaken at times", Burckhardt later reported. Hitler's rhetoric and views, however, came across as clear as ever. He was furious at press accusations that he had lost the war of nerves and that his bluff had been called by the courageous Poles.

"If the slightest incident happens I shall crush the Poles without warning in such a way that no trace of Poland can be found afterwards. . . . If I have to wage war, I would rather do it today than tomorrow." An Anglo-French alliance with Russia, Hitler continued "won't make our flesh creep". In any case, Moscow "will not pull the chestnuts out of the fire for others. . . . For grain, I need space in the East. For timber, I need one colony, one only."

"I came here about Danzig", Burckhardt was finally able to interject into the tirade. Always adept at mixing harangue with the inevitable carrot, Hitler calmly said: "If the Poles leave

Danzig absolutely calm, if they don't try to overtrump me with false cards, then I can wait."

A further carrot Hitler reserved for the British: "I want to live in peace with England and to conclude a definitive pact; to guarantee all the English possessions in the world and to collaborate." A chance to meet a German-speaking Englishman to discuss this would be most welcome.

According to prearranged plans, Burckhardt immediately proceeded to his home in Bâle. There he gave representatives from the British and French Foreign Offices a full description of the conversation. The enlightenment as to German intentions, eagerly awaited in London and Paris, did not materialise. Both capitals agreed that his motives in sending for Burckhardt remained unclear, and the results appeared inconclusive. Despite Hitler's ranting about the supremacy of German arms, the impression created in London was that he was "in a state of some doubt and indecision about the fortunes of war". When news of the meeting was leaked by the Danzig press, despite the elaborate secrecy precautions, Burckhardt's usefulness was irrevocably compromised.[7]

Hitler had presumably wanted to intimidate the Poles and sow suspicion between them and their allies, was William Strang's guess as to the motives for the visit. "I should hope the Poles understand that we are not deceived by such manoeuvres." Hitler must have known of Burckhardt's previous secret briefings to London and Paris. If Strang was right, Hitler's ploy failed. The only advice the British and French sent Colonel Beck, as a direct result, was to keep himself ready at all times to negotiate over Danzig, if there were any prospects of success.[8]

*

What Hitler had hinted to Professor Burckhardt came pouring out in unmistakable terms to an unsuspecting Count Galeazzo Ciano, the Italian Foreign Minister. Alarmed by what appeared to be Hitler's determination to solve the Danzig question by war, Ciano had received Mussolini's approval to go to Germany.

"The moment has come when we must really know how

matters stand", Ciano wrote in his diary. "Before letting me go he [Mussolini] recommends that I should frankly inform the Germans that we must avoid a conflict with Poland, since it will be impossible to localise it, and a general war would be disastrous for everybody." Ciano took to Germany a report, drafted by Mussolini, which begged Hitler to participate in international negotiations to settle European problems.

During a ten-hour meeting with Joachim von Ribbentrop at Schloss Fuschl, near Salzburg, Ciano received probably the scare of his life. He discovered that a clash between Germany and Poland was considered inevitable. According to Ribbentrop, who was impervious to argument, war would be localised. "Europe will be an impassive spectator of the merciless destruction of Poland by Germany." Even if Britain and France wished to intervene, they would not possibly injure Germany or the Axis. What were Germany's immediate plans of action? Ciano asked at last. "All decisions were still locked in the Führer's impenetrable bosom," was the reply. Ciano departed with the profound conviction that Ribbentrop intended to provoke a conflict.

The next day, August 12th, Ciano was taken to see Hitler at the Berghof. He found the Führer in a large drawing-room, standing in front of a table covered with maps. These Hitler used to impress his wobbly guest with the unprecedented military strength of Germany, and his determination not to yield over the Danzig question.

Ciano then stepped forward to pore over the maps. Italy, he explained, believed that a German-Polish war could not be localised. It would develop into a European conflagration for which Italy was not prepared. Hitler disagreed. "He personally was absolutely convinced that the Western democracies would, in the last resort, recoil from unleashing a general war." No time must be lost before resolving the crisis. After September Poland was a vast swamp, unsuitable for military operations. The Danzig question must be settled "one way or the other by the end of August". Therefore, a "move against Poland must be expected at any moment".

Ciano was given an unexpected glimpse of the reason for

Hitler's confident exposition. The USSR, Hitler said, "would probably never intervene on behalf of Poland whom she thoroughly detested."

When their conversation was resumed the following day, Ciano knew he had failed in his mission. Listening to Hitler's elaborate military and political calculations he "folded up like a jack-knife". The plan for a communiqué calling for a peaceful solution was dropped. Ciano only intervened to ask until what date Hitler was prepared to wait. The "end of August must be the time limit" came the categorical reply.

"He has decided to strike, and strike he will", Ciano recorded in his diary. "I return to Rome completely disgusted with the Germans, with their leader, with their way of doing things. They have betrayed us and lied to us."[9]

Count Ciano's visit to Germany was no secret. Nor were the results of his conversations unknown in London. The Foreign Office discovered that a difference of opinion over Danzig existed between Hitler and Mussolini. Hitler was known to be seeking a solution by the end of August. Mussolini intended to intervene late in the crisis with a proposal for a conference, "which Great Britain would be sure to accept". Such a conference would give the Axis Powers all they wanted.

Each stage of Hitler's betrayal of his ally was relayed to Neville Chamberlain in between fishing outings in Scotland. On August 14th, a day after Ciano's return to Rome, Lord Halifax wrote to Chamberlain, giving him information "pretty straight from the horse's mouth". The Ciano–Ribbentrop meeting derived from Mussolini's efforts "to produce good arguments in favour of moderation. . . . I hope to hear soon what passed."

The gist of what transpired at Salzburg soon arrived. As previously, Sir Robert Vansittart had been given the information. On August 17th William Strang minuted: "Dr Kordt has, we gather, been reported as saying that he hears from his brother (who is Ribbentrop's private secretary) that the Italians have *not* given the Germans a blank cheque over Danzig."[10]

While Italy's attitude gave some comfort, the general outlook was bleak. By August 11th the Foreign Office was aware that a state of complete military preparedness had been proclaimed in Germany for August 15th. The deployment of German submarines in the north and south Atlantic, the increase in the number of ships carrying arms to east Prussia, and arrangements for requisitioning private transport in Germany added up to a dangerous picture. "In general," Halifax wrote to Chamberlain on August 14th, "things do not look too good and a good deal of talk is going on about very early action being taken."[11] War Office assessments, based on detailed intelligence of German military plans and preparations, were equally gloomy. Officials counted on the German General Staff to oppose a war involving a two-front campaign. On the political issues involved, the War Office was proving admirably clear-headed: "the Danzig question is really only an incidental part of Germany's ultimate aims at the expense of Poland."[12]

Shooting incidents on the Polish-German frontier increased daily. German troops began to be deployed on Poland's frontiers. The Nazi press campaign mounted in intensity. It rejected any possibility of compromise over Danzig, linked the questions of Danzig and the Corridor, and proclaimed that the honour of the German nation was at stake. Dramatic stories of the persecution of the German minority in Poland covered pages of the press. The situation was getting out of control.

On August 16th Sir Nevile Henderson visited the German Secretary of State. The "situation had very gravely deteriorated since August 4th", Weizsäcker said, at once putting the blame on the shoulders of Poland. In the discussion which followed, the Danzig dispute was forgotten. Weizsäcker, reflecting current propaganda, concentrated instead on the persecution of the German minority in Poland. It was out of the question for Germany to take the initiative and make a peaceful gesture. The point had been reached when events could drift no longer. The absence of any suggestions for a compromise or a solution from the moderate Weizsäcker was ominous.

On the evening of August 18th, Sir Alexander Cadogan's dinner at home was suddenly interrupted. Sir Robert Vansittart, he recorded in his diary, "rang up in high state of excitement". He was soon in Cadogan's home, eating a cold supper and excitedly talking. "*His* source has told him H[itler] has chosen war, to begin between 25th and 28th." It was the same source which had provided what proved to be accurate intelligence in September 1938. "This is the beginning of the 'War of Nerves'," Cadogan mused after Vansittart had departed. He then telephoned to Lord Halifax in Yorkshire, asking him to return to London.[13]

The question of what action to take was answered by sheer coincidence. It was continued in a telegram received that same evening from Sir Nevile Henderson. It was marked "Most Immediate" and began: "I have come to definite conclusion that if peace is to be preserved present situation cannot be allowed to continue any longer." The moment has come, Henderson stated, "for Prime Minister to address secret and personal letter to Hitler setting forth unequivocally England's position and her obligations." Either someone like General Sir Edmund Ironside should carry the letter to Hitler and explain verbally where Britain stood, or, Henderson concluded, he himself should do it.

Henderson's suggestions added the vital impetus to a problem which had been simmering in the Foreign Office for days. During the Burckhardt-Hitler conversation on August 11th, the idea of sending a German-speaking Englishman to Hitler had arisen. Gauleiter Forster strongly supported it and wished to arrange the visit.

No one particularly liked the idea. To Sir Alexander Cadogan all such manoeuvres seemed "part of Hitler's double campaign of intimidation and insincere and specious approaches". The dilemma, as Lord Halifax had written to Neville Chamberlain on August 14th, was acute. For "apart from the difficulty of finding the individual, I find it a bit difficult to imagine what he wld. say, inasmuch as Hitler's whole line of thought seems to be the familiar one of the free hand in the East, and, if he really wants to annex land in the East on wh. he can settle Germans to grow wheat, I confess I don't see any way of accommodating him."[14]

If no reply was made, there was the added danger that Hitler would be in a position to score a propaganda victory. He would claim that his conciliatory gesture had been rebuffed. Halifax was inclined, therefore, to respond and himself outlined a bold message. It laid the burden squarely on Hitler to put forward "any suggestions he might wish to make". These would be gladly considered in London.

The problem was referred on August 17th to the absent Prime Minister. He favoured replying to Hitler, yet he understood the kernel of the approaching crisis. The British had to keep attention focused firstly on a solution of the Danzig question, not detrimental to Polish interests. Wider issues could be dealt with later. Yet Chamberlain was aware that "Hitler would not discuss Danzig alone but wanted to go further & deal with grain and timber", that is, a free hand in the east. Tactfully, the Prime Minister deferred a decision on such delicate issues until his return to London.[15]

The Henderson telegram of August 18th and Vansittart's secret intelligence decided the issue. After a full day of consultations at the Foreign Office, Halifax wrote to the Prime Minister on August 19th. Halifax did not disguise the seriousness of the situation. While the dates set for German action against Poland, August 25th–28th, could be part of the "general nerve storm", they just could not be ignored. The situation was a "black one, and there is no time to lose". Hitler must be made to abandon his belief that Britain would not fight, particularly once Poland was rapidly crushed. With that in mind, Halifax suggested "that we should find means of conveying to him a clear message on behalf of H.M.G. defining our position". Halifax himself favoured a personal letter from the Prime Minister to Hitler.

The intelligence received about the Ciano-Hitler talks also inspired an approach to Rome. Everything had to be done to encourage Mussolini not to abandon his restraining efforts. A telegram was sent on August 19th to Sir Percy Loraine containing a message for urgent transmission to the Duce. It broached several possible means of achieving a peaceful settlement by free negotiations on equal terms between Germany and Poland. Halifax specifically warned Mussolini of the "dangerous illusions" that any war would end with a defeat of Poland. "If Mussolini wants to play at all", Halifax conjectured, "this perhaps gives him some encouragement."[16] During the next two weeks the British were to find Mussolini was desperate to play.

For two more days the draft letter from Chamberlain to Hitler underwent extensive revisions by many hands at the Foreign Office. It was ready in time for Cabinet consideration on August 22nd.

Meanwhile, military preparations went ahead in support of diplomatic efforts. Military advisers were recalled from holiday. On August 18th the Deputy Chiefs of Staff held an emergency meeting. The telegrams coming into the Foreign Office pointed to an approaching crisis in eastern Europe. It was reasonable, therefore, to dismiss the nightmare of the "bolt from the blue". This meant a precautionary period of three to four days would be likely. All service departments were asked to prepare a list of measures which the crisis period would demand. The Deputy Chiefs of Staff also recommended, in strongest possible terms, to pursue a policy of restraint in air bombardment in order not to invite German retaliation.[17] This had been the strategy agreed with the French during their military talks in London in early April. By implication it added another nail to the Polish coffin. For it placed the burden on Britain and France of opening in the west the air war to relieve Poland, and no plans for this existed.

In a series of discussions between the Chiefs of Staff, Lord Halifax, Lord Chatfield and Sir Horace Wilson on August 20th and 21st, both measures were approved. Decisions were made quickly and resolutely. As Sir Horace Wilson told an informal meeting of the Chiefs of Staff on August 20th, the reaction to Chamberlain's proposed letter was unknown. Hitler might regard it as provocative. Britain must be militarily prepared for the worst.[18]

The situation looked even blacker when the Cabinet met at 3 p.m. on August 22nd. The main news that day was of Ribbentrop's coming visit to Moscow. Chamberlain opened the meeting by apologising for having to recall Ministers "in circumstances which could only be described as grave". Lord Halifax then briefed the Cabinet on developments in Moscow since their last meeting on August 2nd.

With the situation in the Soviet capital so suddenly altered, though still confused, intelligent discussion of a possible German-Soviet pact was out of the question. The "moral effect of the conclusion of such an agreement at the present time would be very great", Halifax pointedly remarked. For it was upon the Polish crisis and not the Russian imbroglio that the preservation of peace depended. It was for this reason that Halifax could tell the Cabinet that a German-Soviet pact "was perhaps not of very great importance in itself". A successful Anglo-French-Soviet alliance might have deterred Hitler. It would not by itself have solved the German-Polish dispute.

The discussion of steps to meet the current crisis was next taken up by Chamberlain. Parliament would be recalled on August 24th to pass the Emergency Powers (Defence) Bill. Preliminary steps towards mobilisation would be taken. A statement would at once be issued to the BBC and the press, announcing that whatever form a German-Soviet agreement took, it did not effect Britain's determination to support Poland. "The Prime Minister said that, in his view, it was unthinkable that we should not carry out these obligations." For the next eleven days, Chamberlain stood by these fighting words. Whatever compromise or solution was sought, under inhuman pressure and tension, the final course of action was never in doubt.

There now remained the question of the personal letter to Hitler and the method of conveying it. Chamberlain realised the objections to once again repeating Britain's point of view when it was already known to Hitler and would only irritate him. Nevertheless Chamberlain favoured the idea and had come to the conclusion that General Sir Edmund Ironside would not be the right emissary. Furthermore, in light of the reported agreement between Germany and the USSR, he wanted his letter to reach Hitler through normal diplomatic channels.

There were some Cabinet Ministers who were sceptical of sending Hitler a letter. A general public declaration would be equally effective. Others doubted the wisdom of dropping the idea of a special emissary. Their view was dramatically re-inforced when a telegram from the Consul-General in Danzig, Francis Mitchie Shepherd, was brought into the Cabinet room. Ernst von Weizsäcker had sent Lieutenant-Colonel Count Gerhard von Schwerin by air to Danzig to plead with Professor Burckhardt to support the idea of an emissary to Hitler, prefer-ably to arrive while Ribbentrop was out of the way in Moscow. Yet in the end, the Cabinet supported the Prime Minister. A letter was a personal appeal to Hitler, difficult for him to ignore, and it placed the British position on record.

After consultations between the Foreign Office and the Prime Minister, the text of the letter was finally telegraphed to Berlin at 9.50 that evening. It was firm and unequivocal, yet offered com-plete latitude for compromise and conciliation. Any German-Soviet agreement, Chamberlain wrote to Hitler, would not alter Britain's determination to fulfil her obligations to Poland. Conscious of the weakness of the eastern front, however, Chamberlain also hinted that a German success on any one front would not bring an early end to hostilities.

There were no questions in dispute between Poland and Ger-many which could not be peacefully resolved, the letter con-tinued, "if only a situation of confidence could be restored to enable discussions to be carried on in an atmosphere different from that which prevails today." Then followed the practical suggestions. Let Germany and Poland agree on an initial period of truce, during which minority problems could be discussed, extending eventually to all their outstanding issues. Any settle-ment reached would have to be guaranteed by other powers. That would be followed by a discussion of the wider problems disturbing international relations.[19]

As soon as he had received instructions to seek an interview with Hitler, Henderson set the German Foreign Office in motion.

With Ribbentrop already on his way to the Soviet capital, the letter went directly into Hitler's hands. At 1 p.m. on August 23rd, at the same time as Ribbentrop's plane was landing at Moscow's airport, Henderson was received by Hitler at the Berghof. It was their first meeting since March 1st. After the two afternoon conversations which followed, it would have been reasonable to conclude they would never meet again.

With the knowledge that he was on the point of astonishing the world with a German-Soviet agreement, Hitler viciously criticised British and Polish policy. He was excitable and uncompromising; his language "violent and exaggerated". Britain had "poisoned" the atmosphere by her guarantee to the Poles. This had made a peaceful settlement impossible. Should any further mobilisation measures be taken, he warned, there would be general mobilisation in Germany. "At the next instance of Polish provocation, I shall act. The questions of Danzig and the Corridor will be settled one way or another."

Henderson, at least in his official report of the conversations, stuck to his brief: he emphasised Britain's determination to stand by Poland. But from the German record it is clear he went further in trying to mollify Hitler. The Ambassador stated that he had never believed in an Anglo-French-Soviet pact. Proof of Chamberlain's friendship was to be found in the fact that Winston Churchill had not been taken into the Cabinet. "The hostile attitude to Germany did not represent the will of the British people. It was the work of Jews and enemies of the Nazis."

As he was leaving, Henderson commented that war seemed inevitable and expressed regret that both his mission to Berlin and his visit had ended in failure.

The practical proposals advanced by Chamberlain to end the crisis had been ignored. Hitler was not interested. In the reply which he handed Henderson before parting after their second meeting, Hitler declared his determination to solve the questions of Danzig and the Corridor, and save the German minority in Poland from further "atrocities". A solution to wider European problems rested with the Versailles powers who would have to prove their goodwill towards Germany.

A silent witness to Hitler's obvious attempt to bully Britain into abandoning Poland was Ernst von Weizsäcker. He noticed a change in Hitler's mood as soon as the Ambassador had left the room. Hardly had the door been shut "when Hitler slapped himself on the thigh, laughed and said: 'Chamberlain won't survive that conversation: his Cabinet will fall this evening'."[20]

How little did Hitler really understand the British. He was bubbling over with supreme confidence. Ribbentrop was in Moscow. The propaganda campaign against Poland was developing efficiently. The Italians might cause trouble with their hesitations, but not Mussolini. "The Duce is the man with the strongest nerves in Italy." Hitler was confident he would give no trouble. While the British and French were led by mediocrities who would not stand by Poland.

"Our enemies are small fry. I saw them in Munich", Hitler had jubilantly told his Commanders-in-Chief on August 22nd. He had summoned them to the Berghof to explain his decision to act and to ginger up their confidence. In a brilliant military exposé, he showed why, to his mind, the moment was right to strike successfully against Poland. "Now the probability is still great that the West will not intervene. We must take the risk", Hitler stated. "England and France have undertaken obligations which neither is in a position to fulfil."

Hitler had badly miscalculated. "A quick decision in view of the season" is what he had offered the assembled military chiefs. Without a second front in the east, he assumed the Western Powers would not intervene to help the isolated Poles. He had expressed just one hesitation. "I am only afraid that at the last moment some swine or other will yet submit to me a plan for mediation."

On August 23rd Hitler gave the order to set *Y-Tag* – the day of attack – for 4.15 or 4.30 a.m. on August 26th.[21] He reserved for August 25th the final order to attack, confident the anti-German front would by then be in ruins.

In London, Neville Chamberlain was having a long talk with the American Ambassador, Joseph Kennedy. The Prime Minister appeared terribly depressed. The situation, he said, looked "very bad but I have done everything that I can think of and it seems as if all my work has come to naught."

The "spectre of the impending catastrophe" was over Chamberlain all the time, Kennedy afterwards wrote. To push the Poles to make concessions, Chamberlain had pointed out, would be "disastrous. . . . He says the futility of it all is the thing that is frightful; after all they cannot save the Poles; they can merely carry on a war of revenge that will mean the destruction of the whole of Europe."

Such sentiments must have strongly affected Kennedy. In a conversation earlier that day with Lord Halifax, he had tried to encourage the British government to press the Poles. He was afraid "that there was real danger of the Poles not appreciating their true position" in light of the day's developments in Moscow. Halifax told him this was impossible. Kennedy's behaviour in allowing himself "to be badly jolted" confirmed the Foreign Office in its view that he tended "to lag behind the President & U.S. public opinion in resistance to aggression".[22]

On August 24th, against a background of morning newspaper reports of the German-Soviet agreement and of Sir Nevile Henderson's abortive meeting with Hitler, the British Cabinet was assembled at short notice. Chamberlain had asked for the meeting, not to take decisions, there were none to be made, but to give details of the latest developments.

The shock of these events seemed to have paralysed the Cabinet. The implications seemed not to have yet penetrated. The Cabinet agreed that nothing should be done to press the idea of negotiating with Germany on Warsaw "as this might involve some risk of loss of confidence in us by the Poles". Everyone agreed that the only fruitful avenue appeared to be negotiations between the two powers on the minority question. Here again the Poles must not be pushed too far. Chamberlain's statement of Britain's determination to abide by the guarantee was received, as Captain Euan Wallace, the Minister of Transport, noted in his diary, "with unanimous assent and approbation".[23]

That afternoon Chamberlain addressed a special session of the House of Commons, once again against a crisis background. He spoke with a "studied sobriety" appropriate to the situation, in the "tone of a coroner summing up a murder case". Only for a brief moment, when he declared – "God knows I have tried my best" – did any emotion warm his voice. He briefly described the Henderson-Hitler encounters and once again reaffirmed Britain's determination to honour her obligations. There was no weakness or lack of resolve in his speech.[24]

Europe seemed set for war. Hitler had set his military machine in motion. Chamberlain had spoken. Mussolini's efforts at conciliation had proven futile. Beck had watched impassively, silently. Within twenty-four hours Poland suddenly was to be given a new lease of life. The glimmer of negotiation shone through the gloom. Hitler, it appears, and not the Western Allies, had lost his nerve.

Ribbentrop returned to Berlin, where Hitler was now in residence, to give him details of the Moscow success. Hitler was fascinated but also troubled. The British Parliament had earlier that day approved emergency measures and backed the Prime Minister who had not fallen or resigned. Ernst von Weizsäcker had that day also, in a rare private talk with the Führer, urged him to take one final step to arrive at a reasonable solution with the Polish government. The Italians, Weizsäcker warned, feeding Hitler's own growing doubts, were behaving as if the crisis was no concern of theirs.[25] In the evening Hitler spent long hours in conversation with Ribbentrop, Göring and other advisers. It must then have been decided to give the British another chance to abandon Poland.

For a change of tactics Hitler adopted a change of mood. At 12.45 p.m. on August 25th he sent a message to Sir Nevile Henderson to come to the Reich Chancellery at 1.30. The Ambassador found Hitler "calm and 'normal, speaking with great earnestness and apparent sincerity." Hitler explained that he had "turned things over in his mind once more" and "his conscience compelled him to make this final effort. . . . It was his last attempt." It was, he said, to be as decisive a move towards Britain as he had just made towards the USSR.

Polish provocation had become intolerable, Hitler stated.

"Germany was in all the circumstances determined to abolish these Macedonian conditions on her eastern frontier." The problem of Danzig and the Corridor must be solved. Then and only then, he magnanimously concluded, would he make England a "large comprehensive offer". Subject to certain minor conditions, he was prepared to personally guarantee the continued existence of the British Empire and even place the power of the German Reich at the disposal of the British government. Further proof of his good intentions was that he now regarded Germany's western frontiers as fixed and final.

With the Polish question solved, Hitler assured Henderson, he would settle down. He preferred to end his life "as an artist and not as a war-monger". Henderson tried to make Hitler understand that his country would never abandon Poland. The offer just made still lacked plans for a peaceful settlement with Poland.

"If you think it useless then do not send my offer at all", Hitler said. Sensing the importance of what had just taken place, Henderson accepted Hitler's suggestion to fly at once to London. There he would personally lay these ideas before the British government.[26]

What Hitler had done was to dust off his oldest and most deeply held conviction. Anglo-German peace depended on his having a free hand in the east. Britain was welcome to the seas. The offer had been dangled many times before, and always rejected.

By the time Henderson left the Reich Chancellery, Hitler was already pondering his next step. The attack against Poland was a mere fourteen hours away. The issue of the executive order to attack had already been postponed before Henderson's visit, from 2 to 3.02 p.m.[27] He could not have expected Henderson to return from London with a considered reply in the short period before attacking. His offer was sincere. For in making it, he was already considering a delay to allow the British to accept his bribe and abandon Poland.

Two events within the next few hours led Hitler to humiliate himself before his military commanders. At about 4.30 news reached Berlin, probably as a result of intercepted telephone conversations between the Polish Embassy in London and Warsaw, that Britain and Poland were about to sign their long delayed alliance. With this report before him, Hitler sat brooding at his desk. Britain and Poland were now firmly bound by treaty.

This unwelcome news was followed by even worse. Early that morning Hitler had written to Mussolini, justifying the German-Soviet agreement and advising him that a conflict with Poland was possibly hours away. He asked for the Duce's understanding and support.

Mussolini's reply, handed to Hitler at about 6 p.m., was lavish in its understanding, but meagre in support. Hitler was "considerably shaken". Mussolini had backed out of the conflict and deserted his ally. If Germany attacked Poland and a general war followed Italy would take no initiative. She had neither the military supplies nor raw materials to resist an Anglo-French attack.[28]

Hitler knew he was temporarily beaten. He at once summoned General Keitel, Chief of the High Command of the *Wehrmacht*, who, on leaving moments later, was heard to exclaim: "The order to advance must be delayed again." It was a "miracle that the order stopping the advance got through in time." *Y-tag* was postponed. Further orders would be given the next day.

"I must see whether we can eliminate British intervention", Hitler told Field-Marshal Göring that evening.[29] Hitler had just given the diplomats a final chance to deliver Poland to him.

CHAPTER THIRTEEN

The Coming of the
German-Polish War

PEACE on August 25th rested on the shoulders of two men – an accredited Ambassador and a well-meaning busybody. Hitler had sent Sir Nevile Henderson to London with his official ideas for peace. He had also agreed to another scheme favoured by Field-Marshal Göring. Birger Dahlerus, the Swedish businessman, had lost none of his enthusiasm for personally engineering an Anglo-German settlement. On August 24th Göring had spent several hours with him discussing the situation, first at Karinhall and then in his two-seater car driving to Berlin.

Later that afternoon Dahlerus had telephoned to one of his British businessmen contacts in London and cryptically said: "the Boss, i.e. Field-Marshal Göring, wanted to know whether there was any chance of selling rubber in London". Both Dahlerus and Göring had been satisfied with the reply. The British government had still seemed interested in a reasonable settlement. Hitler gave his official blessing to the secret mission and Dahlerus flew to London, arriving at Croydon at 1.30 p.m. on August 25th. His task was to convince the British government that Germany desired to come to an understanding.

Why should Göring, at this moment of grave crisis, have spent so much time with Dahlerus? The Foreign Office was naturally intrigued. The Secret Intelligence Service believed Göring had replaced Ribbentrop in Hitler's affections. Lord Halifax agreed to see the Swede. By the time the two men met, about 7 o'clock on the evening of August 25th, first reports of Hitler's conversation with Sir Nevile Henderson earlier that day were available.

Halifax was feeling more optimistic. Now that Hitler had reopened the possibility of further discussions, he told Dahlerus, there was no longer any need for his services.

Dahlerus was not to be got rid of so easily. The next morning he was back at the Foreign Office, speaking excitedly to Lord Halifax. It was necessary to send an immediate message to Berlin, Dahlerus advised, in order to calm the situation. He had spoken the previous evening to Field-Marshal Göring who was nervous and agitated. The signing of the Anglo-Polish treaty had been considered as a "slap in the face" by Hitler. Halifax conferred with Chamberlain and concocted a brief letter containing the usual platitudes.[1] With that in his pocket, Dahlerus set off, making part of the journey, from Amsterdam to Berlin, aboard the German plane which had carried Sir Nevile Henderson to London.

———

"They aren't proposals at all" and the "most impudent document I have ever seen" was how Sir Alexander Cadogan and Oliver Harvey, respectively, summed up Hitler's communication to Sir Nevile Henderson on August 25th. Work began at once on drafting a reply. Close consultation between the Foreign Office and 10 Downing Street continued until well past midnight and again the following morning, August 26th.[2]

The first of three Cabinets to grapple with Hitler's communication gathered at 10 Downing Street at 6.30 p.m. Sir Nevile Henderson, who had arrived in London at midday, found himself attending his second Cabinet meeting in twelve months. It proved to be mainly an exploratory meeting. Lord Halifax began by submitting

that two conflicting desires were expressed in Herr Hitler's letter. The first was his keen desire to settle the Polish question. The second, his desire to avoid a quarrel with the British Empire. He referred more than once to the position as it would exist when the Polish question had been settled, but he was careful not to say what kind of settlement he had in mind. . . .

The ultimate question was, of course, whether he wanted a settlement with Poland on his own terms more than he wanted to avoid war with Great Britain.

Halifax "felt no confidence as to the answer to this question." He was impressed, however, by one important act. Despite "fairly precise information" that Germany intended to attack Poland that night or the next morning, it was significant that Hitler had arranged for the Ambassador, bearing a special message, to fly to London in a German plane. Would Hitler have gone to such lengths if his intentions were sinister? Halifax seemed to think not. A reply to Hitler, which suggested the basis of a settlement of the German-Polish dispute, seemed in order.

There was no question that "we had our obligations to Poland which we were bound to honour", Halifax continued. But, if a "solution could be arrived at which had regard to Poland's vital interests, and was subject to an international guarantee, it would be one which we could recommend to Poland."

There was no weakening in such words, nor any illusions about Hitler. Halifax went on to say that it was clearly Hitler's intention to divide Britain from her allies. Neville Chamberlain likewise understood what was being asked of him. Hitler's latest proposals had been made before. "The basic idea was that if Britain would leave Herr Hitler alone in his sphere, (Eastern Europe), he would leave us alone." Chamberlain had never previously accepted this division of the world. Hitler was deluding himself if he believed the Prime Minister would jump at the offer at such a period of crisis.

Sir Nevile Henderson then answered questions put to him by several Cabinet Ministers. He "suggested that, however little faith one might have in Herr Hitler's promises, one might at least test them out." This seemingly fatuous advice had a practical basis and explains all British activity for the next five days. For on August 25th the Chiefs of Staff had decided, as this Cabinet was informed, that if an ultimatum was to be issued with all essential war preparations completed, the earliest date could be August

31st. It appeared to the Cabinet useful, in the meantime, to explore Hitler's proposals and intentions.

This feeling was strongly encouraged by Sir Nevile Henderson. He pleaded with the Cabinet to get Poland and Germany into direct negotiation. The "real value" of the British guarantee was to enable Poland to reach a negotiated settlement with Germany. Hitler, who "was quite well disposed towards Colonel Beck", contended that Britain had given Poland a blank cheque. It might make a considerable difference, Henderson advised, if he was able to tell Hitler that Britain could arrange for the Polish government to enter into direct negotiations with Germany. The Cabinet liked this idea and seemed convinced that the minority question formed a good basis on which to start negotiations. Agreement on this did not prevent the draft reply, which was then circulated, from being criticised as "too deferential" and capable of being "stiffened up".

A reply to Hitler which was "firm yet moderate in tone" is how the minutes record the wishes of the Cabinet. The Prime Minister took notes of all the criticisms and, with Lord Halifax and Sir John Simon, was invited to prepare a revised draft.[3] Sir Alexander Cadogan and R. A. Butler were added to the team which worked on late into the night of August 26th and again the following morning.

Meanwhile Birger Dahlerus was back again. Since leaving England the previous day, he had delivered Lord Halifax's private letter which had pleased Göring. He had also been subjected to the dubious honour of a post-midnight lecture from Hitler in the Reich Chancellery. The Führer had nothing new to say and emphasised that he had made his "last magnanimous offer to England". He had appeared determined to impress Dahlerus with his mastery of the intricacies of Germany's military machine. In his post-war memoirs, Dahlerus described how Hitler's "mental equilibrium was patently unstable" throughout the interview. He "seemed more like a phantom from a story book than a real person."

At 2.15 p.m. on August 27th Birger Dahlerus was ushered into the Cabinet room at 10 Downing Street. Chamberlain, Halifax

and Cadogan were waiting. Dahlerus carried a six-point programme which had been worked out verbally with Hitler the
previous night. It was a rehash of everything Henderson had
already heard with one notable exception. On August 25th Hitler
had shouted that the "problem of Danzig and the Corridor must
be solved." Now he had begun to spell out his demands.
"England was to help Germany to obtain Danzig and the
Corridor." A free harbour in Danzig would be at Polish disposal. Poland would also have a corridor to Gdynia, retaining the
whole of it and adequate surrounding territory.

Dahlerus did not tell Chamberlain, whom he was meeting for
the first time, of his impressions as to Hitler's mental instability.
"I shouldn't like to have him as a partner in my business", was
the only opinion he ventured. And in the record of his Berlin
conversations, shown to the Prime Minister, Dahlerus expressed
the belief that "Hitler himself is not in favour of war".

One personal suggestion made by Dahlerus to Chamberlain
had an important effect. From Sir Alexander Cadogan's room at
the Foreign Office, Dahlerus put through a call to Berlin, where
Hitler consented to wait another day for the British reply. This
would enable Dahlerus to return to Berlin, there to test Hitler's
reaction to "Britain's firm stand".[4]

At 3 p.m. the second Cabinet meeting dealing with the British
reply assembled after several hours' delay. Before settling down
to the tedious problems of drafting, Chamberlain and Halifax
revealed to the Cabinet for the first time the details of Dahlerus'
secret activities. They explained why so much attention was
being paid to this obscure Swede. His talks in Berlin, Halifax
said, seemed to prove that Göring had re-established his influence with Hitler. For more than a year Göring seemed to have
been out of favour. Always a perverse favourite of Lord Halifax,
it was exciting and encouraging to have evidence of Göring's
reinstatement.

Chamberlain added that Dahlerus "was not a man who came
very quickly to the point, and he often spent time in discussing
unimportant details. . . . The use of Mr 'D' was that he was an
intermediary who could talk to the Field Marshal, who, in his

turn, could put points to Herr Hitler." As to the latest German terms, the Prime Minister "could see no prospect of settlement . . . the Poles would fight rather than surrender the Corridor." He thought that the most they could concede would be Danzig, subject to the retention of special Polish rights, and extra-territorial roads for Germany across the Corridor; the whole settlement to be internationally guaranteed.

The Poles would, in fact, hardly have agreed and in any case it was, since August 25th, specifically guaranteed by Britain. But as he had earlier told the Cabinet, "it was desirable that we should work to gain time." The longer negotiations continued, the less likely the chance of war erupting.

It had further been made clear to Dahlerus, Chamberlain explained, that it was "not practicable" to discuss Anglo-German relations with Hitler, so long as there was the possibility that Germany might any day invade Poland.

The Cabinet fully agreed with this tough position. It was also agreed that Dahlerus must make it clear in Berlin that Germany and Poland must negotiate directly; that any agreement reached must be guaranteed by the great powers; "and that while we desired a settlement with Germany, we would certainly not fail to carry out our obligations to Poland."

The secret journeys of Dahlerus had begun to worry Halifax and he so informed his colleagues. He feared the issues might become confused. Chamberlain assured him that Dahlerus would return to Berlin only to prepare the way for the final British reply.

As the Cabinet had deliberated, what slowly emerged as the main stumbling block was the problem of communication. The crux of the projected British reply was to urge the Germans and Poles to negotiate, especially and firstly on the minority question. Yet it had been pointed out during the Cabinet that a telegram received early that morning from Paris made this impossible. On August 26th Hitler had flatly turned down an impassioned plea from the French Prime Minister, Edouard Daladier, to open negotiations with Poland.[5]

Could the British government succeed where the French had failed? If the mood of the Foreign Office at the time was anything to judge by, the answer was yes. The Germans "are wobbling"; "Hitler evidently hesitating"; "Hitler has cold feet"; and "Hitler is in a hole & knows it" were typical euphoric comments.[6]

This confident mood seemed solidly based. On August 27th Dr Reinhold Schairer turned up at the Foreign Office with the latest intelligence from Dr Karl Goerdeler. The Axis was completely broken; the German generals were pressing Hitler to avoid a two-front war; and raw materials and petrol were in short supply, Goerdeler reported. The head of the Secret Intelligence Service, Admiral Sir Hugh Sinclair, confirmed this information. He had just had a report that, on August 22nd, "General Halder and Admiral Raeder [Commander-in-Chief of the German Navy], who were themselves convinced that the British and French would fight, warned Hitler against the danger of fighting on two fronts." The generals considered this inevitable if Poland was attacked. Goerdeler pleaded that Britain and France must at all costs remain firm.[7]

The same advice was volunteered by the Counsellor of the German Embassy in London, Dr Ewart von Selzam, who had for some time been passing information, via Professor Conwell Evans, to the Foreign Office. He told William Strang that the Anglo-Polish treaty had come as a "bombshell" and that there was hesitation in Berlin on what to do next.[8]

All this time Field-Marshal Göring appeared genuinely to be working for a negotiated settlement. Despite Dahlerus' inexperience, his messages were beginning to show the outlines of a possible settlement. Hitler was being kept talking and inching towards making his demands explicit. The Poles were receptive to ideas of population exchanges with Germany. The French were proving firmer than in the previous year's crisis. The Italians were in confusion, working feverishly for peace and almost certainly neutral in any conflict.

A rosy outlook during crisis days had its dangers. "If only we remain firm! I am terrified of another attempt at a Munich and selling out on the Poles," Oliver Harvey, Private Secretary to Lord Halifax, wrote in his diary on August 27th. He suspected Sir Horace Wilson and R. A. Butler were "working like beavers for this". But Harvey received Lord Halifax's definite assurance that the Foreign Office "mustn't be suspicious of any attempt to rat on the Poles."[9]

The Polish government was again taking no chances. Colonel Beck did not intend to be left out in the cold. On August 27th, fearing a possible surprise attack, he ordered full, but not general, mobilisation. On political issues he was being reasonable, though cautious on what was emerging as the key problem: how and on what basis to re-establish contact with Berlin. Sir Nevile Henderson had for weeks been passionate in his pleas for such a get-together: "Even at this eleventh hour", he wrote to Halifax on August 22nd.

Not surprisingly, this idea received its strongest support from Mussolini. On the verge of ratting on Hitler, he must have sensed that the only way to save his honour was to father a negotiated settlement. On August 23rd the Foreign Office received an important telegram from Sir Percy Loraine, conveying a message from Mussolini. It advised the British to urge Warsaw to re-establish direct contact "without delay".[10]

The advice was accepted. On August 19th, Colonel Beck had responded favourably to a British idea, inspired by Lord Halifax, of letting Hitler know that the Polish government was willing to discuss the minorities problem. On August 22nd, and again the next day, Halifax advised Beck "to make an immediate approach" to the German government, "in order to see what sort of reaction it evokes". The firm stand taken in the face of the German-Soviet pact was a guarantee the gesture would not be misinterpreted.[11]

German military preparations profoundly worried Beck. He feared Hitler was no longer bluffing and was anxious to please the British. He decided to let his Ambassador in Berlin, Jozef Lipski, see Field-Marshal Göring. The visit would ostensibly be to thank him for an invitation, sent to the Ambassador on August 11th, to go hunting in the German state forests during the autumn. The Poles hoped to use Göring to restrain Hitler.

On August 23rd Beck told the British Ambassador of the

planned meeting. Any other method of contact, Beck stated, "would be interpreted in Berlin as a sign of weakening". He even went further in response to British advice. That same day, he authorised Lipski to seek out the German State Secretary, Ernst von Weizsäcker, to discuss possibilities of reducing tension.

Both Polish gestures proved of no value. Lipski was invited to Göring's Berlin residence for an hour's cordial, but fruitless conversation. Neither had been given any latitude to negotiate by their governments. Göring, Lipski wrote afterwards, "expressed regrets that he should, on the Führer's order, fight in the opposite camp to me, and he took leave of me with a theatrical gesture." Significantly, Göring had frankly traced the root of German-Polish tension to Poland's alliance with Britain. With that remark, as Roger Makins noticed, Göring "let the cat out of the bag".[12]

The meeting planned between Lipski and Weizsäcker, upon which the British government placed high hopes, never took place. Lipski was not able to find Weizsäcker in Berlin. Henderson had to inform the Polish Ambassador on August 24th that the State Secretary was spending his time in Hitler's entourage at Berchtesgaden.

Sir Nevile Henderson went further than merely providing information. He acted without instructions, though under the impact of his meetings with Hitler. On August 25th he told the Polish Ambassador that the situation demanded a meeting with Ribbentrop. In several telegrams to the Foreign Office, containing his usual mixture of personal anguish and realistic advice, Henderson argued that Weizsäcker would no longer do. Lipski must immediately seek an interview with Hitler.

Once again Henderson's views received coincidental support from Mussolini. On August 25th the Foreign Office was informed that Mussolini wanted Beck to see Ribbentrop, or make an "equally significant" gesture. The Duce thought the "hour is too critical to boggle over normal diplomatic routine".[13]

A brief battle developed between British ambassadors on the continent. Sir Percy Loraine considered it impossible for Colonel Beck to visit Berlin: "it would savour too much of a capitulation."

Sir Howard Kennard agreed: it "would be too much like Canossa." Sir Nevile Henderson, however, repeatedly urged the alternative course. To re-establish contact, he gloomily wrote, was the "*last* hope, if any, of peace: if there is a last hope." The contradictory advice poured into the Foreign Office. It was an agonising decision to evaluate. Sir Alexander Cadogan preferred to ignore Henderson's pleadings.[14]

Sir Nevile Henderson's August 25th conversation with Hitler and his flight to London changed the situation. He now had direct access to the Cabinet and did not hesitate to reiterate his views. Images of former statesmen, returning cowed and defeated from visits to Berlin, must have occurred to every Cabinet Minister as he spoke. Was he advising Beck to follow the same suicidal path?

As the Cabinet deliberated from August 26th–28th they grappled with the problem of how to force Hitler to divulge his terms for a settlement with Poland. There seemed only one way to bring the Führer out into the open: to advise Poland strongly, and this time officially, to open negotiations with Germany.

This was neither coercion of Poland nor appeasement of Germany. It was a clever though dangerous expedient. It could force Hitler to negotiate or bring Poland to her knees. In conversations with Count Edward Raczynski, Lord Halifax emphasised how "doubtful" he was "whether Herr Hitler would be willing to enter upon negotiations with Poland on a fair basis". Nevertheless, any opportunity for discussions about Danzig or the Corridor ought not to be neglected.

The mood of determination and firmness in London was set out on August 26th by Lord Halifax. In a message to Rome, designed to help Mussolini press the case for negotiations with' Hitler, he wrote:

Herr Hitler has often spoken of German honour. There is also such a thing as British honour. We can do nothing incompatible with it, and it would clearly be quite incompatible with it to betray our associates and agree to any solution which must be destruction of Polish independence. On the other hand, if the settlement were confined to Danzig and the Corridor, it did not seem to us that it should be impossible with reasonable time to find a solution without war.[15]

The final Cabinet meeting to discuss the British reply to Hitler was scheduled for noon on August 28th. Much depended on the German reaction to the message conveyed by Birger Dahlerus. At 9.30 that morning Dahlerus' first report came into the Foreign Office, via the British Embassy in Berlin.

Dahlerus had this time been denied another meeting with Hitler. The Führer was "too tired". However, Dahlerus had good news. After consulting with Hitler, Göring was able to report a major breakthrough. The ideas of an international guarantee to Poland and the opening of direct Polish-German conversations were now acceptable in Berlin. Dahlerus could not contain his excitement. Besides briefing the British Embassy, he also telephoned to his friends in London. The Germans were "showing goodwill and conciliatory spirit". The British reply, therefore, should be "Not cold or governessy".

Here was adequate information, almost too good to be true, upon which to settle a final reply. Halifax informed the Cabinet of Dahlerus' news and also that he had urged him to remain in Berlin in case of need. Several last-minute amendments were then hastily incorporated. Chamberlain was the last to speak. He expressed his satisfaction that the reply to Hitler "was now a dignified, firm and yet quite unprovocative document".

As soon as the meeting had ended, Sir Alexander Cadogan entered the room. He was there to draft one of the most crucial telegrams ever sent from London to Warsaw. It was telephoned at 2 p.m. and asked Colonel Beck to authorise the British government to inform Hitler that Poland was "ready to enter at once into direct discussion with Germany."

Everything depended on this reply. It came within two hours. The Foreign Office was not disappointed. Beck gave Britain the authorisation requested. Henderson was soon at Croydon airport on his way to Berlin.[16]

If the latest news at the Foreign Office was any indication, the prospects were not bright. Birger Dahlerus had just forwarded information that the German army would be finally positioned to attack Poland on the night of August 30th–31st. Furthermore, Göring had just indicated how much of the Corridor he wished to revert to Germany. Ivone Kirkpatrick estimated that this meant giving up territory with a 90 per cent Polish population. Both he and Sir Orme Sargent were convinced such a settlement was impossible. Coupled with the prospect of negotiation under the threat of a mobilised German army on the Polish frontier, they agreed that this all amounted to pure blackmail.[17]

Sir Nevile Henderson, "fortified by half a bottle of champagne", as he later recalled, was driven the few hundred yards from the British Embassy to the Reich Chancellery at 10.30 that same evening. Berlin was in complete darkness undergoing a trial blackout. A guard of honour, drawn up in the courtyard, greeted him with a roll of drums, while a silent crowd watched. He was received by Hitler and handed over a German translation of the British reply.

What Hitler read in the document brought by Henderson was a straightforward peace plan. The British government agreed with Hitler's August 25th message that the differences between Germany and Poland must be resolved. However, everything depended upon the "nature of the settlement and the method by which it is to be reached." On both these crucial points Hitler had been silent. The British spelled out how a settlement could be achieved. Its "nature" must be such as to safeguard Poland's essential interests and must be guaranteed by other powers. The "method" should be direct discussions between Germany and Poland, to which Poland had agreed. In the meantime, the tension, the reports over the treatment of minorities and all frontier incidents must be abated.

Once the differences between Poland and Germany were peacefully settled, the reply continued, then could come discussions on Anglo-German relations. "The results of a decision to use force have been clearly set out in the Prime Minister's letter to the Chancellor of the 22nd August."

Hitler finished reading without registering any emotion. Sir Nevile Henderson then began to speak on the basis of notes prepared for him by Lord Halifax and Sir Alexander Cadogan. Several times Henderson repeated that the choice being faced was friendship with Britain or war with Poland. Chamberlain could only carry through his policy of German appeasement if Hitler co-operated. "It was now or never and it rested with Herr Hitler."

Henderson succeeded admirably in drawing Hitler out on what he was after: the return of Danzig and the whole Corridor, together with frontier rectifications in Silesia. He begged Hitler not to raise his demands over that made the previous March for a corridor through the Corridor. Hitler retorted that it had then been "contemptuously" refused and would never be made again. He finally agreed to discuss an exchange of minorities with Poland. However, he needed time to think about direct political negotiations. Turning to Ribbentrop, he said: "we must summon Field-Marshal Göring to discuss it with him." Hitler promised a reply the following day.[18]

Even Sir Robert Vansittart, no friend of Henderson, had to admit he had conducted the interview very well. But there was one dangerous lapse. In reply to a question from Hitler, Henderson had stated that he personally did not exclude the possibility of Britain accepting an alliance with Germany.

"A treaty, Yes; an alliance, No," Vansittart wrote in a minute to Halifax. "An alliance means a military alliance if it means anything. And against whom should we be allying ourselves with such a gang as the present regime in Germany? The merest suggestion of it would ruin us in the United States."

Halifax saw the force of this argument. He also remembered that Henderson was acting contrary to his instructions. When in London, the Ambassador had tried unsuccessfully to convince the Government to offer Hitler a non-aggression pact. It was still distasteful to Halifax. "An alliance", he minuted, "raises all the difficulties in most acute form that we felt yesterday when discussing the 'non-aggression Pact' idea." A strongly worded warning to avoid the subject was sent to Henderson.[19] The damage was presumably done.

Everyone waited expectantly throughout August 29th while Hitler prepared his reply. In London it was a time for reflection. Henderson's record of his conversation with Hitler the previous evening was circulated in the Foreign Office and inspired lengthy comments. The prospect of a settlement with Germany seemed a little brighter. Yet at this eleventh hour, the nightmare of Munich – a bad settlement reached under threat of force – haunted the Foreign Office. World opinion "will of course despise and blame us if we allow Hitler to play his old game of securing concrete concessions in return for purely illusory promises", Ivone Kirkpatrick commented. Sir Orme Sargent remained cautious. He believed Hitler had neither changed his negotiating methods since Munich nor his current objective, which remained the destruction of Poland.

Lord Halifax tried to reassure his subordinates. While a permanent settlement might not be possible with the Nazi regime, this did not mean "a peaceful solution in proper terms" should be avoided. "And when we speak of Munich", Halifax added in a revealing insight, "we must remember the change that has supervened since then in the attitude and strength of this country." He was confident Hitler could be bettered at his own game. His Private Secretary, Oliver Harvey, observed that day: "Halifax thought it very important to get into negotiation and then be very stiff and then Hitler would be beat." This was a strategy which seemed to be working.

During the day further breathless messages arrived from Birger Dahlerus, busy once again in Berlin. He had gathered from a conversation with Field-Marshal Göring that there was a definite possibility of a satisfactory settlement. "Hitler was in fact only considering how reasonable he could be" and was preparing to invite the Poles to Berlin for discussions. Dahlerus "strongly" recommended they accept.[20]

Dahlerus did not know it, but he had overstepped the line. To assist the Foreign Office through his German contacts was tolerable; to begin advising on matters of policy was found distasteful. Patience with the busy Swede was ending. His reassuring messages did in fact bolster confidence. The "Germans are weakening and fear a general war", Roger Makins minuted. "Time is on our side; our morale is high . . . we are gradually rallying opinion in other countries." Ivone Kirkpatrick was again confirmed in his belief that there was a "strong wobble" in Berlin. Britain should not be "rushed" by the Germans. Even if negotiations take place, he advised, "I see no reason why the Poles should have to go to Berlin."

These outspoken minutes reached Sir Orme Sargent's desk and he noted his agreement. He also went further, revealing for the first time what he, if not others in the Foreign Office, thought of the Swedish emissary. Kirkpatrick had already hinted that "in the German atmosphere & dealing with the relatively sane Göring" Dahlerus was naturally pressing for a settlement on Hitler's terms. Sargent was more blunt.

I think we must be on our guard in dealing with these messages from Dahlerus. So long as we treat him as an agent of Goering's it will be all right. But we ought to beware of considering him as an impartial intermediary.[21]

Curiously, Ribbentrop suspected that Dahlerus was a British agent.

––––––––

The Prime Minister, meanwhile, could do little. He sat for a time with Lord Halifax and Sir Alexander Cadogan in St James' Park. Later he went to speak to the House of Commons, where anti-gas doors were being fitted and sandbags heaped against the basement windows. It was five days since Parliament had met, but he wanted to keep Members informed of developments. This he did briefly and discreetly. He praised the calm of the British people, described the various measures taken to prepare the defence of the country, and eloquently concluded: "The issue of peace or war is still undecided, and we still will hope, and still will work, for peace; but we will abate no jot of our resolution to hold fast to the line which we have laid down for ourselves."[22]

Throughout that day, August 29th, Henderson waited in

Berlin for Hitler's summons. From the information reaching him at the Embassy, the atmosphere seemed "well-disposed". He was hopeful the Poles and Germans would soon be negotiating. He had only one nagging worry. Alone among the Ambassadors of the major powers in Berlin, Jozef Lipski had not asked to see him.

Henderson was totally unprepared for the reception Hitler gave him. At 7.15 p.m. he was handed the text of the German reply. Three hours later the Foreign Office was put on alert by his preliminary report of the subsequent conversation: "Interview this evening was of a stormy character and Herr Hitler far less reasonable than yesterday."

Hitler had obviously decided to end what to him was the tedious charade of continuous replies and counter replies. Henderson, for his part, lost his temper, probably embarrassed by how he had misjudged the Berlin atmosphere. "I felt that I must play Herr Hitler at his own game", he later explained. A shouting match developed between the two men, during which, Henderson proudly telegraphed to Lord Halifax, "I glared at Herr Hitler the whole time."

The undiplomatic hysterics did not alter the harshness and rigidity of Hitler's demands. Although sceptical as to the prospects of a successful outcome, he agreed to negotiate directly with Poland. He would also participate, along with the USSR, in a guarantee of Poland. All this was by way of proof of his sincere intentions to enter into a "lasting friendship" with Britain. Then followed the last cruel blow. "The German Government, accordingly, in these circumstances agree to accept the British Government's offer of their good offices in securing the despatch to Berlin of a Polish Emissary with full powers. They count on the arrival of this Emissary on Wednesday, the 30th August, 1939."

"I remarked that this phrase sounded like an ultimatum", Henderson later reported, but Hitler reassured him that it only reflected the urgency of the situation. Meanwhile, the German government would immediately put on paper its proposals for a solution.[23]

The British had at last succeeded in getting Hitler to spell out the nature and method of his peace plan! Now the toughest bargaining could begin.

Henderson's preliminary accounts of this stormy meeting found the British government equally uncompromising. Halifax and Cadogan joined the Prime Minister at 10 Downing Street and, according to Cadogan, "between us we knocked up a fairly hot draft by 12.30 [a.m. on 30th August]."

This draft, which described the reply as "disappointing", was never sent. When the full text reached the Foreign Office in the early morning, it was seen to contain, as Sir Horace Wilson advised Neville Chamberlain, a "*much less* bad impression" than the earlier summary. Nevertheless, a telegram drafted by Cadogan was at once sent to Henderson, instructing him to inform the German government of the first British reaction: "it is of course unreasonable to expect that we can produce a Polish representative in Berlin today and the German Government must not expect this." So outrageous was Hitler's demand that it was not even forwarded to Warsaw until twenty-four hours later. Hitler had said this was not an ultimatum. His word was accepted. At 4 a.m. Henderson informed Ribbentrop as instructed from London. The message came as no surprise. It had already been intercepted by the *Forschungsamt*. *[24]

On the morning of August 30th Birger Dahlerus was secretly back again at 10 Downing Street. He had been sent by Field-Marshal Göring to soften up the British and plead the reasonable-ness of the German government. That task was hourly getting more difficult. "I think M. Dahlerus should now be treated with caution: his favourable glosses are becoming suspicious," Roger Makins minuted when given advance warning of the Swede's arrival.

* The *Forschungsamt* (Research Office) was the most secret of German intelligence agencies. It concentrated on monitoring all public forms of communication. The telephones of the British Embassy in Berlin were a prime target.

Chamberlain, Halifax, Cadogan and Wilson listened to Dahlerus' report of his latest meetings with Göring. Dahlerus did not disguise the fact that, in the current manner of Berlin conversations, Göring was "very excited". The British officials were equally outspoken and critical of the German summons of an emissary from Warsaw.

From the welter of detail Dahlerus poured out, one hopeful sign emerged. It seemed Hitler might propose a plebiscite to decide the future of the Corridor: a corridor across the Corridor would go to the loser.[25] Dahlerus was then asked to leave. The Cabinet was scheduled to meet at 11.30 a.m. to discuss the next step in the dialogue with Hitler.

It was with patience and caution that Neville Chamberlain and Lord Halifax guided the Cabinet which followed. Ministers were once again divided. "There are some people in the Cabinet", Sir Thomas Inskip afterwards noted in his diary, "who see the ghosts of Munich in every sentence that comes from Germany." At least one of those gadflies present, Leslie Hore-Belisha, was suspicious and apprehensive. According to War Office intelligence, he pointed out, Germany had forty-six divisions on the Polish frontier. To the Cabinet as a whole, this "afforded no valid argument against further negotiations" with Germany.

The Foreign Secretary based his appeal on the full text of Hitler's reply. Unlike Henderson's earlier summary, which he described as "most unsatisfactory" and "misleading", the full text was open to several interpretations. It was of course "bombastic, but he thought that, when stripped of its verbiage, it revealed a man who was trying to extricate himself from a difficult position." Hitler had already gone some way towards meeting the British position in agreeing to direct discussions with Poland, respecting her vital interests and participating in an international guarantee.

The British reply, Halifax carefully argued, must "pin Herr Hitler down" on the points he had already conceded "and on the other points to endeavour to safeguard the position of ourselves and our allies." Britain must again be "firm yet unprovocative". Halifax then recounted Dahlerus' latest activities and conversations with Göring. This, too, confirmed the wisdom of the approach being suggested.

Nothing had so far been said about Hitler's demand to see a Polish representative that very day in Berlin. That question was inevitably raised and the picture conjured up, by an unnamed Cabinet Minister, was that Germany possibly intended to repeat the humiliation of the former leaders of Austria and Czechoslovakia.

The Prime Minister himself boldly tackled this problem. "This definitely represented part of the old technique," he stated. "It was essential that we should make it clear that we were not going to yield on this point." Chamberlain's stubborn streak made such a resolution unbreakable. After some rather disjointed discussion of several points in the draft reply, Halifax was asked to settle the final details.

During the course of the Cabinet meeting, Halifax mentioned a suggestion had been made that Chamberlain should send a personal message to Hitler. The idea evoked no recorded comment. The letter, drafted in 10 Downing Street with amendments made in the Foreign Office and approved by Halifax, stated that an official reply would shortly be on its way, and welcomed the continuing exchanges as evidence of the desire for an Anglo-German understanding. It was telegraphed to Hitler at 2.45 p.m.

Later in the afternoon, a last-minute attempt was made to soften the document. Sir Thomas Inskip had been keeping the Dominion High Commissioners in touch with the London–Berlin dialogue. When shown the latest draft reply, they were in an uproar, protesting it was "cold" and "abrupt". Inskip took their complaints to the Foreign Secretary.

For a moment Halifax wavered, acutely sensitive to the need of pacifying these firm advocates of appeasement. Only three days earlier, J. A. Lyons, the Australian Prime Minister, had asked Chamberlain to invite Hitler to a new Munich-type conference. This had been rejected. In his diary, Inskip described what now happened:

Then almost suddenly he [Halifax] said "No! it is meant to be firm & even sharp. The H.C.s only see part of the picture: they dont know about the P.M.'s letter to H. & you may tell them that in confidence – not for their Govt. Also I have a message from Dusseldorf that the crowd is pulling down Nazi posters."

Inskip went off to brief the High Commissioners, who declared they were satisfied.[26] Halifax completed his work on the reply to Hitler and at 5 p.m. went home to bed.

It was not until 9.5 p.m. that the Foreign Office gave Sir Nevile Henderson final permission to act on the British reply to Hitler. That document had already been sent to Berlin, but last-minute objections had been raised by the French government and Sir Robert Vansittart. Further telegrams incorporating several changes, had to be sent to Henderson. When he had at last arranged a meeting with Ribbentrop for 11.30 p.m. there was a further delay. The Embassy decoding staff had not completed their work. Henderson was given another appointment, a half hour later.[27] That was precisely midnight, the hour before which Hitler had asked to see a Polish emissary in Berlin.

Hitler had obviously refused to conduct this midnight meeting. He preferred to leave the dirty work to Ribbentrop. The conversation which followed was in the opinion of the interpreter, Dr Paul Schmidt, the "stormiest" he had presided over. "The atmosphere was highly charged, the nerves of the two men worn by the protracted negotiations."

What developed into a confrontation between "two fighting cocks", began with Henderson handing over the latest British communication. This lightly skipped over Hitler's references to the desirability of an Anglo-German understanding, pinned him down to the common points of agreements, and then deftly highlighted the major outstanding issues. "The method of contact and the arrangements for discussions must obviously be agreed with all urgency between the German Government and the Polish Government, but in His Majesty's Government's view it would be impracticable to establish contact so early as today." Meanwhile, a military standstill and a temporary *modus vivendi* for Danzig ought to be arranged at once.

Henderson then asked whether Germany's proposals were ready to be shown to Britain, as promised. He also advised that they be given to Lipski, according to normal diplomatic practice.

"Up to midnight, Germany had heard nothing from the Poles", Ribbentrop then burst out. "The question of possible proposals therefore no longer arose." For the record, he then read them out – in German – the sixteen points. Danzig was to return to Germany, with Gdynia remaining Polish. Both cities were to be demilitarised. A plebiscite, a year later and under international supervision, would decide the future of the Corridor. The loser would be compensated by an extra-territorial system of communications across the Corridor. An international commission of inquiry would investigate minority complaints from either Germany or Poland.

According to Henderson, the sixteen points were "rather gabbled through", "at top speed" and in a scornful tone. Both Ribbentrop and the interpreter, Schmidt, deny this, adding that some of the points were even elaborated upon. Had the Ambassador only taken less pride in the fluency of his German and requested a translation, he would have properly noted all sixteen points. He then asked for the text of this document. Ribbentrop refused, saying it was now out of date.

Ribbentrop vehemently denied that the deadline of August 30th had in fact been an ultimatum. As Hitler had explained, speed was essential while two mobilised armies faced each other within firing range. The Foreign Minister rejected "in the most violent terms" Henderson's suggestion to summon Lipski. However, Ribbentrop "hinted that if the Polish Ambassador asked him for interview it might be different." A final decision rested with the Führer.[28] Henderson built his hopes on this slender hint. For the next twenty-four hours he waged a futile battle to keep alive the glimmer of further negotiation.

In refusing to press Poland to send a special emissary to Berlin, the British government had finally drawn the line. Here at last was unfolding precisely the sort of diplomatic imbroglio for which, on March 31st, Poland had been guaranteed. For here was the true meaning of the guarantee: negotiations on the basis of equality and free from the threat of force. The British government were standing by their obligations.

Sir Nevile Henderson retreated from his ugly interview with the German Foreign Minister to the British Embassy. He was "convinced that the last hope for peace had vanished." What drove this obviously obsessed man to make a final effort? In a private letter to Lord Halifax on August 31st, he explained: "I feel that we ought in principle to call the German bluff and not give way an inch. Yet I cannot reconcile it with my duty to you and His Majesty's Government not still to do my utmost to avoid war. The German proposals certainly do not endanger the independence of Poland."[29]

Henderson's sweeping opinion about the scope of the German proposals was based only on the six or seven of the sixteen points he had managed to absorb.* He felt it was sufficient to return to the charge. He telephoned the Polish Ambassador and asked him to come at once to the British Embassy.

"I found him highly excited after a violent discussion with Ribbentrop", Lipski later wrote. In what Henderson himself admitted were the "very strongest terms", he told the Polish Ambassador to telephone Beck and obtain approval to receive the sixteen points. Henderson had no faith in his "inert" colleague. Lipski, who for his part did not particularly trust Henderson, hurried back to his Embassy and decided on a compromise. He telegraphed to Warsaw details of three of the sixteen points Henderson had been able to follow. Having already ordered the Embassy Counsellor, Prince Lubomirski, to Warsaw to get permission to see Ribbentrop, the Ambassador felt enough had been done and went to bed.

Henderson was awake and on the telephone again to the Polish Embassy a little after 8 a.m. Lipski was busy and could not

---

* According to Dahlerus, *The Last Attempt*, pp. 100–3, he spent an hour, from 1.30–2.30 a.m., in the company of Göring. During that time, with Göring's permission, he telephoned full details of the sixteen points to Sir George Ogilvie-Forbes at the British Embassy. There is no evidence in the British documents which supports this; and the British government indeed acted as if the information had not been received.

accept the invitation to another urgent conversation. Instead, he sent his First Secretary, Henryk Malhomme, who found Henderson, looking worn out, seated behind his desk in his study.

"Malhomme, I do not like war", were the Ambassador's first words of greeting to a friend from former days in Belgrade. Henderson was uneasy. What he wanted to explain, he said, was "rather in the nature of a personal confidence". Lately he suspected the Poles regarded him as a Nazi sympathiser. This was not so. He had many Polish friends, "he knew Poland well because of his passion for hunting," and he liked the country and its people. He would work to the last possible moment to stop a war which would destroy Poland. Britain and France could not come to her assistance for a long time. He had now lost almost all hope of a peaceful settlement, but would labour on. These were the motives which inspired all his efforts to bring peace between Poland and Germany. Henderson touchingly concluded: "He now considered that his mission had come to an end, and he would like me, when the war was over, to repeat his motives to my compatriots." The two men parted with a long handshake.[30]

From the activity which Henderson pursued during that day, one could never have guessed he considered his mission ended. Over breakfast, in fact, he was spurred on even more. At the instigation of Ernst von Weizsäcker, both Dr Bernardo Attolico, the Italian Ambassador, and Ulrich von Hassell, a former German Ambassador in Rome, pleaded with Henderson to apply pressure on the Poles. Hitler would only wait to midday at the latest before declaring war.[31]

Soon after 10 a.m. Dahlerus turned up at the British Embassy with the full notes of the sixteen points which he had obtained from Göring. The Ambassador, "tired and depressed", listened to the latest account of Göring's strenuous efforts to preserve peace. Henderson decided to press Lipski by despatching Sir George Ogilvie-Forbes and Dahlerus to the Polish Embassy. There Dahlerus – introduced as "neutral intermediary in the confidence of the Cabinet, of the Embassy, and of the German Government" – read aloud the German proposals and proclaimed they were a reasonable basis for an honourable settlement. Once

361

negotiations began, he added encouragingly, Lipski would be able to shoot stags with Göring.

Lipski was astonished at "this ghastly business". It threatened to undermine his position. He ordered Dahlerus out of the room to dictate the proposals to his secretary. Left alone with Ogilvie-Forbes, he warned that the whole procedure was a breach of Polish sovereignty. "It would be fatal for M. Beck or a Polish representative to come to Berlin. We must for heaven's sake stand firm and show a united front and Poland if deserted by her allies was prepared to fight and die alone. This German offer was a trap."[32]

In London there were some indications which gave ground for confidence. During the day Neville Chamberlain was shown a terse telegram from Goerdeler, now in Stockholm. His last peacetime message read: "Chief Manager's attitude weakening. Remain completely firm. No compromise. Take initiative only for general settlement under strong conditions." Another telegram, from Sir Nevile Henderson, eventually proved a cruel delusion. It brought news that a Ministerial Council for the Defence of the Reich had been set up. The members included Göring, General Keitel and Rudolf Hess, and were empowered to pass laws without reference to Hitler, who was not on this executive body.

"This seems to me a most surprising development and a most hopeful sign", Sir Orme Sargent excitedly minuted. He actually believed that a "Palace revolution" had occurred and that Göring and the generals had taken charge. Admiral Sir Hugh Sinclair later gave his experienced judgement: "it is the coping stone of the German war preparations."[33]

Determination to see the crisis through without weakening was matched by an equal desire to see no opportunity, however slim, wasted. At 11 a.m. Count Ciano telephoned Lord Halifax with Mussolini's latest brainwave. If Poland would at once renounce her rights in Danzig, Mussolini would invite Hitler to a "conference or free negotiation on the other questions". Halifax flatly turned this down. The immediate problem remained for Germany and Poland to make their initial contact, Halifax replied to Ciano. The Poles were refusing to come and ask the German government what their terms were and "His Majesty's Government could not press them to do it". After consulting the Prime Minister, Halifax telephoned to Ciano. Chamberlain, too, could not co-operate with Mussolini under such conditions. The Poles could hardly be pressed to give away in advance the main point of the dispute.[34]

Such a firm stand took a powerful battering in the following hours. Sir Nevile Henderson sent one telegram after another to Lord Halifax, giving details of his activities in Berlin and offering endless advice. He wanted the Foreign Office to force Warsaw towards a negotiating position by instructing Lipski to go at once and receive the German proposals. "Can procedure be allowed to stand in the way of such a moment?" Henderson asked.

The pressure mounted. By 12.30 p.m. the Foreign Office knew the details of the German proposals. Henderson considered them "moderate". At that moment, too, Dahlerus telephoned from the British Embassy in Berlin to 10 Downing Street. He told Sir Horace Wilson, who had answered, that the sixteen points were "extremely liberal". Dahlerus then repeated what had transpired during his meeting with Lipski. Wilson, realising the conversation was being tapped, told Dahlerus to stop talking. He went on to say, however, that "it was 'obvious to us' that the Poles were obstructing the possibilities of negotiation. I [Wilson] told D. to shut up, but as he did not do so I put down the receiver." At Wilson's suggestion a telegram was sent to Henderson, warning him about the use of the telephone and denying that the Poles were being obstructive.[35]

No sooner had this conversation ended than Count Ciano was again on the telephone. Would the British and French governments agree to a conference for September 5th to revise the disputed clauses of the Treaty of Versailles? No mention was made this time of previously handing Hitler, what Ciano had called, the "fat prize: Danzig". This proposal was to lurk in the back-stages of the major European capitals for another two days. On

August 31st Chamberlain would have nothing to do with it. He sensed the similarities to events the previous year and felt it impossible to agree to a conference under the threat of mobilised armies. The French Prime Minister, Edouard Daladier, was equally opposed to a "second 'Munich'". He remarked that he would rather resign than accept this invitation.[36]

The continuing silence from Warsaw remained the one outstanding dilemma. While Henderson was having his stormy interview with Ribbentrop, Sir Howard Kennard had asked the Polish Foreign Minister to enter into direct discussions with Germany. The method and arrangement for this had been left open. Colonel Beck had promised a reply by noon. When it did not arrive at that time, but when it was clear there was no Polish objection, a further telegram was sent to Warsaw at 1.45 p.m. It asked that instructions be sent to Lipski to ask the German government for their proposals.[37] Ribbentrop had hinted he would agree to such a procedure.

These instructions were superfluous. At 12.40 p.m. Beck had put through a telephone call in code to Lipski. He was instructed to see either Ribbentrop or Weizsäcker and say the Polish government was "favourably considering" Britain's suggestion to open direct negotiations, and that a formal reply would follow shortly. An additional secret order, intended for Lipski alone, concluded the message: "Please do not engage in any concrete discussions, and if the Germans put forward any concrete demands, say you are not authorized to accept or discuss them and will have to ask your government for further instructions."

The British Ambassador was at once informed of the full instructions to Lipski. The details "as to where, with whom, and on what basis" negotiation would begin, Beck confided, must first be arranged. However, "if invited to go to Berlin he would of course not go, as he had no intention of being treated like President Hacha." What remained a well-kept secret was that a meeting had taken place on August 29th at Beck's private residence. It had then been decided to conduct any negotiations somewhere on the Polish-German frontier and with Lipski as representative.[38]

The highly efficient German intelligence system proved its worth that afternoon in Berlin. Beck's telephone call, including the secret message, was instantly decoded. Here was proof to the German government of Poland's delaying tactics and refusal to negotiate seriously.

Ambassador Lipski telephoned the German Foreign Ministry at 1 p.m. There was no reason for Ribbentrop to hasten his reception. Lipski was not received until 6.30. He walked through the halls of the Foreign Ministry, along which ss guards in uniform were posted. In the reception room he glanced at the desk on which less than six years earlier he had signed the German-Polish Non-Aggression Pact. Then, standing before Ribbentrop, Lipski read out his instructions.

"Have you authority to negotiate with us now on the German proposals?" Ribbentrop asked. No, Lipski replied. The brief interview was ended.[39] The Ambassador returned to his Embassy. His telephone line to Warsaw was soon cut.

Was all this effort in vain? Hitler's military timetable actually allowed for the possibility of negotiation – German style. In his diary on August 29th, General Halder described Hitler's last-minute strategy:

Führer wants them [Poles] to come tomorrow.
Basic principles: Raise a barrage of demographic demands. . . .
30.8 Poles in Berlin.
31.8 Blow up. [*Zerplatzen*]
  1.9 Use of force.

On August 30th, while awaiting the arrival of a Polish emissary, Hitler ordered a slight delay. If negotiations started, he was prepared to wait until the early morning of September 2nd. After the 2nd the attack would have to be called off. The uncompromising stand of the Poles, unknown to them, came very close to spoiling Hitler's timetable.

On August 31st Hitler became impatient. He could not face the humiliation of ordering another delay, perhaps even a complete cancellation of his military plans. At 6.30 a.m. he gave the order for the German army to take up positions. At 4 p.m. the High

Command of the *Wehrmacht* released the orders to attack at 4.45 a.m. the following morning.[40]

For German diplomacy there remained a small matter to clear up. The world had to be informed of the German version of events. At 9 p.m. Berlin Radio broadcast a communiqué and the text of the sixteen points. Within the next hour Weizsäcker handed copies of both documents to the British, French and Japanese Ambassadors, and the American and Russian Chargé d'Affaires. The communiqué blamed the Poles for refusing to open negotiations. German reasonableness had only been met "with empty subterfuges and meaningless declarations". After waiting for two days the German government regarded its proposals as rejected.[41] It was the first time the official text of the sixteen points had been released. The world had been informed before the diplomats.

Astonishingly the German broadcast was not taken as the final word. The American radio and press expressed relief and claimed Germany was giving way. Mussolini thought negotiation was still possible. Colonel Beck was unsure whether it was a final attempt at blackmail or the last act before war. In London, Sir Thomas Inskip, in the company of Sir Horace Wilson and several secretaries, listened to the broadcast at 10 Downing Street. "It looked rather odd but we weren't depressed," Inskip noted in his diary. Sir Alexander Cadogan felt Hitler was hesitating "trying all sorts of dodges, including last-minute bluff. We have got to stand firm."[42]

At 10.45 p.m. exciting and important news came from Rome in a coded telephone call from Sir Percy Loraine. "Italy will not fight against either England or France", Ciano had told Loraine under seal of secrecy. The Ambassador received the news in tears.[43] The British policy of courting Italy, despite criticism, had paid off. This news bolstered confidence still further.

Was there any hope? Two late night telegrams again revealed a clash of opinion between British Ambassadors in Warsaw and Berlin. "Stripped of legalistic language", Sir Howard Kennard argued, the sixteen points were "clearly calculated to undermine the existence of the Polish State." Method and procedure were important. Failure to continue supporting the Poles would be "catastrophic". This advice was followed by yet another plea from Sir Nevile Henderson to force the Poles to send their plenipotentiary.[44]

Lord Halifax sat at his desk, pondering this conflicting advice. If anything was to be done at this last minute, he wanted it tried. In short note form he personally drafted a telegram to Warsaw. As with all similar advisory telegrams since March, it politely asked Colonel Beck to instruct Jozef Lipski to receive the sixteen points. They did not contain any ultimatum, Halifax pointed out, and Ribbentrop had vigorously denied that August 30th had been a deadline. If the contrary proved true, the Poles should then refuse any discussion. Sir Alexander Cadogan added some corrections. William Strang prepared the final draft and it was telegraphed to Warsaw at 1.45 a.m. on September 1st.

This telegram was never acted upon. It was deciphered at 4 a.m. The Polish government would in any case have never agreed. Less than an hour later, the full force of Germany's armed forces was launched across the eastern frontier.[45]

CHAPTER FOURTEEN

The Hours to World War

LONDON awoke slowly on September 1st to the news of the German-Polish conflict gathering momentum in eastern Europe since 4.45 that morning. Lethargic reactions replaced the expected outburst of indignation and declaration of war. That was not surprising. The nightmare which had haunted the minds of responsible Ministers and officials since the previous March was a reality. It took another 54¼ hours to change the German-Polish war of 1939 into the Second World War. The momentum of diplomatic machinery, acting at high speed, and the dictates of long term strategy coloured the character of these last agonising hours of peace.

The news of the fighting in eastern Europe trickled out slowly. Hitler did not declare war on Poland. At 5.30 a.m. Leslie Hore-Belisha received this terse message: "Germans are through."[1] Minutes later, Berlin Radio carried Hitler's proclamation to his army: Poland had refused to negotiate and had violated the frontiers of the Reich. "In order to put an end to this lunacy I have no other choice than to meet force with force from now on." The text of this broadcast – sent from Berlin by Reuter news agency to Lord Halifax and Neville Chamberlain – and a single telegram from Warsaw, briefly describing air and ground action, were the main official documents of the morning's activities available to the Foreign Office.[2]

The first foreign diplomat to see Lord Halifax was the Polish Ambassador, Count Edward Raczynski. They met in a small office on the ground floor of 10 Downing Street.

Raczynski carried with him no written documents. He was acting on information telephoned to him from Paris that major

Polish cities, including Warsaw, had been bombed, and that the
Wehrmacht had crossed the Polish frontier at four points.

After repeating this to Halifax, Raczynski concluded: "The
Polish Government considers this to be a case of aggression
under Article 1 of the Anglo-Polish Treaty of Mutual Assistance." Halifax replied: "I have very little doubt of it."

In the corridor Raczynski met Sir John Simon, who grasped
the Ambassador's hand and "said something to the effect that
'We can shake hands now – we are all in the same boat. . . .
Britain is not in the habit of deserting her friends'." From the
Minister, who to many was the epitome of appeasement, the
warm words were a touching gesture of encouragement.[3]

Halifax at once summoned Theo Kordt, the German Chargé
d'Affaires, to 10 Downing Street and gave him Raczynski's
information. "These reports create a very serious situation,"
Halifax said. To Kordt's question as to what points on the
frontier had been crossed, Halifax could not reply. Otherwise,
Kordt played innocent and ignorant. He returned to his Embassy to listen to the remainder of Hitler's speech before the
Reichstag, where the Führer declared: "I am from now on just
first soldier of the German Reich. I have once more put on that
coat that was the most sacred and dear to me. I will not take it off
again until victory is secured, or I will not survive the outcome."[4]

Even while the *Wehrmacht* continued its advance into Poland,
diplomacy was having its last flutter in Berlin. It had failed to
drive a wedge between Poland and her allies. Could it now succeed in the larger task of containing the German-Polish war and
avoiding a world war? Hitler was very anxious to try. His first
military directive, issued on August 31st, confined the conflict
to Poland. He cleverly laid the responsibility for action in the
west on the shoulders of Britain and France. Whereas alleged
frontier violations by Poland were the excuse to attack in the
east, similar incidents on the western frontier were to be played
down. He intended to bring Poland speedily to her knees. In
support of this strategy, stiff instructions were sent to German

Embassies, on September 1st, to describe the hostilities not as war, but as "engagements" caused by Polish attacks.[5]

Two suggestions for a peaceful solution arrived at the Foreign Office almost simultaneously. They were available before the Cabinet meeting scheduled for 11.30 a.m. on September 1st. Birger Dahlerus, seemingly addicted to air travel, produced a scheme of flying to London and bringing back to Berlin General Sir Edmund Ironside to act as mediator. On this Cadogan minuted: "Not to be contemplated in present circumstances."[6] The second plan came from Sir Nevile Henderson. He wanted Marshal Smigly-Rydz to go to Berlin "as soldier and plenipotentiary" for talks with Field-Marshal Göring. With Smigly-Rydz involved in fighting off a German attack, it is not surprising that Roger Makins here minuted: "Impossible at this stage."[7]

Later that afternoon Henderson, who had struggled so passionately to avoid war, was finally to admit defeat. "Mutual distrust of Germans and Poles is so complete", he advised the Foreign Office, "that I do not feel I can usefully acquiesce in any further suggestions from here. . . . Last hope lies in inflexible determination on our part to resist force by force."[8]

For the other man who had struggled equally hard and suffered galling disappointment, similar words and feelings easily welled up. Neville Chamberlain was the first to address the morning's Cabinet meeting.

THE PRIME MINISTER said that the Cabinet met under the gravest possible conditions. The event against which we had fought so long and so earnestly had come upon us. But our consciences were clear, and there should be no possible question now where our duty lay.

THE SECRETARY OF STATE FOR FOREIGN AFFAIRS said that the position was still confused in many respects, but the main lines were clear. In the last two days the principal obstacle to progress had been the difficulty of establishing contact between the Germans and the Poles. . . . All this, however, was rather ancient history . . . reports had been received of the invasion of Poland.

Halifax then recounted his conversations with Raczynski and Kordt. He added that the American Ambassador, Joseph Kennedy, had telephoned a message with information that Warsaw had been bombed. Later in the meeting, further messages arrived and were read out. Warsaw, it now appeared, had not been bombed.

Confusion over the exact military position in Poland added to the difficulties of framing precise action. One Cabinet Minister, unnamed, argued that with the lack of "definite information . . . it was desirable not to take any irrevocable action". For even while this discussion continued, Hitler was addressing the Reichstag, and Henderson had indicated a German peace move might follow.

There was no hesitation, however, in dealing with the account Halifax gave of the latest telephone message from Birger Dahlerus. The reply must be "stiff". It must emphasise that a world war could be stopped only if Germany ceased hostilities and withdrew her troops from Poland. Every other last minute peace solution was to be handled with similar firmness.

The moment had come to discuss the communication to Germany which the situation obviously demanded. Should it contain a time limit and what should it say? On the first question, Chamberlain called on Lord Chatfield who had just been meeting with the Chiefs of Staff. They favoured a very brief time limit. They felt that if the moment had come to fulfil the guarantee to Poland, "the right course would be that we should despatch to Germany a communication in the nature of an ultimatum without any undue delay."

The Chiefs of Staff had no plans to help Poland. Her fate depended on the outcome of the war – the defeat of Germany. That was the long and difficult task they were anxious to begin.

Copies of a draft communication were then handed round the Cabinet. What it contained is not recorded. But it was an obviously strong document and possibly contained an ultimatum with a time limit. On the information available as to hostile action, the draft was rejected, despite the opposition of some unnamed Ministers. The "view generally held" was that this would give a "false sense of security". Hitler might bomb London in the meantime.

The communication adopted referred to the German attack against Poland, and concluded that unless Germany stopped her aggressive action and promptly withdrew her troops, "His Majesty's Government will without hesitation fulfil their obligations to Poland."

The Prime Minister himself dramatically raised the question as to the next step. If the German reply was "unfavourable", he asked, should Sir Nevile Henderson "then ask for his passport?" The answer to this, as well as any other outstanding points, was left to be settled with the French government. It had already been agreed that Britain and France should declare war together. That decision, more than any other, was to delay for another two days the declaration of war.

Before adjourning, the Cabinet heard of the mobilisation of the Army, Air Force, and most of the Navy. They agreed secretly to send at once both the advanced air striking force and the first contingent of the British field force to France. Good news finally came in the form of a message from the Canadian Prime Minister, William Lyon Mackenzie King. Once war broke out, Canada would march with Britain.[9]

Trouble between Britain and France erupted that afternoon. It was totally unexpected, embarrassing and dangerous. It almost brought down the Chamberlain government. At their Council of Ministers, meeting at the same time as the British Cabinet, the French decided for immediate mobilisation and to summon Parliament for 3 p.m. the next day. Only Parliament could approve the war budget and, until it met, war could not be declared.

Speaking to Halifax on the telephone that afternoon, Georges Bonnet, the French Foreign Minister, refused to insert a time limit into the communication. That would be an ultimatum, he pointed out, for which Parliament alone could give authorisation. For the same reason he refused to permit the Ambassadors in Berlin to ask for their passports.

There seemed no alternative but to send the communication to the German government without a time limit. Work at the Foreign Office began meanwhile on a second note – a simple ultimatum. Henderson was advised to ask for an immediate reply. Should any questions be asked, he was instructed to explain that the communication "is in the nature of warning and is not to be considered as an ultimatum".[10]

Chamberlain rose to address the House of Commons at 6 p.m. "The time has come when action rather than speech is required", he told the dimly-lit chamber. Besides reviewing recent events, there was little else he could tell the assembled MPs. He read aloud the communication to be made to the German government.

"Time limit?" an MP suddenly cried out as Chamberlain finished reading. The Prime Minister then added that if the German reply to the warning was unfavourable, Henderson had instructions to ask for his passport. That temporarily satisfied the Commons. According to one MP, Harold Nicolson, Chamberlain was "evidently in real moral agony and the general feeling in the House is one of deep sympathy for him and of utter misery for ourselves".[11]

Henderson carried out his instructions at 9.30 p.m. Ribbentrop was in no hurry to receive the Ambassador. German intelligence already knew he was conveying only a warning. The German Foreign Minister was this time "courteous and polite". He attempted to resume with Henderson the debate about Polish responsibility. But the British Ambassador hardly answered. He was through trying to reason with German officials. Earlier that afternoon, he had ordered his Embassy ciphers and confidential documents burnt.

Before parting, Henderson stated he would be available at any time to receive Hitler's reply.[12] The French Ambassador, Robert Coulondre, then followed to hand in a similar communication.

———

The second day of the Polish-German war – September 2nd – dawned. The German *Wehrmacht* continued pounding the Poles. From Berlin there was still no reply to the Anglo-French communication.

Lord and Lady Halifax, accompanied by Sir Alexander Cadogan, walked in the gardens of Buckingham Palace. The King had generously given the Foreign Secretary a key. Their thoughts were occupied with more than just waiting for Hitler's reply. There was serious trouble with the French government. The British Ambassador in France, Sir Eric Phipps, was instructed "to infuse courage and determination into M. Bonnet". The weakest link in French resistance was already singled out for stiffening. Otherwise, for the rest of the morning, Lord Halifax "was occupied with making preparations for what now seemed inevitable."

The French government began to give trouble when, at 1.30 p.m., they demanded that the ultimatum to Germany must contain a forty-eight-hour time limit. The French general staff needed this time to complete evacuation and general mobilisation.[13]

Before that problem could be solved, Lord Halifax received a telephone call from Rome. Count Ciano, with the British and French Ambassadors at his side, revealed to Halifax what had been going on behind the backs of the British. The Italian government, encouraged by the French, had suggested an armistice to Hitler – to be immediately followed by a five-power conference. After being assured that the Anglo-French communication was not an ultimatum, Hitler had been surprisingly amenable. He wanted until noon on September 3rd to consider the question. The French government had already agreed. What was the British reaction? Ciano asked Halifax.

Halifax's immediate, but personal, reply was negative and firm. It was the same as his reaction on August 31st, when another conference call had come from the Duce. Halifax told Ciano "that the indispensable condition of the convening of a conference would be the evacuation by the German armies of Polish territory." The Germans would never listen to such a demand, Ciano said. Halifax replied that he would consult Chamberlain and the Cabinet and then give a definite answer.

Never could a proposal have been more inconvenient nor, at least in London, less likely to succeed. Chamberlain had asked

Sir John Simon to speak for him at 3 p.m. to the Commons. Simon was to give the latest war news, announce that Hitler's reply had not yet been received and reassure Parliament that the Government was not prepared to wait much longer. An ultimatum would follow as soon as the French parliament had finished its meeting.

Simon described in his diary what had happened: "Two or three minutes before the House met a message came to me, just as I was going into the Chamber, that a communication had just been received from Italy which made it essential to make no statement at all about the international situation at the beginning of business." Instead, Simon asked the Commons to await a later statement from the Prime Minister himself.

In his "Record of Events Before the War, 1939", a brief diary of the last days of peace compiled in October, Lord Halifax recorded:

> I managed to rush over to the House of Commons to stop John Simon making the statement that had been prepared for 2.45, in order to give time to get in touch with the French about the conference proposal and to synchronise with them any action we may decide to take with Germany. I never remember spending such a miserable afternoon and evening. From 3 to 5.30 we were telephoning to Bonnet, who I suspect had committed himself rather further than he was willing to admit to the conference. . . .[14]

At 3 p.m. Halifax had had his first direct telephone conversation with Bonnet. They exchanged information about the Italian proposals. Bonnet did not admit he had already backed Ciano. Halifax, however, stood firm. His government would reply shortly to the Italians. "It was very difficult to imagine a conference while German troops remained on Polish soil." Halifax added: "You seem to me to believe that one can resuscitate a corpse with holy water!" Georges Bonnet, nevertheless, was unabashedly trying his hardest.

This was all the more surprising as Bonnet already knew the Polish government would have nothing to do with a conference.

Colonel Beck had informed him on September 1st: "We are in the thick of war as the result of unprovoked aggression. The question before us is not that of a conference but the common action which should be taken by the Allies to resist." A tactful indiscretion by the French Ambassador in Warsaw, Léon Noël, had insured that the Foreign Office shortly knew of Bonnet's backstage manoeuvring.[15]

Amidst such frantic activity, Chamberlain hastily summoned a Cabinet meeting at 4.15. The quick exit of Ministers from the Government front bench alerted the Commons to the fact that something was afoot. Sir Horace Wilson and Sir Alexander Cadogan were also invited to attend. Halifax had no time to prepare a general statement. He began by reading aloud the records of his conversations with Count Ciano and Georges Bonnet. He then put to the Cabinet several conclusions, "provisionally" agreed with the Prime Minister prior to the meeting. These conclusions were firm, yet conciliatory; taking into account the upsetting afternoon schemes of Bonnet and Ciano.

If the German government asked for more time to consider their reply, "we should be prepared to allow them until 12 noon to-morrow for this purpose, subject to their agreeing to an armistice." Furthermore, the "primary condition for any conference would be that German troops should first withdraw from Polish soil." To help matters, Halifax added, the time limit might be extended from 12 noon to midnight on September 3rd. Clarifying these remarks later in the discussion, Chamberlain added that both he and Halifax had felt that "there should be no discussion of terms" until German troops had left Polish soil. He himself had no illusions. "It was not very likely that Herr Hitler would accept this condition."

A fierce debate followed. The Cabinet Ministers were, as Halifax typically understated, "in an extremely difficult mood". The Cabinet minutes record by name the opinions of almost half the members. The Chamberlain–Halifax ideas just put forward for discussion received almost no support. Instead, as Minister after Minister was called on to speak, it became clear that Chamberlain was about to be overruled by his Cabinet. He had badly misjudged their mood, determination and impatience with Hitler's methods.

The Service Ministers, voicing the opinions of their respective Chiefs of Staff, were opposed to any delay whatever in issuing a deadline to Hitler. The Naval Staff was eager to reconnoitre the latest position of the German fleet. The Chief of Air Staff, Air Chief Marshal Sir Cyril Newall, was anxious for the "moral effect of redeeming our pledge to Poland". Leslie Hore-Belisha feared that further delay would shatter the unity of the country. British public opinion "was strongly against our yielding an inch. . . . The Dictators had made demand after demand and if we were to hesitate now", he eloquently pleaded, "we might well find ourselved faced with war in a year's time, but in the mean-time we should have lost ground by hesitation." Malcolm MacDonald was equally outspoken. He wryly commented that the "Germans could make up their minds quickly enough on occasions and had been known to ask other people to make up their minds in a very short time."

If any further evidence was needed of where the decision of the Cabinet lay, it was introduced into the discussion by Chamberlain himself. The Polish Ambassador had just handed in an urgent personal message and a telegram from Warsaw. Chamberlain first read aloud the message. It requested the "immediate fulfilment of British obligations to Poland". Then the telegram which spoke for itself:

> Battle to-day over the whole of the front has increased in intensity and has acquired very serious character. Our troops are opposing strong resistance. The whole of German Air Force is engaged against Poland. Villages and factories bombarded. The engagement of German aircraft by allied forces of greatest urgency.

There is no recorded comment on this. Every Minister knew Poland was to be crushed as there were no allied plans to come to her defence. Assessing the determined mood of the Cabinet, Chamberlain summarised its conclusions. There should be no negotiations with Germany until she agreed to withdraw her troops from Poland and Danzig. Hitler was to have only until midnight to make up his mind on all questions. This "clearly constituted an ultimatum", Chamberlain stated, and a communication in this sense would be sent to the German government.

The final agreed conclusion provided Chamberlain within a few hours with the most serious Cabinet revolt he ever faced in peacetime. Ministers had already been warned twice that the French were stubbornly insisting on a forty-eight-hour time limit. Nevertheless, the Cabinet willingly consented to let Chamberlain and Halifax settle the terms of the communication after consultation with the French.[16] That proved a disaster which nearly brought down the Government. The Cabinet then adjourned, its members believing Britain would be at war by midnight.

Georges Bonnet was at once informed over the telephone of the Cabinet conclusions. He "put forward every wiggle in favour of delay". A midnight ultimatum, he flatly stated, was "impossible". Evacuation was not yet complete. He was told that, if Hitler had not replied by midnight, the British intended to fulfil their obligations to Poland.

Unable to budge Bonnet, Halifax decided to appeal directly to the French Prime Minister, Edouard Daladier. Surely his reputation for firmness would ensure the desired result? Daladier temporised. He would have to summon his Council of Ministers.[17]

In Rome, Count Ciano was impatiently awaiting a reply to his conference proposal. At 6.38 p.m. Halifax telephoned to give him the Cabinet view. So long as German troops were on Polish territory and Danzig was occupied, Halifax stated, a conference was impossible. Ciano replied that Hitler would not acccept this condition. An exhortation to Ciano "to do his best" were Halifax's parting words. But with such a definite restatement of British views, the conference proposal was dead. Within three hours, both the British and German governments were informed of Mussolini's decision to abandon his peace efforts.[18]

Meanwhile the House of Commons was temporarily suspended

from a little after 6 p.m. Members waited for the summons to hear the Prime Minister's statement. They moved from group to group, into the smoking room, on to the terrace and back to the lobbies. They were restless, tense and anxious. Rumours, spread from the diplomatic gallery, gave an inkling of the causes of delay. But every MP expected the Prime Minister to enter the chamber at any moment to announce Britain would soon be at war.

Chamberlain finally entered, carrying a statement agreed with Daladier, and began to speak at 7.45 p.m. One MP, Brigadier-General Edward Spears, later recalled how, as members of Parliament listened, their "amazement turned into stupefaction, and stupefaction into exasperation". When Chamberlain had finished, "members sat as if turned to stone". Captain Euan Wallace, the Minister of Transport, recorded in his diary: "Our own people were flabbergasted and the Opposition infuriated." For instead of an ultimatum, he mentioned the delay caused by the Italian conference proposal. Instead of a time limit, he was forced to admit that agreement with the French had still not been reached. Instead of an assurance of immediate military help to Poland, came a reiteration of a willingness to negotiate should Germany's forces withdraw from Poland.

As Arthur Greenwood, the deputy Labour leader, slowly rose to speak, there were suddenly loud shouts: "Speak for England", "Speak for the working classes", and "Speak for Britain". Those words carried the anguish and fury of a parliament determined to end the era of Anglo-German negotiation. Having been previously briefed by Chamberlain, Greenwood spoke with restraint and polite consideration for the Prime Minister's difficulties.

"An act of aggression took place thirty-eight hours ago." From that moment "one of the most important treaties of modern times automatically came into operation. There may be reasons why instant action was not taken." But every minute's delay, Greenwood continued, imperilled Britain's interest and national honour. "I hope, therefore, that tomorrow morning . . . we shall know the mind of the British Government, and that

379

there shall be no more devices for dragging out what has been dragged out too long." Greenwood sat down to universal cheers.

Chamberlain soon rose again to speak, to soothe the angry Commons. "I should be horrified if the House thought for one moment that the statement that I have made to them betrayed the slightest weakening either of this Government or of the French Government", he said. Difficult telephone communications with Paris were causing some delay. But a definite statement would be made tomorrow. He left no doubt that it would be an announcement of war.[19]

Members of the Commons dispersed with the impression that Britain was heading for another Munich conference. Henry Channon, the Chicago-born Parliamentary Private Secretary to R. A. Butler, recorded in his diary: "All the old Munich rage all over again; all the resentment against Chamberlain; All those who want to die abused Caesar." Afterwards in the lobbies, Hugh Dalton wrote, "there was a terrific buzz. It had seemed almost as though on a free vote of the House, Chamberlain and Simon would have been overthrown."[20]

What Parliament did not know and what would have given them comfort, was that many members of Chamberlain's Cabinet were equally aghast at the Prime Minister's performance and statement. His words had contradicted the Cabinet decision to impose a midnight time limit.

A group of dissident Cabinet Ministers took action.* They staged a "sit-down strike." They hurriedly met in Sir John Simon's room in the House of Commons. A late-comer to this gathering, Sir Reginald Dorman-Smith, appointed Minister of Agriculture and Fisheries just seven months before, afterwards recalled:

---

* The Ministers in revolt included the following: Leslie Hore-Belisha, Sir John Simon, Lord De La Warr, Captain Euan Wallace, Sir John Anderson, Ernest Brown, Leslie Burgin, Sir Reginald Dorman-Smith, Malcolm MacDonald, Walter Elliot, Oliver Stanley, William Morrison, John Colville, and Sir Kingsley Wood. Malcolm MacDonald and Lord De La Warr have broadly confirmed for the author the written accounts by their former Cabinet colleagues of the incident.

My colleagues already there had decided they would not leave that room until such time as war had been declared. As we sat there and waited by the phone and nothing happened, I felt like a disembodied spirit. It didn't seem real. We were on strike . . . there was a feeling of great emotion. All of us were getting back to our natural selves. I became more Irish, and Hore-Belisha more Jewish – talking of rights and indignities and so on. . . . As we waited, we got scruffier and sweatier.

In his diary Simon described the discussion and what then happened:

> . . . one and all expressed their surprise that the statement made differed fundamentally from the Cabinet decision, and yet had been announced without another Cabinet being called. They felt that this was putting them in a false position, and, more-over, they were consumed with the fear that the announce-ment just made would throw the Poles into dejection, and be exploited by the Germans as a proof that Poland was too sanguine if she expected prompt British support.
>
> The language and feeling of some of my colleagues were so strong and deep that I thought it right at once to inform the Prime Minister, who was still in his room at the House. He asked me to bring in the protesting disappointed Ministers, and invited me to state the difficulty.

The rebels trooped into Chamberlain's room, looking to him, "very sullen". Simon put their case briefly, but forcibly. He added, in what must have been painful words from so loyal a Minister, that he "shared the feeling of the others that it was surprising to have so grave a variation adopted and publicly announced when the Cabinet had decided otherwise."

Chamberlain did not deny the charge; nor does he appear to have reminded the rebels of the actual Cabinet conclusions. Instead, he pleaded the "heavy pressure under which these constant messages from Italy and France had put Halifax and himself". He had been unable to synchronise an Anglo-French ultimatum. And he had felt, according to Euan Wallace's diary, "that the grave disadvantage of declaring war without France more than counterbalanced the probable effect of further delay upon the House of Commons and the country." The Ministers advised Chamberlain that he could not face the House of Commons again unless he could announce the expiry of an ultimatum and that Britain was in the process of fulfilling her guarantee to Poland.

Immediately afterwards, the protesting Ministers met again and reiterated their views in a letter to Chamberlain. They made one concession. If the price of French co-operation was time, the Ministers would be willing to extend the expiry of the ultimatum until noon on the following day. "Otherwise we ought to make our own declaration at once."[21]

Chamberlain was terrified and desperately needed help. He hurried back to 10 Downing Street. There he met Sir Thomas Inskip who, unlike his militant colleagues, had come to press the case for giving Hitler more time. Chamberlain poured out his woes; describing the scenes by his Cabinet, according to Inskip's diary, as

> a state of semi revolt. He sent for them: they came in looking very sullen, & Simon made their point clear. The P.M. told them the French wouldn't agree, & he had to make some statement. The P.M. seemed a little rattled, & his face was deeply lined. I felt sorry for him; it may have a bad effect on a man who is past seventy, & has borne a very heavy burden. Moreover he seems to be conducting the foreign policy & I wonder if Halifax will stand it. The P.M. *is* a man of peace. He spoke to me tonight about the hundreds of thousands of children in France that would be killed if war came.

Inskip tried to console him.[22]

Chamberlain then telephoned to Halifax, who was just going out to dine and ordered him to 10 Downing Street. There had been an "unpleasant scene" in the Commons, Chamberlain said, with the Government being accused of half-heartedness and hesitation. "I had never heard the Prime Minister so disturbed", Halifax later recorded. "I accordingly went straight off to No. 10, where he gave me dinner. He told me that the statement infuriated the House and that he did not believe, unless we could clear the position, that the Government would be able to maintain itself when it met Parliament the next day."

Sir Alexander Cadogan was eating his dinner when his phone rang. The call was from 10 Downing Street, ordering him there "At once: at once". He shortly arrived to continue his meal with Chamberlain, Halifax and Sir Horace Wilson also present. When they had finished, Charles Corbin, the French Ambassador, was summoned.[23]

Meanwhile, still in their stuffy room at the House of Commons, the rebel Ministers were meeting at 10 p.m. for further talk. According to Sir John Simon's diary, a message came from 10 Downing Street, asking him to go there at once. Hore-Belisha's diary mentions no message, only that Simon was delegated to go and see what was happening. In fact, Sir John Anderson, the Lord Privy Seal, accompanied Simon who was not fully trusted by the others. Simon's diary continues the story:

> On going into the Cabinet room, I saw at once what the Prime Minister wanted of me. The French Ambassador was there as well as Halifax. The Prime Minister asked me to tell the French Ambassador my own impression of the state of feeling which the last announcement had made. I said that the most serious feature of it undoubtedly was that the statement contained no time limit, and was therefore consistent with an indefinite delay, and that, I was quite certain neither the House of Commons nor the country would support. For the first time since the crisis loomed up there were signs of cleavage in the House, and the Prime Minister's position as leader of the nation was in danger of being challenged.

There followed an argument in which Simon stated the rebel Ministers' case for a short time limit before the expiry of an ultimatum. When Parliament met at noon tomorrow, he told Corbin, a definite announcement had to be made: "either that Hitler had agreed to withdraw, or that a state of war had begun."[24]

Having failed to impress Corbin, Chamberlain telephoned the French Prime Minister, Edouard Daladier, to describe the "angry scene" in the Commons and to admit that "it would be impossible for the Government to hold the situation here." He had decided that it would be impossible to wait any longer. A British ultimatum would be presented at 8 a.m. on September 3rd. During a telephone conversation with Georges Bonnet minutes later, the final decision was made. Britain must act alone. The French would follow at noon with a deadline yet to be fixed.

Neither Frenchman was prepared to budge or compromise. Both, however, spoke the harshest words to an Englishman. As Daladier told Chamberlain: "unless the British bombers were ready to act at once, it would be better for France to delay".[25] British bombers were just arriving on French soil. But they never flew over Poland in her defence and only briefly, months later, in defence of France.

Unaware of the defensive nature of Anglo-French strategy, Colonel Beck had already appealed during the day for air raids on the western front. He hoped this would draw off some of the German aircraft operating mercilessly against Polish military and civil targets. Kennard supported this plea and appealed for an immediate declaration of war.

The Polish Ambassador, Count Edward Raczynski, saw Lord Halifax at 10 p.m., in the middle of the telephone calls to Paris. It was an awkward moment to be inquiring when the British would be sending their ultimatum. Even more awkward was the question of whether Britain would act without France. Halifax replied with generalities as best he could. Raczynski left reassured and aware a final decision was taking place. The Polish Embassy now had no doubt that the French were causing the difficulties.[26]

At the very moment Halifax was speaking to Raczynski, an astonishing scene was taking place in the private office of Sir Horace Wilson. He was deeply absorbed in conversation with a secret contact, Fritz Hesse, press adviser to the German Embassy. Hesse was acting on the direct instructions of Hitler in making an approach to what, in Berlin, seemed the weakest link

in English resistance. Hitler still hoped to confine the war to
Poland. For this the British and French must still be kept talking
and negotiating. "Links must not be broken," he told General
Halder. That is why he asked for time to consider Mussolini's
conference proposal. That is also why Hesse was now facing
Wilson with an offer, according to Hesse's memoirs, to withdraw German forces from Poland and pay reparation for
damages. In return, Germany would get Danzig and a road
across the Corridor. Britain would act as mediator in the
German-Polish dispute.

Sir Horace Wilson's brief record of this meeting is even more
astonishing. According to Wilson, "Hesse . . . was told by
Ribbentrop shortly after 8 p.m. to try to see me to ask whether
H.M. Govt. would agree that I should be authorised to go to
Berlin secretly to meet him and Hitler . . . to discuss the whole
position, heart to heart, including Poland." An undated minute
by Cadogan on this record reads: "You seem to have given the
correct answer, to which we must stick. (These attempts at indirect approaches rather reassure me: the Germans must be
feeling the draught)."[27]

The Germans had seriously underestimated Wilson. His reply
to this preposterous scheme was unequivocal. There could be no
conversations until Germany had withdrawn her forces from
Poland and restored the *status quo*.

———————

There remained now only one decision to make: the exact hour
for the presentation and expiry of an ultimatum to the German
government. Sir Nevile Henderson was ordered to stand by to
deliver this communication.

At 11.20 a message came through to Sir John Simon's room at
the House of Commons. There the Ministers on "sit-down
strike" had been occupying themselves by reading copies of the
latest Foreign Office telegrams. As time had passed, Euan
Wallace later recorded in his diary, "our anxiety increased and
one or two made suggestions of a united advance on Downing
Street". This had been rejected by a majority. Now the Secretary

to the Cabinet was summoning them to 10 Downing Street for a meeting. Through the driving rain of a heavy thunderstorm they arrived, "scruffy and smelly", to find Chamberlain, Halifax, in his evening clothes, and Cadogan waiting.

Other Ministers also arrived, some hastily redressing after going to bed. The Marquess of Zetland was awoken and told to go immediately to the meeting. "I flung on some clothes and sallied forth into a perfectly filthy night. Not only was the black-out complete but a terrific thunderstorm was in progress and I had great difficulty in finding my way along the streets."

The Cabinet which finally met at 11.30 lasted only 45 minutes. Chamberlain patiently explained once more the reasons which had led him to depart from the earlier Cabinet conclusions. But he "now recognised the strength of feeling" shown in the Commons, even among his most loyal supporters. He intended immediately to correct the position. After describing the latest telephone conversations with Daladier and Bonnet, Chamberlain led an involved discussion of the time of presentation and expiry of the ultimatum. He wanted the Cabinet to make this decision.

The advice from the Chiefs of Staff was to shorten the period of uncertainty before the expiry of the ultimatum. This would make a surprise air attack on London less likely. It was also pointed out by Chamberlain that he must be able to make a definite statement when the Commons met the next day at noon. Furthermore, to lessen the interval between the delivery of the British and French ultimatums, the Chiefs of Staff had no objection to its presentation at 9 a.m. next morning. This would help the French, Chamberlain said, "who after all would bear the main part of the burden."

The Cabinet was painfully aware that every hour's delay would sow further "doubt and suspicion" of the Government. For that reason, Leslie Hore-Belisha argued without support for a 2 a.m. ultimatum to expire at 6 a.m. However, the Cabinet stoically accepted that further criticism was inevitable. At last a decision was reached. Britain would declare war independently of France. Sir Nevile Henderson was instructed to see Ribbentrop at 9 a.m. on Sunday, September 3rd. He was to state that if the German government had not replied favourably by 11 a.m. to the communication of September 1st a state of war would exist between Britain and Germany from that hour.

The Dominion Prime Ministers were to be informed at 9 a.m. that an ultimatum was to be delivered. Sir Thomas Inskip decided on a little revolt of his own against a Cabinet decision. He sent the information at 1.30 a.m. He "thought it impossible to leave the Dominions in the dark" for so long.

Throughout the meeting, Sir Reginald Dorman-Smith recalled later, Chamberlain "was calm, even icy-cold". He had accepted this "plain dictat" from the rebel Ministers. The climax of the meeting – not recorded in the minutes – came dramatically.

"The P.M. said quietly: 'Right, gentlemen, this means war.' Hardly had he said it, when there was the most enormous clap of thunder and the whole Cabinet Room was lit up by a blinding flash of lightning. It was the most deafening thunder-clap I've ever heard in my life. It really shook the building."[28]

The Cabinet meeting then broke up. The Chiefs of Staff, waiting in uniform outside the Cabinet room, were told of the decision. Charles Corbin was also given the news. Cabinet Ministers left No. 10 into the almost flooded street to return home. Henry Channon observed that Chamberlain, looking "almost relieved that the dread decision was taken", was left talking to R. A. Butler, before retiring.[29]

Rushing up the large central staircase of the Foreign Office, Sir William Malkin was stopped by the Labour MP, Hugh Dalton. "How are things going?" Dalton asked. The breathless reply came: "I have got the declaration in the bag now. It is settled now." Coming out of the side door of the Foreign Office into Downing Street, Dalton then met Lord Halifax. Warned about the "explosion" to expect in Parliament in case of further delay, Halifax gently replied: "It has been very difficult. But it will be all right tomorrow." Dalton was reassured and said, "Thank God!"

Halifax returned to his office and sat with some of his staff. A telegram ordering Henderson to ask for an appointment with

Ribbentrop at 9 a.m. had already been sent to Berlin. The Foreign Secretary "seemed relieved" that the decision had been taken. "He called for beer, which was brought down by a sleepy Resident Clerk in pyjamas."[30] Exhausted officials then went home to bed.

Looking back at the crisis two days later, the Foreign Office had no hesitation when assessing the blame. "M. Bonnet was the villain of the piece . . . he is, we know, the rallying point of French *defaitisme*," Sir Orme Sargent minuted. He feared Bonnet would "intrigue" to get France out of the war and, therefore, advised "discreet measures" should be taken to get rid of the French Foreign Minister. Sir Alexander Cadogan agreed. Bonnet "is entirely untrustworthy, and we know that on occasions he has lied and misrepresented us." Before British plans for Bonnet's removal matured, he was replaced at the Quai d'Orsay.[31] On September 14th Edouard Daladier took on the additional post of Foreign Minister and Georges Bonnet became Minister of Justice.

When Lord Halifax arrived at the Foreign Office on the morning of September 3rd, he found nothing to do but wait. At 9 a.m. Sir Nevile Henderson delivered the British ultimatum. He entered Ribbentrop's office to find not the Foreign Minister, but the interpreter Dr Paul Schmidt. Ribbentrop had preferred to spare himself the disagreeable task of being presented with a document whose contents he could accurately guess. Henderson, looking very serious, shook hands but remained standing. "I thought it somewhat ridiculous for two friends to stand like tin soldiers in front of each other", Schmidt later recalled. Then "with deep emotion" Henderson read the ultimatum and left.

Schmidt rushed to the Reich Chancellery and translated the document to Hitler. When he had finished, Hitler turned to Ribbentrop standing near him and said: "What now?"[32]

The real answer was astonishing. Hitler could still not abandon a last minute hope of confining the war to Poland. He gave his blessing to a scheme originating from the obsessedly optimistic

mind of Birger Dahlerus. At 10.50 a.m. the silence of the telephone lines between London and Berlin was broken. Dahlerus
spoke to Frank Roberts: "As a last resort, might he suggest that
Field-Marshal Göring should fly over to London to discuss
matters." Dahlerus waited on the phone while Halifax was consulted. The reply was a flat rejection. The British government
was still waiting for a definite answer from Hitler. Dahlerus
reported this back to Göring who was "annoyed". He had
already ordered an airplane to stand at a nearby airfield to fly him
to London.[33]

At 11 a.m. Halifax and Cadogan walked through the crowds in
Downing Street to join the Prime Minister. Ten minutes later, a
telephone call to the Berlin Embassy confirmed that no reply had
been received. The Polish-German war was now the Second
World War. It was already fifteen minutes old when Chamberlain broadcast to the country his first wartime speech:

> You can imagine what a bitter blow it is to me that all my long
> struggle to win peace has failed . . . we have done all that any
> country could do to establish peace, but a situation in which
> no word given by Germany's ruler could be trusted, and no
> people or country could feel themselves safe, had become
> intolerable.

To Alvar Liddell, the BBC announcer witnessing this historic
event, the Prime Minister "looked crumpled, despondent and old".

At noon, having already experienced a first air raid warning –
a false alarm – and while the French Ambassador in Berlin was at
last presenting an ultimatum to expire at 5 p.m., Chamberlain
spoke to the House of Commons. He read the British ultimatum.
No reply had been received within the stipulated time, he said,
"and, consequently, this country is at war with Germany." Then
he added: "Everything that I have worked for, everything that I
have hoped for, everything that I have believed in during my
public life, has crashed into ruins."[34]

During both speeches Chamberlain's words lingered on his
personal tragedy. It was appropriate. He had taken his country
into war.

To mounting cries of indignation he had delayed the announcement of a second world war for 56¼ hours. It was a brief delay for the nation which was to participate for more than five years – longer than any other – in the war against Nazi Germany.

*

Could war have been avoided? That was the question plaguing the minds of two diplomats, among others, who had hastily fled from the battle areas. The British Consul-General, Francis Michie Shepherd, and the League of Nations High Commissioner, Professor Carl Burckhardt, both having escaped the destruction of the Danzig flashpoint, considered that the Polish government had taken one fatal step. The ultimatum it had sent to the Danzig Senate on August 4th had been a terrible mistake. It had provoked Hitler and precipitated the crisis. It had destroyed any chance of a peaceful settlement of German-Polish differences and led to war.

The views of Shepherd and Burckhardt reached the Foreign Office in late September. There was ample time, now that war had begun, to indulge in leisurely post-mortems. Sir Orme Sargent carefully read what they had to say, but was unconvinced. He minuted in his florid handwriting: "If it had not been one thing it would have been another. Hitler wanted his pretext and he would have found it even if he had been dealing with the Archangel Gabriel." From Sargent's desk the file was then delivered to Sir Alexander Cadogan. "*Nothing* wd. have made any difference – except complete surrender to Herr Hitler's demands," Cadogan wrote.[35] The file was closed.

Notes* to Chapters

pp. 19–37   CHAPTER ONE

1. Koloman Gajan and Robert Kvaček, eds., *Germany and Czechoslovakia 1918–1945, Documents on German Policies* (Prague 1965), no. 56; War Office memorandum, 9 May, FO371/22997, C7007/19/18.
2. Radomir Luza, *The Transfer of the Sudeten Germans, A Study of Czech-German Relations, 1933–1962* (1964), 174; Minute by Makins, 22 Mar., FO371/22995, C3832/19/18.
3. Minute by Makins, 14 Mar., FO371/22897, C3243/7/12.
4. Newton to Halifax, 7 Mar., no. 123, FO371/22958, C2837/13/18; Letter, Newton to Strang, 29 Mar., FO371/22996, C4756/19/18.
5. David Dilks, ed., *The Diaries of Sir Alexander Cadogan, 1938–1945* (1971), 155; Minute by Cadogan, 11 Mar., FO371/22897, C3156/7/12.
6. Minute by Speaight and Makins, 10 Mar., FO371/22896, C2774/7/12; Minutes by Makins, 8, 13 Mar., *ibid.*, C2567, 2927/7/12. See also Minutes in FO371/22897, C3117/7/12.
7. *H.C.Deb.*, 339, 4 Oct., 1938, col. 303.
8. Cabinet Paper 258(38), 12 Nov. 1938, CAB24/280; Record of Anglo-French conversations, *DBFP*, III, no. 325; Minutes, CAB57(38), 30 Nov. 1938, CAB23/96; Minutes, FPC, 34th meeting, 6 Dec. 1938, CAB27/624.

* The following abbreviations have been used: *DBFP* – *Documents on British Foreign Policy*, Third Series; *H.C.Deb.*, *H.L.Deb.* – Parliamentary Debates, Fifth Series; House of Commons, House of Lords; *DGFP* – *Documents on German Foreign Policy 1918–1945*, Series D; *FRUS* – *Foreign Relations of the United States, Diplomatic Papers*; CID – Committee of Imperial Defence; COS – Chiefs of Staff Sub-committee; FPC – Foreign Policy Committee; DCOS – Deputy Chiefs of Staff; SAC – Strategic Appreciation Committee; JPC – Joint Planning Sub-committee; AFC – Anglo-French Conversations.

All references to dates, unless otherwise indicated, are to 1939. Foreign Office documents printed in *DBFP*, Third Series, are cited by their published reference numbers.

9. Newton to Halifax, 11 Dec. 1938, *DBFP*, III, no. 423; Minutes in FO371/22992, C717, 2141/19/18.
10. Minute by Strang, 9 Jan., FO371/22991, C646/17/18; Record of conversation, 12 Jan., *DBFP*, III, no. 500; Malcolm Muggeridge, ed., *Ciano's Diplomatic Papers* (1948), 265–6.
11. Phipps to Halifax, 11 Jan., *DBFP*, III, no. 496; Minute by Strang, 9 Jan., FO371/22991, C320/17/18.
12. Minutes by Halifax, Chamberlain and Cadogan, 18, 20, 26 Jan., *ibid.*, C659/17/18.
13. Henderson to Halifax, 3 Mar., *DBFP*, IV, no. 171; Minutes by Makins and Strang, 11 Mar., FO371/22991, C2657/17/18; Minutes by Sargent and Cadogan, 6 Mar., FO371/22992, C2340/19/18.
14. Notes by Halifax, n.d., *ibid.*; Minutes by Makins and Strang, 14, 16 Mar., *ibid.*, C3287, 3289/17/18; Draft telegram to Phipps, 14 Mar., *ibid.*, C3532/17/18.
15. Minutes, Cab 11(39), 15 Mar., CAB23/98.
16. *Cadogan Diaries, 1938–1945*, 157; H.C.Deb., 345, 15 Mar., cols. 438–40.
17. Halifax to Henderson, 15 Mar., *DBFP*, VI, no. 279; Herbert von Dirksen, *Moscow, Tokyo, London* (1951), 230; Dirksen to Foreign Ministry, 15 Mar., *DGFP*, IV, no. 244.
18. Minute by Vansittart, 15 Mar., FO371/22966, C3102/15/18.
19. Minute by Peake, 15 Mar., FO371/22993, C3313/19/18.
20. Phipps to Halifax, 14 Mar., *DBFP*, IV, no. 234; Minutes by Cadogan, 16, 17 Mar., FO371/22994, C3318/19/18; Minute by Sargent, 17 Mar., FO371/22966, C3102/15/18.
21. Nigel Nicolson, ed., *Harold Nicolson, Diaries and Letters, I, 1930–1939* (1966), 393.
22. Draft telegram to Henderson, 17 Mar., FO371/22994, C3318/19/18. Cf. *DBFP*, IV, no. 308.
23. Keith Feiling, *The Life of Neville Chamberlain* (1946), 400; Minute by Cadogan, 16 Mar., FO371/22993, C3313/19/18; *Cadogan Diaries, 1938–1945*, 157.
24. Letter, Chamberlain to Lord Beaverbrook, 11 June 1934, Lord Beaverbrook Papers; Neville Chamberlain, *The Struggle for Peace* (1939), 167–77; *The Times*, 18 Mar.

pp. 38–60   CHAPTER TWO

1. Entry of 17 Jan., A. L. Kennedy Diaries.
2. Minutes, Cab51(38), 31 Oct. 1938, CAB23/96. See also, Memorandum

by Lord Samuel of a conversation with Chamberlain, Lord Samuel Papers, A/111/1.

3. A. P. Young, *Across the Years* (1971), 17–46; "X" Document no. 3, 15 Oct. 1938, Young Papers. Information from Goerdeler and records of conversations with him were circulated by Young in memoranda entitled "X" Documents. Goerdeler was always referred to as "X".

4. "X" Document no. 4, 6–7 Nov. 1938, *ibid.*

5. Minutes, FPC, 32nd meeting, 14 Nov. 1938, CAB27/624.

6. Minute by Jebb, 6 Jan., FO371/22961, C939/15/18.

7. Minutes by Cadogan, 14 Oct., 8 Nov. 1938, FO371/21659, C14471/42/18.

8. Ogilvie-Forbes to Halifax, 3 Jan., *DBFP*, III, no. 515; Henderson to Halifax, 9 Mar., *DBFP*, IV, no. 195; Minutes, Cab56(38), 22 Nov. 1938, CAB23/96; Minute by Makins, 10 Jan., FO371/22912, C150/90/17; Letter, Vereker to Collier, 24 Dec. 1938, FO371/23677, N17/17/38.

9. Memorandum by Jebb, 19 Jan., FPC Paper(36)74, CAB27/627.

10. Minute by Collier, 19 Jan., FO371/22961, C528/15/18. Cf. Memorandum by Speaight, 16 Jan., *ibid.*, C609/15/18.

11. Letter, Lady Kirkpatrick to the author, 29 Aug. 1972; Sir Ivone Kirkpatrick, *The Inner Circle* (1959), 136–9; Letter, Kirkpatrick to Godfrey, 15 Feb., FO371/22958, C2164/13/18; *Cadogan Diaries, 1938–1945*, 130, 131; Minutes in FO371/22961, C939/15/18; Minutes, CID, 342nd, 343rd meetings, 16, 22 Dec. 1938, CAB2/8; Entries of 15–16 Dec. 1938, General Sir Henry Pownall Diaries.

12. Minute by Cadogan, 24 Jan., FO371/22961, C835/15/18; Letter, Beaumont-Nesbitt to Strang, 24 Jan., *ibid.*, C1194/15/18.

13. Entry of 25 Oct. 1938, Kennedy Diaries; Minutes, Cab57(38), 30 Nov. 1938, CAB23/96; *H.C.Deb.*, 342, 19 Dec. 1938, col. 2524; Minutes by Strang and Roberts, 5 Jan., FO371/22988, C204/16/18; Minute by Vansittart, 10 Jan., FO371/22960, C15/15/18.

14. Minute by Ashton-Gwatkin, 3 Dec. 1938, FO371/21655, C14809/62/18; "X" Document no. 5, 4 Dec. 1938, Young Papers. Cf. FO371/22961, C938/15/18.

15. Memorandum by Jebb, 19 Jan., FPC Paper(36)74, CAB27/627.

16. Ewan Butler, *Mason-Mac, The Life of Lieutenant-General Sir Noel Mason-Macfarlane* (1972), 74–5; Ogilvie-Forbes to Halifax, 29 Dec. 1938, *DBFP*, III, no. 505; Minute by Cadogan, 6 Jan., FO371/22960, C15/15/18.

17. "Memorandum based on most trustworthy information received before January 15th, 1939", Young Papers; "Summary of information from Dr Goerdeler", 21 Jan., FO371/22961, C864/15/18. Cf. FO371/22963, C1290/15/18.

18. Entry of 16 Jan., Sir Thomas Inskip Diaries, INKP1/2; Memorandum by Roberts, 13 Jan., FO371/22957, C1095/13/18.

19. Memoranda by Halifax and Jebb, 19 Jan., FPC Paper(36)74, CAB27/627.

20. Minutes, FPC, 35th meeting, 23 Jan., CAB27/624; Minutes, Cab2(39), 25 Jan., CAB23/97; Minutes, FPC, 36th meeting, 26 Jan., CAB27/624.

21. Minute by Vansittart, 25 Jan., FO371/22962, C1096/15/18; Minutes by Jebb and Cadogan, 26 Jan., *ibid.*, C1196/15/18.

22. Minutes, Cab3(39), 1 Feb., CAB 23/97; *H.C.Deb.*, 343, 6 Feb., col. 623. *Nicolson Diaries and Letters, I, 1930–1939*, 390; Minutes, Cab53(38), 7 Nov. 1938, CAB 23/96.

23. Minute by Roberts, 19 Jan., FO371/22961, C658/15/18; Memorandum by Roberts, 24 Apr., FO371/22971, C6143/15/18; Minutes by Kirkpatrick and Cadogan, 20, 21 Feb., FO371/22965, C2139/15/18; Minute by Strang, 6 Feb., FO371/23005, C1323/53/18.

24. Raoul de Roussy de Sales, ed., *Adolf Hitler, My New Order* (New York 1941), 559–94; Minute by Kirkpatrick, 31 Jan., FO371/22963, C1295/15/18; Minute by Jebb, 16 Feb., FO371/22965, C1979/15/18.

25. Note of a meeting at the Dominions Office, 17 Feb., FO371/22966, C2622/15/18; Minute by Cadogan, 11 Mar., *ibid.*, C2533/15/18; Memorandum by Roberts, 14 Feb., FO371/22958, C2058/13/18. Cf. Fritz Hesse, *Hitler and the English* (1954), 62.

26. Letter, Beaumont-Nesbitt to Strang, 8 Feb., FO371/22958, C1822/13/18; Letter, Col. W. C. van Cutsem to Strang, 28 Feb., *ibid.*, C2450/13/18.

27. Lindsay to Halifax, 20 Feb., *DBFP*, IV, no. 122; Minute by Jebb, 21 Feb., FO371/22965, C2431/15/18; Halifax to Lindsay, 27 Feb., *DBFP*, IV, no. 158.

28. Letter, Cadogan to Henderson, 28 Feb., FO800/270, 39/9.

29. Sir Nevile Henderson, *Water Under the Bridges* (1945), 209; Henderson to Halifax, 16, 18 Feb., *DBFP*, IV, nos. 109, 118; Minutes by Vansittart, 21, 22 Feb., FO371/22965, C2139/15/18; Minutes in FO371/23006, C2762/53/18; Minute by Cadogan, 26 Feb., FO800/294, C2/39/3.

30. Letters, Chamberlain to Hilda and Ida Chamberlain, 12, 19, 26 Feb., Neville Chamberlain Papers, (copies of Chamberlain's letters were for a short time available in the Lord Templewood Papers, XIX: (C) 11); Kennedy to Hull, 17 Feb., *FRUS, 1939*, I, 14–17.

31. Letter, Chamberlain to Henderson, 19 Feb., *DBFP*, IV, appendix 1, 591–2; Letter, Halifax to Henderson, 20 Feb., *ibid.*, 592; *Cadogan Diaries, 1938–1945*, 151.

32. Minute by Halifax, 26 Jan., FO371/22962, C1196/15/18; Minute by Sargent, 12 Feb., FO371/22963, C1290/15/18; Minute by Cadogan, 2 Feb., *ibid.*, C1277/15/18.

33. Entry of 16 Feb., Pownall Diaries; Minutes by Vansittart, 17 Feb., FO800/315, H/XV/124; 20 Feb., FO371/22965, C2209/15/18; 21, 24 Feb., 6 Mar., FO371/23006, C2762/53/18; 13 Mar., FO371/22966, C3234/15/18; Minute by Cadogan, 26 Feb., FO800/294, C2/39/3.

34. Feiling, *Neville Chamberlain*, 396–7; Earl of Halifax, *Fulness of Days* (1957), 232.

35. Ulrich von Hassell, *D'Une Autre Allemagne, Journal Posthume 1938–1944* (Neuchatel 1948), 29, 36; Ernst von Weizsäcker, *Memoirs* (1951), 172.

36. Minute by Vansittart, 8 Mar., FO371/22951, C2762/53/18.

37. Directive by Hitler, 21 Oct. 1938, *DGFP*, IV, no. 81; Directive by Keitel, 17 Dec. 1938, *ibid.*, no. 152.

pp. 61–78   CHAPTER THREE

1. V. V. Tilea, interview in *The Times*, 18 Nov. 1968; Halifax to Hoare, 17 Mar., *DBFP*, IV, no. 395. Gafencu's telegram was sent on March 16th but received by Tilea on the 17th. Cf. Viorica Moisuc, "Orientations dans la Politique Extérieure de la Roumanie après le Pacte de Munich", *Revue Roumaine d'Histoire*, V, no. 2, 1966, 336; and his *Diplomatia României si Problema Apararii Suveranitatii si Independentei Nationale în Perioada Martie 1938–Mai 1940* (Bucharest 1971), 137–9.

2. Minute by Sargent, 16 Mar., *DBFP*, IV, no. 298; Hoare to Halifax, 16 Mar., no. 37; Minutes by Sargent and Cadogan, 17 Mar., FO371/23752, R1733/1733/67.

3. Author's interviews with the late V. V. Tilea, 1970–2; Kennedy to Hull, 17 Mar., *FRUS, 1939*, I, 72.

4. Halifax to Hoare, 17, 18 Mar., *DBFP*, IV, nos. 395, 409; John Harvey, ed., *The Diplomatic Diaries of Oliver Harvey, 1937–1940* (1970), 263. Cf. Robert Rhodes James, ed., *Chips, The Diaries of Sir Henry Channon* (1967), 186–7; Sir Basil Liddell Hart, *Memoirs*, II, (1965), 217–18.

5. Minute by Jebb, 18 Mar., FO371/23061, C3576/3356/18; Minute by Vansittart, 17 Mar., *ibid.*, C3749/3356/18; A. A. Gromyko, *et al.*, eds., *SSSR v Borbe za Mir Nakanune Vtoroi Mirovoi Voini, Sentyabr 1938g.–Avgust 1939g., Dokumenti i Materiali* (Moscow 1971), no. 155; Minute by Hore-Belisha, 17 Mar., FO371/23832, R2195/113/37.

6. Halifax to Seeds, Kennard, Knatchbull-Hugessen, Waterlow and Campbell, 17 Mar., *DBFP*, IV, nos. 389–90; *Cadogan Diaries, 1938–1945*, 160.

7. Rumania: Personalities Report for 1938, FO371/23855, R5695/5695/37; Author's interviews with V. V. Tilea. Tilea's activities during February can be followed in FO371/23831–2.

8. Minutes, FPC, 37th meeting, 8 Feb., CAB27/624; Letter, Leith-Ross to Sargent, 2 Feb., FO371/23831, R827/113/37; Minute by Cadogan, 1 Feb., *ibid.*, R858/113/37; Halifax to Hoare, 3 Feb., *ibid.*, R826/113/37.

9. Moisuc, "Politique Extérieure de la Roumanie", 335; Halifax to Hoare, 10 Mar., no. 82, FO371/23840, R1634/122/37.

10. Minute by Sargent, 14 Mar., FO371/23739, R2032/114/67.

11. Ogilvie-Forbes to Halifax, 20 Mar., no. 146, FO800/294, C2/39/7.

12. Hoare to Halifax, 18 Mar., *DBFP*, IV, nos. 397, 399; Minute by Cadogan, 18 Mar., FO371/23060, C3538/3356/18.

13. Letter, Lord Lloyd to Halifax, 20 Mar., FO371/23062, C4105/3356/18; Unpublished Letter, Tilea to the *Daily Telegraph*, 21 Feb. 1963.

14. Letter, Hoare to Ingram, 13 June, FO371/23847, R5123/464/37; Hoare to Halifax, 21 Nov., no. 352; Minutes by Nichols and Vansittart, 1, 7 Dec., *ibid.*, R10674/464/37.

15. Memorandum by Roberts, 14 Feb., FO371/22958, C2058/13/18; Minute by Strang, 28 Jan., FO371/22965, C2106/15/18; Macnab to Hoare, 16 Mar., FO371/23852, R2135/1417/37.

16. Memorandum by Jebb, 18 Mar., FO371/22958, C3565/13/18.

17. Letter, Chamberlain to Ida Chamberlain, 8 Jan., Chamberlain Papers; Halifax to Lindsay, 17 Mar., *DBFP*, IV, no. 394.

18. *Cadogan Diaries, 1938–1945*, 157, 161.

19. Minutes, COS, 283rd, 284th meetings, 18 Mar., CAB53/10. Cf. Minutes, JPC, 242nd meeting, 18 Mar., CAB55/3.

20. Minutes, Cab12(39), 18 Mar., CAB23/98.

pp. 79–114   CHAPTER FOUR

1. Minutes, Cab12(39), 18 Mar., CAB23/98.

2. Minutes of the two meetings of Ministers on March 19th are in FO371/22967, C3858–9/15/18.

3. Letter, Chamberlain to Ida Chamberlain, 19 Mar., Chamberlain Papers.

4. For the debate on the letter to Mussolini, see Minutes by Cadogan, Wilson and Chamberlain, PREM1/327; Minutes by Nichols, Cadogan and Halifax, 17, 18, 19 Mar., FO371/22967, C3858/15/18; *Cadogan Diaries, 1938–1945*, 162. The letter as finally sent is in *DBFP*, IV, no. 448.

5. Halifax to Seeds, 19 Mar., *ibid.*, no. 433; Note of a meeting with the Dominion High Commissioners, 22 Mar., FO371/22968, C4415/15/18. Cf. *SSSR v Borbe za Mir*, no. 164.

6. Minutes, Cab13(39), 20 Mar., CAB23/98.

7. Malcolm Muggeridge, ed., *Ciano's Diary, 1939–1943* (1947), 45–6;

Perth to Halifax, 18 Mar., nos. 189, 193, FO371/22994, C3366,3425/19/18.

8. Minute by Noble, 23 Mar., FO371/22995, C3716/19/18; Perth to Halifax, 22 Mar., no. 203, *ibid.*, C3730/19/18; Minute by Nichols, 23 Mar., FO371/23797, R2115/9/22; Minutes by Nichols and Cadogan, 24 Mar., FO371/22996, C3865/19/18; Minute by Cadogan, 24 Mar., FO371/22944, C4311/421/62; Perth to Halifax, 21 Mar., *DBFP*, IV, nos. 375–6.

9. *Ciano's Diary, 1939–1943*, 52, 54; Letter, Mussolini to Chamberlain, 31 Mar., *DBFP*, IV, no. 596; Minutes in PREM1/327.

10. *Cadogan Diaries, 1938–1945*, 161–2; Halifax to Campbell, 23 Mar., *DBFP*, IV, no. 506; Halifax to Phipps, Seeds and Kennard, 20 Mar., *ibid.*, no. 446.

11. Records of conversations, 21, 22 Mar., *ibid.*, nos. 458, 484; Minutes, Cab14(39), 22 Mar., CAB23/98.

12. Letter, Chamberlain to Hilda Chamberlain, 26 Mar., Chamberlain Papers; Feiling, *Neville Chamberlain*, 403.

13. Halifax to Kennard, 24 Mar., *DBFP*, IV, no. 518.

14. Memoranda by Ribbentrop, 21, 26 Mar., *DGFP*, VI, nos. 61, 101; Polish Ministry for Foreign Affairs, *The Polish White Book, Official Documents Concerning Polish-German and Polish-Soviet Relations, 1933–1939* (1940), nos. 61–3; Waclaw Jedrzejewicz, ed., *Diplomat in Berlin 1933–1939, Papers and Memoirs of Jozef Lipski, Ambassador of Poland* (1968), 501–8; Directive from Hitler to Brauchitsch, 25 Mar., *DGFP*, VI, no. 99.

15. *Cadogan Diaries, 1938–1945*, 163–4; *Harvey Diaries, 1937–1940*, 268; Minute by Sargent, 26 Mar., FO371/23062, C4655/3356/18.

16. Minutes, FPC, 38th meeting, 27 Mar., CAB27/624; Letter, Hoare to Beaverbrook, 15 Feb., 1943, Beaverbrook Papers.

17. JPC Paper 384, 21 Mar., CAB55/15; Minutes, JPC, 246th meeting, 28 Mar., CAB55/3; Minutes, COS, 285th meeting, 28 Mar., CAB53/10; COS Paper 870, 28 Mar., CAB53/47. COS Paper 872 (revise), 3 April, *ibid.*, toned down the more outspoken criticisms of a guarantee recorded in JPC Paper 388, 28 Mar., CAB55/15.

18. Minutes, Cab15(39), 29 Mar., CAB23/98; Halifax to Kennard and Hoare, 27 Mar., *DBFP*, IV, no. 538.

19. See letters, minutes and notes exchanged between Hore-Belisha, Wilson and Chamberlain in PREM1/296; and R. J. Minney, *The Private Papers of Hore-Belisha* (1960), 186–7.

20. Minute by Sargent, 29 Mar., FO371/23015, C4505/54/18; Kennard to Halifax, 31 Mar., *DBFP*, IV, no. 577. References to this American information were included, but then omitted from the telegram to

Phipps informing the French government of the decision to guarantee Poland. See FO371/23015, C4525/54/18.

21. Minute by Strang, n.d., FO371/22989, C5269/16/18; Henderson to Halifax, 19 Feb., no. 66; Minute by Kirkpatrick, 21 Feb., FO371/22988, C2109/16/18; Ian Colvin, *Vansittart in Office* (1965), 298–311; *Cadogan Diaries, 1938–1945*, 164–5.

22. Ogilvie-Forbes to Halifax, 1, 3 Apr., nos. 215, 220, 221, FO371/22989, C4579, 4640, 4658/16/18; Letter, Cadogan to Ogilvie-Forbes, 18 Apr., FO800/294, C2/39/9; Letter, Ogilvie-Forbes to Strang, 19 Apr., FO371/22989, C5702/16/18.

23. Letter, Holman to Strang, 3 Mar.; Minute by Roberts, 15 Mar., FO371/22958, C2882/13/18; Minute by Roberts, 24 Apr., FO371/22971, C6143/15/18.

24. For summaries of information regarding a German coup in Danzig, see Minute by Speaight, 29 Mar., FO371/23016, C4859/54/18; War Office memorandum, 30 Mar., *ibid.*, C4622/54/18.

25. Knox to Halifax, 23 Mar., no. 67, FO371/23061, C3823/3356/18.

26. Minute by Roberts, 25 Mar., FO371/22967, C3894/15/18; Clive to Halifax, 21, 25 Mar., *DBFP*, IV, nos. 477, 527; Minute by Roberts, 31 Mar., FO371/22969, C5567/15/18.

27. Notes of meeting of Ministers, 21 Mar.; Note of an informal conference in Sir Warren Fisher's room, 22 Mar., CAB21/592.

28. Minutes, Cab16(39), 30 Mar., CAB23/98.

29. Letter, Ismay to Strang, 3 Apr., FO371/22969, C5041/54/18; COS Paper 872 (revise), 3 Apr., CAB53/47; Liddell Hart, *Memoirs*, II, 221. Cf. Message from Lord Beaverbrook, 21 Apr., Sir Basil Liddell Hart Papers, LH.B2/5.

30. Minutes, COS, 286th meeting, 30 Mar., CAB53/10.

31. Letter, Zetland to Linlithgow, 4 Apr., Marquess of Zetland Papers, MSS, EUR, D609, XI.

32. Minutes, FPC, 39th meeting, 30 Mar., CAB27/624.

33. War Office, Summary of information, no. 9 (new series), 30 Mar.; Minute by Cadogan, 30 Mar., FO371/22996, C4745/19/18; Ogilvie-Forbes to Halifax, 29 Mar., no. 116, FO371/22958, C4399/13/18.

34. Minute by Speaight, 29 Mar., FO371/23066, C4859/54/18; Minute by Kirkpatrick, 30 Mar., FO371/22968, C4621/15/18.

35. Minutes, FPC, 40th meeting, 31 Mar., CAB27/624.

36. Minutes, Cab 17(39), 31 Mar., CAB23/98; Halifax to Perth, 31 Mar., *DBFP*, IV, no. 581; *Cadogan Diaries, 1938–1945*, 167; Halifax to Lindsay, 31 Mar., no. 311, FO371/23015, C4529/54/18.

37. Crozier interview with Vansittart, 13 Oct., W. P. Crozier Papers, C/5; Halifax to Seeds, 31 Mar., *DBFP*, IV, no. 589; *SSSR v Borbe za Mir*,

no. 200; Minute by A. J. Sylvester, 31 Mar., David Lloyd George Papers, G/130. Cf. Ivan Maisky, *Who Helped Hitler?* (1964), 107–8.

38. *H. C. Deb.*, 345, 31 Mar., 3 Apr., cols. 2421–2, 2487–92.

pp. 115–151   CHAPTER FIVE

1. Letter, Chamberlain to Ida Chamberlain, 3 Apr., Chamberlain Papers; Letter, Chamberlain to Lloyd George, 31 Mar., Lloyd George Papers, G/4/2/1; *SSSR v Borbe za Mir*, no. 202. Cf. Entry of 2 Apr., Hugh Dalton Diaries.

2. Notes by Kirkpatrick, 30 Mar., FO371/23062, C4472/3356/18; Letter, D. V. Kelly to Sir Miles Lampson, 18 Apr., FO371/23007, C5566/53/18; Minute by Roberts, 30 Mar., FO371/23062, C4289/3356/18.

3. Letter, Ogilvie-Forbes to Strang, 29 Mar., *DBFP*, IV, appendix 5, 623–7; Minute by Cadogan, 31 Mar., FO371/22958, C4760/13/18; Ogilvie-Forbes to Cadogan, 10 Apr., FO800/294, C2/39/8; Minute by Sargent, 20 May, *ibid.*, C2/39/15.

4. COS Paper 843, 20 Feb., CAB53/45.

5. COS Paper 885, 20 Apr., CAB53/48; Sir Hughe Knatchbull-Hugessen, *Diplomat in Peace and War* (1949), 145–6.

6. Minutes, SAC, 3rd meeting, 17 Mar., CAB16/209; Minutes, COS, 283rd meeting, 18 Mar., CAB53/10; COS Papers 873(JP), 872 (revise), 1, 3 Apr., CAB53/47.

7. Minutes, Cab12, 15(39), 18, 29 Mar., CAB23/98.

8. Knatchbull-Hugessen to Halifax, 17 Mar., no. 67, FO 371/22994, C3365/19/18; 25 Mar., nos. 83–4, FO371/23061–2, C4050–1/3356/18; Halifax to Knatchbull-Hugessen, 21 Mar., *DBFP*, IV, no. 472.

9. Minutes by Sargent, Oliphant and Cadogan, 27, 28 Mar., FO371/23063, C5257/3356/18; *Cadogan Diaries, 1938–1945*, 163–4. Cf. Minute by Nichols, 28 Mar., FO371/23753, R2311/2311/67.

10. Halifax to Hoare, 31 Mar., *DBFP*, IV, no. 583; Minutes by Sargent, Cadogan and Halifax, 1, 2, 3 Apr., FO371/23063, C5258/3356/18.

11. Count Edward Raczynski, *In Allied London* (1962), 4, 15; *Cadogan Diaries, 1938–1945*, 168; Briefs for Beck's visit, FO371/23016, C4860, 5047/54/18; Minute by Jebb, 4 Apr., *ibid.*, C4758/54/18.

12. *Lipski Papers and Memoirs*, 527.

13. Record of Anglo-Polish conversations, 4 Apr., *DBFP*, V, nos. 1–2; *Cadogan Diaries, 1938–1945*, 169; Minutes, Cab18(39), 5 Apr., CAB23/98.

14. Records of Anglo-Polish conversations, 5–6 Apr., *DBFP*, V, nos. 10, 16; Minute by Cadogan, 7 Apr., FO371/23016, C5055/54/18.

15. *Cadogan Diaries, 1938–1945*, 170; *Ciano's Diary, 1939–1943*, 44–64.

16. Minute by Noble, 24 Mar., FO371/23711, R1908/725/90; Minute by Sargent, 29 Mar., *ibid.*, R1989/725/90; Minute by Noble, 3 Apr., *ibid.*, R2227/1335/90.

17. Halifax to Campbell, 22 Mar., no. 48, FO371/23816, R1910/399/22; Campbell to Halifax, 23 Mar., no. 54, *ibid.*, R1967/399/22; War Office, Summary of Information, no. 13 (new series), 4 Apr., FO371/22996, C4835/19/18; Admiral J. H. Godfrey, *Naval Memoirs*, VIII, 159, 164, Godfrey Papers, GDFY 1/11. Cf. Perth to Halifax, 23 Feb., no. 127, FO371/23816, R1301/399/22; Phipps to Halifax, 4 Apr., no. 142, FO371/23711, R2326/1335/90.

18. Minutes, Cab18(39), 5 Apr., CAB23/98; Halifax to Lindsay, 6 Apr., no. 330, FO371/23711, R2389/1335/90; Halifax to Perth, 6, 7, 8 Apr., *DBFP*, V, nos. 77, 81, 86, 90; Perth to Halifax, 4, 7, 9 Apr., *ibid.*, nos. 72, 82, 104; Minute by Sargent, 6 Apr., FO371/23711, R2333/1335/90.

19. *Ciano's Diary, 1939–1943*, 51.

20. COS Paper 885, annex 5, 20 Apr., CAB53/48.

21. Notes of a conference of Ministers, 8 Apr., CAB23/98; *Cadogan Diaries, 1938–1945*, 170; Minute by Ingram, 4 Apr., FO371/23711, R2342/1335/90; Minute by Jebb, 7 Apr., *ibid.*, R2531/1335/90; Minute by Halifax, 8 Apr., FO371/23712, R2548/1335/90.

22. Letter, Phipps to Cadogan, 8 Apr., *DBFP*, V, no. 96; Phipps to Halifax, 9 Apr., *ibid.*, no. 106; Waterlow to Halifax, 9 Apr., *ibid.*, no. 97; Letter, Churchill to Chamberlain, 9 Apr., PREM1/323.

23. Halifax to Perth, 9 Apr., *DBFP*, V, nos. 101, 109–10; Halifax to Waterlow, 9 Apr., *ibid.* no. 105; Waterlow to Halifax, 10 Apr., *ibid.*, no. 118; Perth to Halifax, 11 Apr., *ibid.*, no. 131; Phipps to Halifax, 9 Apr., *ibid.*, no. 103; Waterlow to Halifax, 13 Apr., no. 137, FO371/23780, R2718/1877/19.

24. Minutes, Cab10(39), 10 Apr., CAB23/98; Minutes, FPC, 41st meeting, 10 Apr., CAB27/624; Minutes, SAC, 5th meeting, 11 Apr., CAB16/209.

25. Minutes, FPC, 42nd meeting, 11 Apr., CAB27/624; Knatchbull-Hugessen to Halifax, 10, 13 Apr., *DBFP*, V, nos. 119–21, 124, 149, 152–3; Halifax to Knatchbull-Hugessen, 11, 12 Apr., *ibid.*, nos. 128, 138.

26. Halifax to Hoare, 10 Apr., *ibid.*, no. 37; Author's interviews with V. V. Tilea, 1970–2.

27. Minutes, FPC, 41st meeting, 10 Apr., CAB27/624.

28. Entry of 12 Apr. Dalton Diaries; Minute by T. W. Dupree, 12 Apr., FO371/23063, C5105/3356/18; *Cadogan Diaries, 1938–1945*, 173; Minutes, Cab20(39), 13 Apr., CAB23/98; Letter, Chamberlain to Ida

Chamberlain, 15 Apr., Chamberlain Papers; Minutes by Jebb and Cadogan, 12 Apr., FO371/23063, C5290/3356/18.

29. Halifax to Phipps, 13 Apr., *DBFP*, V, no. 66; Minute by Jebb, 13 Apr., FO371/23048, C5796/454/18; Minutes, Cab20(39), CAB23/98; Hoare to Halifax, 13 Apr., *DBFP*, V, no. 54.

30. Minute by Wilson, 9 Apr., CAB21/653; Minutes of a meeting with the TUC, 26 Apr., PREM1/387.

31. JPC Paper 378, 20 Mar. CAB55/15; Minutes, AFC(J), 1st meeting, 29 Mar., CAB29/160.

32. AFC(J) Paper 29, 4 Apr.; Minutes, AFC(J), 4th meeting, 30 Mar.; AFC(J) Paper 14, 29 Mar., *ibid.*

33. AFC Paper 6, CAB29/159; (also COS Paper 872 (revise), 3 Apr., Cab53/47); AFC(J) Paper 44, 25 Apr., CAB29/160.

34. AFC(J) Paper 56, 4 May; Minutes, AFC(J), 12th–13th meetings, 26 Apr., 3 May, *ibid.*; Minutes, COS, 292nd meeting, 1 May, CAB53/11.

35. Minutes, COS 290th, 292nd, 294th meetings, 19 Apr., 1, 10 May, CAB53/11.

36. Minutes, JPC, 253rd, 256th meetings, 15 May, 14 June, CAB55/3; Minutes, COS, 297th meeting, 17 May, CAB53/11; COS Papers 903(JP), 15 May, 927, 12 June, 940(JP), 7 July, CAB53/49, 50, 51.

37. DCOS Paper 108, 24 June, CAB54/7; Minutes, DCOS, 47th, 53rd meetings, 3, 24 Aug., CAB54/2.

38. Minutes, COS, 299th meeting, 1 June, CAB53/11; Minutes, CID, 360th meeting, 22 June, CAB2/8.

39. Minutes, COS, 306–309th meetings, 11, 12, 18, 19 July, CAB53/11; COS Papers 938(JP), 7 July, 939, 18 July, CAB53/51; Minutes, CID, 368th meeting, 24 July, CAB2/9.

40. Minutes, COS, 312th meeting, 24 Aug., CAB53/11; COS Paper 963, 23 Aug., CAB53/54; Minutes, COS, 311th meeting, 21 Aug., CAB53/11; COS Papers 960–1, 20 Aug., CAB53/53.

41. Minutes, JPC, 269–70th meetings, 25, 28 Aug., CAB55/3; JPC Papers, 529 (revise), 27 Aug., 535, 28 Aug., CAB55/19.

42. Minutes, COS, 314–317th meetings, 28–31 Aug., CAB53/11; COS Papers 968, 31 Aug., 970, 28 Aug., CAB53/54; Minutes, CID, 374th meeting, 1 Sept., CAB2/9; Minutes, WM1(39), 3 Sept., CAB65/1; JPC Paper 529(revise), 27 Aug., CAB55/19.

pp. 152–187   CHAPTER SIX

1. Seeds to Halifax, 28 Jan., *DBFP*, IV, no. 46; Minutes in FO371/23683, N751/105/38.

2. Letter, Sir William Seeds to the author, 17 Sept. 1972; Author's interview with Seeds, 18 Sept. 1968; Entry of 12 July, Dalton Diaries.

3. Letter, Robert Boothby to Lloyd George, 18 Sept., Lloyd George Papers, D/3/13/12.

4. Minutes by Lascelles, Ashton-Gwatkin, Halifax and Vansittart, 5, 14, 18, 20 Jan., FO371/23677, N57/57/38.

5. Minute by A. J. Sylvester, 23 Feb., Lloyd George Papers, G/23/1/8; Entry of 16 Feb., Sir Harold Nicolson Diaries; Minutes, Cab6(39), 8 Feb., CAB23/97; Chamberlain to Ida Chamberlain, 8 Jan., Chamberlain Papers; Sidney Aster, "Ivan Maisky and Parliamentary Anti-Appeasement, 1938–1939", in A. J. P. Taylor, ed., *Lloyd George, Twelve Essays* (1971), 338.

6. Letter, Collier to Lieut.-Col. N. C. D. Brownjohn, 2 Jan., FO371/22299, N6201/924/38; Letter, Collier to Vereker, 14 Jan.; Minute by Collier, 25 Jan., FO371/23686, N464/243/38; Author's interview with Brigadier R. C. Firebrace, 6 Aug. 1968.

7. Seeds to Halifax, 26 Jan., *DBFP*, IV, no. 24.

8. Halifax to Seeds, 14 Feb., *ibid.*, no. 103; *Nicolson Diaries and Letters*, I, *1930–1939*, 391–2; Memorandum by Lord Strabolgi, 20 Sept., Dalton Papers.

9. Foreign Policy archives of the USSR, quoted in V. I. Popov, *Diplomaticheskie Otnosheniya Mezhdu SSSR i Angliei, 1929–1939gg.* (Moscow 1965), 384; Minute by Butler, 9 Mar., *DBFP*, IV, no. 194; Liddell Hart, *Memoirs*, II, 222; *SSSR v Borbe za Mir*, no. 141.

10. Letter, Brownjohn to Collier, 30 Jan., FO371/23684, N559/190/38; Joseph Stalin, *Leninism* (1940), 630.

11. Minutes, Cab14, 15(39), 20, 29 Mar., CAB23/98; Minutes, FPC, 38th, 40th meetings, 27, 31 Mar., CAB27/624.

12. Perth to Halifax, 22 Mar., no. 205; Minute by Roberts, 23 Mar., FO371/23061, C3777/3356/18; Minutes by Makins and Cadogan, 23 Mar., *ibid.*, C3905/3356/18.

13. Minutes, FPC, 40th meeting, 31 Mar., CAB27/624.

14. Seeds to Halifax, 1 Apr., *DBFP*, IV, no. 597; Minutes by Strang, Halifax and Speaight, 3, 4 Apr., FO371/23016, C4575/54/18; Halifax to Seeds, 6 Apr., *DBFP*, V, no. 19.

15. Seeds to Halifax, 6 Apr., *ibid.*, no. 13.

16. Minute by Peake, 5 Apr.; Memorandum by Ewer, 4 Apr.; Minutes by Sargent, Cadogan and Halifax, 6,7,8 Apr., FO371/23063, C5430/3356/18.

17. Halifax to Seeds, 11 Apr., *DBFP*, V, no. 42; *SSSR v Borbe za Mir*, no. 226; Seeds to Halifax, 14 Apr., *DBFP*, V, no. 161.

18. Seeds to Halifax, 13 Apr., *ibid.*, no. 52; Minutes, Cab20(39), 13 Apr., CAB23/98.

19. Halifax to Seeds, 14 Apr., *DBFP*, V, nos. 166, 170, 176; *SSSR v Borbe za Mir*, nos. 230–1.

20. *Ibid.*, nos. 217–18.

21. Phipps to Halifax, 20 Apr., *DBFP*, V, no. 241; *SSSR v Borbe za Mir*, no. 232; Georges Bonnet, *Défense de la Paix*, II, *Fin d'une Europe* (Geneva 1948), 180.

22. Seeds to Halifax, 18 Apr., *DBFP*, V, no. 201; Halifax to Phipps, 18, 20 Apr., *ibid.*, nos. 210, 240; *Cadogan Diaries, 1938–1945*, 175; Minute by Strang, 19 Apr., FO371/22969, C5460/15/18.

23. Maisky, *Who Helped Hitler?*, 116–19; A. A. Gromyko, *et al.*, ed., *Istoriya Diplomatii*, III, (Moscow 1965), 771–2.

24. *SSSR v Borbe za Mir*, no. 218.

25. Letter, Sir William Seeds to Martin Gilbert, 12 Feb. 1968, Martin Gilbert Archive.

26. Note by Cadogan, 19 Apr., FO371/22969, C5460/15/18; Minutes, FPC, 43rd meeting, 19 Apr., CAB27/624; COS Paper 890, 22 Apr., CAB53/48.

27. Minutes, COS, 291st meeting, 21 Apr., CAB53/11; COS Paper 887, 24 Apr., CAB53/48; Minutes, FPC, 44th meeting, 25 Apr., CAB27/624.

28. Records of conversations between Ribbentrop, Hitler and Gafencu, 18, 19 Apr., *DGFP*, V, nos. 227, 234; Grigore Gafencu, *The Last Days of Europe* (1947), 48–72.

29. Records of conversations, 24, 25, 26 Apr., *DBFP*, V, nos. 278–9, 285, 295; Gafencu, *Last Days of Europe*, 92–106.

30. Minutes, Cab24(39), 26 Apr., CAB23/99.

31. Halifax to Phipps, 28 Apr., *DBFP*, V, no. 305. Chamberlain personally revised and approved this telegram. See Minutes in FO371/23064, C5838/3356/18.

32. Maisky, *Who Helped Hitler?* 124; Seeds to Halifax, 4 May, *DBFP*, V, no. 353; Minute by Halifax, 3 May, FO371/23065, C6743/3356/18.

33. Memorandum by Strabolgi, 20 Sept., Dalton Papers.

34. Memorandum by Weizsäcker, 17 Apr., *DGFP*, V, no. 215.

35. Maisky, *Who Helped Hitler?* 119–21; George Bilainkin, *Maisky, Ten Years Ambassador* (1944), 246; *SSSR v Borbe za Mir*, no. 218; Entry of 8 Apr., Beatrice Webb Diaries.

36. P. N. Pospelov, *et al.*, eds., *Istoriya Velikoi Otechestvennoi Voiny Sovetskogo Soyuza, 1941–1945*, I, (Moscow 1960), 161–2, 260.

37. Letter, Hitler to Mussolini, 25 Aug., *DGFP*, VII, no. 266; Kirk to Hull, 4 May, *FRUS*, *Soviet Union*, 757–9; Davies to Hull, 10 May, *ibid.*, 760–1; Mario Toscano, "La Politique Russe de l'Italie au Printemps 1939", *Revue d'Histoire de la Deuxième Guerre Mondiale*, II, no. 6, Apr. 1952,

11–14; Ministère des Affaires Etrangères, *Le Livre Jaune Français, Documents Diplomatiques, 1938–1939* (Paris 1939), no. 123.

38. Minutes by Lascelles and Collier, 5 May, FO371/23685, N2282/233/38. The significance of Litvinov's dismissal is analysed *ibid.*, various files; and FO371/23697, N2752/1459/38.

39. Osborne to Halifax, 6, 10 May, nos. 24, 26, FO371/22972, C6698, 6918/15/18; Loraine to Halifax, 9, 11 May, nos. 447, 161, FO371/23018, C6864/54/18; FO371/23686, N2446/243/38.

40. Minute by Strang, 6 May, FO371/22972, C6794/15/18; Henderson to Halifax, 5, 8 May, *DBFP*, V, nos. 377, 413; *Livre Jaune Français*, no. 123.

41. Minute by Cadogan, 6 May, FO371/22972, C6794/15/18; Minute by Roberts, 8 May, *ibid.*, C6698/15/18; Minute by Makins, 12 May, *ibid.*, C6987/15/18; Minute by Lascelles, 13 May, FO371/23018, C6864/54/18.

42. Memorandum by Schnurre, 5 May, *DGFP*, V, no. 332.

43. Seeds to Halifax, 4, 9, 12 May, *DBFP*, V, nos. 359, 421–2, 509; Letter, Seeds to Oliphant, 16 May, *ibid.*, no. 533.

44. Entry of 14 June, Dalton Diaries.

45. Minutes, Cab26(39), 3 May, CAB23/99.

46. Phipps to Halifax, 3 May, *DBFP*, V, nos. 350–1; Minutes, FPC, 45th meeting, 5 May, CAB27/624.

47. Seeds to Halifax, 9 May, *DBFP*, V, nos. 421, 436; Letter, Seeds to Oliphant, 16 May, *ibid.*, no. 533; Minute by Cadogan, 21 May, FO371/23066, C7614/3356/18.

48. Seeds to Halifax, 10 May, *DBFP*, V, no. 441; Minutes by Strang and Butler, 10 May, FO371/23065, C6923/3356/18.

49. Minutes, Cab27(39), 10 May, CAB23/99; Cabinet Paper 108(39), 10 May, CAB24/286. This paper was discussed by the JPC on 8 May, and by the COS on 10 May. Cf. JPC Paper 410, 8 May, CAB55/16; COS Paper 902, 10 May, CAB53/49.

50. Letter, Seeds to Oliphant, 16 May, *DBFP*, V, no. 533; Seeds to Halifax, 15, 16 May, *ibid.*, nos. 520, 530; Memorandum by Ewer, 10 May, FO371/23066, C7108/3356/18.

51. Letter, Sargent to Chatfield, 15 May, *ibid.*, C7246/3356/18; Minutes, COS 295–6th meetings, 16 May, and aide-mémoire, attached as annex to minutes of 296th meeting, CAB53/11; Minutes, FPC, 47th meeting, 16 May, CAB27/625; Minute by Vansittart, 16 May, FO371/23066, C7268/3356/18; Letter, Burgin to Margaret Burgin, 17 May, Leslie Burgin Papers.

52. See Minute by Vansittart, 16 May, FO371/20366, C7169/3356/18; Minutes in Lord Vansittart Papers, VNST3/2; and Crozier interview with Vansittart, 13 Apr., Crozier Papers, C/5.

53. Minutes, Cab28(39), 17 May, CAB23/99.
54. Minutes, FPC, 48th meeting, 19 May, CAB27/625. Cf. Minutes by Gwilym Lloyd George, 17, 18 May, Lloyd George Papers, G/130; Minutes in PREM1/409.
55. *H.C.Deb.*, 347, 19 May, cols. 1839–59; Maisky, *Who Helped Hitler?* 125–7; Notes by Strang, 19 May, FO371/23066, C7316/3356/18; Admiral Sir R. P. Ernle-Erle-Drax, "Mission to Moscow, August 1939", *Naval Review*, XL, no. 3, Aug. 1952, 253.
56. Foreign Office memorandum, 22 May, *DBFP*, V, no. 589. See also, Letter, Loraine to Ingram, 23 May, FO371/23067, C7872/3356/18.
57. Minute by Strang, 16 May, *DBFP*, V, no. 528; Letter, Corbin to Halifax, 16 May, *ibid.*, no. 531; Minute by Strang, 21 May, FO371/23066, C7266/3356/18; Halifax to Phipps, 17 May, *DBFP*, V, no. 539.
58. Minute by Vansittart, 17 May, FO371/22972, C7253/3356/18; Letter, Henderson to Cadogan, 18 May, *DBFP*, V, no. 552; Minute by Cadogan, 19 May, FO371/22972, C7457/15/18. See also, Memorandum by Dr P. M. Papirnik, 4 May, *ibid.*, C6746/15/18; Joseph E. Davies, *Mission to Moscow* (1942), 284.
59. Minutes by Cadogan and Halifax, 3 May; Halifax to Seeds, 10 May, no. 105, FO371/23065, C6743/3356/18; Halifax to Cadogan, 21 May, *DBFP*, V, no. 576; *Harvey Diaries 1937–1940*, 290.
60. Bilainkin, *Maisky*, 256; Letter, Gwilym Lloyd George to David Lloyd George, 1 June, Lloyd George Papers, G/130; Maisky, *Who Helped Hitler?* 128–31; Halifax to Cadogan, 22 May, *DBFP*, V, nos. 581–2; *SSSR v Borbe za Mir*, no. 302.
61. *Cadogan Diaries, 1938–1945*, 182; Cadogan to Halifax, 21 May, *DBFP*, V, no. 574; Seeds to Cadogan, 22 May, *ibid.*, no. 583; Schulenburg to Weizsäcker, 20, 22 May, *DGFP*, V, nos. 414, 424.
62. Letter, Cadogan to Halifax, 23 May, FO371/23066, C7469/3356/18; *Cadogan Diaries, 1938–1945*, 183–4.
63. Letters, Chamberlain to Hilda and Ida Chamberlain, 9 Apr., 14 May, Chamberlain Papers; Feiling, *Neville Chamberlain*, 408; Letter, Cadogan to Hoare, 26 Oct. 1951, Lord Templewood Papers, XIX:12; *Cadogan Diaries, 1938–1945*, 182.
64. Minutes, Cab30(39), 24 May, CAB23/99; Letter, Cadogan to Hoare, 19 May, FO371/23066, C7499/3356/18. See also, Note of a meeting between Inskip and the Dominion High Commissioners, 23 May, FO371/23067, C7870/3356/18.
65. Letter, Chamberlain to Hilda Chamberlain, 28 May, Chamberlain Papers.

Notes to Chapters

1. See Letter, Lieutenant-General Adrian Carton de Wiart to Ismay, 26 June, General Lord Ismay Papers, IV/Car/1.
2. "Brief for Colonel Beck's visit", by Makins, n.d., FO371/23016, C4860/54/18.
3. *Polish White Book*, nos. 48–9; Memoranda by Schmidt and Ribbentrop, 5, 9, Jan., *DGFP*, V, nos. 119–20; Jozef Beck, *Final Report* (New York 1957), 171–3.
4. Minute by Speaight, 9 Jan., FO371/23015, C259/54/18; Kennard to Simon, 11 Jan., *DBFP*, III, no. 531; Minutes by Speaight and Strang, 13, 14 Jan., FO371/23015, C403/54/18; U K. Delegation (Geneva) to Halifax, 18 Jan., no. 3, *ibid.*, C833/54/18.
5. Henderson to Halifax, 1 Mar., no. 73, *ibid.*, C2496/54/18; Minute by Makins, 3 Mar., *ibid.*, C2596/54/18; Henderson to Halifax, 2 Mar. *DBFP*, IV, no. 166; Letter, Kennard to Cadogan, 7 Mar., *ibid.*, no. 187.
6. Minutes of a meeting of Ministers, 19 Mar., FO371/22967, C3858/15/18; Minutes, Cab13(39), 20 Mar., CAB23/98; Halifax to Kennard, 21, 24 Mar., *DBFP*, IV, nos. 471, 518.
7. Minutes, Cab16(39), 30 Mar.; Cab17(39), 31 Mar., CAB23/98.
8. Chamberlain to Hilda Chamberlain, 3 Apr., Chamberlain Papers.
9. Entry of 4 Apr., Kennedy Diaries; Entry of 3 Apr., Geoffrey Dawson Diaries.
10. Letters, Ogilvie-Forbes to Strang, 23, 29 Mar.; Minutes by Kirkpatrick, 31 Mar., FO371/22967–8, C3978, 4669/15/18; Letter, Kennard to Halifax, 4 Apr.; Minutes by Roberts and Strang, 14 Apr., FO371/23016, C5032/54/18. Colvin later admitted that the stories about Beck were circulated by the Germans. Ian Colvin, *Chief of Intelligence* (1951), 78.
11. Briefs for Beck's visit, FO371/23016, C4860, 5047/54/18; Records of conversations, 4 Apr., *DBFP*, V, nos. 1–2.
12. Record of conversations, 6 Apr., *ibid.*, no. 16; Letter, Strang to C. G. L. Syers, 7 Apr., PREM1/331; Minute by Strang, 5 May, FO371/23017, C6457/54/18; Raczynski, *In Allied London*, 342; *Cadogan Diaries, 1938–1945*, 170.
13. Ogilvie-Forbes to Halifax, 6 Apr., *DBFP*, V, no. 14; Directive by Keitel, 3 Apr., *DGFP*, VI, no. 149; Directive by Hitler, 11 Apr., *ibid.*, no. 185.
14. Ogilvie-Forbes to Halifax, 8 Apr., no. 259, FO371/22968, C4908/15/18.
15. Ogilvie-Forbes to Halifax, 14 Apr., *DBFP*, V, no. 163; Minutes by Sargent, Cadogan, Halifax and Jebb, 17 Apr., FO371/23017, C5349/

54/18; Halifax to Kennard, 17, 20 Apr., *DBFP*, V, nos. 197, 237; Kennard to Halifax, 18, 22 Apr., *ibid.*, nos. 208, 263.

16. Ogilvie-Forbes to Halifax, 17 Apr., no. 307; Minute by Kirkpatrick, 19 Apr., FO371/23017, C5469/54/18.

17. Minute by Makins, 20 Apr., *ibid.*

18. Minutes, Cab25(39), 1 May, CAB23/99; Halifax to Kennard, 3 May, *DBFP*, V, no. 346; Kennard to Halifax, 4 May, *ibid.*, no. 355.

19. Minutes by Kirkpatrick, Cadogan, Halifax and Strang, 5, 8, 9 May, FO371/23017, C6457/54/18; Halifax to Kennard, 10 May, *DBFP*, V, no. 442.

20. Kennard to Halifax, 10 May, *ibid.*, no. 459; Minutes by Strang, Sargent and Halifax, 12, 13 May, FO371/23018, C6910/54/18; Halifax to Kennard, 19 May, *DBFP*, V, no. 558.

21. Norman H. Baynes, ed., *The Speeches of Adolf Hitler, April 1922–August 1939*, II, (1942), 1605–56.

22. Henderson to Halifax, 2 May, *DBFP*, V, no. 334; Shepherd to Halifax, 4 May, no. 39, FO371/23017, C6588/54/18; Minutes by Kirkpatrick, Jebb, Sargent and Cadogan, 8, 9 May, FO371/23018, C6861/54/18.

23. Halifax to Henderson, 9, 11 May, *DBFP*, V, nos. 431, 475, 489; Halifax to Loraine, 9 May, *ibid.*, no. 432; Letter, Henderson to Cadogan, 10 May; Halifax to Henderson, 11 May, no. 158, FO371/23018, C7045/54/18.

24. Minute by Strang, 11 May, FO371/23018, C6914/54/18; Halifax to Henderson, 13 May, *DBFP*, V, no. 513; Henderson to Halifax, 16, 30 May, *ibid.*, nos. 525, 671.

25. Letter, Strang to Beaumont-Nesbitt, 18 May, FO371/23019, C7204/54/18.

26. *Cadogan Diaries, 1938–1945*, 170; Letter, Henderson to Cadogan, 10 May, FO800/294, C2/39/11; Letter, Henderson to Halifax, 17 May, *DBFP*, V, no. 542.

27. *Harvey Diaries, 1937–1940*, 286.

28. Letter, Henderson to Halifax, 4 May, *DBFP*, V, no. 364; Letter, Henderson to Wilson, 24 May, PREM1/331; Letter, Henderson to Sargent, 2 Aug., FO371/23024, C10934/54/18.

29. Minutes by Makins and Speaight, 23, 24 May, FO371/23019, C7317, 7324/54/18; Minutes by Vansittart, 20 May, FO371/23018, C7096/54/18; 21 May, FO371/23020, C8757/54/18.

30. Kennard to Halifax, 13 June, *DBFP*, VI, no. 44; Minutes by Makins, Sargent and Cadogan, 16, 17 June, FO371/23020, C8484/54/18.

31. Memorandum by Jebb, 9 June; Letter to Jebb, 15 June, *ibid.*, C8336/54/18. Cf. Entry of 21 June, Dalton Diaries.

32. Minutes by Sargent, Cadogan and Halifax, 23, 24 May, FO371/23019, C7326/54/18; Minute by Cadogan, 23 May, *ibid.*, C7557/54/18; Cadogan to Kennard, 23 May, *DBFP*, V, no. 596; *Cadogan Diaries, 1938–1945*, 182; Kennard to Halifax, 24 May, *DBFP*, V, no. 607.

33. Minutes, Cab30(39), 24 May, CAB23/99; Note of a meeting of Ministers, 25 May, FO371/23019, C7728/54/18.

34. Halifax to Kennard, 26 May, *DBFP*, V, no. 636; Kennard to Halifax, 31 May, *ibid.*, no. 675; Minute by Cadogan, 25 May, FO371/23019, C7517/54/18.

35. Minute to Cadogan, 2 June; Letter, Sargent to Ismay, 7 June, *ibid.*, C7887/54/18; Letter, Ismay to Sargent, 8 June, FO371/23020, C8238/54/18.

36. Minutes by Sargent and Cadogan, 5, 6 June, FO371/23019, C7589/54/18; Halifax to Kennard, 7 June, *DBFP*, V, no. 732; Minute by Strang, 9 June, *DBFP*, VI, no. 16; Minutes by Cadogan, Wilson and Chamberlain, 9, 16, 17, 18 June, FO371/23020, C8261/54/18.

37. Letter, Kennard to Sargent, 11 June, *DBFP*, VI, no. 27; Halifax to Kennard, 16 June, *ibid.*, no. 68.

38. Shepherd to Halifax, 24 June, *ibid.*, no. 141; Henderson to Halifax, 19 June, no. 261, FO371/23020, C8753/54/18; Shepherd to Halifax, 28 June, *DBFP*, VI, no. 155; Minute by Troutbeck, 30 June, FO371/23021, C9127/54/18; Halifax to Shepherd, 1 July, *DBFP*, VI, no. 201; Minute by Halifax, 13 July, FO371/23022, C9561/54/18; Minute by Makins, 26 July, FO371/23023, C10332/54/18.

39. Minutes by Roberts and Troutbeck, 30 June, FO371/23021, C9127/54/18; Aide-Mémoire by Roland de Margerie, 29 June, *ibid.*, C9138/54/18; Halifax to Kennard, 29 June, *DBFP*, VI, no. 170.

40. Letter, Holman to Kirkpatrick, 29 June, *ibid.*, no. 180; Henderson to Halifax, 30 June, 1 July, *ibid.*, nos. 183, 211.

41. Phipps to Halifax, 30 June, *ibid.*, no. 186.

42. Minute by Cadogan, 26 June, FO371/23021, C8981/54/18; Minute by Roberts, 3 July, *ibid.*, C9191/54/18; Phipps to Halifax, 1 July, *ibid.*, C9232/54/18. See also, Minute by Ashton-Gwatkin, 25 Aug., FO371/22981, C12787/15/18.

43. Norton to Halifax, 1 July, *DBFP*, VI, no. 209; Minutes, Cab35(39), 5 July, CAB23/100; Minute by Cadogan, 5 July, FO371/23022, C9838/54/18; Letter, Cadogan to Norton, 6 July, *DBFP*, VI, no. 257; Entry of 1 July, Dalton Diaries; Entry of 1 July, Dawson Diaries; Entry of 4 July, Kennedy Diaries.

44. Phipps to Halifax, 1 July, *DBFP*, VI, no. 212.

45. Minutes by Kennard and Sargent, 1, 3 July, FO371/23021, C9348/54/18; Minutes, *ibid.*, C9235/54/18.

46. Phipps to Halifax, 3 July, no. 417; Minutes by Troutbeck and John Balfour, 4 July, *ibid.*, C9280/54/18.
47. Minutes, FPC, 55th meeting, 4 July, CAB27/625.
48. Halifax to Loraine, 5 July, *DBFP*, VI, no. 234; Loraine to Halifax, 7 July, *ibid.*, no. 261; Minute by Sargent, 14 July, FO371/22974, C10037/15/18. See also, Letter, Wilson to Cadogan, 4 July, *ibid.*, C9471/15/18.
49. Minute by Vansittart, 17 July, FO371/23022, C9959/54/18. For the Foreign Office draft of the Prime Minister's speech on 10 July, see *ibid.* C9706/54/18.
50. Halifax to Kennard, 30 June, *DBFP*, VI, no. 184; Norton to Halifax, 1 July, *ibid.*, nos. 209, 264.
51. Minute by Sargent, 1 July, FO371/23021, C9348/54/18.
52. Colonel Roderick Macleod and Denis Kelly, eds., *The Ironside Diaries, 1937–1940* (1962), 76.
53. Minutes, Cab35(39), 5 July, CAB23/100; Minute by Sargent, 10 July, FO371/23022, C9748/54/18; *Ironside Diaries, 1937–1940*, 77–8, 80; Visit of Ironside to Warsaw, 12 July, FO371/23022, C9748/54/18. For details regarding Ironside's controversial instructions see *ibid.*, C9834, 9839/54/18; PREM1/331.
54. Norton to Halifax, 20, 25 July, *DBFP*, VI, nos. 361, 445; Letter, Norton to Oliphant, 21 July, *ibid.*, no. 397.
55. Ironside's Report on his Visit, 28 July, FO371/23024, C10949/54/18; Norton to Halifax, 20 July, *DBFP*, VI, no. 374; Minutes by Makins and Oliphant, 26, 29 July, FO371/23023, C10289/54/18; Minute by Sargent, 3 Aug., FO371/23024, C10977/54/18.
56. Minutes, Cab38(39), 19 July, CAB23/100; Henderson to Halifax, 5 July, no. 771, FO371/22974, C9524/15/18; Letter, Henderson to Sargent, 14 July, *ibid.*, C9996/15/18; Minutes by Vansittart, 18, 21 July, *ibid.*, C9524, 9996/15/18.
57. Minute by SIS, n.d. FO371/22981, C12878/15/18. In a minute on 3 Aug., Sargent referred to "Red Paper No. 350, which reports that Hitler shows signs of faltering as regards Danzig." FO371/23024, C10977/54/18. An SIS "Red Paper" contained a specific intelligence report.
58. Shepherd to Halifax, 19 July, *DBFP*, VI, no. 353; Minutes, Cab39(39), 26 July, CAB23/100; Lindsay to Halifax, 14 July, no. 4, FO371/23023, C10278/54/18; Minutes by Makins and Kirkpatrick, 21 July, *ibid.*, C10163/54/18.
59. Minutes by Oliphant and Sargent, 21 July, *ibid.*; Minute by Sargent, 18 July, FO371/23022, C10017/54/18.

Notes to Chapters

1. Minutes, Cab12(39), 18 Mar., CAB23/98.
2. *Ironside Diaries, 1937–1940*, 77.
3. Letter, Chamberlain to Lieutenant-Colonel Lord Francis Scott, 12 June, PREM1/304.
4. Letters, Chamberlain to Ida Chamberlain, 26 Mar., 23 July, Chamberlain Papers; David Dilks, "Appeasement Revisited", *University of Leeds Review*, XV, no. 1, May 1972, 47.
5. Letter, Lloyd George to Strabolgi, 15 May, Lloyd George Papers, G/19/4/2; Minute by Butler, 22 Mar., FO371/22966, C2533/15/18.
6. Minutes by Butler and Halifax, 19, 20 Apr., FO371/22970, C5864/15/18; Letter, Duke of Buccleuch to Wilson, 1 May; Minutes by Cadogan and Vansittart, 2, 5 May, FO371/23018, C6744/54/18.
7. Letter, Sir Francis Fremantle to Halifax, 2 May; Letter, Halifax to Fremantle, 8 May, FO371/22989, C6670/16/18.
8. Letter, Chamberlain to Scott, 12 June, PREM1/304.
9. Minutes by D. J. Scott, Sargent and Cadogan, 15 Apr., FO371/22969, C5523/15/18.
10. William L. Langer and S. Everett Gleason, *The Challenge to Isolation* (New York 1952), 104; Kennedy to Hull, 22 Mar., *FRUS, 1939*, I, 88.
11. Minute by Ingram, 15 Apr., FO371/23753, R3018/2613/67; Minute by Sargent, 15 Apr., FO371/22970, C5592/15/18; Press communiqué, *DBFP*, V, no. 188; Feiling, *Neville Chamberlain*, 325.
12. Circular by Ribbentrop, 17 Apr., *DGFP*, VI, no. 213; Memorandum by Weizsäcker, 17 Apr., *ibid.*, no. 216, *Ciano's Diary, 1939–1943*, 70; Perth to Halifax, 20 Apr., no. 376, FO371/22970, C5624/15/18.
13. Minutes by Roberts, in FO371/22971, C6063, 6231, 6345, 6396/15/18.
14. Minutes, Cab26(39), 3 May, CAB23/99.
15. Minutes, FPC, 51st meeting, 13 June, CAB27/625; Halifax to Henderson, 23 June, *DBFP*, VI, no. 136.
16. *Harvey Diaries, 1937–1940*, 286; *Cadogan Diaries, 1938–1945*, 178; Entry of 8 May, Nicolson Diaries.
17. Letter, Wilson to Henderson, 12 May, PREM1/331.
18. *H. C. Deb.*, 346, 26 Apr., col. 1111; *The Times*, 12 May.
19. Halifax to Henderson, 19 May, *DBFP*, V, no. 559; Minutes, Cab30(39), 24 May, CAB23/99.
20. Letter, Chamberlain to Scott, 12 June, PREM1/304.
21. Notes of meetings with Dominion High Commissioners, 30 Mar., FO371/22969, C5265/15/18; 23 May, FO371/23067, C7870/3356/18.

22. Minutes, Cab30(39), 24 May, CAB23/99; Letter, Cadogan to Chatfield, 9 June, FO371/22973, C8300/15/18.
23. Telegram to Dominion Prime Ministers, 25 May, copy in CAB21/551; Letter, Hankinson to Harvey, 31 May; Letter, Halifax to Inskip, 21 June, FO371/22973, C8410/15/18; Letter, Inskip to Halifax, 26 June, FO371/22974, C10031/15/18.
24. Minute by Roberts, 7 June, FO371/22973, C8004/15/18.
25. Memorandum recording a conversation with "X", 16 Mar., Young Papers.
26. Minute by Cadogan, 10 Dec. 1938, FO371/21659, C15084/42/18; Minute by Ashton-Gwatkin, 29 Aug., FO371/22981, C12878/15/18; Minute by Vansittart, 7 Dec. 1938, FO371/21659, C15084/42/18.
27. Memoranda by Ashton-Gwatkin on conversations with Goerdeler, 25, May, FO371/23008, C7729, 7769/53/18; 30 May, FO371/22973, C8004/15/18; "A Plan for Peace Partnership in Europe", Memorandum by Goerdeler, *ibid.*
28. Minutes by Roberts, Sargent and Cadogan, 7, 8, 9 June, FO371/22973, C8004/15/18; Minute by Cadogan, 3 May, FO371/23008, C6329/52/18.
29. Letter, C. E. Steel to Kirkpatrick, 31 May; Minute by Roberts, 8 June, FO371/22973, C7972/15/18.
30. Henderson to Halifax, 28 May, *DBFP*, V, no. 658; Letters, Henderson to Halifax, 28, 30 May, *ibid.*, nos. 659, 671; Minutes by Halifax, 2, 13 June, FO371/22989, C8046/16/18; *H. L. Deb.*, 113, 8 June, cols. 350–64; Letter, Butler to Halifax, 13 June, FO800/315, H/XV/177; Halifax to Henderson, 16 June, *DBFP*, VI, no. 72. See also, Letter, Lord Lothian to Halifax, 5 June, Lord Lothian Papers.
31. H. H. E. Craster, ed., *Viscount Halifax, Speeches on Foreign Policy* (1940), 287–97.
32. Memorandum by Makins, 12 June, *DBFP*, VI, no. 36.
33. Letter, Holman to Kirkpatrick, 3 June; Minutes by Kirkpatrick, Sargent and Jebb, 8, 12 June, FO371/23020, C8062/54/18; Minute by Kirkpatrick, 8 June, *DBFP*, VI, no. 4. See also Letter, Sir Horace Rumbold to Halifax, 9 June, FO800/315, H/XV/174.
34. Fabian von Schlabrendorff, *The Secret War Against Hitler* (1966), 95–8.
35. Author's interview with the Hon. David Astor, 19 Sept. 1972; Minute by R. H. Hadow, 1 Mar., FO371/22966, C2639/15/18; Letter, Beaumont-Nesbitt to Strang, 3 Apr., FO371/22968, C4819/15/18; Minutes of a conference, 23 May, *DGFP*, VI, no. 433.
36. Godfrey, *Naval Memoirs*, V, part 1, 17–18, Godfrey Papers, GDFY1/6; Minute by Kirkpatrick, 26 June, FO371/23022, C9576/54/18; Report by Lieutenant-General Marshall-Cornwall, 7 July, *DBFP*, VI, no. 269.

Further details in FO371/22974, C9758, 9818–9/15/18; FO371/22990–1, C9275, 9287, 11448/16/18; David Astor, "Why the Revolt Against Hitler was Ignored", *Encounter*, June 1969.

37. Minute by Cadogan, 29 June, FO371/22990, C9275/16/18; Minute by Vansittart, 10 July, FO371/22974, C9819/15/18.

38. Letter, Chamberlain to Hilda Chamberlain, 9 Apr., Chamberlain Papers; Entry of 6 July, Dawson Diaries; Minute by Cadogan, 21 June, FO371/22974, C9818/15/18.

39. Entries of 29, 30 June, 3–5 July, Nicolson Diaries, Letter; Chamberlain to Ida Chamberlain, 8 July, Chamberlain Papers; Letter, Kennedy to Roosevelt, 20 July, Roosevelt Papers, PSF, Great Britain, Kennedy.

40. Godfrey, *Naval Memoirs*, V, part 1, 18, Godfrey Papers, GDFY1/6; Letter, Godfrey to Jebb, 28 June, FO371/22990, C9275/16/18.

41. Memorandum by Trott, 1–8 June, *DGFP*, VI, no. 497; Entries of 4–6 June, Dawson Diaries; Dirksen to Ribbentrop, 24 June, *DGFP*, VI, no. 564; Weizsäcker to Dirksen, 28 June, *ibid.*, no. 577.

42. Letter, Crown Prince of Sweden to Chamberlain, 31 May; Minute by Syers, 1 June, PREM1/328; Record of conversation, 6 June, *DBFP*, VI, appendix 3, 736–8. See also FO371/23020, C8497/54/18.

43. Minute by Roberts, 30 June, *DBFP*, VI, no. 192; Notes of interview, 6 July, *ibid.*, appendix 4, 744–5; Minute by Kirkpatrick, 13 July, FO371/22975, C10165/15/18; Author's interview with Major-General Sir Harold Wernher, 31 May 1972.

44. Letter, Henderson to Cadogan, 29 June, *DBFP*, VI, no. 177; Minutes by Cadogan, Halifax and Sargent, 2, 3, 4 July, FO371/22974, C9475/15/18.

45. *Harvey Diaries, 1937–1940*, 302; Letter, Henderson to Halifax, 9 July, *DBFP*, VI, appendix 1, 711–13; Note of discussion with Dominion High Commissioners, 11 July, FO371/22975, C10103/15/18.

pp. 243–259   CHAPTER NINE

1. See FO371/23661, N2889/337/63.

2. Minute by Chamberlain, 9 Dec. 1938, PREM1/344. For Hudson's plans and views on economic appeasement, see T160/866/F.15447/021/1–2; BT11/1050.

3. *Cadogan Diaries, 1938–1945*, 150, 156–7, 174; Seeds to Halifax, 28 Feb., no. 29, FO371/23653, N1087/64/63.

4. Minutes by H. H. Hankey and Kirkpatrick, 12, 13 July, FO371/23661, N3395/337/63.

5. Minute by Ashton-Gwatkin, 7 June, *DBFP*, V, no. 741; Minute by Ashton-Gwatkin, 7 June, FO800/315, H/XV/170.
6. Record of conversation, 19 July, *DBFP*, VI, no. 354.
7. Record of conversation, 20 July, *ibid.*, no. 370.
8. Memorandum by Wohlthat, 24 July, *DGFP*, VI, no. 716.
9. Letter, Wilson to Anthony Bevir, 1 Oct. 1950, FO371/22990, C10521/16/18.
10. Letter, Chamberlain to Ida Chamberlain, 23 July, Chamberlain Papers; Letter, Beaverbrook to Lord Rothermere, 24 July, Beaverbrook Papers.
11. Entry of 21 July, Dalton Diaries; *The Week*, no. 325, 26 July; Memorandum by Hesse, 24 July, Ministry of Foreign Affairs, *Documents and Materials Relating to the Eve of the Second World War*, II (Moscow 1948), no. 16.
12. Letter, R. Reid Adam to A. N. Rucker, 24 July, PREM1/330.
13. Memorandum by Dirksen, 24 July, *Documents and Materials*, II, no. 15; Minute by Sargent, 24 July, *DBFP*, VI, no. 426; *Harvey Diaries, 1937–1940*, 303; Minute by Wilson, n.d., PREM1/330; Minute by Vansittart, 26 July, FO371/22990, C10521/16/18.
14. Letters, Chamberlain to Ida and Hilda Chamberlain, 23, 30 July, Chamberlain Papers; Feiling, *Neville Chamberlain*, 409; *H. C. Deb.*, 350, 24 July, col. 1027. Cf. letters and minutes in FO371/22990, C10698/16/18.
15. Ribbentrop to Dirksen, 31 July, *DGFP*, VI, no. 743; Dirksen to Foreign Ministry, 31 July, 11 Aug., *ibid.*, nos. 746, 752.
16. See Minutes of the ACIQ for 1938–9 and its memoranda nos. 484A, 489, Labour Party Papers.
17. Minutes, ACIQ, 19 July; and memoranda nos. 493A, 489A.
18. Dirksen to Weizsäcker, 1 Aug., *Documents and Materials*, II, no. 22.
19. Letter, Mackenzie King to Chamberlain, 24 July; Chamberlain to Mackenzie King, 7 Aug., William Lyon Mackenzie King Papers, 264, 224772–9, 224782.
20. Ernest W. D. Tennant, *Account Settled* (1957), 215–26; Letter, Tennant to Chamberlain, 4 July; Record of conversation by Wilson, 10 July; Minute by Wilson, 24 July; Report by Tennant, 31 July, PREM1/335.
21. Note of conversation between Kemsley and Hitler, 27 July; Minute by Wilson, 1 Aug., PREM1/332; *Cadogan Diaries, 1938–1945*, 193.
22. Minute by Wilson, 1 Aug.; Letter, Kemsley to Otto Dietrich, 1 Aug.; Note of conversation with Dietrich, 3 Aug.; Letter, Dietrich to Kemsley, 17 Aug., PREM1/332.
23. Letter, Butler to Wilson, 2 Aug., PREM1/330; Record of conversation, 3 Aug., *DBFP*, VI, no. 533.

Notes to Chapters

24. Dirksen to Ribbentrop, 3 Aug., *Documents and Materials*, II, no. 24; Minutes by Wilson, 3, 4 Aug., PREM1/330.

25. Minute by Dirksen, 9 Aug., *Documents and Materials*, II, no. 25; Memorandum by Dirksen, Sept., *ibid.*, no. 29; Minute by Wilson, 20 Aug., PREM1/331.

pp. 260–280   CHAPTER TEN

1. *H. C. Deb.*, 347, 24 May, col. 2267.
2. Halifax to Seeds, 24 May, *DBFP*, V, no. 609; Seeds to Halifax, 25 May, *ibid.*, no. 623; *SSSR v Borbe za Mir*, no. 309.
3. Seeds to Halifax, 27, 28, 30 May, *DBFP*, V, nos. 648, 657, 665, 670.
4. Seeds to Halifax, 1, 2 June, *ibid.*, nos. 681, 697; Minute by Makins, 2 June, FO371/23067, C7895/3356/18.
5. *Cadogan Diaries, 1938–1945*, 184; Minutes by Cadogan, 10 June, FO371/23067, C7936–7/3356/18; Kennedy to Hull, 9 June, *FRUS, 1939*, I, 272.
6. Minute by Chamberlain, n.d.; see note by E. L. Woodward, 14 Mar. 1944, FO371/23069, C9295/3356/18.
7. Minutes, FPC, 49th meeting, 5 June, CAB27/625; *Cadogan Diaries, 1938–1945*, 185; Halifax to Seeds, 6, 7 June, *DBFP*, V, nos. 720, 734; Seeds to Halifax, 7 June, *ibid.*, no. 729.
8. Davies to Hull, 18 Apr., *FRUS, Soviet Union*, 756–7; Langer and Gleason, *Challenge to Isolation*, 128; The Earl of Avon, *The Eden Memoirs, The Reckoning* (1965), 55. Cf. Minute by Cadogan, 12 June, FO371/23069, C8861/3356/18.
9. Halifax to Seeds, 8, 12 June, *DBFP*, VI, nos. 5, 38; *SSSR v Borbe za Mir*, nos. 322–3; Memorandum by Ewer, 9 June, FO371/23068, C8701/3356/18.
10. Lord Strang, *Home and Abroad* (1956), 158; Maisky, *Who Helped Hitler?* 141.
11. Minutes, FPC, 50th meeting, 9 June, CAB27/625.
12. Phipps to Halifax, 6 June, *DBFP*, V, no. 719; Minutes, Cab31(39), 7 June, CAB23/99.
13. Foreign Office memoranda, 12 June, *DBFP*, VI, no. 35; Seeds to Halifax, 15, 16, 20 June, *ibid.*, nos. 60, 69, 73, 103; *SSSR v Borbe za Mir*, no. 331; Letter, Sir William Seeds to the author, 17 Sept. 1972.
14. Minutes, Cab33(39), 21 June, CAB23/100; Entry of 12 July, Dalton Diaries; Halifax to Seeds, 19 June, *DBFP*, VI, no. 89; Minute by H. W. Malkin, 15 June, FO371/23068, C8618/3356/18.

15. Minutes, FPC, 53rd meeting, 20 June, CAB27/625; Seeds to Halifax, 21, 22, 24 June, *DBFP*, VI, nos. 119, 123, 126, 139.

16. Minutes, FPC, 54th meeting, 26 June, CAB27/625; Halifax to Seeds, 27, 29, 30 June, 1 July, *DBFP*, VI, nos. 151, 171, 185, 199; Seeds to Halifax, 28, 30 June, *ibid.*, nos. 156, 181; Minute by Cadogan, 30 June, FO371/23069, C9154/3356/18.

17. Entry of 28 June, Dalton Diaries. Cf. Record of conversation, 28 June, PREM1/325.

18. Seeds to Halifax, 1, 4 July, *ibid.*, nos. 221, 225, 226–7; *SSSR v Borbe za Mir*, no. 361; Minutes, FPC, 56th meeting, 4 July, CAB27/625.

19. Letters, Halifax to Henderson, 14, 30 June, *DBFP*, VI, nos. 55, 194; Sir Nevile Henderson, *Failure of a Mission, Berlin 1937–1939* (1940), 236.

20. Letter, Chamberlain to Hilda Chamberlain, 2 July, Chamberlain Papers; Aster, "Ivan Maisky", 352.

21. *Livre Jaune Français*, no. 182; Phipps to Halifax, 8 June, *DBFP*, VI, no. 2; Minute by Roberts, 10 June, FO371/23067, C8212/3356/18. Cf. Letter, Henderson to Kirkpatrick, 22 June, FO371/23069, C8915/3356/18; Letter, Sargent to Henderson, 23 June, *DBFP*, VI, appendix 1, 708; Minute by Peake, 9 June, FO371/23068, C8641/3356/18.

22. Letter, Godfrey to Jebb, 2 June, FO371/23008, C8006/53/18; Memorandum by Stafford Cripps, 9 June, FO371/22973, C8347/15/18; Letter, Henderson to Cadogan, 13 June, *DBFP*, VI, appendix 1, 702.

23. Letter, Berlin Chancery to Central Department, 23 June, FO371/23687, N3099/411/38; Seeds to Halifax, 10, 15 June, *DBFP*, VI, nos. 19, 57.

24. Minute by Vansittart, 16 June, FO371/23009, C8923/53/18; Memorandum by Ridsdale, 16 June, *DBFP*, VI, appendix 1, 705–6; Minute by Cadogan, 7 Apr., FO371/22969, C5062/15/18. Cf. Erich Kordt, *Nicht aus den Akten* (Stuttgart 1950), 313–19.

25. See e.g., Snow to Halifax, 21 June, no. 136, FO371/22973, C9101/15/18; Minute by Lascelles, 26 June, FO371/23686, N3110/243/38; Letter, Holman to Halifax, 30 June, FO371/23069, C9365/3356/18; Campbell to Halifax, 27 June, no. 133, *ibid.*, C9075/3356/18; Minute by Halifax, 29 June, FO371/23021, C9205/54/18.

26. War Office memorandum, 4 July, FO371/23686, N3335/243/38.

27. Weizsäcker to Schulenburg, 30 May, 12 June, *DGFP*, VI, nos. 453, 514; Schulenburg to Foreign Ministry, 2 June, *ibid.*, nos. 465, 499; Tippelskirch to Foreign Ministry, 18, 25 June, *ibid.*, nos. 543, 568.

28. Schulenburg to Foreign Ministry, 29 June, *ibid.*, no. 579; Memorandum by Hewel, 29 June, *ibid.*, no. 583; Weizsäcker to Schulenburg, 30 June, *ibid.*, no. 588.

29. Minutes, FPC, 56th meeting, 4 July, CAB27/625; Minutes, Cab35(39), 5 July, CAB23/100.
30. Halifax to Seeds, 6 July, *DBFP*, VI, nos. 251–3; Seeds to Halifax, 9, 10 July, *ibid.*, nos. 279, 281–2.

pp. 281–319 CHAPTER ELEVEN

1. Minutes, Cab38(39), 19 July, CAB23/100; Kennedy to Hull, 17 Feb., *FRUS, 1939*, I, 17; Minutes, CID, 348th meeting, 24 Feb., CAB2/8.
2. Minutes, FPC, 57th meeting, 10 July, CAB27/625.
3. Letter, Chamberlain to Hilda Chamberlain, 15 July, Chamberlain Papers; Feiling, *Neville Chamberlain*, 412.
4. Halifax to Seeds, 12 July, *DBFP*, VI, no. 298; Seeds to Halifax, 18 July, *ibid.*, no. 338; Minutes in FO371/23070, C9709, 9889/3356/18; *SSSR v Borbe za Mir*, no. 376.
5. Weizsäcker to Schulenburg, 7 July, *DGFP*, VI, no. 628; Schulenburg to Foreign Ministry, 10, 16 July, *ibid.*, nos. 642, 677; Memorandum by Schnurre, 18 July, *ibid.*, no. 685.
6. Minutes, Cab38(39), 19 July, CAB23/100; Kennedy to Hull, 20 July, *FRUS, 1939*, I, 288.
7. Minutes, FPC, 58th meeting, 19 July, CAB27/625.
8. Notes from French Embassy, 18, 19 July, *DBFP*, VI, nos. 346, 357; Letter, Campbell to Halifax, 19 July, *ibid.*, no. 358; Bonnett, *Fin d'une Europe*, 198–201.
9. Halifax to Seeds, 22 July, *DBFP*, VI, no. 378.
10. *SSSR v Borbe za Mir*, nos. 372, 377, 381.
11. Seeds to Halifax, 24, 28 July, *DBFP*, VI, nos. 414–15, 473; Halifax to Seeds, 25 July, *ibid.*, no. 435.
12. Dirksen to Foreign Ministry, 21 July, *DGFP*, VI, no. 695; Weizsäcker to Schulenburg, 22 July, *ibid.*, no. 700.
13. Minutes, Cab39(39), 26 July, CAB23/100.
14. Hugh Dalton, *Hitler's War, Before and After* (1939), 119. Cf. Letter, Ismay to Churchill, 30 Sept., 1947, Ismay Papers, Ismay II/3/35/1; General Lord Ismay, *Memoirs* (1960), 97.
15. Letter, Strang to Sargent, 20 July, *DBFP*, VI, no. 376; Maisky, *Who Helped Hitler?* 164–5; Entry of 2 Aug., Pownall Diaries; Memorandum by Boothby, 17 Sept., Dalton Papers.
16. Minutes by Kirkpatrick and Oliphant, 25 July, FO371/23071, C10525/3356/18. See also, Minutes, DCOS, 43rd meeting, 27 July, CAB54/2; JPC Paper 483, 26 July, CAB55/18.
17. "A Fragment of Autobiography", Drax Papers, DRAX6/7; further

details, *ibid.*, DRAX2/9–13, 19; information from the Major-General Thomas G. G. Heywood Papers.

18. *SSSR v Borbe za Mir*, no. 411, fn. 142.

19. JPC Paper 483, 26 July, CAB55/18; DCOS Paper 144(JP), 27 July, CAB54/10.

20. Minutes, JPC, 266th meeting, 29 July, CAB55/3; Minutes, DCOS, 45th, 46th meetings, 31 July, CAB 54/2.

21. The final version of the instructions, CID Paper DP(P)71, CAB16/183B, is in *DBFP*, VI, appendix 5, 762–89. For earlier drafts see JPC Paper 488, 28 July, CAB55/18; DCOS Paper, 154 (revise), 31 July, CAB54/10.

22. Entry of 14 June, Dalton Diaries.

23. Draft, "Mission to Moscow, August 1939", 4–7, Drax Papers, DRAX 6/5; Minutes, CID, 372nd meeting, 2 Aug., CAB2/9.

24. Minute by Stevenson, 25 July, FO371/23071, C10634/3356/18; Minutes, DCOS, 45th meeting, 31 July, CAB54/2; Minutes, FPC, 60th meeting, 1 Aug., CAB27/625.

25. Campbell to Halifax, 29 July, *DBFP*, VI, nos. 489–90; Minute by Ismay, 29 July, FO371/23072, C10811/3356/18; Minute by Roberts, 2 Aug., *DBFP*, VI, no. 520; Henderson to Halifax, 31 July, *ibid.*, no. 495.

26. Draft, "Mission to Moscow, August 1939", 4, Drax Papers, DRAX 6/5; Minutes, FPC, 60th meeting, 1 Aug., CAB27/625; "Diary of the Military Mission to Moscow", Major-General Francis Davidson Papers.

27. General André Beaufre, *1940, The Fall of France* (1967), 96. The instructions to the French delegation are *ibid.*, 92–5.

28. Memorandum by Schnurre, 27 July, *DGFP*, VI, no. 729; Welczeck to Foreign Ministry, 28, 30 July, *ibid.*, nos. 731, 741.

29. Weizsäcker to Schulenburg, 29 July, *ibid.*, no. 736.

30. Schnurre to Schulenburg, 2 Aug., *ibid.*, no. 757; Memorandum by Otto von Erdmannsdorff, 8 Aug., *ibid.*, no. 784; Ribbentrop to Schulenburg, 3 Aug., *ibid.*, nos. 758, 760.

31. Ministry of Defence and Foreign Policy archives of the USSR, quoted in *Istoriya Velikoi Otechestevennoi Voiny*, I, 174–5.

32. Memorandum by Schnurre, 3 Aug., *DGFP*, VI, no. 761; Schulenburg to Foreign Ministry, 4 Aug., *ibid.*, no. 766.

33. *SSSR v Borbe za Mir*, nos. 395, 397–8; Seeds to Halifax, 3 Aug., *DBFP*, VI, nos. 525, 527; Halifax to Seeds, 4 Aug., *ibid.*, no. 540; Minutes by Roberts, 4 Aug., FO371/23072, C10815, 10821/3356/18; Minutes by Strang and Cadogan, 10, 11 Aug., *ibid.*, C11524/3356/18.

34. Memorandum by Schnurre, 5 Aug., *DGFP*, VI, no. 772; Memorandum by Schnurre, 10 Aug., *DGFP*, VII, no. 18.

35. Schnurre to Schulenburg, 14 Aug., *ibid.*, no. 50; Record of conversation between Hitler and Ciano, 12 Aug., *ibid.*, no. 43; Halder Diary, *ibid.*, appendix 1, 552–6.

36. Draft, "Mission to Moscow, August 1939", 11, Drax Papers, DRAX 6/5; Seeds to Halifax, 13 Aug., *DBFP*, VI, no. 647; Author's interview with Brigadier R. C. Firebrace, 6 Aug. 1968.

37. All references to the military talks are taken from both the British and Soviet published records: *DBFP*, VII, appendix 2, 561–614; "Negotiations between the Military Missions of the U.S.S.R., Britain and France in August 1939", *International Affairs* (Moscow), nos. 2–3, Feb., Mar. 1959, 110–23, 106–22; and from French documents, captured by the Germans in 1940 and then by the Russians in 1945, in *SSSR v Borbe za Mir*, nos. 416, 418–19, 424, 430–1, 433–5, 440.

38. Seeds to Halifax, 3, 12 Aug., *DBFP*, VI, nos. 525, 638; Minutes by Roberts and Sargent, 4 Aug., FO371/23072, C10821/3356/18; Minute by Roberts, 14 Aug., *ibid.*, C11276/3356/18.

39. Beaufre, *1940*, 110.

40. Seeds to Halifax, 13 Aug., *DBFP*, VI, no. 647.

41. Minutes by Strang, 14, 15 Aug., FO371/23072, C11275/3356/18; DCOS Paper 167, 14 Aug., CAB54/11; Minutes, DCOS, 49th, 50th meetings, 14, 15 Aug., CAB54/2; Halifax to Seeds, 15 Aug., DBFP, VII, nos. 6, 8.

42. Seeds to Halifax, 15 Aug., *ibid.*, nos. 1–2.

43. Halifax to Seeds, 25 July, 1 Aug., *DBFP*, VI, nos. 432, 504; Seeds to Halifax, 26 July, *ibid.*, no. 456; Instructions to the British Military Mission, *ibid.*, appendix 5, 764, 772, 783.

44. Léon Noël, *L'Agression Allemande Contre la Pologne* (Paris 1946), 422–3; Paul Reynaud, *In the Thick of the Fight* (1955), 212.

45. Minute by Strang, 16 Aug., FO371/23072, C11323/3356/18; Waclaw Jedrzejewicz, ed., *Diplomat in Paris 1936–1939, Memoirs of Juliusz Lukasiewicz* (1970), 249–50; *SSSR v Borbe za Mir*, no. 416.

46. Minutes, DCOS, 51st meeting, 16 Aug., CAB54/2; DCOS Paper 179, 16 Aug., CAB54/11; Halifax to Kennard, 17 Aug., *DBFP*, VII, nos. 38–9; Kennard to Halifax, 18 Aug., *ibid.*, no. 52.

47. Ribbentrop to Schulenburg, 14 Aug., *DGFP*, VII, no. 56; Schulenburg to Foreign Ministry, 16 Aug., *ibid.*, nos. 70, 79; Schulenburg to Weizsäcker, 16 Aug., *ibid.*, no. 88; Foreign Policy archives of the USSR, quoted in *Istoriya Velikoi Otechestvennoi Voiny*, I, 175.

48. Ribbentrop to Schulenburg, 16 Aug., *DGFP*, VII, no. 75; Schulenburg to Foreign Ministry, 18 Aug., *ibid.*, no. 105.

49. Letter, Burnett to Newall, 16 Aug., *DBFP*, VII, appendix 2, 597; Draft, "Mission to Moscow, August 1939", 38–9, Drax Papers, DRAX6/5.

50. Ribbentrop to Schulenburg, 18, 20 Aug., *DGFP*, VII, nos. 113, 142; Schulenburg to Foreign Ministry, 19, 20, 21 Aug., *ibid.*, nos. 125, 132–3, 158–9.

51. Halifax to Kennard, 20 Aug., *DBFP*, VII, no. 91; Kennard to Halifax, 19, 20, 21 Aug., *ibid.*, nos. 70, 87–8, 90, 94, 108; Letter, Kennard to Cadogan, 21 Aug., *ibid.*, no. 119; Bonnet, *Fin d'une Europe*, 282.

52. Record of conversation, 22 Aug., *DBFP*, VII, appendix 2, 609–13; General Doumenc, "The Inside Story of the Moscow Talks, 1939", *Tribune*, 11 July 1947.

53. Minutes by Ridsdale, 22, 23 Aug., FO371/22976–7, C11744,11898/ 15/18; Minute by Vansittart, 23 Aug., *ibid.*, C12027/15/18; Steinhardt to Hull, 23 Aug., *FRUS*, *1939*, I, 343; Seeds to Halifax, 22 Aug., *DBFP*, VII, nos. 128, 164, 187.

54. Halifax to Kennard, 22 Aug., *ibid.*, no. 150; Kennard to Halifax, 23 Aug., *ibid.*, no. 176; Halifax to Seeds, 23 Aug., *ibid.*, no. 198; Bonnet, *Fin d'une Europe*, 289–90.

55. Memorandum by Hencke, 24 Aug., *DGFP*, VII, no. 213; Treaty of non-aggression and secret additional protocol, *ibid.*, nos. 228–9; Seeds to Halifax, 11 Sept., no. 258, FO371/22983, C13871/15/18.

56. Record of conversation, 25 Aug., *DBFP*, VII, appendix 2, 613–14; Ministry of Defence archives of the USSR, quoted in *Istoriya Velikoi Otechestvennoi Voiny*, I, 172; Halifax to Seeds, 22 Aug., *DBFP*, VII, no. 136; Seeds to Halifax, 23, 25, 29 Aug., *ibid.*, nos. 165, 291, 499.

57. Langer and Gleason, *Challenge to Isolation*, 124–5; Cordell Hull, *Memoirs*, I (1948), 656–7.

58. Lindsay to Halifax, 29 Apr., no. 197, FO371/22971, C6217/15/18; W. G. Krivitsky, *I was Stalin's Agent* (1940), 17–42; Whittaker Chambers, *Witness* (1953), 321–7.

59. Minutes by Lascelles, 24, 25 May; Letter, Collier to Jebb, 24 May, FO371/23697, N2594/1459/38; Letters, Moscow Chancery to Northern Department, 21 June; Collier to Moscow Chancery, 27 June, *ibid.*, N3082/1459/38; Letter, Washington Embassy to Northern Department, 14 July; Minute by Collier, 3 Aug., *ibid.*, N3496/1459/ 38.

60. Davies, *Mission to Moscow*, 287; Letter, Welles to Steinhardt, 4 Aug., *FRUS*, *1939*, I, 293–4; Steinhardt to Welles, 16 Aug., *ibid.*, 296–9; *SSSR v Borbe za Mir*, nos. 359, 427.

61. Lindsay to Halifax, 17 Aug., *DBFP*, VII, no. 41; Lindsay to Halifax, 17 Aug., no. 6, FO371/22976, C11733/15/18; Letter, Seeds to Sargent, 5 Oct., FO371/23074, C16704/3356/18.

62. Minute by Roberts, 22 Aug., FO371/22976, C11723/15/18; Letter, Seeds to Sargent, 5 Oct., FO371/23074, C16704/3356/18; Letter,

Sargent to Seeds, 19 Sept., *ibid.*, C13842/3356/18; Entry of 23 Aug., Pownall Diaries.

63. Minute by Butler, 25 Aug.; Memorandum by Collier, 25 Aug.; Minute by Sargent, 3 Sept., FO371/23686, N4146/243/38. See also, Minutes by Lascelles and Sargeant, 22, 24 Aug., FO371/22980, C12741/15/18.

64. Letter, Sir William Seeds to the author, 23 Mar. 1970.

pp. 320–338   CHAPTER TWELVE

1. Shepherd to Halifax, 4 Aug., *DBFP*, VI, nos. 542–3; *Polish White Book*, no. 82; *Livre Jaune Français*, no. 178.

2. Halifax to Norton, 4 Aug., *DBFP*, VI, no. 549; Kennard to Halifax, 5 Aug., *ibid.*, no. 565; *Polish White Book*, nos. 83–4; Kennard to Halifax, 6 Aug., *DBFP*, VI, no. 576; Minute by Makins, 9 Aug., FO371/23024, C11062/54/18.

3. Memorandum by Erdmannsdorff, 8 Aug., *DGFP*, VI, no. 784; Memorandum by Weizsäcker, 9 Aug., *DGFP*, VII, no. 5; *Lipski Papers and Memoirs*, 554; *Polish White Book*, no. 86.

4. Kennard to Halifax, 10 Aug., *DBFP*, VI, no. 606; Halifax to Kennard, 10, 12 Aug., *ibid.*, nos. 610, 645; Minutes by Makins, 7 Aug., FO371/23024, C10979/54/18; 17 Aug., FO371/22976, C11491/15/18; 21 Aug., FO371/22977, C11901/15/18.

5. Minute by Halifax, 10 Aug., FO371/23025, C11185/54/18; Minute by Syers, 11 Aug., PREM1/331.

6. Feiling, *Neville Chamberlain*, 410; Letter, Chamberlain to Syers, 13 Aug., PREM1/331.

7. Minute by Makins, 14 Aug., *DBFP*, VI, no. 659; Letters, Makins to Frank Walters, 14 Aug.; Strang to Beaumont-Nesbitt, 17 Aug., FO371/23025, C11266/54/18; Shepherd to Halifax, 14, 17 Aug., nos. 129, 204, FO371/23025–6, C11325, 11761/54/18.

8. Letter, Strang to Kennard, 16 Aug., FO371/23025, C11338/54/18; Halifax to Kennard, 15 Aug., *DBFP*, VII, no. 4.

9. *Ciano's Diplomatic Papers*, 297–304; *Ciano's Diary, 1939–1943*, 123–5; Memoranda by Schmidt, 12, 13 Aug., *DGFP*, VII, nos. 43, 47.

10. Letter, Syers to Chamberlain, 12 Aug.; Letter, Halifax to Chamberlain, 14 Aug., PREM1/331; Minute by Strang, 17 Aug., FO371/22976, C11375/15/18.

11. Minutes by Syers, 11, 12, 15 Aug.; Letter, Halifax to Chamberlain, 14 Aug., PREM1/331; Entry of 7 Aug., Pownall Diaries.

Notes to Chapters

12. War Office memoranda, 4 Aug., FO371/22960, C11122/13/18; 8 Aug., FO371/23025, C11330/54/18.

13. Henderson to Halifax, 16 Aug., *DBFP*, VII, no. 32; *Cadogan Diaries, 1938–1945*, 196; Halifax, "A Record of Events before the War, 1939", FO800/317, H/XV/312. This was based on extracts from Cadogan's diaries in FO371/22978, C12122/15/18.

14. Henderson to Halifax, 18 Aug., *DBFP*, VII, no. 56; Shepherd to Halifax, 15 Aug., *ibid.*, no. 10; Minute by Cadogan, 16 Aug., FO371/22976, C11573/15/18; Letter, Halifax to Chamberlain, 14 Aug., PREM1/331.

15. Minute by Halifax, 17 Aug., FO371/23025, C11382/54/18; Minutes by Cadogan and Chamberlain, 17, 18 Aug., FO371/22976, C11573/15/18.

16. Letter, Halifax to Chamberlain, 19 Aug., *DBFP*, VII, no. 83; Halifax to Loraine, 19 Aug., *ibid.*, no. 79. Cf. Minute by Halifax, 18 Aug., FO371/22976, C11452/15/18.

17. Minutes, DCOS, 52nd meeting, 18 Aug., CAB54/2.

18. Minutes of meeting at Air Ministry, 20 Aug., COS Paper 960, CAB53/53.

19. Minutes, Cab41(39), 22 Aug., CAB23/100; Halifax to Henderson, 22 Aug., *DBFP*, VII, nos. 142, 145.

20. Record of Interview, 23 Aug., *DGFP*, VII, no. 200; Henderson to Halifax, 23, 24 Aug., *DBFP*, VII, nos. 178, 200, 248; Hitler to Chamberlain, 23 Aug., *DGFP*, VII, no. 201; Weizsäcker, *Memoirs*, 203.

21. Memorandum of Speech by Hitler, 22 Aug., *DGFP*, VII, nos. 192–3; Halder Diaries, *ibid.*, appendix 1, 557–60.

22. Kennedy to Hull, 23 Aug., *FRUS, 1939*, I, 355; Halifax to Lindsay, 23 Aug., no. 948; Minutes by John Balfour and Roberts, 30, 31 Aug., FO371/22977, C11836/15/18. Cf. Kennedy to Hull, 23 Aug., *FRUS, 1939*, I, 339–42; Minutes in FO371/22827, A6561/1090/45.

23. Minutes, Cab42(39), 24 Aug., CAB23/100; Entry of 24 Aug., Captain Euan Wallace Diaries.

24. *H. C. Deb.*, 351, 24 Aug., cols. 3–10; Entry of 24 Aug., Nicolson Diaries.

25. Weizsäcker, *Memoirs*, 204–5.

26. Statement by Hitler to Henderson, 25 Aug., *DGFP*, VII, no. 265; Henderson to Halifax, 25 Aug., *DBFP*, VII, nos. 283–4, 288.

27. Halder Diaries, *DGFP*, VII, appendix 1, 560–1.

28. Hitler to Mussolini, 25 Aug., *ibid.*, no. 266; Mussolini to Hitler, 25 Aug., *ibid.*, no. 271; Halder Diaries, *ibid.*, appendix 1, 561.

29. Paul Schmidt, *Hitler's Interpreter* (1951), 146; Field-Marshal Wilhelm Keitel, *Memoirs* (1965), 89–90; Weizsäcker, *Memoirs*, 207.

Notes to Chapters

1. Birger, Dahlerus, *The Last Attempt* (1948), 49–55; Minute by Roberts, 24 Aug., *DBFP*, VII, no. 237; Memoranda by Dahlerus, 24, 25 Aug., *ibid.*, no. 285; Reply by Halifax, 26 Aug., *ibid.*, no. 349; Entry of 26 Aug., Pownall Diaries.

2. *Cadogan Diaries, 1938–1945*, 201–2; *Harvey Diaries, 1937–1940*, 305–6; "Record of Events before the War, 1939", FO800/317, H/XV/312.

3. Minutes, Cab43(39), 26 Aug., CAB23/100; Minutes and notes in PREM1/330. See COS Minutes, 313th meeting, 25 Aug., CAB53/11; and COS Paper 966, 25 Aug., CAB53/54.

4. Dahlerus, *The Last Attempt*, 55–74; Memorandum by Dahlerus, 27 Aug., *DBFP*, VII, no. 349.

5. Minutes, Cab44(39), 27 Aug., CAB23/100; Phipps to Halifax, 27 Aug., *DBFP*, VII, no. 359; *Livre Jaune Français*, nos. 253, 261.

6. Minute by Kirkpatrick, 27 Aug., *DBFP*, VII, no. 397; *Harvey Diaries, 1937–1940*, 307; *Cadogan Diaries, 1938–1945*, 203; Minute by Kirkpatrick, 29 Aug., FO371/22978, C12825/15/18.

7. Minutes by Jebb and SIS, 27 Aug., *ibid.*, C12211/15/18; Minute by SIS, n.d., FO371/22981, C12875/15/18.

8. Minute by Strang, 26 Aug., PREM1/331.

9. *Harvey Diaries, 1937–1940*, 307–8.

10. Letter, Henderson to Halifax, 22 Aug., *DBFP*, VII, no. 158; Loraine to Halifax, 23 Aug., *ibid.*, no. 166.

11. Minute, unsigned, 18 Aug., FO371/23026, C11576/54/18; Halifax to Kennard, 18, 22, 23 Aug., *DBFP*, VII, nos. 58, 140, 170; Kennard to Halifax, 19 Aug., *ibid.*, no. 89.

12. Jean Szembek, *Journal, 1933–1939* (Paris 1952), 491; *Lipski Papers and Memoirs*, 556, 563–4, 587, 590–2; Kennard to Halifax, 23, 24, 25 Aug., *DBFP*, VII, nos. 180, 196, 228, 263; Minute by Makins, 25 Aug., FO371/23026, C11970/54/18.

13. Henderson to Halifax, 24, 25 Aug., *DBFP*, VII, no. 233, 241, 271, 293; Loraine to Halifax, 25 Aug., *ibid.*, no. 262.

14. *Ibid.*; Letter, Kennard to Cadogan, 26 Aug., *ibid.*, no. 357; Letter, Henderson to Halifax, 24 Aug., *ibid.*, no. 257; Minute by Makins, 25 Aug., FO371/23026, C11948/54/18.

15. Halifax to Kennard, 25, 26 Aug., *DBFP*, VII, nos. 309, 354; Halifax to Loraine, 26 Aug., *ibid.*, no. 327.

16. Ogilvie-Forbes to Halifax, 28 Aug., *ibid.*, no. 402; Minutes, Cab45(39), 28 Aug., CAB23/100; Halifax to Kennard, 28 Aug., *DBFP*, VII, no.

411; Kennard to Halifax, 28 Aug., *ibid.*, no. 420; *Cadogan Diaries, 1938–1945*, 203.

17. Ogilvie-Forbes to Halifax, 28 Aug., *DBFP*, VII, no. 418; Minutes by Kirkpatrick and Sargent, 28 Aug., FO371/22978, C12234/15/18.

18. Henderson, *Failure of a Mission*, 262–4; Henderson to Halifax, 29 Aug., *DBFP*, VII, nos. 450, 455, 472, 501; Memorandum by Schmidt, 29 Aug., *DGFP*, VII, no. 384.

19. Minute by Vansittart, 29 Aug., *DBFP*, VII, no. 455; Minute by Halifax, 29 Aug., FO371/22978, C12253/15/18; *Cadogan Diaries, 1938–1945*, 203; Halifax to Henderson, 30 Aug., *DBFP*, VII, no. 545.

20. Henderson to Halifax, 29 Aug., *ibid.*, nos. 455, 467; *Harvey Diaries, 1937–1940*, 309; Minute by Roberts, 29 Aug., *DBFP*, VII, no. 459; Dahlerus, *The Last Attempt*, 82–5.

21. Minutes by Makins, Kirkpatrick and Sargent, 29 Aug., FO371/22979, C12338/15/18; Dahlerus, *The Last Attempt*, 84.

22. *H. C. Deb.*, 351, 29 Aug., cols. 111–16.

23. Henderson, *Failure of a Mission*, 264; Henderson to Halifax, 29, 30 Aug., *DBFP*, VII, nos. 470, 490, 493, 502, 508, 565.

24. *Cadogan Diaries, 1939–1945*, 204; Minute by Wilson, 30 Aug., PREM1/331; Halifax to Henderson, 30 Aug., *DBFP*, VII, no. 504; Henderson to Halifax, 30 Aug., *ibid.*, no. 520; David Irving, ed., *Breach of Security* (1968), 101–2.

25. Minute by Makins, 30 Aug., FO371/22979, C12389/15/18; Dahlerus, *The Last Attempt*, 88–99; Foreign Office minute, 30 Aug., *DBFP*, VII, no. 514; Note of telephone conversation, 30 Aug., *ibid.*, no. 519.

26. Minutes, Cab46(39), 30 Aug., CAB23/100; Halifax to Henderson, 30 Aug., FO371/22979, C12467/15/18; Entry of 30 Aug., Inskip Diaries, INKP1/2; Lyons to Chamberlain, 27 Aug., PREM1/300.

27. Halifax to Henderson, 30 Aug., *DBFP*, VII, nos. 534, 538, 543, 547–8; *Cadogan Diaries, 1938–1945*, 205; Henderson, *Failure of a Mission*, 269. See also, Minutes in FO371/22979, C12486–7/15/18.

28. Schmidt, *Hitler's Interpreter*, 150–3; Henderson to Halifax, 31 Aug., *DBFP*, VII, nos. 570–1, 574; Schmidt to German Embassy in London, 30 Aug., *DGFP*, VII, no. 458; Memorandum by Schmidt, 31 Aug., *ibid.*, no. 461; Joachim von Ribbentrop, *Memoirs* (1954), 122–4.

29. Henderson, *Failure of a Mission*, 273; Letter, Henderson to Halifax, 31 Aug., *DBFP*, VII, no. 628.

30. Henderson to Halifax, 31 Aug., *ibid.*, no. 575; *Lipski Papers and Memoirs*, 569–71, 605–7.

31. Henderson to Halifax, 31 Aug., *DBFP*, VII, nos. 577, 579, 628; Hassell, *D'Une Autre Allemagne*, 74–6.

32. Dahlerus, *The Last Attempt*, 104–5; Henderson to Halifax, 31 Aug., *DBFP*, VII, no. 597; *Lipski Papers and Memoirs*, 608–9.

33. Telegram from Goerdeler, 30 Aug., FO371/22981, C12789/15/18; Henderson to Halifax, 31 Aug., no. 521; Minutes by Sargent and Cadogan, 31 Aug., FO371/23010, C12519/53/18.

34. Minutes by Halifax, 31 Aug., *DBFP*, VII, nos. 580, 627.

35. Henderson to Halifax, 31 Aug., *ibid.*, no. 587; Minutes by Cadogan and Wilson, 31 Aug., *ibid.*, no. 589; Halifax to Henderson, 31 Aug., *ibid.*, nos. 591–2.

36. Minute by Halifax, 31 Aug., *ibid.*, no. 590; *Ciano's Diary, 1939–1943*, 140; Phipps to Halifax, 31 Aug., *DBFP*, VII, no. 604.

37. Halifax to Kennard, 30, 31 Aug., *ibid.*, nos. 539, 596; Kennard to Halifax, 31 Aug., *ibid.*, no. 576.

38. *Lipski Papers and Memoirs*, 572, 601; Kennard to Halifax, 31 Aug., *DBFP*, VII, no. 608.

39. *Lipski Papers and Memoirs*, 609–10; Memorandum by Schmidt, 1 Sept., *DGFP*, VII, no. 476; Schmidt, *Hitler's Interpreter*, 154.

40. Halder Diaries, *DGFP*, VII, appendix 1, 566–70.

41. Memorandum by Weizsäcker, 31 Aug., *DBFP*, VII, no. 482.

42. Thomsen to Foreign Ministry, 1 Sept., *DGFP*, VII, no. 494; *Ciano's Diary, 1939–1943*, 142; *Livre Jaune Français*, no. 319; Entry of 31 Aug., Inskip Diaries, INKP1/2; *Cadogan Diaries, 1938–1945*, 206.

43. Loraine to Halifax, 31 Aug., *DBFP*, VII, no. 621; *Ciano's Diary, 1939–1943*, 141.

44. Kennard to Halifax, 31 Aug., *DBFP*, VII, no. 618; Henderson to Halifax, 1 Sept., *ibid.*, no. 631.

45. Halifax to Kennard, 1 Sept., no. 356, FO371/22980, C12543/15/18; *DBFP*, VII, no. 632; Kennard to Halifax, 1 Sept., *ibid.*, no. 675.

pp. 368–390   CHAPTER FOURTEEN

1. *Hore-Belisha Papers*, 224–5. Cf. J. R. Colville, *Man of Valour, The Life of Field-Marshal the Viscount Gort* (1972), 141.

2. Reuter to Halifax, 1 Sept., *DBFP*, VII, no. 637; and to Chamberlain, PREM1/331, Kennard to Halifax, 1 Sept., *DBFP*, VII, no. 638.

3. Raczynski, *In Allied London*, 25; Halifax to Kennard, 1 Sept., *DBFP*, VII, no. 689.

4. Halifax to Henderson, 1 Sept., *ibid.*, no. 690; Memorandum by Kordt, 1 Sept., *DGFP*, VII, no. 501; *Adolf Hitler, My New Order*, 683–90.

5. Directive by Hitler, 31 Aug., *DGFP*, VII, no. 493; Circular by Weizsäcker, 1 Sept., *ibid.*, no. 512.

6. Record of conversation, 1 Sept., *DBFP*, VII, no. 639; Minute by Cadogan, n.d., FO371/22980, C12647/15/18.
7. Henderson to Halifax, 1 Sept., *DBFP*, VII, no. 645; Minute by Makins, 1 Sept., FO371/22980, C12622/15/18.
8. Henderson to Halifax, 1 Sept., *DBFP*, VII, no. 658.
9. Minutes, Cab47(39), 1 Sept., CAB23/100. See Minute by Butler, 1 Sept., FO371/23092, C12928/12590/18.
10. Phipps to Halifax, 1 Sept., no. 289; Minutes by Barclay and Makins, 1 Sept., FO371/22913, C12616/90/17; Georges Bonnet, *Quai d'Orsay* (Isle of Man 1965), 263; his *Fin d'une Europe*, 349–50; Kennedy to Hull, 1 Sept., *FRUS, 1939*, I, 405–6; Halifax to Henderson, 1 Sept., *DBFP*, VII, nos. 664, 669.
11. *H. C. Deb.*, 351, 1 Sept., cols. 126–33; *Nicolson Diaries and Letters, I, 1930–39*, 417.
12. Henderson to Halifax, 1 Sept., *DBFP*, VII, nos. 682, 648; Memoranda by Schmidt, 2 Sept., *DGFP*, VII, nos. 513, 515; Irving, *Breach of Security*, 118.
13. Halifax to Phipps, 1 Sept., *DBFP*, VII, no. 699; "A Record of Events Before the War, 1939", FO800/317, H/XV/312; Phipps to Halifax, 2 Sept., *DBFP*, VII, no. 708.
14. Minutes by Loraine and Harvey, 2 Sept., *ibid.*, nos. 709–10; Halifax to Phipps, 2 Sept., *ibid.*, no. 700; Entry of 2 Sept., *Sir John Simon Diaries*; "A Record of Events Before the War, 1939", FO800/317, H/XV/312.
15. Minute by Cadogan, 2 Sept., *DBFP*, VII, no. 716; (an earlier draft of this conversation was read to the first Cabinet on 2 Sept.); Georges Bonnet, *Dans la Tourmente, 1938–1948* (Paris 1971), 187; *Livre Jaune Français*, no. 343; Kennard to Halifax, 2 Sept., *DBFP*, VII, no. 693.
16. Minutes, Cab48(39), 2 Sept., CAB23/100; Minute by Rucker, 2 Sept., PREM1/331; "A Record of Events Before the War, 1939", FO800/317, H/XV/312.
17. Record of conversation, 2 Sept., *DBFP*, VII, no. 718; Minutes by Cadogan and Mallet, 2 Sept., *ibid.*, nos. 727, 730; *Harvey Diaries, 1937–1940*, 314.
18. Minute by Jebb, 2 Sept., *DBFP*, VII, no. 728; Loraine to Halifax, 2 Sept., *ibid.*, no. 739; Memorandum by Brücklmeier, 2 Sept., *DGFP*, VII, no. 554.
19. Major-General Sir Edward Spears, *Assignment to Catastrophe, I, Prelude to Dunkirk* (1954), 19–22; Entry of 2 Sept., Wallace Diaries; *H. C. Deb.*, 351, 2 Sept., cols. 280–5; Notes by Hugh Dalton, 2 Sept., Lord Henderson Papers, HEN/16/1; Jasper Rootham, *Demi-Paradise* (1960), 174.

20. *Channon Diaries*, 212–13; Notes by Dalton, 2 Sept., Lord Henderson Papers, HEN/16/1.
21. Sir Reginald Dorman-Smith, interview in *The Sunday Times*, 6 Sept., 1964; Entry of 2 Sept., Simon Diaries; Entry of 2 Sept., Wallace Diaries.
22. Entry of 2 Sept., Inskip Diaries, INKP1/2.
23. "A Record of Events Before the War, 1939", FO800/317, H/XV/312; *Cadogan Diaries, 1938–1945*, 212.
24. Author's interview with Sir Reginald Dorman-Smith, 28 Apr. 1972; Entry of 2 Sept., Simon Diaries.
25. Minutes by Cadogan, 2 Sept., *DBFP*, VII, nos. 740–1.
26. Kennard to Halifax, 2 Sept., *ibid.*, no. 734; Halifax to Kennard, 2 Sept., *ibid.*, no. 751; Entry of 2 Sept., Dalton Diaries.
27. Halder Diaries, *DGFP*, VII, appendix 1, 571; Hesse, *Hitler and the English*, 83–8; Hesse and Kordt to Foreign Ministry, 3 Sept., *DGFP*, VII, no. 558; Minute by Wilson, 2 Sept., PREM1/331.
28. Entry of 2 Sept., Wallace Diaries; Dorman-Smith, interview in *The Sunday Times*, 6 Sept. 1964; Letter, Zetland to Linlithgow, 4 Sept., Zetland Papers, MSS. Eur. D.609, 11; Minutes, Cab49(39), 2 Sept., CAB23/100; Entry of 3 Sept., Inskip Diaries, INKP1/2.
29. *Channon Diaries*, 214.
30. Notes by Dalton, 3 Sept., Lord Henderson Papers, HEN/16/1; "A Record of Events Before the War, 1939", FO800/317, H/XV/312; Kirkpatrick, *The Inner Circle*, 144.
31. Minutes by Sargent and Cadogan, 4 Sept., FO371/22982, C13021/15/18; Minutes, *ibid.*, C13356/15/18.
32. Schmidt, *Hitler's Interpreter*, 157–8; Schmidt, interview in *The Listener*, 16 Apr., 1970.
33. Dahlerus, *The Last Attempt*, 128–30; Minute by Cadogan, 3 Sept., *DBFP*, VII, no. 762; Minute by Roberts, 3 Sept., FO371/22982, C12967/15/18.
34. *Harvey Diaries, 1937–1940*, 316; Alvar Liddell, interview in *The Daily Express*, 4 Sept., 1967; *H. C. Deb.*, 351, 3 Sept., cols. 291–2.
35. Shepherd to Halifax, 4 Sept., *DBFP*, VII, no. 767; Letter, Sir Edmund Monson to Collier, 11 Sept.; Minutes by Sargent and Cadogan, 22 Sept., FO371/23028, C14016/54/18; Report by Burckhardt, n.d., *ibid.*, C21050/54/18.

Sources

1. *Unpublished Documents:*
Public Record Office.

CABINET OFFICE AND COMMITTEE OF IMPERIAL DEFENCE: Cabinet minutes – CAB23/94–100; Cabinet papers – CAB24/278–88; War Cabinet minutes – CAB65/1; War Cabinet papers – CAB66/1–2; Foreign Policy Committee minutes and papers – CAB27/624–7; Cabinet Office, registered files – CAB21; Committee of Imperial Defence minutes – CAB2/8–9; Committee of Imperial Defence papers – CAB4/28–30; Chiefs of Staff Sub-committee minutes and papers – CAB53/9–11, 41–54, CAB79/1, CAB80/1–3; Deputy Chiefs of Staff Sub-committee minutes and papers – CAB54/2, 4–11, CAB82/1, 4; Joint Planning Sub-committee minutes and papers – CAB55/3, 13–19, CAB84/1, 7; Strategic Appreciation Sub-committee minutes and papers – CAB16/209; Defence Policy (Plans) Sub-committee minutes and papers – CAB16/180, 182, 183A–B; Anglo-French Conversations minutes and papers – CAB29/159–62.

PRIME MINISTER'S OFFICE: correspondence and papers – PREM1.

FOREIGN OFFICE: Chief Clark's Department – FO366; political files –FO371; Private Office, individual files – FO794; Ministers and Officials, private collections – FO800.

TREASURY: finance files – T160; supply files – T161.

BOARD OF TRADE: Commercial Department correspondence and papers – BT11; Department of Overseas Trade correspondence and papers – BT60; Industries and Manufactures Department correspondence and papers – BT64.

ADMIRALTY: Admiralty and Secretariat papers – ADM1; Admiralty and Secretariat, Cases – ADM116.

WAR OFFICE: Registered Papers, general series – WO32; reports and miscellaneous papers – WO33; Directorate of Military Operations and Intelligence papers – WO106; Director of Military Intelligance, appreciation files – 190; Director of Military Operations, collation files – WO193.

AIR MINISTRY: correspondence – AIR2; unregistered papers – AIR20.

Sources

2. Unpublished Documents:
Private Papers.

Major S. Vyvyan ADAMS Papers – British Library of Political and Economic Science, London.

1st Earl (A. V.) ALEXANDER Papers – Churchill College, Cambridge.

1st Earl (Clement) ATTLEE Papers – Churchill College; and University College, Oxford.

1st Baron BEAVERBROOK (Sir William Maxwell Aitken) Papers – Beaverbrook Library, London.

Edward Leslie BURGIN Papers – by courtesy of Mrs Dorothy Burgin.

Charles Roden BUXTON Papers – McGill University, Montreal.

Sir Alexander CADOGAN Papers – Public Record Office (FO800/294), London.

1st Viscount CALDECOTE (Sir Thomas Inskip) Diaries and Papers – Churchill College; and Public Record Office (CAB64/14–28).

1st Viscount (Lord Robert) CECIL Papers – British Museum, London.

Neville CHAMBERLAIN Papers – *See* Note 30, p. 394.

Admiral of the Fleet 1st Baron (Alfred E. M.) CHATFIELD Papers – by courtesy of 2nd Baron Chatfield.

Sir Stafford CRIPPS Papers – Nuffield College, Oxford.

1st Viscount CROOKSHANK Papers – Bodleian Library, Oxford.

W. P. CROZIER Papers – Beaverbrook Library.

Admiral of the Fleet 1st Viscount (Sir Andrew) CUNNINGHAM Papers – British Museum.

1st Baron (Hugh) DALTON Diaries and Papers – British Library of Political and Economic Science.

Major-General Francis H. M. DAVIDSON Papers – King's College, London.

Geoffrey DAWSON Diaries – by courtesy of Mr Michael Dawson.

Admiral Sir Barry DOMVILE Diaries – National Maritime Museum, Greenwich.

Air Marshal Sir Thomas ELMHIRST Papers – Churchill College.

Admiral Sir R. P. ERNLE-ERLE-DRAX Papers – Churchill College.

H. A. L. FISHER papers – Bodleian Library.

Major-General J. F. C. FULLER Papers – King's College.

Admiral J. H. GODFREY Papers – Churchill College.

1st Earl of HALIFAX Papers – by courtesy of 2nd Earl of Halifax; and Public Record Office (FO800/309–28).

Lieutenant-Colonel Sir Cuthbert HEADLAM Diaries and Papers – County Record Office, Durham.

Sir Nevile HENDERSON Papers – Public Record Office (FO800/270–1).

Sources

1st Baron (William W.) HENDERSON Papers – Transport House, London.

Major-General Thomas G. G. HEYWOOD Papers – by courtesy of Mrs Joan Heywood.

Sir Richard HOPKINS Papers – Public Record Office (T175).

General 1st Baron (Hastings) ISMAY Papers – King's College.

A. L. KENNEDY Diaries – *The Times* Archives, London.

1st Baron and Lady KENNET Diaries and Papers – by courtesy of 2nd Baron Kennet.

William Lyon Mackenzie KING Papers – Public Archives of Canada, Ottawa.

LABOUR PARTY Papers – Transport House.

George LANSBURY Papers – British Library of Political and Economic Science.

LEAGUE OF NATIONS UNION Papers – British Library of Political and Economic Science.

Sir Basil LIDDELL HART Papers – by courtesy of Lady Liddell Hart.

1st Earl (David) LLOYD GEORGE Papers – Beaverbrook Library.

11th Marquess of LOTHIAN (Philip Henry Kerr) Papers – Scottish Record Office, Edinburgh.

Colonel Roderick MACLEOD Papers – King's College.

1st Viscount (David) MARGESSON Papers – Churchill College.

Gilbert MURRAY Papers – Bodleian Library.

Air Chief Marshal Sir Cyril L. N. NEWALL Papers – Public Record Office (AIR8/235–299).

Sir Harold NICOLSON Diaries – Balliol College, Oxford.

Lady PASSFIELD (Beatrice Webb) Diaries – British Library of Political and Economic Science.

General Sir Henry POWNALL Diaries – by courtesy of Colonel J. W. Pownall-Gray.

Franklin D. ROOSEVELT Papers – Franklin D. Roosevelt Library, Hyde Park, New York.

Dr George H. ROSSDALE Papers – King's College.

1st Viscount (Walter) RUNCIMAN Papers – University Library, Newcastle-upon-Tyne.

1st Baron (Sir Arthur) SALTER Papers – by courtesy of Lord Salter.

1st Viscount (Sir Herbert) SAMUEL Papers – House of Lords Library, London.

Sir Orme SARGENT Papers – Public Record Office (FO800/278).

1st Viscount (Sir John) SIMON Diaries and Papers – by courtesy of 2nd Viscount Simon.

Sir John SLESSOR Papers – Public Record Office (AIR9/78–138).

J. A. SPENDER Papers – British Museum.

1st Viscount TEMPLEWOOD (Sir Samuel Hoare) Papers – University Library, Cambridge.

Sources

1st Viscount THURSO (Sir Archibald Sinclair) Papers – Churchill College.

THE TIMES Archives – Printing House Square, London.

1st Baron (Sir Robert) VANSITTART Papers – Churchill College.

Captain Euan WALLACE Diaries – Bodleian Library.

Sir Charles WEBSTER Papers – British Library of Political and Economic Science.

Sir John WHEELER-BENNETT Papers – St Anthony's College, Oxford.

Sir Kingsley WOOD Papers – Public Record Office (AIR19/25–72).

Arthur Primrose YOUNG Papers – by courtesy of Mr Young.

2nd Marquess of ZETLAND Papers – India Office Library, London.

3. Published Documents.*

BRITAIN: E. L. Woodward and Rohan Butler, eds., *Documents on British Foreign Policy, 1919–1939*, Third Series, I–IX, 1949–55.

Parliamentary Debates, Fifth Series. *House of Commons; House of Lords.*

GERMANY: *Documents on German Foreign Policy, 1918–1945*, Series D, I–VII, 1949–56.

FRANCE: Ministère des Affaires Étrangères, *Le Livre Jaune Français, Documents Diplomatiques, 1938–1939*, Paris 1939.

Les Evénements Survenus en France de 1933 à 1945, Témoignages et Documents Recueillis par la Commission d'Enquête Parlementaire, 9 vols., Paris 1947–51.

USSR: A. A. Gromyko, *et al.*, eds., *SSSR v Borbe za Mir Nakanune Vtoroi Mirovoi Voini, Sentyabr 1938g. – Avgust 1939g.*, Dokumenti i Materiali [The USSR in the Struggle for Peace on the Eve of the Second World War, September 1938 – August 1939, Documents and Materials], Moscow 1971.

Ministry of Foreign Affairs, *Documents and Materials Relating to the Eve of the Second World War*, 2 vols., Moscow 1948.

Milestones of Soviet Foreign Policy, 1917–1967, Moscow 1971.

"Negotiations between the Military Missions of the USSR, Britain and France in August 1939", *International Affairs* (Moscow), nos. 2–3, Feb., Mar. 1959.

Jane Degras, ed., *Soviet Documents on Foreign Policy, III, 1933–1941*, 1953.

USSR AND POLAND: I. A. Khrenov, *et al.*, eds., *Dokumenti i Materiali po Istorii Sovetsko-Polskich Otnoshenii, VI, 1933–1938gg.* [Documents and Materials on the History of Soviet-Polish Relations, VI, 1933–1938], Moscow 1969.

POLAND: Polish Ministry for Foreign Affairs, *The Polish White Book, Official Documents Concerning Polish-German and Polish-Soviet Relations, 1933–1939*, 1940.

* All books are published in London, unless otherwise indicated.

Sources

USA: Department of State, *Foreign Relations of the United States, The Soviet Union, 1933–1939*, Washington, D.C., 1952.

Foreign Relations of the United States, Diplomatic Papers, 1938, I, Washington, D.C., 1955; *1939*, I, Washington, D.C., 1956.

OTHERS: Académie Royale de Belgique, Commission Royale d'Histoire, *Documents Diplomatiques Belges, 1920–1940, La Politique de Sécurité Extérieure*, V, *1938–1940*, Brussels 1966.

Magda Adam, *et al.*, eds., *Allianz Hitler–Horthy–Mussolini, Dokumente zur Ungarischen Aussenpolitik 1933–1944*, Budapest 1966.

Pierre Blet, *et al.*, eds., *Records and Documents of the Holy See Relating to the Second World War*, I, *The Holy See and the War in Europe, March 1939–August 1940*, 1968.

Koloman Gajan and Robert Kvaček, eds., *Germany and Czechoslovakia, 1918–1945*, Prague 1965.

Ministero Degli Affari Esteri, *I Documenti Diplomatici Italiani*, 8th Series, *1935–1939*, XII–XIII, Rome 1952–3.

Trial of the Major War Criminals Before the International Military Tribunal, Nuremburg, 14 Nov. 1945–1 Oct. 1946, Proceedings and Documents, 42 vols., Nuremburg 1947–9.

Office of the U.S. Chief of Counsel for Prosecution of Axis Criminality, *Nazi Conspiracy and Aggression*, 10 vols., Washington 1946–7.

RIIA, *Documents on International Affairs, 1938*, 2 vols., *1939–46*, I, 1951.

4. Biographies, Diaries, Memoirs, Speeches, etc.

A. BRITISH

AMERY, L. S., *My Political Life, II, The Unforgiving Years, 1929–1940*, 1955.
ADAM, Colin Forbes, *Life of Lord Lloyd*, 1948.
ATTLEE, C. R., *As It Happened*, 1954.
AVON, The Earl of, *The Eden Memoirs, The Reckoning*, 1965.
BIRKENHEAD, The Earl of, *Halifax, The Life of Lord Halifax*, 1965.
BOOTHBY, Robert, *I Fight to Live*, 1947.
BUTLER, Ewan, *Mason-Mac, The Life of Lieutenant-General Sir Noel Mason-Macfarlane*, 1972.
BUTLER, Lord, *The Art of the Possible*, 1947.
CHAMBERLAIN, Neville, *The Struggle for Peace*, 1939.
CHATFIELD, Admiral of the Fleet Lord, *It Might Happen Again*, II, *The Navy and Defence*, 1947.
CHURCHILL, Winston S., *The Second World War*, I, *The Gathering Storm*, 1949.
COLVILLE, J. R., *Man of Valour, The Life of Field-Marshal the Viscount Gort*, 1972.

431

Sources

COLVIN, Ian, *Vansittart in Office*, 1965.

COOTE, Sir Colin, *A Companion of Honour, Walter Elliot*, 1965.

CRASTER, H. H. E., ed., *Viscount Halifax, Speeches on Foreign Policy*, 1940.

CUNNINGHAM, Admiral of the Fleet Viscount, *A Sailor's Odyssey*, 1951.

DALTON, Hugh, *Memoirs, II, The Fateful Years, 1931–1945*, 1957.

DILKS, David, ed., *The Diaries of Sir Alexander Cadogan, 1938–1945*, 1971.

DOUGLAS-HOME, Sir Alec, " 'I Was There', The Munich Conference", Transcript of BBC Broadcast Talk, 19 Feb. 1968.

DUFF COOPER, Alfred, *Old Men Forget*, 1953.

ERNLE-ERLE-DRAX, Admiral Sir R. P., "Mission to Moscow", *Naval Review*, XL, nos. 3–4, Nov. 1952; XLI, no. 1, Feb. 1953.

FEILING, Keith, *The Life of Neville Chamberlain*, 1946.

GLADWYN, Lord, *Memoirs*, 1972.

HALIFAX, The Earl of, *Fulness of Days*, 1957.

HARVEY, John, ed., *The Diplomatic Diaries of Oliver Harvey, 1937–1940*, 1970.

HENDERSON, Sir Nevile, *Failure of a Mission, Berlin 1937–1939*, 1940.

— *Water under the Bridges*, 1945.

HOLLIS, General Sir Leslie, *One Mariner's Tale*, 1956.

ISMAY, General Lord, *Memoirs*, 1960.

JAMES, Robert Rhodes, ed., *Chips, The Diaries of Sir Henry Channon*, 1967.

JOHNSON, Allen Campbell, *Viscount Halifax*, 1941.

JONES, Thomas, *A Diary with Letters, 1931–1950*, 1954.

KELLY, Sir David, *The Ruling Few*, 1952.

KENNEDY, Major-General Sir John, *The Business of War*, 1957.

KIRKPATRICK, Sir Ivone, *The Inner Circle*, 1959.

KNATCHBULL-HUGESSEN, Sir Hughe, *Diplomat in Peace and War*, 1949.

LEASOR, James, and General Sir Leslie Hollis, *War at the Top*, 1959.

LEITH-ROSS, Sir Frederick, *Money Talks*, 1968.

LIDDELL HART, Sir Basil, *Memoirs*, 2 vols., 1965.

MCLACHLAN, Donald, *In the Chair, Barrington-Ward of The Times, 1927–1948*, 1971.

MACDONALD, Malcolm, *People and Places*, 1969.

MACLEOD, Iain, *Neville Chamberlain*, 1961.

MACLEOD, Colonel Roderick, and Denis Kelly, eds., *The Ironside Diaries, 1937–1940*, 1962.

MAUGHAM, Viscount, *At the End of the Day*, 1954.

MINNEY, R. J., *The Private Papers of Hore-Belisha*, 1960.

NEWMAN, Aubrey, *The Stanhopes of Chevening*, 1969.

NICOLSON, Nigel, ed., *Harold Nicolson, Diaries and Letters*, I, *1930–1939*, 1966.

PETERSON, Sir Maurice, *Both Sides of the Curtain*, 1950.

ROOTHAM, Jasper, *Demi-Paradise*, 1960.

RYAN, Sir Andrew, *The Last of the Dragomans*, 1951.

Sources

SALTER, Lord, *Memoirs of a Public Servant*, 1961.

SIMON, Viscount, *Retrospect*, 1952.

SLESSOR, Sir John, *The Central Blue*, 1956.

SPEARS, Major-General Sir Edward, *Assignment to Catastrophe*, I, *Prelude to Dunkirk*, 1954.

STRANG, Lord, *Home and Abroad*, 1956.

— *The Moscow Negotiations*, Leeds 1968.

STRONG, Major-General Sir Kenneth, *Intelligence at the Top*, 1968.

TEMPLEWOOD, Viscount, *Nine Troubled Years*, 1954.

TENNANT, Ernest W. D., *Account Settled*, 1957.

VANSITTART, Lord, *Lessons of my Life*, 1943.

— *The Mist Procession*, 1958.

WHEELER-BENNETT, Sir John W., *John Anderson, Viscount Waverly*, 1962.

— *King George VI, His Life and Reign*, 1958.

WERNHER, Major-General Sir Harold A., *World War II, Personal Experiences*, Private Circulation, 1950.

WINTERTON, Earl, *Orders of the Day*, 1953.

WRENCH, John Evelyn, *Geoffrey Dawson and Our Times*, 1955.

YOUNG, Arthur Primrose, *Across the Years*, 1971.

ZETLAND, Marquess of, *"Essayez"*, 1956.

B. GERMAN

ABSHAGEN, Karl Heinz, *Canaris*, 1956.

ABETZ, Otto, *Das Offene Problem*, Cologne 1951.

BAYNES, Norman H., ed., *The Speeches of Adolf Hitler, April 1922–August 1939*, 2 vols., 1942.

BULLOCK, Alan, *Hitler, A Study in Tyranny*, 1953.

COLVIN, Ian, *Chief of Intelligence*, 1951.

DIETRICH, Otto, *The Hitler I Knew*, 1957.

DIRKSEN, Herbert von, *Moscow, Tokyo, London*, 1951.

GISEVIUS, Hans Bernd, *To the Bitter End*, 1948.

HASSELL, Ulrich von, *D'Une Autre Allemagne, Journal Posthume, 1938–1944*, Neuchatel 1948.

HESSE, Fritz, *Hitler and the English*, 1954.

HILGER, Gustav, and A. C. Meyer, *The Incompatible Allies, A Memoir–History of German-Soviet Relations, 1918–1941*, New York 1953.

HITLER, Adolf, *Mein Kampf*, 1939.

KEITEL, Field-Marshal Wilhelm, *Memoirs*, 1965.

KLEIST, Peter, *European Tragedy*, Isle of Man 1965.

KORDT, Erich, *Nicht aus den Akten*, Stuttgart 1950.

MEISSNER, Otto, *Staatssekretar unter Ebert–Hindenburg–Hitler*, Hamburg 1950.

Sources

PAPEN, Franz von, *Memoirs*, 1952.

RIBBENTROP, Joachim von, *Memoirs*, 1954.

RITTER, Gerhard, *The German Resistance, Carl Goerdeler's Struggle Against Tyranny*, 1958.

ROON, Ger van, *German Resistance to Hitler, Count von Moltke and the Kreisau Circle*, 1971.

SALES, Raoul de Roussy de, ed., *Adolf Hitler, My New Order*, New York 1941.

SCHACHT, Hjalmar, *Account Settled*, 1949.

— *My First Seventy-Six Years*, 1955.

SCHLABRENDORFF, Fabian von, *Revolt Against Hitler*, 1948.

— *The Secret War Against Hitler*, 1966.

SCHMIDT, Paul, *Hitler's Interpreter*, 1951.

SYKES, Christopher, *Troubled Loyalty, a Biography of Adam von Trott zu Solz*, 1968.

WEIZSÄCKER, Ernest von, *Memoirs*, 1951.

C. FRENCH

BEAUFRE, General André, *1940, The Fall of France*, 1967.

BONNET, Georges, *Dans la Tourmente, 1938–1948*, Paris 1971.

— *Défence de la Paix*, II, *Fin d'une Europe*, Geneva 1948.

— *Quai d'Orsay*, Isle of Man 1965.

COULONDRE, Robert, *De Stalin à Hitler, Souvenirs de Deux Ambassades, 1936–1939*, Paris 1950.

DALADIER, Edouard, *Défence du Pays*, Paris 1939.

DOUMENC, General Joseph, "The Inside Story of the Moscow Talks, 1939", *Tribune*, 11 July 1947.

FRANCOIS-PONCET, André, *Souvenirs d'une Ambassade à Berlin*, Paris 1946.

GAMELIN, General M. G., *Servir*, 2 vols., Paris 1946.

MASSIGLI, René, *La Turquie Devant la Guerre, Mission à Ankara, 1939–1940*, Paris 1964.

MONZIE, Anatole de, *Ci-Devant*, Paris 1941.

NOEL, Léon, *L'Agression Allemande contre la Pologne*, Paris 1946.

REYNAUD, Paul, *In the Thick of the Fight*, 1955.

STEHLIN, General Paul, *Témoignage pour l'Histoire*, Paris 1964.

WEYGAND, General Maxime, *Mémoires, Rappelé au Service*, Paris 1950.

ZAY, Jean, *Carnets Secrets*, 1942.

D. RUSSIAN

BILAINKIN, George, *Maisky, Ten Years Ambassador*, 1944.

DEUTSCHER, Isaac, *Stalin, A Political Biography*, 1949.

Sources

KRIVITSKY, W. G. *I was Stalin's Agent,* 1940.
KUZNETSOV, N. G., *Pered Voina* [Before the War], Moscow 1968.
MAISKY, Ivan, *Vospominaniya Sovetskogo Posla* [Memoirs of a Soviet Ambassador], 2 vols., Moscow 1964.
— *Who Helped Hitler?* 1964.
POPE, Arthur Upham, *Maxim Litvinoff,* 1943.
STALIN, Joseph, *Leninism,* 1940.
TALBOTT, Strobe, ed., *Khrushchev Remembers,* 1971.

E. AMERICAN

BLUM, John Morton, *From the Morgenthau Diaries, Years of Urgency, 1938-1941,* Boston 1965.
BURNS, James MacGregor, *Roosevelt, The Lion and the Fox,* 1956.
CHAMBERS, Whittaker, *Witness,* 1953.
DAVIES, Joseph E., *Mission to Moscow,* 1942.
HOOKER, Nancy, ed., *The Moffat Papers,* Cambridge, Mass. 1956.
HULL, Cordell, *Memoirs,* 2 vols., 1948.
ICKES, Harold L., *The Secret Diary of Harold Ickes, II, The Inside Struggle, 1936-1939,* 1954.
KENNAN, George F., *From Prague after Munich, Diplomatic Papers, 1938-1940,* 1968.
— *Memoirs, 1925-1950,* 1968.
PHILLIPS, William, *Ventures in Diplomacy,* 1955.
WELLES, Sumner, *The Time for Decision,* 1944.
WHALEN, R. J., *The Founding Father,* New York 1964.

F. OTHERS

BECK, Jozef, *Final Report,* New York 1957.
BURCKHARDT, Carl J., *Meine Danziger Mission, 1937-1939,* Munich 1960.
CRETZIANU, Alexandre, *The Lost Opportunity,* 1957.
DAVIGNON, Vicomte Jacques, *Berlin 1936-1940, Souvenirs d'une Mission,* Paris 1951.
GAFENCU, Grigore, *The Last Days of Europe,* 1947.
— *Prelude to the Russian Campaign,* 1945.
GRIPENBERG, G. A., *Finland and the Great Powers, Memoirs of a Diplomat,* Lincoln, Nebraska 1965.
GUARIGLIA, Raffaele, *La Diplomatie Difficile,* Paris 1955.
JEDRZEJEWICZ, Waclaw, ed., *Diplomat in Berlin 1933-1939, Papers and Memoirs of Jozef Lipski, Ambassador of Poland,* 1968.
— *Diplomat in Paris 1936-1939, Memoirs of Juliusz Lukasiewicz,* 1970.

435

Sources

MASSEY, Vincent, *What's Past is Prologue*, 1963.
MUGGERIDGE, Malcolm, ed., *Ciano's Diary, 1939–1943*, 1947.
— *Ciano's Diplomatic Papers*, 1948.
RACZYNSKI, Count Edward, *In Allied London*, 1962.
SZEMBEK, Jean, *Journal, 1933–1939*, Paris 1952.

G. SECONDARY STUDIES*

ALSOP, Joseph, and Robert Kintner, *American White Paper*, New York 1940.
ASSMAN, Kurt, "Stalin and Hitler, Part I, The Pact with Moscow", *U.S. Naval Institute Proceedings*, LXXV, June 1949.
ASTER, Sidney, "Ivan Maisky and Parliamentary Anti-Appeasement, 1938–1939", in A. J. P. Taylor, ed., *Lloyd George, Twelve Essays*, 1971.
ASTOR, David, "Why the Revolt Against Hitler was Ignored", *Encounter*, June 1969.
BULLOCK, Alan, *Hitler and the Origins of the Second World War*, 1967.
CIENCIALA, Anna M., *Poland and the Western Powers, 1938–1939*, 1968.
DALTON, Hugh, *Hitler's War, Before and After*, 1939.
DILKS, David, "Appeasement Revisited", *University of Leeds Review*, XV, no. 1, 1972.
EASTERMAN, A. L., *King Carol, Hitler and Lupescu*, 1942.
FIELDHOUSE, Noel, "The Anglo-German War of 1939–42: Some Movements to End it by a Negotiated Peace", *Transactions of the Royal Society of Canada*, IX, 1971.
GILBERT, Martin, and Richard Gott, *The Appeasers*, 1963.
GILBERT, Martin, *The Roots of Appeasement*, 1966.
GROMYKO, A. A., *et al.*, eds., *Istoriya Diplomatii*, III, [History of Diplomacy, 2nd edn.], Moscow 1965.
HILLGRUBER, Andreas, *Hitler, König Carol und Marschall Antonescu, die Deutsch-Rumänischen Beziehungen 1938–1944*, Wiesbaden 1954.
IRVING, David, ed., *Breach of Security*, 1968.
LANGER, William L., and S. Everett Gleason, *The Challenge to Isolation, 1937–1940*, New York 1952.
LUZA, Radomir, *The Transfer of the Sudeten Germans, A Study of Czech-German Relations, 1933–1962*, 1964.
METZMACHER, Helmut, "Deutsch-Englische Ausgleichsbemühungen im Sommer 1939", *Vierteljahrshefte für Zeitgeschichte*, XIV, no. 4, Oct. 1966.
MOISUC, Viorica, *Diplomatia României si Problema Apararii Suveranitatii si*

* This very brief selection contains secondary studies cited in footnotes; or those which are of special interest for their use of important archival sources.

Sources

Independentei Nationale în Perioada Martie 1938–Mai 1940 [Rumania's Diplomacy and the Question of the Defence of National Sovereignty and Independence, March 1938–May 1940], Bucharest 1971.

— "Orientations dans la Politique Extérieure de la Roumanie après le Pacte de Munich", *Revue Roumaine d'Histoire*, V, no. 2, 1966.

PONOMARYOV, B. N., A. A. Gromyko and V. M. Khvostov, eds., *Istoriya Vneshnei Politiki SSSR, I, 1917–1945gg.* [History of the Foreign Policy of the USSR, I, 1917–1945], Moscow 1966.

POPOV, V. I., *Diplomaticheskie Otnosheniya Mezhdu SSSR i Angliei 1929–1939 gg.* [Diplomatic Relations between the USSR and Britain, 1929–1939], Moscow 1965.

POSPELOV, P. N., *et al.*, eds., *Istoriya Velikoi Otechestvennoi Voiny Sovetskogo Soyuza, 1941–1945*, I [History of the Great Patriotic War of the Soviet Union], Moscow 1960.

RIIA, *Survey of International Affairs, 1938*, III, 1953; *The World in March 1939*, 1952; *The Eve of War, 1939*, 1958.

ROBERTSON, E. M., *Hitler's Pre-War Policy and Military Plans, 1933–1939*, 1963.

ROTHFELS, Hans, *The German Opposition to Hitler*, 1961.

STRONG, Major-General Sir Kenneth, *Men of Intelligence*, 1970.

TAYLOR, A. J. P., *The Origins of the Second World War*, 1961.

TOSCANO, Mario, "La Politique Russe de l'Italie au Printemps 1939", *Revue d'Histoire de la Deuxième Guerre Mondiale*, II, no. 6, Apr. 1952.

— *Designs in Diplomacy, Pages from European Diplomatic History in the 20th Century*, 1971.

TREUE, Wilhelm, "Rede Hitlers vor der Deutschen Presse, 10 Nov. 1938", *Vierteljahrshefte für Zeitgeschichte*, VI, no. 2, Apr. 1958.

WHEELER-BENNETT, Sir John W., *The Nemesis of Power: The German Army in Politics 1918–1945*, 1953.

Index

Index

Index

453

Index

455

Index